Dark Age Naval Power

A Reassessment of Frankish and Anglo-Saxon Seafaring Activity

John Haywood

Anglo-Saxon Books

First published 1991 by Routledge

This revised and extended edition published in 1999 by
Anglo-Saxon Books
Frithgarth
Thetford Forest Park
Hockwold-cum-Wilton
Norfolk England

Printed by
Antony Rowe Ltd
Chippenham
Wiltshire England

© Copyright John Haywood 1999

All rights reserved. No part of this publication may be reproduced or transmitted in any form or by any means, electronic or mechanical including photo-copying, recording, or any information storage or retrieval system, without prior permission in writing from the publisher, except for the quotation of brief passages in connection with a review written for inclusion in a magazine or newspaper.

This book may not be lent, resold, hired out or otherwise disposed of by way of trade in any form of binding or cover other than that in which it is published, without the prior consent of the publishers.

British Library Cataloguing-in-Publication Data. A catalogue record for this book is available from the British Library.

ISBN 1–898281–22–X

In memory of my father,
James Rowland Haywood

Preface

I would like to thank the following individuals and institutions without whose help this work could not have been completed: Professor Graham Caie for ensuring that the time I spent in research at the University of Copenhagen was both enjoyable and profitable; Charlotte Culmsee for her linguistic help; Dr Edward James for his advice and constructive criticism and my mother for her unfailing moral support. For their financial support I would like to thank the British Academy, the Erasmus Bureau of the European Community and the Danish Ministry of Education. Finally, I would like to record my especial thanks to my research supervisor at the University of Lancaster, Dr P. D. King. His friendship and encouragement, advice, constructive criticism and, above all, his own exemplary standards of scholarship, have been an inspiration to me.

Preface to the Second Edition

Maritime archaeology has not stood still since the first edition of this book was published in 1991. Excavations and sea trials with sailing replicas of early ships have provided much new evidence and made necessary extensive revision of some sections of the book. I am grateful to Tony and Pearl Linsell of Anglo-Saxon Books for their considerable assistance in preparing this revised edition which, I believe, presents an even stronger case than the first. Additional thanks are due to Edwin and Joyce Gifford, for their advice on nautical archaeology, practical boatbuilding and some enjoyable and instructive trips out in *Sæ Wylfing*, (their half-scale sailing model of the Sutton Hoo ship), and to the Department of History at the University of Lancaster for its continuing support for my research through an Honorary Research Fellowship.

Contents

ABBREVIATIONS 11

INTRODUCTION 13

1 THE BEGINNINGS OF GERMANIC PIRACY 12 BC TO C. AD 240 17
   The Earliest Germanic Naval Activity 17
   The Raids of the Chauci 19
   The Ships of the Early Germanic Seafarers 31

2 THE 3RD & 4TH CENTURY RAIDS OF THE FRANKS & SAXONS 41
   The Causes of 3rd Century Piracy 41
   The Earliest Frankish Pirate Raids 49
   The Roman Coastal Defences 55
   Frankish and Saxon Pirate Raids in the Late 3rd and 4th Centuries 59
   The Ships of the Franks 70

3 ANGLO-SAXON PIRACY AND THE MIGRATIONS TO BRITAIN 77
   The Saxon Shore 77
   From Raiding to Settlement and Conquest; the 5th to 7th Centuries 81
   The Ships of the Angles and Saxons 93
   Anglo-Saxon Naval Power on the Eve of the Viking-Age 110

4 FRANKISH NAVAL POWER FROM CLOVIS TO PIPPIN III 113
   The Decline of Frankish Piracy 113
   Hygelac's Raid and the 6th Century 114
   Frankish Naval Activity in the Later Merovingian Period 126
   Merovingian Warships 131

Contents (continued)

5 FRANKISH NAVAL POWER UNDER CHARLEMAGNE & LOUIS THE PIOUS....135
    Charlemagne's Use of Fleets on Inland Waterways 136
    The Regnitz-Altmühl Canal 147
    The Frankish-Byzantine Naval Conflict in the Adriatic 152
    The Frankish-Moslem Naval War in the Mediterranean.........................156
    The Defence of the Northern Coasts against the Vikings 163
    Diplomacy and War in Frankish-Danish Relations................................172
    The Ships of the Northern Coast-Defence Fleets...................................178
    The Fate of the Coast Defences after Louis the Pious 181

CONCLUSIONS 185

GLOSSARY 189

BIBLIOGRAPHY OF WORKS CITED..191
    Primary Sources 191
    Secondary Sources 196

INDEX 211

Maps and Illustrations

Maps

1. The southern North Sea region first and second centuries AD 20
2. The southern North Sea region third and fourth centuries AD 47
3. The lower Rhine area in the early Middle Ages 117
4. The Carolingian Empire 137
5. The Fossa Carolina 148

Illustrations

1. The Hjortspring boat's method of construction 32
2. Hjortspring-type boat from an Iron Age rock carving, Ostfold, Norway 33
3. First–second century AD clay bowl, Vendyssel, Denmark 34
4. Reconstruction of the Bruges boat 36
5. Late Roman merchant ship inscribed on a bone from the River Weser 37
6. Reconstruction of a late Roman type-A warship ('lusoria') from Mainz 71
7. Barbarian warship from a Roman potsherd, Trier, fourth century AD 76
8. The Nydam ship 94
9. Rowing vessel from Gotland picture stone c. AD 400–600 96
10. The Karlby ship-carving 97
11. The Sutton Hoo ship (British Museum) 99
12. *Sæ Wylfing* general arrangement 102
13. Figureheads from the River Scheldt 132
14. A ship from a Merovingian strap end found in northern France 133
15. A dromon from an early medieval graffito at Malaga, Spain 162
16. Early ninth-century coins from Dorestad and Hedeby 179
17. Warships from the *First Bible of Charles the Bald* (c. 845–6) and the *San Paolo Bible* (c.846) 180

Photograph (E & J Gifford) half-scale Sutton Hoo ship under sail 103

Abbreviations

ARF	*Annales Regni Francorum*
ASC	*Anglo Saxon Chronicle*
BAR	British Archaeological Reports
BAR BS	British Archaeological Reports, British Series
BAR IS	British Archaeological Reports, International Series
BAR Supp. Ser.	British Archaeological Reports, Supplementary Series
CBA	Council for British Archaeology
IJNA	*International Journal of Nautical Archaeology*
JRGZM	*Jahrbuch des Römisch-Germanischen Zentralmuseums, Mainz*
MGH. AA	*Monumenta Germaniae Historica, Auctores Antiquissimi*
MGH. Epp.	*Monumenta Germaniae Historica, Epistolae*
MGH. LL	*Monumenta Germaniae Historica, Leges*
MGH. SS	*Monumenta Germaniae Historica, Scriptores*
MGH. SSRG	*Monumenta Germaniae Historica, Scriptores Rerum Germanicarum in Usum Scholarum*
MGH. SSRL	*Monumenta Germaniae Historica, Scriptores Rerum Langobardicarum et Italicarum*
MGH. SSRM	*Monumenta Germaniae Historica, Scriptores Rerum Merovingicarum*
Rev.	Reviser (Annales qui dicuntur Einhardi).
Settimane	*Settimane di Studio del Centro Italiano di Studi sull'Alto Medioevo (Spoleto)*
SHA	*Scriptores Historiae Augustae*
TRHS	*Transactions of the Royal Historical Society*

Introduction

In 793 terrible portents were seen over Northumbria, flashes of lightning, thunderbolts and fiery dragons terrified the inhabitants. Then on 8th June pagan Scandinavian pirates – Vikings – plundered the monastery of St Cuthbert on the island of Lindisfarne, despoiling the altars, killing some monks and taking others captive. The sacking of this, one of the holiest places in the British Isles, caused widespread shock and alarm. The Northumbrian scholar Alcuin, still reeling from news of the attack, famously wrote 'never before has such terror been seen in Britain as we have suffered by this pagan people nor was such a voyage thought possible'.[1] This passage has been taken as a sign that the Vikings possessed some hitherto unsuspected seafaring ability.[2] However, Alcuin goes on to criticise the Northumbrians for adopting the hairstyles of the very people who now threatened them.[3] The Vikings were clearly, therefore, already familiar to the Northumbrians so their seafaring abilities must have been well known. Alcuin's shock is, in fact, purely theological; why, he asks, had St Cuthbert not intervened to protect his monastery? Was not the attack God's punishment for some terrible sin? If somewhere as holy as Lindisfarne could not expect the protection of the saints, Alcuin concludes, then nowhere was safe. Over the next century the Vikings were to prove that to be true time and again but their seaborne raids were by no means an unprecedented phenomenon in the history of northern Europe. Alcuin's own pagan forefathers had once been regarded with the same degree of fear and horror by the Romans.

Between the third and seventh centuries Germanic barbarian peoples – Franks, Saxons, Angles, Heruls, Frisians and Danes – were all too frequently active as pirates in the North Sea. Indeed, in the third and fourth centuries, the raids of the Franks and Saxons, extending to the Channel, the Atlantic and even the Mediterranean, rivalled those of the Vikings in audacity and created for the Romans a security problem which, despite the commitment of considerable resources, they were never able permanently to solve. At different times in the

---

[1] Alcuin, *Epistolae*, ed. E. Duemmler, *MGH. Epp.* 4 (Berlin, 1895), pp. 18-481, no. 16: 'et numquam talis terror prius apparuit in Britannia, veluti modo pagana gente perpessi sumus, nec eiusmodi navigium fieri posse putabatur'. The exact meaning of this passage depends upon the reading of *navigium*, which unfortunately does not have a well-defined meaning in Carolingian Latin. *Navigatio* is usually used to describe a voyage, *navigium* more usually to describe a fleet or ferry. It may be that *navigium* is here a corruption of *naufragium* meaning 'shipwreck' or 'disaster'.

[2] P. H. Sawyer, *The Age of the Vikings* (London, 1962), p. 79, and also his *Kings and Vikings* (London, 1982), pp. 78–9.

[3] Alcuin, *Epp.* no. 16: 'Ecce tonsura, quam in barbis et in capillis paganis adsimilaris voluistis. Nonne illorum terror inminet, quorum tonsuram hebere voluistis'.

same period Goths, Heruls and Vandals launched pirate raids in the Black Sea and the Mediterranean. Earlier still, in the first and second centuries, the Chauci, Canninefates, Usipi and other Germanic barbarian tribes had been engaged in piracy in the North Sea. In fact, Germanic naval activity can be traced back almost to the dawn of the recorded history of barbarian Europe and no doubt raiding and piracy had gone on for centuries before that.

No comprehensive history of Germanic barbarian seafaring before the Viking age has been written, probably for two main reasons. Firstly, the long term continuity of barbarian seafaring activity has gone largely unrecognised because it straddles one of the great, artificial, dividing lines of history, the end of the ancient world and the beginning of the Middle Ages. Secondly, a series of remarkable ship finds from Scandinavia, dating to the period 700–1000, have served to concentrate the attention of maritime historians and archaeologists alike on the development of Viking shipbuilding and seafaring. Though the importance of Viking seafaring in European history is undeniable, this concentration on Viking activities has resulted in a distorted view of European maritime history, with the Vikings occupying a far too prominent position: they were in fact only the last in a long line of barbarian pirates to harass western Europe. Moreover, it has caused pre-Viking ships from northern Europe, such as those from Nydam and Sutton Hoo, to be treated only as stages in the evolution of the Viking ship and not, as they should be, as fully developed ships in their own right. The failure of maritime historians and archaeologists to give proper attention to primary historical source material has served only to entrench this distortion: it seems almost as if the belief has taken root that the literary sources can have nothing more to tell us, yet valuable nuggets of information can still be discovered even in the works of such well known writers as Tacitus.

Though the lack of a comprehensive history of early Germanic seafaring is a deficiency which needs to be remedied, and which I would have liked to have remedied myself, it is a subject which proved to be too large to be given adequate treatment within the time and funding I had available. In narrowing my field of investigation I have chosen to concentrate on the activities of the barbarian peoples who were, in the Roman period, settled between the Rhine and the Jutland peninsula both because their activities show long-term continuity and because of the wide range of literary and archaeological evidence which is available. In effect, this means that this study is concerned primarily with the seafaring activities of the Franks and Anglo Saxons and those Germanic peoples who were directly related to them. The Frisians are also treated at some length but, with the exception of the Heruls, the Scandinavian peoples are only dealt with in so far as their activities affected the Franks, Anglo-Saxons and Frisians. Again, in order to keep the study within manageable proportions, I have had to limit the range of seafaring activities which are examined to the closely related matters of warfare, piracy and migration: trade has been omitted as this would properly demand a study in its own right and also a quite different methodological approach.

Introduction

The study begins with the earliest recorded Germanic barbarian naval activity, an unsuccessful attack by a fleet of the Bructeri against a Roman fleet on the Ems in 12 BC, and ends with the collapse of the Carolingian coastal defence system after the death of Louis the Pious. The temporary dominance which the Vikings established in north European waters following this makes a decisive break with the past for both Anglo-Saxon and Frankish seafaring history and is the natural point at which to end the study.

The method I have adopted has been to reconstruct as far as possible the historical context of the different phases of barbarian naval activity from literary sources, from archaeological evidence of fortifications, coin hoards, destruction layers and sea level changes and from analyses of the strategic and tactical thinking which lay behind the Roman and Carolingian coastal defence systems. The evidence for barbarian shipbuilding from maritime archaeology is also considered in detail but only in the light of conclusions drawn from a study of the other sources of evidence mentioned above. This approach, which runs counter to the recent tendency for early maritime history to concentrate on the study of ship finds, has been most rewarding. Firstly, it has allowed proper prominence to be given to the impressive seafaring achievements of the Franks which have been largely overlooked by historians, no doubt partly because no Frankish ship has yet been identified. Secondly, it has highlighted the shortcomings in the present state of our knowledge of barbarian shipbuilding by allowing us to compare what barbarian seafarers actually achieved with what they might have achieved if the ships which we actually know of are representative of the best that were available to them. For example, an examination of the literary evidence shows that the raids of the Saxon pirates between the third and fifth centuries are comparable to those of the Vikings in both range and tactics, yet maritime archaeology has as yet provided evidence only for the use of large, relatively unseaworthy, open rowing boats by the Anglo-Saxons. The discrepancy is too great to be reconciled, so we must question whether the archaeological evidence as it stands is truly representative of Anglo-Saxon shipbuilding.

There are also some limitations to this approach, though they do not outweigh the advantages. These mainly derive from the nature of archaeological evidence itself. Coin hoards, destruction layers and fortifications all speak of insecurity, and if these show marked distributions in coastal areas we may fairly conclude that the threat came from the sea. However, such evidence can rarely put a name to the origin of that threat. This is a particularly acute problem in the third and fourth centuries when both Saxon and Frankish pirates were active. How are we to distinguish between them or determine their relative importance? The problems of interpreting the different types of archaeological evidence are discussed at the appropriate places in the text. The sources of archaeological evidence are, then, circumstantial rather than specific; but they are plentiful and so we should not be deterred from drawing conclusions from them, provided it is recognised that there must remain in them an element of doubt.

Apart from their sparseness, the literary sources also pose an important problem: the question of barbarian tribal names. It is clear that the Germanic barbarian tribes were not unchanging entities. Some of the most important tribes, like the Franks, were confederations; others, like the Saxons, have complex and little understood origins. It is clear that the Franks of the eighth century were a very different cultural and ethnic mix from the Franks of the third century: how much continuity can we assume? Also, how sure can we be that the Roman writers on whom we rely for many of our sources knew what they were talking about when they identified an invading Germanic force as being *Franci* or *Saxones*? These are important questions but they are ones which I have, by and large, chosen not to address because of their immense complexity and the ultimate impossibility of reaching any definite answers. Except where there is clear evidence to the contrary, I have assumed that the continuity of a name is indicative also of a meaningful degree of ethnic and cultural continuity. Similarly, unless there is an obvious reason to doubt its reliability, I have also assumed that a literary source correctly identifies the tribe or tribes it mentions. Before the migration period, the barbarian peoples with whom this study is largely concerned fell into two archaeologically distinct cultural groupings: to distinguish them in generalised discussion, I use the term 'north German' to cover the peoples who were settled between the Zuyder Zee and southern Jutland, i.e. the Frisians, Chauci, Saxons, and Angles, and 'Rhine German' to cover those settled on the river Rhine between the sea and the Main, i.e. the Canninefates, the Batavians and the Frankish tribes.

It should be pointed out, finally, that throughout the period in question (and, indeed, for centuries afterwards) naval warfare in the modern sense was very rare. Ships had relatively poor sea-keeping abilities and offered little protection for their crews. Regular patrolling and blockading were effectively impossible and the interception of an enemy ship on the open sea was an unusual occurrence. As a result, the initiative usually lay with the attacker and such ship to ship naval battles as did occur generally took place in confined waters such as rivers, estuaries or harbours. Most offensive naval activity in this period consisted of the transport of armies or raiding parties by ship; in other words, it was the type of military activity that would now be classed as amphibious warfare.

1 The Beginnings of Germanic Piracy

12 BC to c. AD 240

The Earliest Germanic Naval Activity

It would be quite impossible now to determine the date at which the Germanic barbarians settled along the coast of the North Sea first took to seafaring but they were already active at the time of the first Roman contacts with them. The earliest recorded Germanic pirate raids date from the mid-first century AD and the earliest known Germanic naval activity dates from the late first century BC. Most prominent among the early Germanic seafarers were the Chauci, but the Canninefates, Batavi, Frisians, Bructeri and Usipi were also active to a lesser extent. The early activities of the Bructeri and Usipi are particularly worth noting; both tribes became part of the Frankish confederacy in the third century so that it may fairly be said that their activities represent the earliest evidence of Frankish naval power.

The Bructeri, in fact, provide us not only with our earliest evidence of 'Frankish' naval power but also with the earliest evidence of Germanic naval power. When, in 12 BC, Augustus's stepson Drusus led a Roman fleet along the North Sea coast of Germany as far as the Elbe, the only recorded naval opposition came from the Bructeri who fought, and lost, a naval battle against the Romans on the river Ems.[1] Unfortunately, we know nothing more about the incident than this so it is obviously impossible to draw any general conclusions on the state of Germanic seafaring abilities in the first century BC.[2] However, it

---

[1] Strabo, *Geography*, ed. and trans. H. L. Jones, Loeb Classical Library (vol. 3, London, 1924), VII. 1. 3. See also C. G. Starr, *The Roman Imperial Navy*, 2nd edn (Cambridge, 1960), p. 142.

[2] L. Schmidt, *Geschichte der deutschen Stämme bis zum Ausgang der Völkerwanderung: Die Westgermanen* (2 vols, Munich, 1938–40), vol. 2, p. 200, does not think that this incident can be taken as evidence that the Bructeri were a seafaring people. Though a degree of doubt must be admitted, ruling this evidence out altogether seems to be going too far. If E. Norden, *Die germanische Urgeschichte in Tacitus Germania* (Leipzig Berlin, 1923), p. 290, is correct and the island of Borkum derives its name from the Bructeri it would seem that they must have been a seafaring people: Schmidt, *op. cit.* questions this identification, however.

seems unlikely that the Germans were complete strangers to naval warfare even then.

The Usipi were a tribe of the middle Rhine, settled between Cologne and the river Lippe,[3] and they are not obviously a people from whom one would expect great feats of seamanship. Yet it was members of this tribe who performed the earliest historically attested circumnavigation of the coast of northern Britain. This occurred in AD 83 when an auxiliary cohort of Usipi serving under Agricola on the west coast of Britain rebelled.[4] After killing their officers they seized three Liburnian galleys and kidnapped their three helmsmen, two of whom were murdered after the third had escaped. The Usipi took the rest of the Roman fleet by surprise and they had made good their escape by the time anyone realised what was happening. The rebels sailed north along the British coast, around the north of Scotland and back down the east coast of Britain, before crossing the North Sea. On their way they pillaged for supplies but local resistance was determined, if not always victorious, and the constant attrition depleted their numbers to the point where the Usipi found foraging difficult. After suffering terrible privations from hunger, the Usipi were shipwrecked on the coast of Germany or Denmark, presumably while attempting to reach the Rhine and return to their homeland. The survivors eventually fell into the hands of the Frisians who treated them as pirates, killing some and selling the others as slaves.

---

[3] Schmidt, *op. cit.*, p. 195.

[4] Tacitus, *Agricola*, ed. R. M. Ogilvie and I. Richmond (Oxford, 1967), ch. 28:

> Eadem aestate cohors Usiporum per Germanias conscripta et in Britanniam transmissa magnum ac memorabile facinus ausa est. occiso centurione ac militibus, qui ad tradendam disciplinam immixti manipulis exemplum et rectores habebantur, tres liburnicas adactis per vim gubernatoribus ascendere; et uno remigante, suspectis duobus eoque interfectis, nondum vulgato rumore ut miraculum praevehebantur. mox ubi aquam atque utilia raptum exissent, cum plerisque Britannorum sua defensantium proelio congressi ac saepe victores, aliquando pulsi, eo ad extremum inopiae venere, ut infirmissimos suorum, mox sorte ductos vescerentur. atque ita circumventi Britanniam, amissis per inscitiam regendi navibus, pro praedonibus habiti, primum a Suebis, mox a Frisiis intercepti sunt. ac fuere quos per commercia venumdatos et in nostram usque ripam mutatione ementium adductos inicium tanti casus inlustravit.

The meaning of the passage 'et uno remigante, suspectis duobus eoque interfectis', which hinges on the interpretation of *uno remigante*, is unclear but it seems likely that the text should be emended to *uno remigrante*, i.e. 'with one escaping'. On this and other possible interpretations see Ogilvie and Richmond, p. 246).

Tacitus wrote the *Agricola* in AD 97–8 but an earlier account certainly existed which the Roman poet Pompullus drew on as a source for one of his works, now also lost but for two lines quoted by Martial (*Epigrammata*, ed. W. M. Lindsay (Oxford, 1929), VI, lxi. 3 4) in a mocking epigram written *c.* AD 90. Tacitus' account is complemented by that of Cassius Dio, *Histories*, ed. and trans. E. Cary, Loeb Classical Library (9 vols, London, 1960–1), LXVI. 20. Dio's account makes it clear that the Usipi must have been on the west coast of Britain when they rebelled and that their voyage took them north around Scotland and down the east coast where they made a number of landfalls. There is a very useful discussion of the sources for this incident in Ogilvie and Richmond, *op.cit.* pp. 321–2. S. S. Frere, *Britannia*, 3rd edn (London, 1987), p. 209, suggests that the mutiny may have taken place on the Clyde.

Some of those who were sold as slaves eventually finished up, by way of trade, back in the Roman Empire where their story came out.

Tacitus attributes the disastrous end of the voyage to the inexperience and incompetence of the Usipi. Though Tacitus's explanation has been unquestioningly accepted by modern historians,[5] it does not really stand up to examination. The Liburnian was the standard warship of the Roman fleet in the first and second centuries AD. They were usually biremes (i.e. with two banks of oars) but they could have only a single bank of oars: propulsion was by sail and 40–60 oarsmen.[6] A Liburnian galley would therefore have been a complex ship for an untrained and inexperienced crew to operate, yet the Usipi stole three of them from under the noses of the rest of the Roman fleet, evaded recapture, and successfully navigated the completely uncharted waters of the west coast of Scotland and the notoriously difficult Pentland Firth before making the earliest known crossing of the North Sea by a Germanic tribe, ironically, from west to east. If these men were ignorant of navigation, they must have been extremely lucky to get so far before being wrecked when the most dangerous part of their voyage was over. In fact the Usipi were probably wrecked by being blown on to a lee shore by a gale at a time when, because of hunger or scurvy, they had simply become too weak to handle their ships properly – a fate which befell the crew of many a homecoming East Indiaman in the seventeenth and eighteenth centuries. While the Usipi were, no doubt, inexperienced in marine navigation, they must have been skilful boat handlers, used to disciplined rowing (as opposed to paddling) and, probably, using sail. In the hands of bold and resourceful men, these skills, learned on rivers, were readily adaptable to seafaring. It is more likely that Tacitus has attributed the shipwreck of the Usipi to incompetence so as not to detract from his father-in-law Agricola's achievement in subsequently ordering a Roman fleet to circumnavigate Britain.[7]

The Raids of the Chauci

Significant though the activities of the Bructeri and Usipi are for the light which they shed on the development of Frankish naval power, they are of minor importance beside the activities of the Chauci, who are the most prominent of the early Germanic seafarers. Since the Chauci were one of the tribes which were ancestral to the Saxons, their pirate raids are of more than passing interest.

In the first and second centuries AD the Germanic tribes who inhabited the North Sea coast, between the Zuyder Zee and the border of modern Denmark, shared a common material culture. Consequently, the settlement areas of the individual tribes who made up this North Sea coastal grouping, which included

---

[5] For example Schmidt, *op. cit.*, vol. 2, p. 195, and Frere, *op. cit.*, p. 209.

[6] See Starr, *op. cit.*, pp. 8, 54, and L. Casson, *Ships and Seamanship in the Ancient World* (Princeton, 1971), pp. 133–4, 142.

[7] Tacitus, *Agricola*, 38.

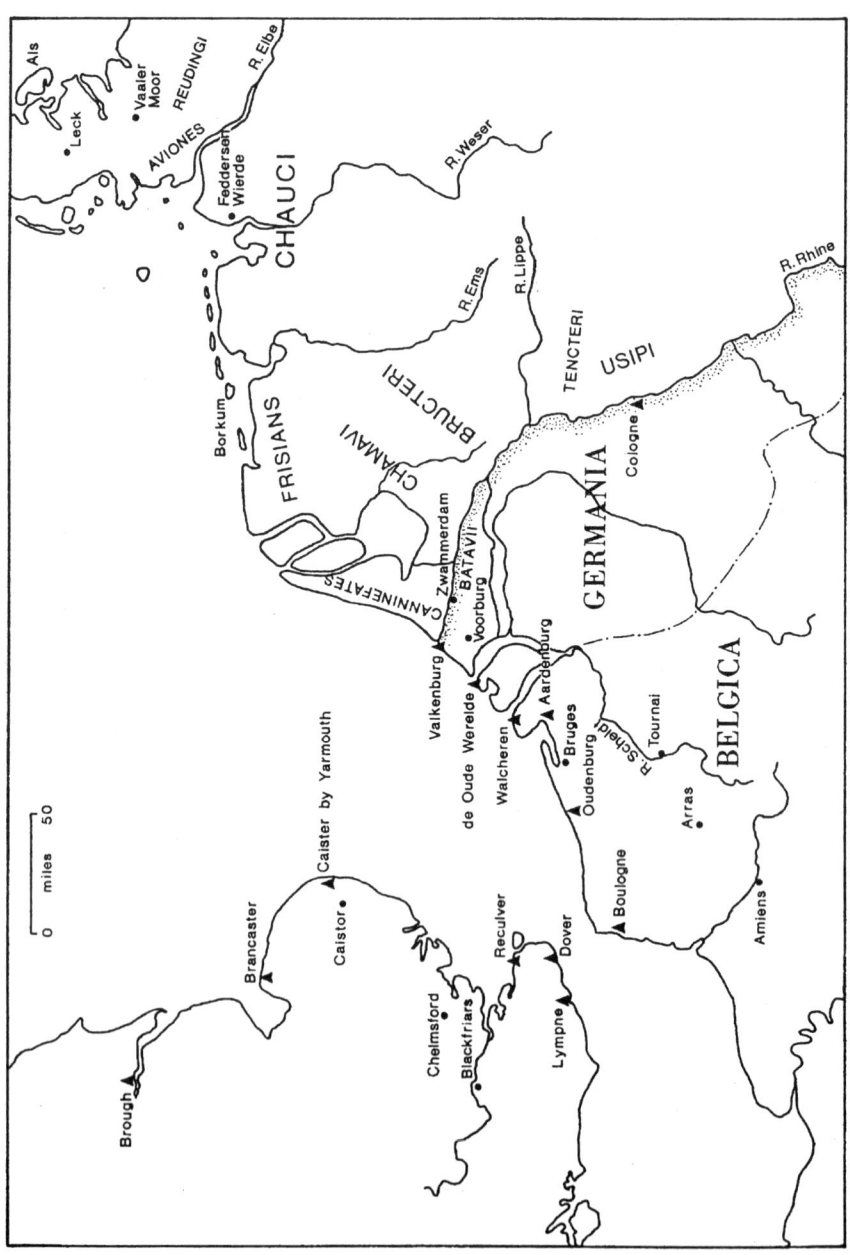

Map 1 The southern North Sea region, first to second centuries AD (John Haywood) Key: ▲ = military site

the Chauci and the Frisians, cannot be archaeologically defined.[8] As a result we must rely on contemporary literary sources to define the homeland of the Chauci. According to Tacitus, the Chauci were one of the most numerous of the Germanic peoples at the end of the first century AD. Their homeland was centred on the Weser and the Elbe, but by the time Tacitus was writing, *c*. AD 100, they had expanded westwards as far as the river Ems, to border directly onto the Frisians.[9] It is also possible that Chaucian seafarers had settled some of the islands at the mouth of the Rhine.[10]

The environmental conditions across the whole of this North Sea coastal province are very uniform and it seems reasonable to suppose that this was an important factor behind the cultural unity of the area. In its natural state, the low lying coastal area of this region is marshy, prone to flooding and dissected by innumerable creeks, inlets, fens and shallow lakes. It is a characteristic of the area that settlements are sited on raised mounds to protect them from flooding. Usually known from their Dutch name as *terpen* (German: *Wurten*), these mounds are formed partly from the accumulation of the debris of human settlement and partly from the deliberate piling up of layers of clay to form a building platform clear of the flood level.[11]

The exploitation of the wetlands formed a vital part of the agricultural economy of the region.[12] They provided grazing for livestock, especially cattle, and they were an important source of game and fish. It is possible also that coastal trade played a part in the economy, though this is difficult to demonstrate. What is certain is that the inhabitants of this area would have found the early acquisition of boat building and boat handling skills a social and economic necessity.

Little is known of the social organisation of the Chauci. In the first century AD, the settlement patterns and burial practices of the inhabitants of the Elbe-Weser coastal area, which we can be fairly certain was the heartland of the Chauci, point to a society which was neither highly centralised nor highly stratified.[13] In the later second century there are signs that the structure of Chaucian society was beginning to change. A small number of apparently

---

[8] M. Todd, *The Northern Barbarians 100 BC–AD 300*, revised edn (Oxford, 1987), pp. 44–48.

[9] Tacitus, *Germania*, ed. and trans. M. Hutton, Loeb Classical Library, rev. edn (London, 1970), ch. 35. On the Chaucian homeland, see also Schmidt, *op. cit.*, vol. 1, p. 33, E. Demougeot, *La formation de l'Europe et les invasions barbares: Des origines germaniques á l'avènement de Dioclétien* (Paris, 1969), p. 50, and J. N. L. Myres, *The English Settlements* (Oxford, 1986), p. 50.

[10] Pliny, *Natural History*, ed. and trans. H. Rackham, Loeb Classical Library, revised edn (London, 1968), IV. 15.101. See also Schmidt, *op. cit.*

[11] In general on the *terpen* see S. Lebecq, 'De la proto histoire au haut moyen âge: le paysage des "*terpen*" le long des côtes de la Mer du Nord', *Revue du Nord* LXII (1980), pp. 125–54. Also Todd, *op. cit.*, pp. 79–88. The *terpen* are described by Pliny, *Natural History*, XVI. 2–4, who paints a miserable picture of the lives of their inhabitants.

[12] On the economy of the region see Todd, *op. cit.* pp. 23, 84, 87–8. See also Pliny, *Nat. Hist.* XVI 2–4.

[13] Characteristic of the area between the Elbe and Weser are huge cemeteries of cremation urn burials containing a uniform range of poor quality grave goods: Todd, *op. cit.*, p. 46.

aristocratic cemeteries appear, with burials accompanied by rich grave goods,[14] while the settlement patterns of the villages show evidence of the emergence of permanent dominant families. The clearest evidence for this comes from the *terp* settlement of Feddersen Wierde, near Bremerhaven. In the first century AD there is no evidence of social stratification but after *c.* AD 100 it is clear that one family achieved a position of greater status and wealth than its neighbours. Their *Herrenhof* was situated in a palisaded compound on the edge of the village which contained a complex of craftsmens' workshops, farm buildings, storehouses and a large meeting or banqueting hall. This family, or at least the occupants of the site, continued to dominate the village until the fifth century when it was abandoned.[15] This movement towards a more hierarchical society coincides with the period which probably saw the most intense Chaucian piracy.

What the immediate causes of Chaucian piracy were cannot be determined. Neither population pressure nor marine transgression seems to have played a part.[16] The underlying cause, however, is certainly the simple desire to acquire the material products of Roman civilisation to shore up the status and prestige of the emerging ruling class. Whatever their feelings towards the Roman Empire itself, the Germanic tribes were certainly not hostile to Roman products. Roman goods, from luxury items like glass and silverware to everyday objects like pottery and iron tools, together with gold, silver and even bronze coins and perishable items like wine and foodstuffs, were distributed widely in the Germanic area;[17] Scandinavia, especially the Danish islands, has produced very rich finds of Roman goods from the whole imperial period.[18] Whether these

---

[14] K. Weidmann, 'Zur Interpretation einiger kaiserzeitlicher Urnenfriedhöfe in Nordwestdeutschland', *JRGZM* XII (1965), pp. 84–92. Six such cremation cemeteries have been identified on the lower Weser and in Hadeln which date from the second to the third centuries. They are distinguished from other contemporary cemeteries in the same area by their small size and rich grave goods, including bronzes, pottery, weapons and riding gear. Many of these rich burials are accompanied by simple urn burials. Weidmann, *ibid.*, p. 89, interprets these as the graves of retainers buried alongside their masters.

[15] See Todd, *op. cit.*, p. 85.

[16] Sea level was probably slightly lower than the present day in the early imperial period, and though the Chaucian population was growing, the surplus was absorbed by a progressive reclamation of the wetlands for agriculture: Todd, *op. cit.* pp. 87–8.

[17] On trade contacts between the Germans and the Romans see L. Hedeager, 'A quantitative analysis of Roman imports in Europe north of the *limes* (0–400 AD), and the question of Roman Germanic exchange', in K. Kristiansen and C. Paludan-Müller (eds), *New Directions in Scandinavian Archaeology*, Studies in Scandinavian Prehistory and Early History 1 (Copenhagen, 1979), pp. 191–216 (esp. 211–13). Also E. A. Thompson, *The Early Germans* (Oxford, 1965), pp. 18–28, and Todd, *op. cit.*, pp. 22–29.

[18] On the trade of Roman goods in Denmark in this period see J. Brønsted, *Danmarks oldtid III, Jernalderen* (Copenhagen, 1966), pp. 168–76, 200–8. Brønsted claims that the marked concentration of finds on the eastern Danish islands indicates that there was a direct sea trade with the Roman Empire via the North Sea and the Kattegat. Though Brønsted's ideas have been widely accepted (e.g. by Hedeager, 'Processes', see n. 19 below), I fail to find his conclusions convincing. Could not such a distribution pattern just as easily have been created by a trade

products were distributed by genuine long range trade by land and sea or by a succession of exchanges between merchants operating in relatively limited areas is impossible to say; quite probably both played a part.[19]

The material culture of those tribes which bordered directly onto the Roman Empire became considerably enriched by their contact. The obvious wealth of the Empire acted as a magnet and drew the barbarians to attempt to acquire a share, both by trade and by raiding across the frontier. Roman subsidies to friendly barbarians were probably also an important mechanism in distributing Roman wealth beyond the frontiers. In turn, the increased wealth of the border tribes acted as a magnet upon those tribes who were more distant from the Empire and they in their turn raided, or traded with, their wealthier neighbours.[20] Except for a short period in the first century when both they and the Frisians had fallen under Roman domination, the Chauci belonged to this second group of barbarians whose lands did not border directly onto Roman territory. For the Chauci, raiding by sea was simply a means of gaining direct access to the Roman Empire by turning the flank not only of the Roman defences but of their own Germanic neighbours.[21]

The earliest recorded raids by the Chauci on Roman territory occurred in AD 41 when they attacked the coastal area of Belgica.[22] Though the raids were beaten off, we may suspect that they were not a minor affair as Gabinius, the governor of Belgica, was permitted to take the surname *Cauchus* by the emperor Claudius in honour of his part in defeating the raiders.[23] However the Chauci were not discouraged by their defeat for they returned to raid Belgica again in AD 47.[24] The leader of the Chauci on these raids was Gannascus, a deserter from a Roman auxiliary unit who belonged to the Canninefates, a Germanic tribe of the lower Rhine.[25] No doubt the Chauci benefited greatly from Gannascus's

---

route which ran overland (and possibly through many intermediaries) through Germany and over the short Baltic crossing to the Danish islands?

[19] See Hedeager, *op. cit.* and also *idem*, 'Processes towards state formation in early Iron Age Denmark', in Kristiansen and Paludan-Müllar, *op. cit.*, pp. 217–23.

[20] G. Kossack, 'The Germans', in F. Millar, *The Roman Empire and its Neighbours*, 2nd edn (London, 1981), pp. 294–320. Also A. R. Birley, 'The third century crisis in the Roman Empire', *Bulletin of the John Rylands University Library of Manchester* LVIII (1975), p. 279.

[21] A good, but much later (fourth century), example of this motivation in action is recorded by Zosimus, *New History*, ed. and trans. F. Paschoud, *Zosime: Histoire Nouvelle*, Collection des universités de France (3 vols, Paris, 1971–9), IV. 6. See below chapter 2, p. 66.

[22] Cassius Dio, LX. 8.7. On the Roman naval expeditions in the North Sea see Starr, *op. cit.*, pp. 141–6.

[23] Suetonius, *De Vita Caesarum*, ed. and trans. J. C. Rolfe, Loeb Classical Library (2 vols, London, 1914), *Divus Claudius*, XXIV. 3. The form of the name is unusual but it is certain that it refers to the Chauci.

[24] Tacitus, *Annales*, ed. and trans. C. H. Moore, Loeb Classical Library (4 vols, London, 1963), XI. 18–19, Schmidt, *op. cit.*, vol. 1, p. 34, Kossack, *op. cit.*, p. 301.

[25] On the Canninefates generally see Schmidt, *op. cit.* vol. 2, pp. 147–8. They probably had affinities with the Frisians.

knowledge of the wealthy coastal communities.[26] The Roman auxiliary fort at Valkenburg, guarding the mouth of the Old Rhine,[27] was destroyed by fire around this time and it has been suggested that the Chauci may have been responsible for this.[28] The raiders were eventually defeated by the *classis Germanica* which had probably been called down the Rhine from its main base at Cologne.[29] This fleet included a number of triremes and it seems to have made short work of the Chaucian pirate fleet. Gannascus himself escaped and took refuge with the Chauci, only to be killed a short time later by a Roman punitive expedition.[30]

The Chauci also took part in the revolt of the Batavian Civilis in the years AD 69 to 70.[31] This began as a rebellion of the Batavi and the Canninefates against Roman rule but it quickly turned into a general rising of the northern Germans as first the Chauci and the Frisians joined in, and then the proto-Frankish tribes of the Bructeri, Tencteri and Usipi.[32] Both barbarian and Roman naval forces were heavily engaged in this revolt which centred for the most part on the lower Rhine. There is no explicit evidence for Chaucian naval activity in this revolt but it seems reasonable to suppose, in the light of their earlier piracy, that some of their aid to the rebels took the form of naval forces. In any case, Tacitus is sometimes vague about the tribal origins of the various rebel groups and often calls them simply *Germani*,[33] so it is often not possible to identify the individual tribes involved in any particular incident. For all that, it seems likely that the Canninefates were the leading naval power among the barbarian allies, and their naval forces were certainly active early on in the revolt when, with Frisian assistance, they destroyed the isolated Roman garrisons in the Rhine delta area.[34] Soon after this the Canninefates' fleet was reinforced when a mutiny by Batavian oarsmen in Roman service helped the rebels to capture 24 galleys of the

---

[26] Tacitus, *Annales*, XI. 19.

[27] In Roman times the Old Rhine was the main channel of the Rhine. On the changes in the course of the lower Rhine in Roman and early medieval times see S. Lebecq, *Marchands et navigateurs frisons du haut moyen âge* (2 vols, Lille, 1983), vol. 1, p. 124.

[28] H. Schönberger, 'The Roman frontier in Germany: an archaeological survey', *Journal of Roman Studies* LIX (1969), p. 152, but see also n. 34 below for an alternative interpretation.

[29] Cologne was the main base of the *classis Germanica* between the first and third centuries: see O. Höckmann, 'Romische Schiffsverbände auf dem Ober und Mittelrhein und die Verteidigung der Rheingrenze in der Spätantike', *JRGZM* XXXIII (1986), p. 379. For a general history of the *classis Germanica*, see Starr, *op. cit.*, pp. 141–52.

[30] Tacitus, *Annales*, XI. 19.

[31] Tacitus, *Historiarum libri*, ed. C. D. Fisher (Oxford, 1911), IV. 79, V. 19. Also Schmidt, *op. cit.*, vol. 1, p. 35.

[32] Tacitus, *Hist.* IV. 21.

[33] As for example in *Hist.* IV. 27.

[34] Tacitus, *Hist.* IV. 15. A. van Doorselaer, 'De Romeinen in de Nederlanden', in D. P. Blok *et al.* (eds.), *Algemene Geschiedenis der Nederlanden 1, Middeleeowen* (Haarlem, 1981), p. 80, suggests that it was during the course of these attacks, rather than the Chaucian raids of 47, that the auxiliary fort at Valkenburg was destroyed. Also generally on this revolt see Starr, *op. cit.*, pp. 144–6, and Schmidt, *op. cit.*, vol 1, pp. 35, 159–60.

classis Germanica.[35] No doubt these ships took part in a subsequent engagement in which the Canninefates attacked a Roman fleet off the North Sea coast and won a resounding victory; most of the Roman ships were sunk or captured.[36] More Roman ships, including a trireme which was serving as the flagship of the Rhine fleet, were captured in an attack on the Romans when they were camped on the bank of the Rhine for the night.[37] The jubilant Germans took the trireme up the Rhine and into the Lippe to present it as a gift to an influential priestess of the Bructeri. In another skirmish the Germans captured a Roman grain ship that had run aground.[38]

In the final naval engagement of the revolt it seems as if Civilis had brought all the barbarian naval forces together on the open sea at the mouth of the Rhine to intercept a Roman troop convoy approaching from the Channel.[39] The Germans' fleet was made up of a variety of ships; captured biremes, smaller galleys with a single bank of oars and a multitude of small ships carrying crews of about 40 men.[40] Most of the ships in this fleet were probably sailing ships as, Tacitus tells us, the Germans used cloaks to make improvised sails to improve the performance, and appearance, of some of their captured Roman vessels.[41] This is the earliest evidence which exists for the use of the sail among the Germans and is discussed in greater detail below.

The engagement when it came was a desultory affair which, nevertheless, represented a success for the Romans.[42] The Germans' fleet was the more numerous but the Romans had larger ships and formed a more disciplined battle formation. The Roman fleet had the advantage of the current but the Germans had the wind behind them. The last point is another indicator of the importance of sailing ships in the German fleet. Both sides appear to have been evenly matched because neither seems to have been willing to force a close engagement, though clearly both were in a position to have done so. After a brief exchange of missiles the fleets separated; Civilis withdrew north of the Rhine and the Romans used the opportunity to ravage Batavia unopposed.

---

[35] Tacitus, *Hist.* IV. 16.

[36] *Ibid.* IV. 79.

[37] *Ibid.* V. 22.

[38] *Ibid.* IV. 27.

[39] *Ibid.* V. 23. Tacitus says that the engagement took place at the mouth of the *Mosae* (the Meuse) but the Lek or the Waal are more likely locations in the opinion of H. Goelzer (ed. and trans.), *Tacite; Histoires* (2 vols. Paris, 1965–8), vol 2, p. 310, n. 2.

[40] Tacitus, *Hist.* V. 23.

Civilem cupido incessit navalem aciem ostendanti: complet quod biremium quaeque simplici ordine agebantur; adiecta ingens luntrium vis, tricenos quadragenosque ferunt, armamenta Liburnicis solita.

[41] *Ibid.*: 'et simul captae luntres sagulis versicoloribus haud indecore pro velis iuvabantur'.

[42] *Ibid.*

Following Civilis's revolt the Chauci seem to have settled down, and Tacitus, writing *c*. 98, describes them as a peaceful people.[43] However, in the later second century Chaucian piracy once again broke out. These raids appear to have been both more destructive and more wide-ranging than the first-century raids. The raids probably were at their most serious in the period 170 to 175 when Didius Julianus, then governor of Belgica and later emperor, was forced to the expedient of raising local levies to drive off the Chaucian attacks.[44] But it is unlikely that Julianus's victory marked the suppression of the pirates;[45] in fact Chaucian piracy was probably to remain endemic in the North Sea and Channel until, in the next century, it was replaced by Frankish and Saxon piracy.

Archaeological evidence, though by its nature not conclusive, presents a consistent picture of a state of insecurity in the coastal areas of Belgica and south-eastern Britain in the last three decades of the second century and areas as far away as the Bay of Biscay may have been affected. Of three villas excavated recently on the coast of Brittany two had been destroyed by fire in this period and not subsequently rebuilt while a third had been temporarily abandoned.[46] The coastal distribution of coin hoards of this period in Brittany is marked and points to a threat from the sea rather than from *bagaudae* type banditry which would have produced a more even distribution.[47] In Britain the phenomenon of the 'Antonine fires' in Essex has been associated with Germanic piracy.[48] So many rural sites and small towns, including Chelmsford, Billericay, Gestingthorpe, Braintree, Wickford, Kelvedon, Great Chesterford and Harlow, suffered destruction or damage by fire in the period between 170 and *c*. 200 that accident can be safely ruled out as the cause on the grounds that it would have been too much of a coincidence.[49] A similar pattern of destruction has also been built up from rural and urban sites in northern and north-western Belgica in this period and this too has been linked to Chaucian piracy.[50] Here Amiens, Thérouanne,

---

[43] Tacitus, *Germania*, 35.

[44] *Scriptores Historiae Augustae* (henceforward SHA), ed. E. Hohl (2 vols, Leipzig, 1965), *Didius Julianus*, I. 7: 'inde Belgicam sancto ac diu rexit ibi Cauchis, Germaniae populis qui Albam fluvium adcolebant, erumpentibus restitit tumultuariis auxiliis provincialium.'

[45] For a contrary view see J. F. Drinkwater, *Roman Gaul: The Three Provinces 58 BC–AD 260* (London, 1983), p. 76. Drinkwater does not appear to have taken the archaeological evidence into account. For other brief accounts of these raids see L. Musset, *The Germanic Invasions* (London, 1975), p. 100, and P. Salway, *Roman Britain* (Oxford, 1981), pp. 257–9.

[46] P. Galliou, 'Western Gaul in the third century', in A. King and M. Henig (eds), *The Roman West in the Third Century*, BAR IS 109 (Oxford, 1981), p. 262.

[47] *Ibid.*

[48] W. Rodwell, 'Trinovantian towns in their setting: a case study', in W. Rodwell and T. Rowley (eds), *The Small Towns of Roman Britain*, BAR 15 (Oxford, 1975), p. 93, and P. J. Drury, 'Roman Chelmsford: *Caesaromagus*', *ibid*. p. 172, note the lack of any other historical context to account for the widespread destruction.

[49] Rodwell, *op. cit.* p. 93. Rodwell, pp. 100–1, notes the absence of a complementary pattern of coin hoards.

[50] G. Jelski, 'Les niveaux antiques et la céramique du chartier du commissariat central d'Arras', *Revue du Nord* LXII (1980), pp. 844, 855–6. The valley of the Scheldt seems to have been the

Vendeuil-Caply, Beauvais, Bavai, Tournai and Arras have all produced evidence of destruction by fire in the later second century. At Arras the damage has been fairly precisely dated to between 160 and 180. Naturally, it does not follow automatically that the widespread destruction in Belgica shares the same cause as the 'Antonine fires' in Essex simply because the two phenomena are contemporary. If, in the future, a similar pattern of destruction emerges in areas which could not have been exposed to piracy a different explanation will have to be sought. But as the evidence stands, especially as it is supported by Roman defensive measures, serious Chaucian piracy does seem to be the most likely cause.

The Romans responded to the threat by building civil and military fortifications to protect the exposed coastal areas and vulnerable estuaries of Britain and Belgica. Chelmsford was given earth and timber ramparts *c.* 160–75 which were destroyed by fire along with much of the town between 170 and 200.[51] Further north the small but strategically important town of Brough-on-Humber had also been furnished with earth and timber ramparts by the end of the second century and may have served as a naval base to guard the Humber estuary.[52] The exposed East Anglian town of Caistor by Norwich, which suffered two serious fires in the late second-early third century, was given stone walls *c.* 200.[53] In the same period Voorburg (near The Hague), the *civitas* of the Canninefates, was fortified with a wall and double ditch.[54]

The system of coastal fortifications which the Romans built is a precursor of the later 'Saxon Shore' defences and could perhaps be styled the 'Chaucian Shore' defences. The construction of forts seems to have begun slightly earlier in Belgica than in Britain. The coastal plain of Belgica was protected by a number of military fortifications, the earliest of which is the fort at Aardenburg, built

---

main target for raiders in this period: see W. A. van Es, *De Romeinen in Nederland* (Bussum, 1972), p. 48.

[51] Drury, 'Roman Chelmsford', pp. 170–2. A number of other small defended sites in Essex are also thought to have been a response to piracy in this period, though there is no conclusive evidence to confirm this view: see J. Crickmore, *Romano British Urban Defences* BAR BS 126 (Oxford, 1984), p. 49. The incomplete defences at Wickford do certainly date from late in the second century (p. 136). This is one of the sites that shows major fire damage (see note 49 above); possibly the small settlement was attacked while it was in the process of being fortified. Urban defences in general, however, provide the least satisfactory evidence for piracy as the late second century saw defences built at a number of British towns, for example Dorchester on Thames, which could hardly have felt threatened by piracy. For alternative contexts for urban defences, such as civic prestige, see pp. 61–7.

[52] J. S. Wacher, *The Towns of Roman Britain* (2nd, revised edn, London, 1995), pp. 79, 394–401, and also *idem*, *Roman Britain* (London, 1978), p. 52. A naval presence at Brough has not been universally accepted, though it was certainly a primarily military settlement after *c.* 270: see H. Ramm, *The Parisi* (London, 1978), pp. 39–40, 60. On the towns' defences see also Crickmore, *op. cit.*, pp. 79, 140–1.

[53] Crickmore, *op. cit.* p. 143, and G. Webster, 'Small towns without defences', in Rodwell and Rowley, *op. cit.*, p. 53.

[54] Van Doorselaer, *op. cit.*, p. 80.

c. 170–3.[55] The earliest phases of the fort at Oudenburg, which was later incorporated into the Saxon Shore system, may also date from as early as the end of the second century.[56] A third fort is believed to have been built between these two, at Bruges, but firm evidence for this is lacking.[57] It is also possible that additional forts were built to cover the mouths of the Rhine and the Scheldt. Roman sites with proven military connections are known to have existed at Walcheren, de Oude Werelde and Brittenburg. All have been destroyed by marine erosion in early modern times, but finds from the shoreline, including *classis Germanica* stamped tiles, point to a date no later than the early third century.[58] It is difficult to believe that the defences could have been effective without forts to cover these vulnerable river mouths and the significant volume of merchant and military shipping which used them.[59]

In Britain a fort was built at Reculver c. 220 to cover the Thames estuary.[60] A little earlier than this, possibly before the end of the second century, a fort had been built at Brancaster on the Wash, presumably to protect the rich and densely

---

[55] H. Thoen, *De Belgische kustvlakte in de Romeinse tijd*, Verhandelingen van de Koninklijke Academie voor wettenschappen. Letteren en schone kunsten van Belgie. Klasse der Letteren, XL (1978) no. 88. pp. 144 5. Also, in less detail, *idem*, 'The third century Roman occupation in Belgium: the evidence of the coastal plain', in King and Henig (eds), *op. cit.*, p. 246.

[56] Thoen, *Belgische kustvlakte*, pp. 128–33, and *idem*, 'Roman occupation', p. 246. The earliest building phases at Oudenburg are not securely dated. J. Mertens, 'Oudenburg and the northern sector of the continental *litus Saxonicum*', in D. E. Johnston (ed.), *The Saxon Shore* CBA Research Report 18 (London, 1978), p. 60, argues that the fort was not begun before the start of the mid third century Dunkirk II marine transgression and the position of the fort gives credibility to his claim. However Mertens's date has not been universally accepted: see, for example, E. Wightman, *Gallia Belgica* (London, 1985), pp. 160, 207.

[57] Thoen, *Belgische kustvlakte*, pp. 145–7.

[58] The finds suggest that the sites had all been abandoned by c. 270: see Mertens, *op. cit.*, pp. 51–3. The fact that the *classis Germanica* disappears as an organised unit from the literary sources c. 235 must make a second or early third century date more likely. There were possibly two further forts built on the Gallic coast in this period. S. Johnson, *The Roman Forts of the Saxon Shore* (London, 1976), p. 111, tentatively suggests the possibility of an early third century foundation for two unidentified Saxon Shore forts named in the *Notitia Dignitatum*, ed. O. Seeck (Berlin, 1876), as *Grannona* (Occ. xxxvii. 14) and *Marcis* (Occ. xxxviii. 7) on the grounds that they have comparable garrisons to the two British Saxon Shore forts which are known to date from the early third century, *Branodunum* (Brancaster) and *Regulbium* (Reculver) (Occ. xxviii. 16, 18). Johnson argues that Le Havre, for *Grannona*, and Marck, near Calais, for *Marcis*, are the most likely sites for these forts. On the locations of the other British Saxon Shore forts named in the *Notitia* see Johnson, *op. cit.* pp. 60–8.

[59] On Roman shipping from the lower Rhine to Britain see M. Hassal, 'Britain and the Rhine provinces: epigraphic evidence for Roman trade', in J. du Plat Taylor and H. Cleere (eds), *Roman Shipping and Trade: Britain and the Rhine Provinces*, CBA Research Report 24 (London, 1978), pp. 41–8.

[60] The foundation stone of Reculver has been partially preserved but still cannot be dated more closely than the late second or early third century. The bulk of pottery evidence points to a foundation c. 220. See J. C. Mann, 'The Reculver inscription – a note', in Johnston (ed.), *op. cit.*, p. 15, and Salway, *op. cit.*, pp. 253–4.

populated Fenland.[61] A third fort at Caister by Yarmouth has also been associated with these measures.[62] It has been noted that both Reculver and Brancaster were well sited as bases for naval patrols to protect coastal and cross Channel shipping from piracy.[63] However, nothing definite is known about the operations of the *classis Britannica* or *classis Germanica* in this period. Through most of the second century the main fleet bases of the *classis Britannica* seem to have been Dover, Lympne and Boulogne, reflecting its primary role of transporting troops and military supplies between Britain and the continent.[64] The status of Lympne *c*. 200 is uncertain and though the fleet base at Boulogne was still occupied, Dover had been abandoned *c*. 210, perhaps in favour of Reculver and Brancaster.[65] Such a move to more forward positions might indicate a shift in emphasis for the fleet from transport towards patrolling against pirates. It is reasonable to expect that the *classis Germanica* would have been deployed at the Rhine mouths,[66] a conclusion which is supported to some extent by the few finds from Walcheren, de Oude Werelde and Brittenburg. Tentative evidence for Roman naval activity against Chaucian pirates comes from a funerary inscription of *c*. 200 from Rome which mentions that the deceased had seen action against a Germanic fleet.[67]

---

[61] D. A. Edwards and C. J. S. Green, 'The Saxon Shore fort and settlement at Brancaster, Norfolk', in Johnston (ed.), *op. cit.*, pp. 25, 29. Both Reculver and Brancaster lack the thick walls and bastion towers of later third and fourth century fortifications and this has led to their being dated on typological grounds to before 230: see B. Cunliffe, 'The Saxon Shore: some problems and misconceptions', in *ibid.*, p. 3. Salway, *op. cit.*, pp. 257–8, suggests that the Fenlands may have formed a large imperial estate which would have given the Romans an added incentive to protect the region.

[62] Salway *op. cit.*, p. 258.

[63] Wacher, *Roman Britain*, p. 52, and Salway, *op. cit.* pp. 257–8. Salway points out that these two sites would also have been useful in controlling internal traffic.

[64] H. Cleere, 'The *classis Britannica*', in Johnston (ed.), *op. cit.*, pp. 16–19.

[65] The limited evidence for early third century occupation of Lympne is reviewed in B. Cunliffe, 'Excavations at the Roman fort at Lympne, Kent 1976 78', *Britannia* XI (1980), pp. 284–5. See also *idem*, 'Lympne: a preparatory comment', in Johnston (ed), *op. cit.*, pp. 29–30. On Boulogne see C. Seiller, 'Fouilles de Boulogne sur Mer (*Bononia*)', *Revue du Nord* LIII (1971), pp. 670–3, and on Dover, B. J. Philp, *The Excavations of the Roman Forts of the Classis Britannica at Dover, 1970 1977*, Kent monograph series no 3 (Dover, 1981), pp. 94–9. Also *idem*, 'Dover', in Johnston (ed.), *op. cit.*, pp. 20–1.

[66] Starr, *op. cit.*, p. 151.

[67] A. V. Domaszewski, 'Inschrift eines Germanenkrieges', *Mitteilungen des kaiserlich deutschen archäologischen Instituts, Römische Abteilung* XX (1905), pp. 156 63. The inscription, as restored by Domaszewski, p. 158, reads:

[Huic senatus auctore imperatore ... quod ... rebellionem ...]rum bello [devictarum] Germaniae gentiu[m suppressit, et aedific[ata mox incredibili cel[eritate classe defectores cu]m a barbaris classem habu[issent ... subiecit ... statuam armatam poni in foro divi Traiani pecunia publica censuit].

Domaszewski, pp.162–3, identifies the German fleet as Chaucian and, while Schmidt, *op. cit.*, vol. 1, p. 36, points out that this association cannot be established with any certainty, it does

Dark Age Naval Power

These Roman defensive measures suggest that by 200 the Chauci, and quite possibly other Germanic tribes too, had become expert seafarers. Perhaps they were not as bold and confident as the Saxons and Franks were to become before the end of the next century but they were nevertheless capable of crossing the North Sea, eluding Roman naval patrols in the Channel to raid as far as Brittany and penetrating well organised coastal defences to raid inland along the river systems. However, the apparent prosperity of Britain and northern Gaul in the early third century indicates that the Roman defences were by then successful in preventing major pirate incursions.[68] The threat of piracy must have remained real, though, for the Romans never abandoned the coastal defences as one would expect if the threat had passed; rather they were periodically strengthened and refined over the next two centuries as Chaucian piracy invisibly blended into Frankish and Saxon piracy.

The raids of 170–5 are the last recorded activities of the Chauci; by the fourth century their area of Germany was completely occupied by the Saxons. The disappearance of such a major people has naturally led to extensive, but ultimately inconclusive, speculation as to their fate. One theory is that they migrated westwards under Saxon pressure and were absorbed by the Franks but the literary evidence on which this is based falls well short of demonstrating any connection between the Chauci and the Franks.[69] Much more widespread is the view that, at some unidentifiable point in the third century, the Chauci lost their separate identity by becoming merged, either by peaceful confederation or by conquest, with the Saxons, though they may have preserved it into the fourth century within the Saxon grouping.[70] This conclusion is strongly supported by archaeological evidence which points to continuity of population in the Elbe-

---

seem to be a reasonable conclusion considering that no other German tribe is known from the literary sources to have been active in piracy in this period.

[68] Galliou, *op. cit.*, pp. 261, 264–71; Thoen, 'Roman occupation', p. 246.

[69] The main exponents of this theory are M. Lintzel, 'Zur Entstehungsgeschichte des sächsichen Stammes', *Sachsen und Anhalt* III (1927), pp. 10–17, and R. Wenskus, *Stammesbildung und Verfassung* (Cologne Graz, 1961), pp. 527–30. Neither is very convincing as their arguments are, unavoidably, given the lack of hard evidence, wholly speculative. Particularly weak is Lintzel's assertion that it is inconceivable that the small Saxon tribe could have conquered the powerful Chaucian people and that the Chauci must therefore have migrated out of the area (p. 15). In the first place we know next to nothing about the relative strengths of the two tribes; in the second, one is forced to ask how, if the Chauci were so strong that the Saxons could not have conquered them, the Saxons could have persuaded them to evacuate their territory. For a concise criticism of the literary evidence see W. Goffart, 'Hetware and Hugas: datable anachronisms in *Beowulf*', in C. Chase (ed.), *The Dating of Beowulf*, Toronto Old English series 6 (Toronto, 1981), p. 90.

[70] Schmidt, *op. cit.*, vol. 1, p. 37, W. Lammers, 'Die Stammesbildung bei den Sachsen', in *idem* (ed.), *Entstehung und Verfassung des Sachsenstammes* (Darmstadt, 1967), pp. 297 301, Myres, *op. cit.*, pp. 50–1. See also chapter 2, pp. 43–4, on this question.

Weser coastal region throughout the Roman Iron Age: such continuity rules out the possibility of any extensive migration either out of, or into, the area.[71]

The Ships of the Early Germanic Seafarers

Unfortunately we know little for certain about the boats which the Chauci, or other early Germans, used for their raids. Of the earlier Chaucian raids, Tacitus says simply that they raided 'in levibus navigiis',[72] which could be translated as in either light or swift boats. Elsewhere he calls the Germans' boats *luntres* (*leg. lintres*), which could mean anything from rowing boats to small sailing ships and which Tacitus uses indiscriminately to describe both Roman and barbarian boats.[73] Pliny the Elder, who was serving with the Roman army in Germania at the time of Gannascus's raids,[74] tells us that the Germanic *praedones* used large dug-outs, sometimes capable of carrying over 30 men.[75] Two large expanded logboats, dating from the first to third centuries, have been found in northern Germany, though neither is as large as the boats Pliny describes. These boats, from Vaaler Moor, near Rendsburg, and from Leck, near Schleswig, were both approximately 38 feet long and were strengthened internally with transverse ribs fastened to the hull with trenails.[76] The Vaaler Moor boat is particularly well preserved and was probably a fairly sophisticated vessel. Earlier reconstructions of the boat, such as Åkerlund's,[77] suggested that it was basically a canoe, paddled by a crew of 18–20 sitting on thwarts which were fastened to the gunwales of the

---

[71] Myres, *op. cit.*, pp. 50–1. P. Schmid, 'Some bowls from the excavations of the terp at Feddersen Wierde near Bremerhaven', in V. I. Evison (ed.), *Angles, Saxons and Jutes* (Oxford, 1981), pp. 47–8, points out that the development of pottery styles offers no evidence of an immigration of people into the area between the first century BC and the mid fifth century AD. See also Weidmann, *op. cit.*, on burial customs, which show similar continuity.

[72] Tacitus, *Annales*, XI. 18.

[73] See for example Tacitus, *Hist.* V. 23. On the use of the word *linter* see Casson, *op. cit.*, pp. 333-6.

[74] Norden, *op. cit.*, p. 308.

[75] Pliny, XVI. 76. 203: 'Germaniae praedones singulis arboribus cavatis navigant, quarum quaedam et XXX homines ferunt. Another example of the use of dug-outs by the Germans, in this case on the Elbe, is given by Velleius Paterculus, *Res gestae divi Augusti*, ed. and trans. J. Hellegouarc'h, *Histoire Romaine* (2 vols, Paris, 1982), II. 107. This was presumably a small dug-out of the type used widely throughout Europe on lakes and rivers right up to modern times as it had a crew of just one man. On dug-out boats in general see S. McGrail, *Log Boats of England and Wales* BAR BS 51 (Oxford, 1978), which contains considerable comparative material from other European countries.

[76] On the Vaaler Moor boat see H. Åkerlund, *Nydamskeppen* (Gothenburg, 1963), p. 120, and S. McGrail, *Ancient Boats in North-West Europe* (London, 1987), pp. 65, 78–80, 138, 211. On the Leck boat see D. Ellmers, 'Nautical archaeology in Germany', *IJNA* III (1974), pp. 139–40. Also F. Rieck and O. Crumlin-Pedersen, *Både fra Danmarks Oldtid* (Roskilde, 1988), pp. 88–9. This boat, which has been dated to *c.* AD 200, was beamier than the Vaaler Moor boat and blunter ended. It had a crew of 22 and was paddled.

[77] Åkerlund, *op. cit.*; Rieck and Crumlin-Pedersen, *op. cit.*

boat. But such a boat would have been top heavy when fully loaded and rather unstable; given also its low freeboard, it could not have been a seagoing vessel in any but the calmest weather.[78] Recently, McGrail has reassessed the boat and concluded that the thwarts were fitted eight inches below the gunwale and that the boat was actually rowed by a crew of only 8–10.[79] This interpretation presents a more seaworthy boat, as it is one with lighter loading and a lower centre of gravity: but the crew would have been too small for it to have made a useful warship. The dug-outs which Pliny describes were clearly much larger than the Vaaler Moor boat and had perhaps been extended by the addition of washstrakes to the top of the basic dug-out hull to increase their capacity and freeboard.[80]

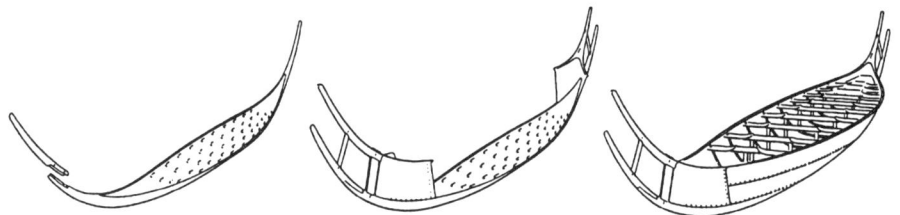

Figure 1 Schematic drawing of the Hjortspring boat's method of construction (National Museum, Copenhagen)

Though it is quite possible that some of the early, tentative, raids in sheltered coastal or estuarine waters could have been carried out in dug-out boats,[81] the Chauci must also have possessed more seaworthy craft by the time of their wider ranging raids in the second century. In fact, far more sophisticated boats were already being built in northern Europe centuries earlier. Evidence for this comes from the Hjortspring boat from Als in southern Denmark.[82] This boat was sunk with a hoard of weapons as a votive deposit in a peat bog *c.* 350 BC. The boat had distinctive double beaked prows and was 56 feet long by 6 feet broad. It was built from five lime wood planks: a broad bottom plank with two broad overlapped planks on either side. This method of building a hull from overlapping planks, known variously as clinker, lapstrake or Nordic construction,

---

[78] Åkerlund's belief, *op. cit.*, p. 120, that this was the kind of boat which took the Anglo-Saxon settlers to Britain is surely misconceived.

[79] McGrail, *Ancient Boats*, pp. 80, 211.

[80] On this common and ancient technique see McGrail, *ibid.* pp. 71–5, and for a global view see B. Greenhill, *The Archaeology of the Boat* (London, 1976), pp. 129–52.

[81] This seems to be fairly widely accepted, e.g. Schmidt, *op. cit.*, vol. 1, p. 34. Norden, *op. cit.*, p. 308. Rieck and Crumlin-Pedersen, *op. cit.*, p. 78.

[82] See Rieck and Crumlin-Pedersen, *op. cit.*, pp. 56–74, and J. Jensen, 'The Hjortspring boat reconstructed', *Antiquity* LXIII (1989), pp. 531–5, and also F. Kaul, *Da våbnene tav* (Copenhagen, 1988), pp. 15–22, 89–90, which also examines the background to the find. Kaul's attempt to reconstruct the specific circumstances in which the boat came to be sacrificed goes much further than the evidence allows.

is one of the distinctive characteristics of Anglo-Saxon and Viking shipbuilding. The Hjortspring boat therefore provides the earliest evidence for the origins of this tradition of shipbuilding. The ends of the boat were closed with two carved wooden blocks which served the same function as stem posts. No metal was used in its construction; the planks were sewn together and fastened to transverse strengthening ribs with ropes made of lime tree bast. The boat was paddled by a crew of 20 who sat on thwarts set at the level of the gunwale. It is thought that the boat was equipped with a steering oar at both ends so that it could be sailed in either direction. The Hjortspring boat was skilfully made to be as light as possible and would have been a fast, stable, flexible and relatively seaworthy vessel. Rock carvings and other depictions of similar ships, dating to the early Iron Age, are abundant in southern Scandinavia so presumably the type was widespread.[83]

Figure 2 Hjortspring-type boat from an Iron Age rock carving, Ostfold, Norway

It is probable, however, that by *c*. AD 100, boats of the Hjortspring type had been superceded in northern Europe by more sophisticated clinker-built boats while the find of a rowlock dated to *c*. 30 BC-AD 250 in a bog in Norway shows that rowing was replacing paddling as a means of propulsion.[84] The Björke boat of *c*. AD 100, discovered on an island west of Stockholm, is a simple clinker-built boat a little over 23 feet long. The hull is based on a light log-boat to which planks have been added, one on each side. The planks fully overlap the sides of the log-boat to which they are fastened with iron clench nails. Cleats were left outstanding on the inner surface of the planks to which six frames were lashed to give the vessel greater strength.[85] A more sophisticated clinker-built boat is represented by fragmentary remains of the Norwegian Halsnøy boat, dated to *c*. AD 200. Though the stem posts have not survived, the shape of the planks indicates that they were raked, not unlike those of the fourth century oak ship from Nydam on Als in Denmark.[86] In an interesting example of long-term

---

[83] A. E. Christensen, 'Proto-Viking, Viking and Norse craft' in A. E. Christensen (ed.) *The earliest ships* (London, 1996), 72–88, p. 74.

[84] Ø. Ekroll, 'Båt I myr – eit eldre jernalders båtfunn fra Nordhordland' in *Arkaeologiske Skrifter. Historisk Museum, Bergen* 4 (1988), 390–401, p. 390.

[85] B. Greenhill and J. Morrison, *The Archaeology of Boats and Ships* (London, 1995), pp. 176–7.

[86] A. E. Christensen, 'Scandinavian Ships from Earliest Times to the Vikings' in G. F. Bass, *A History of Seafaring Based on Underwater Archaeology* (London, 1972), p. 162.

continuity, the rowlocks of the Halsnøy boat are identical to ones still used by traditional boatbuilders in Norway.[87] A unique first or second century boat shaped clay bowl from Vendsyssel in Jutland is modelled on a plank built ship with raking stems and animal figureheads which, allowing for the limitations of the medium, shows, like the Halsnøy boat, a marked similarity with the oak ship from Nydam.[88] The Nydam ship, which is discussed in greater detail in chapter 3 (pp.93–8), was a flat keeled clinker-built oared longship with a length of about 70 feet, including the long raked stems The Nydam ship shows a number of structural similarities to the Hjortspring boat, but it was a very much more sophisticated and seaworthy vessel, capable of carrying a crew of 30–40 men. It seems far more realistic to conclude that the first and second century raids of the Chauci were carried out in comparable types of plank built oared ships than in dug-out canoes.

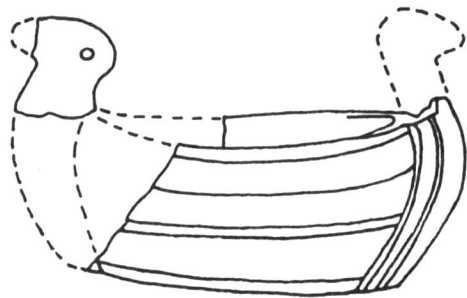

Figure 3 First-second century AD clay bowl in the shape of a boat. Vendyssel, Denmark

The shipbuilding traditions of the Germanic tribes on the lower and middle Rhine were quite different from those used by the tribes of the North Sea coast and the Baltic. The lower Rhine area has produced many ship finds from the Roman period, such as the logboats and large flat-bottomed river barges from Zwammerdam and Kapel Avazath,[89] which are built in a method which is neither Mediterranean nor 'Nordic' and has been styled 'Celtic' or 'continental' by maritime archaeologists. The main characteristics of this technique are that the side planks are all flush, with their edges laid close together (i.e. carvel-built), and that clenched iron nails are used to fasten the ribs to the planks.[90] Although this classification is widely accepted, the name has probably served to obscure the extent to which 'Celtic' boat-building may also have been practised by the Germanic tribes on both banks of the Rhine as well as by the ethnic Celts of

---

[87] Christensen, 'Proto-Viking, Viking and Norse craft', p. 76.

[88] On the bowl see J. Brønsted, *op. cit.*, pp. 165–6.

[89] On Kapel Avazath see P. Johnstone, *The Seacraft of Prehistory* (London, 1980), pp. 161–6. On Zwammerdam see M. D. de Weerd, 'Ships of the Roman period at Zwammerdam/*Nigrium Pullum inferior*', in du Plat Taylor, *op. cit.*, pp.15–21.

[90] D. Ellmers, 'Keltischer Schiffbau', *JRGZM* XVI (1969), pp. 73–122.

The Beginnings of Germanic Piracy

Britain and Gaul. For example, the three barges from Zwammerdam, all dating to the second half of the second century, have Celtic features but were certainly built in the province of Germania Inferior ('Lower Germany') which was inhabited by Germanic tribes who had settled the west bank of the Rhine before the Roman conquest of Gaul. Both they and some of the Germanic tribes on the east bank of the Rhine had already adopted many Gallic practices by Caesar's time and it would be surprising if this influence did not extend to shipbuilding techniques. One of these tribes, the Ubii, offered to transport Caesar's army across the Rhine by boat in 55 BC, which certainly suggests they possessed something more substantial than simple dug-out canoes.[91]

All of the barges from Zwammerdam had mast steps. In two cases the masts they supported were small and were probably used primarily to anchor a tow line; if they did carry a sail it could only have been an auxiliary means of propulsion.[92] The third barge (Zwammerdam 4) was a very large vessel, about 105 feet long by 15 feet broad, and the massive mast step was intended to support a heavy mast and sail.[93] The largest of the logboats (Zwammerdam 3) also had a mast step. This 33 feet long boat was extended by the addition of washstrakes on either side which increased the beam, giving the boat enough stability to have carried a light sail.[94] None of these ships was either a warship or a sea-going ship but their sophistication is such that we can be certain the Rhine Germans were not dependent on simple dug-out canoes as warships.

There is no literary evidence for shipbuilding on the lower Rhine in the first century AD but Pliny notes the use of reeds as caulking between the planks of their ships by the inhabitants of Belgica, which is the same method as was employed in the Zwammerdam finds.[95]

Another ship which should be considered here is a sailing ship from Bruges which has been radio-carbon dated to AD 180±80.[96] The ship was a sea going cargo vessel, probably originally about 45 feet long, carvel-built and flat-bottomed with a sharp transition to steep sides. The ship has been placed in the 'Celtic' tradition and it has some technical similarities with the Zwammerdam

---

[91] Caesar, *The Gallic War*, ed. and trans. H. J. Edwards, Loeb Classical Library (London, 1917), IV. 1.

[92] De Weerd, *op. cit.* pp. 16–17, thinks that the masts of these two barges (Zwammerdam 2 and 6) were for tow lines only. McGrail, *Ancient Boats*, p. 218, disagrees and concludes that the mast steps, and other fittings, of both these barges were massive enough to have been intended to carry sails.

[93] De Weerd, *op. cit.* p. 17; McGrail, *Ancient Boats*, p. 218.

[94] McGrail, *Ancient Boats*, p. 218. On the use of sails on extended logboats in other parts of the world see Greenhill, *op. cit.*, pp. 129–52.

[95] Pliny, *Natural History*, XVI. 64.158; Johnstone, *op. cit.*, pp. 163–4.

[96] For a description of the boat see P. Marsden, 'Ships of the Roman period and after in Britain' in G. F. Bass (ed.), *A History of Seafaring Based on Underwater Archaeology* (London, 1972), pp. 122–3. On the date see Johnstone, *op. cit.*, p. 90. Also of interest is R. Morcken, *Langskip, knarr og kogge* (Bergen, 1983), pp. 110–2, 180.

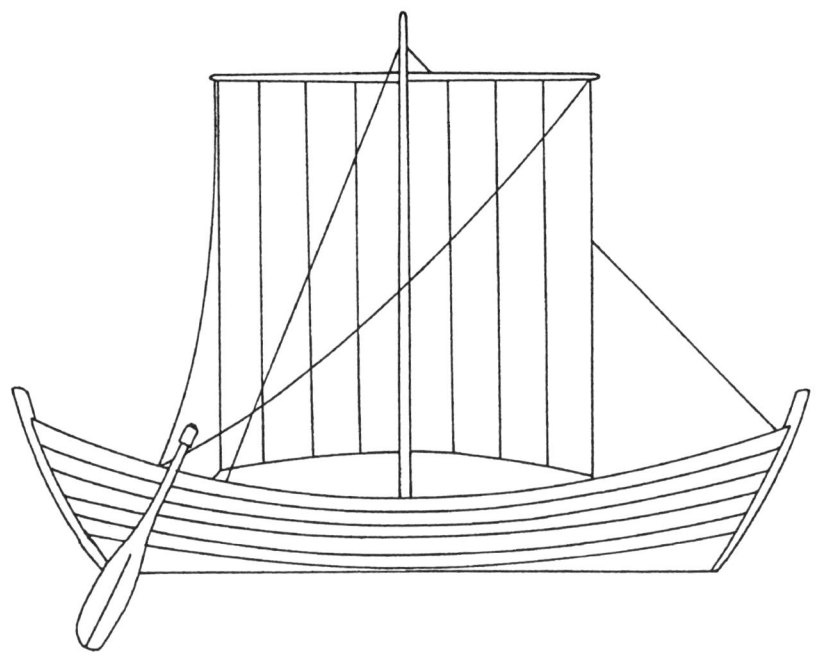

Figure 4 A Reconstruction of the Bruges boat

barges and another second century boat from Blackfriars in London,[97] such as the use of massive iron clench nails and the mast step which takes the form of a heavy transverse frame with a rectangular socket for the mast. Both the Bruges boat and the Blackfriars boat are now seen as being ancestral to the cog, which became the dominant ship type for trade and war in north-west Europe in the Middle Ages.[98] Whatever the geographical and ethnic origins of the Bruges boat, the type had passed into widespread use along the North Sea coast of Germany by the early Middle Ages and the cog is now often thought of as being the typical vessel of the Frisians.[99] It is quite possible that the Germanic peoples of the Low

---

[97] On the Blackfriars ship see P. Marsden, 'A re-assessment of Blackfriars ship 1', in S. McGrail (ed.) *Maritime Celts, Frisians and Saxons* CBA Research Report 71 (London, 1990), pp. 66–74. A similar ship, dating to the late third century, was discovered in 1986 at St Peter Port on Guernsey: see M. Rule, 'The Romano Celtic ship excavated at St Peter Port, Guernsey', in S. McGrail (ed.), *Maritime Celts*, pp. 49–56.

[98] For a general history of the development of the cog see D. Ellmers, 'Frisian and Hanseatic merchants sailed the cog', in A. Bang-Andersen (ed.), *The North Sea* (Stavanger-Oslo, 1985), pp. 79–95.

[99] For example, Ellmers, *op. cit.*, and S. Lebecq, *op. cit.*, vol. 1, pp. 181–3. Also, R. Unger, *The Ship in the Medieval Economy 600–1600* (London-Montreal, 1980), pp. 60–1.

Countries were already building similar sea going sailing ships in the second century.

Though our sources have nothing specific to say about the use of the sail among the Chauci, it seems possible that they had adopted it by the second century. It is impossible to say exactly when the Germanic peoples first learned of the sail but it was certainly in widespread use among their Celtic neighbours by *c.* 100 BC.[100] Roman naval expeditions in 12BC, AD 5 and AD 12 had explored the coasts of Germany and Denmark so it is impossible that the Germans of the North Sea coast were still ignorant of the sail in the first century AD.[101] Graphic evidence that Roman sailing ships continued to be seen along the German coast comes from a beautifully drawn Roman merchant ship on a bone of 4th or 5th century date found in the Weser. A runic inscription on the bone reads LOKOM:HER, probably meaning 'look here', may be a charm against enemy fleets.[102] It is thought that the common Germanic word *segel* is derived from the Celtic word *seklo* (Irish *seól*). As the word must have entered the Germanic vocabulary long before the first century AD, this would seem to indicate that the Germans had learned of the sail from their Celtic neighbours long before their first contacts with the Romans.[103] Of course, acquaintance and adoption are not the same thing (though why would the word be adopted if the device was not?) and current orthodox opinion has it that the sail was not adopted into common use by the Germanic tribes on the North Sea coast until as late as the seventh century, or even later in Scandinavia.[104] Even if there was no evidence to the contrary it is hard to believe that such an obviously useful and, in its basic form,

Figure 5 Late Roman merchant ship inscribed on a bone from the River Weser (Göttlicher)

---

[100]On the Celts' use of sailing ships in this period see, S. McGrail, 'Boats and boatmanship in the late prehistoric southern North Sea and Channel', in *idem, Maritime Celts*, pp. 36–47. McGrail's article clearly demonstrates the widespread use of the sail by the Celts by the first century BC. McGrail, however, also makes a good circumstantial case for Celtic use of the sail by *c.* 300 BC. The earliest known date at which the north Germans could have seen a sail is presumably *c.* 350 BC when the Greek Pytheas explored the northern seas: Johnstone, *op. cit.*, p. 155.

[101]On these expeditions see Starr, *op. cit.*, pp. 141–6.

[102]A. Göttlicher, Roman ship on Runic bone', *IJNA* 18 (1989), p. 73.

[103]Vogel, *op. cit.*, pp. 66–7.

[104]For example recently R. Hodges, *Dark Age Economics* (London, 1982), p. 95, Unger, *op. cit.*, pp. 62–4, Lebecq, *op. cit.*, vol. 1, pp. 177–81. See further below chapter 3, pp. 105–9.

technologically simple device as the sail had not been adopted rapidly by the seafaring peoples of the north German coast, especially as the finds from Zwammerdam and elsewhere show that the sail was in widespread use by their fellow Germans on the Rhine by the later second century. This has certainly been the case among other primitive seafaring peoples in early modern times. For example, the Indian tribes of the north-west coast of North America were skilled seafarers who had never used the sail. Yet within a few years of their first contacts with European seafarers in the eighteenth century they had learned to step masts on their dug-out canoes and make sails from woven cedar bark.[105]

One piece of literary evidence which has often been cited in support of the view that the sail was unknown to the Germans is Tacitus's account in the *Germania* of the Scandinavian *Suiones* (i.e. the Lake Malaren Swedes) whose ships, he says, used neither sails nor oars but were paddled instead.[106] While this was no doubt true of the *Suiones* in their remote Baltic homeland, it cannot be used as evidence that it was true of all the Germanic peoples at this time. The fact that in the *Germania*, the *Suiones* are the only people whose ships are discussed may simply be a sign that they were unusual and thus noteworthy. The archaeological evidence discussed above shows that in their continuing reliance on paddles, at least, the *Suiones* were probably rather backward by the time Tacitus wrote the *Germania* in AD 98. In any case Tacitus' curiously neglected account, discussed above (p. 25), of the indecisive naval encounter between Civilis's barbarian fleet and the Romans proves beyond doubt that the sail had begun to be used among the Germans by the mid-first century AD. The fact that the Germans fitted improvised sails, made from cloaks, on their captured Roman boats in preparation for an engagement at sea shows that, to at least one of the Germanic tribes involved, a sail was an essential part of a seagoing vessel. The simplicity of the improvisation is significant in itself; it demonstrates the ease with which any seafaring people could have begun to experiment with the use of the sail. It is frequently claimed that before the seventh or eighth century the keel structures of Germanic clinker-built ships were too weak to permit mast and sail to be carried.[107] But the loads imposed on a hull by a single masted square sail rig are in fact very modest. The keel structure can, therefore, hardly have been the serious obstacle to the adoption of the sail that many archaeologists claim, as

---

[105]P. Drucker, *Indians of the Northwest Coast* (New York, 1963), pp. 62–77. Unfortunately a wider survey is not possible as nearly all seafaring societies appear to have adopted the sail into use in relatively ancient times. Even in South America the sail had been adopted before AD 1000, probably from contacts, which can only have been occasional, with stray Polynesian seafarers: see Johnstone, *op. cit.*, pp. 224–31.

[106]Tacitus, *Germania*, 44: 'forma navium eo differt, quod utrique prora paratam semper adpulsi frontem agit. nec velis ministrant nec remos in ordinem lateribus adiungunt: solutum, ut in quibusdam fluminum, et mutabile, ut res poscit, hinc vel illinc remigium'.

[107]The most influential exponents of this theory are A. W. Brøgger and H. Shetelig, *The Viking Ships*, 2nd edn (Oslo and London, 1971), pp. 38–40. McGrail, *Ancient Boats*, p. 111, cautions against the uncritical acceptance of these views. Further on this question below, chapter 3, pp. 95–6, 100–101.

even a cursory look at the shipbuilding traditions of other European and non European cultures will confirm. The type and sophistication of a seafaring people's shipbuilding traditions seems to be completely irrelevant to the question of the adoption of the sail: almost anything that can float, from a log raft to a reed boat or a dug-out canoe, can be, and has been, successfully sail driven.[108] Conclusions drawn from ethnographical comparisons are necessarily open to doubt, but it seems that the Germanic barbarians will have been unique in world history if they waited for the invention of the keel before they experimented with the use of the sail. As Zwammerdam 3 shows, the Rhine Germans almost certainly successfully adapted logboats to the sail. Again neither Zwammerdam 4 nor the boat from Bruges had a keel; yet both carried mast and sail.

The decisive factor in the adoption of the sail by the northern Germans will have been a perceived need for it. As we have seen, the earliest ships from German settled areas to provide evidence for the use of mast and sail are all traders. It may well be that sails were first used on trading ships, where there would have been an immediate economic benefit from reduced crew sizes, and were adopted more gradually on warships which had to have large crews anyway. However, the demands of piracy would have made the benefits of sailing increasingly obvious. The close cultural ties which existed between the Germanic tribes of the North Sea coast made possible the close military co-operation demonstrated during Civilis's revolt and these ties must also have aided the diffusion of technological innovation among the tribes. If we accept that the Chauci may not have used the sail in the mid-first century, it would be surprising if they had not begun to experiment with it after their experiences fighting alongside Germans, like Gannascus and Civilis, who were certainly already familiar with sailing ships.

While the first century raids of the Chauci were apparently limited in range, the second century raids seem to have been more serious affairs, foreshadowing in their tactics the later raids of Saxons, Franks and Vikings. The change can be interpreted as indicating a growing confidence and competence on the part of the Germanic seafarers of the North Sea which would be consistent with an enhanced seafaring capacity gained by the introduction of the sail.

---

[108]For examples of the vast variety of vessels that have been sail-driven see Johnstone, *op. cit.*, especially chs 13–15, and the well illustrated J. Hornell, *Water Transport; Origins and Early Evolution* (Cambridge, 1946), *passim*. Perhaps the most relevant comparative material comes from the voyaging canoes of the Pacific. These sophisticated extended logboats and large keel-less plank-built canoes are highly efficient ocean-going sailing vessels and have been used to perform quite remarkable voyages of settlement and conquest. For accounts of the construction and use of these vessels in Polynesia see P. H. Buck, *Vikings of the Pacific* (Chicago, 1959), pp. 27–41, and, D. Lewis, *We, the Navigators* (Canberra, 1973), pp. 253–75.

2 The 3rd & 4th Century Raids of the Franks & Saxons

The middle of the third century saw a sudden increase in Germanic piracy on the North Sea, Channel and Atlantic coasts of the Roman Empire, far more wide-ranging and far more serious than anything which had been known, or at least recorded, before. The Chauci by this time had disappeared from history and the pirates who now set out from the Rhine and the North Sea coast of Germany to raid the coasts of the Roman Empire were called Franks and Saxons. Even the Mediterranean was not safe from these raiders. In a separate but short-lived movement in the east, Gothic and Herul pirates launched massive raids across the Black Sea: primary sources speak improbably of forces of up to 320,000 warriors and 6,000 ships! Between 253 and 276 a series of raids devastated the coastal cities of Asia Minor and Greece.[1] As newcomers to the Black Sea coast the Goths seem not to have possessed any native traditions of shipbuilding as their fleets were initially built and crewed by subject native Bosporans. While the pirate raids in the east died out fairly soon after the Roman abandonment of the trans-Danubian province of Dacia in 271 opened up new lands for barbarian settlement, the raids in the west remained a permanent threat until after the end of the Roman Empire in the west, with ultimately far-reaching consequences.

The Causes of 3rd Century Piracy

There seem to be three main causes for the third century upsurge in Germanic piracy on the northern and western coasts of the Roman Empire: first, changes in

---

[1] For Gothic and Herul piracy in the Black Sea and the Aegean Sea see the detailed narrative in G.Gaggero, *Le invasioni scito germaniche nell' oriente romano dal 251–282 DC* (Genoa, 1973), pp. 29–124. There are shorter accounts in E. Demougeot, *La formation de l'Europe et les invasions barbares: Des origines germaniques à l'avènement de Dioclétien* (Paris, 1969), pp. 416–28, and, A. Alföldi, 'The invasions of peoples from the Rhine to the Black Sea', in *The Cambridge Ancient History*, vol. 12 (Cambridge, 1939), pp. 138–49. The short account in H. Wolfram, *History of the Goths* (Berkeley-Los Angeles, 1988), pp. 48–57, is also very good. The most detailed ancient authority is Zosimus, *New History*, ed. and trans. F. Paschoud, *Zosime: Histoire Nouvelle*, Collection des universités de France (3 vols, Paris, 1971–9), I. 31. To raid across the Danube the Goths, and other Danube Germans, relied mostly on dug-out boats, though rafts and other kinds of boats are sometimes mentioned: see Ammianus Marcellinus, *Rerum gestarum libri*, ed. and trans. J. C. Rolfe, Loeb Classical Library (3 vols, London, 1935), XVII. 13.16-17, 13.27, XXXI. 4.5, 5.3. Also Zosimus, IV. 35.1, 38.5.

the tribal structure of the west Germans; second, a political and economic crisis in the Roman Empire; third, the start of a marine transgression.

The Franks, Saxons and Alamanni who first appeared on the western borders of the Empire during the course of the third century were not newcomers to the area from deeper within Germania; they were confederations of culturally related tribes who had lived in those areas for generations. The mechanics of the processes of confederation are hidden from us and it is impossible to know whether they were essentially peaceful or whether the smaller tribes were coerced into confederation by more powerful neighbours. The ultimate cause of the movement towards confederation was probably the need for greater effectiveness in war. The larger the confederation, the better it could defend itself if attacked by other Germanic tribes and the more effectively it could attack the Roman Empire for plunder or in the hope of winning lands to settle. Success would cement the confederation, giving it a prestige which would draw in tribes which were still outside. Success also weakened the Romans, making future success even more likely and leading to further consolidation of the confederation.

The Alamanni seem to have been the first of these confederations to form, first appearing on the upper Rhine in 213.[2] Though they possessed large numbers of boats which they used on their sorties across the Rhine,[3] the Alamanni were not a seafaring people and will concern us no more.

The Frankish confederation probably began to coalesce in the 230s.[4] Their earliest recorded activity was a raid across the Rhine near Mainz which was repulsed by Aurelian *c.* 245 and their earliest recorded pirate raids occurred *c.* 260.[5] The tribes who made up the Franks lived along the Rhine between the Zuyder Zee and the river Lahn and extended eastwards as far as the Weser, but they were settled most thickly around the Ijssel and between the Lippe and the Sieg. The material culture and burial practices of the pre Frankish inhabitants of this area are very uniform and they develop with uninterrupted continuity throughout the Roman period, ruling out the possibility of any large migrations

---

[2] K. F. Stroheker, 'Die Alamannen und das spätrömische Reich' in W. Müller (ed.), *Zur Geschichte der Alemannen* (Darmstadt, 1975), p. 21. The main tribes of the Alamanni were the Semnones, Hermunduri and Juthungi but they were, as the name 'All men' implies, a mixed bag. On the Alamanni in general see Stroheker, *ibid.*, R. Wenskus, *Stammesbildung und Verfassung* (Cologne-Graz, 1961), pp. 494–512, and Demougeot, *Invasions barbares*, pp. 335-7.

[3] See Ammianus Marcellinus, XVI. 11.9 and 12.58. The fragmentary remains of what may be a third century Alamannic plank built boat, about 4½ ft broad and containing weapons and tools, has been found in an old channel of the Rhine at Wantzenau near Strasbourg: see D. Ellmers, *Frühmittelalterliche Handelsschiffahrt in Mittel- und Nordeuropa* (Neumünster, 1972), p. 284.

[4] For the formation of the Frankish confederation see, primarily, E. Zöllner, *Geschichte der Franken bis zum Mitte des sechsten Jahrhunderts* (Munich, 1970), pp. 1–7, and Wenskus, *op. cit.*, pp. 512–41. Also E. James, *The Franks* (Oxford, 1988), pp. 35–7, and Demougeot, *op. cit.*, pp. 472–6.

[5] *SHA*, ed. E. Hohl (2 vols, Leipzig, 1965): Divus Aurelianus, 7. 1–2. The *SHA* is not a contemporary work but dates from the late fourth century: see T. D. Barnes, *The Sources of the Historiae Augustae*, Collections Latomus vol. 155 (Brussels, 1978), p. 30.

into the area during the period immediately before the Frankish name first appears in the sources.[6] Most of the tribes which formed the Franks retained their old tribal identities for a long time after the confederation had formed, in the case of the Salian Franks, even as late as the eighth century.[7] Because of this we have an unusually clear idea of which tribes joined the confederacy. The earliest tribe which is mentioned in the Roman sources as being Frankish is the Chamavi, whose lands centred on the river Ijssel, and this was probably the nucleus around which the confederacy formed. The other main tribes, who may not necessarily have joined the confederation at the same time, were the Bructeri, the Chattuari (the Hetware of *Beowulf*), the Salians, the Amsivari, the Twihantes, the Usipi and the Tubantes.[8] It is possible that other groups, from the Frisians, Canninefates, Heruls and perhaps even the Chauci, were also absorbed.[9] The name 'Frank' is presumably one which they gave to themselves as the word means 'bold' in their own language.

Though the sources do not tell us so, it is probably safe to conclude that the main seafaring Franks were the tribes of the lower Rhine, especially the Chamavi and the Salians who lived closest to the open sea. In the low coastal wetlands which were their homelands, these tribes would have quickly developed boat handling and boat building skills to a greater extent than their southern neighbours. However, there is no reason to conclude that the Salians and Chamavi monopolised Frankish pirate activity. As we saw in the previous chapter, other Frankish tribes such as the Bructeri and the Usipi had gained considerable boat handling skills in river navigation which had proved adaptable to the sea.

The origins of the Saxons are more obscure than those of the Franks but like the Franks they were a confederation of closely related tribes. Tacitus does not mention the Saxons in the *Germania* and the earliest reference to them comes from *c.* 150 in Ptolemy's *Geography* which places them next to the Chauci, on the North Sea coast between the Elbe and the neck of the Jutland peninsula.[10]

---

[6] R. von Uslar, *Westgermanische Bodenfunde* (Berlin, 1938), p. 179; Todd, *The Northern Barbarians*, pp. 41–4, 96–9.

[7] James, *op. cit.*, p. 7. By the mid-fourth century the Romans were referring to the Franks of the middle Rhine as the Ripuarii so it may be that these tribes began to lose their individual identities earlier than the tribes of the lower Rhine. However the Franks themselves did not use the term until the eighth century: R. A. Gerberding, *The Rise of the Carolingians and the Liber Historiae Francorum* (Oxford, 1987), p. 76.

[8] See James, *op. cit.*, p. 35, on the earliest dates that the various tribes are first recorded as belonging to the Franks. Further on the individual tribes see L. Schmidt, *Geschichte der deutschen Stämme bis zum Ausgang der Völkerwanderung: Die Westgermanen*, (2 vols, Munich, 1938-40), passim.

[9] Wenskus, *op. cit.*, pp. 527–30; James, *op. cit.*, p. 35.

[10] Ptolemy, *Geography*, II. ii. 7: text and trans. in H. M. Chadwick, *The Origins of the English Nation* (Cambridge, 1907), pp. 39–40. S. Johnson, 'Late Roman defences and the *limes*', in D. E. Johnston (ed.), *The Saxon Shore*, CBA Research Report 18 (London, 1997), p. 67, points out that only one of the surviving manuscripts has the reading *Saksones*, most of the others having *Aksones* which he suggests may be a derivative of Tacitus's *Aviones*.

How long the Saxons had existed as a group before then depends on the age of Ptolemy's sources. It is widely assumed that he relied on accounts from the Roman naval expeditions in the North Sea of 150 years before[11] but this raises the question of why, if the Saxons existence was already known to the Romans, Tacitus omits them from his account of the Germans. By and large it seems most sensible to agree with Lintzel, who believes that Ptolemy relied upon more recent sources and that Tacitus's omission of the Saxons is an indication that c. 100 the name was not yet known to the Romans.[12] If so, it would seem that the Saxons were a confederation, including the Reudingi and the Aviones,[13] which began to form north of the Elbe in the second century and which spread, in the third century, westwards to the Ems to include the Chauci and perhaps part of the Frisians.[14] The alternative view, which relies more heavily on unsupported assumptions than Lintzel's, is that the Saxons did already exist in the first century but were omitted by Tacitus by an oversight and that in the course of the second or third century they expanded their territory by conquering their neighbours.[15] Unfortunately, evidence on which to base a firm conclusion is lacking but it would be in keeping with developments elsewhere in Germany if the Saxons had originated as a confederation, even if they eventually completed their expansion to the west by conquest.

Large scale Saxon piracy seems to have begun rather later than Frankish piracy. The earliest recorded Saxon piracy occurred in the 280s,[16] some twenty years after the first known Frankish raids. Such is the poverty of sources for third century history that the delay may well be more apparent than real but, if the Chauci resisted amalgamation, it could be because it took the Saxons longer than the Franks to achieve the unity necessary for successful offensive action. Once

---

[11] For example, Johnson, 'Late Roman defences'; J. N. L. Myres, *The English Settlements*, (Oxford, 1986), p. 50; Schmidt, *op. cit.*, vol. 1. p. 38.

[12] M. Lintzel, 'Zur Entstehungsgeschichte des sächsichen Stammes', *Sachsen und Anhalt* III (1927), pp. 2–3.

[13] *Ibid.*, pp. 4–8, thinks that the Reudingi were the original core of the Saxons.

[14] Wenskus, *op. cit.*, p. 550. Chadwick, *op. cit.*, pp. 87–97, argues that the partial or total absorption of the Frisians into the Saxons would explain their absence from the later Roman sources. Other minor tribes which were probably absorbed by the Saxons were the Ampsivari, Chasuari, Angrivari and perhaps the Lombards of the Bardengau: see Lintzel, *op. cit.*, p. 16. The individual tribes of the Saxon grouping do not seem to have preserved their individual identities to the same extent as did the Frankish tribes. The Chauci may still have preserved their identity to some degree in the fourth century (see chapter 1, n. 70) and the Aviones may still have been a recognised group in Anglo-Saxon times: see Lintzel, *op. cit.*, p. 5, and, more generally, A. Bliss, 'The Aviones and *Widsith* 26a', in p. Clemoes (ed.), *Anglo-Saxon England* 14 (Cambridge, 1985), pp. 97–106.

[15] This is the conclusion preferred by Schmidt, *op. cit.*, vol. 1, p. 39, Wenskus, *op. cit.*, p. 542, and Demougeot, *op. cit.*, pp. 50–1 (though see chapter 1, n. 70, on Demougeot's case which is certainly unacceptable).

[16] Eutropius, *Breviarium ab urbe condita*, ed. F. Ruehl (Stuttgart, 1975), IX. 21. Orosius, *Historiarum adversum paganos libri VII*, ed. C. Zangmeister (Leipzig, 1889), VII. 25.3.

The 3rd and 4th Century Raids of the Franks and Saxons

started on a course of successful piracy, the prestige of the Saxons would steadily have increased, gradually welding the confederation together.

As with the Franks, the tribes which made up the Saxons had been culturally similar. All belonged to the North Sea coast group and the process of amalgamation, whether peaceful or violent, did not disrupt the continuity of material culture or burial practices in the group area.[17] Numerically, the Chauci were probably the most important constituent of the third century Saxons[18] and their long tradition of seafaring and piracy must have played an important part in determining the character of the Saxons. However, the Chauci cannot have been the only seafaring element incorporated into the Saxons as Ptolemy records that the North Frisian islands were inhabited by Saxons in the middle of the second century.[19]

If success bred success for the new barbarian confederations, that success was made more likely by the parlous state in which the Roman Empire found itself in the mid-third century. Certainly, barbarian pressure on the empire's frontiers had been constant since *c.* 160; the later outbreaks of Chaucian piracy had formed just a small part of this. Though the Romans had generally been successful in holding the Germans off until the middle of the third century, the persistent pressure had taken its toll on the Empire. The legions came to dominate the political life of the Empire with destabilising results. The constant financial demands of the army concentrated wealth in the border provinces, where the great bulk of the troops were stationed. The increased wealth of these provinces made them even more attractive to barbarian raiders and reinforced one of the main causes of the barbarian pressure; the desire for plunder.

In these conditions of almost continual war, the emperor had to be first and foremost a good soldier who could command the support of the army. But the legions soon learned that they had the power to make and unmake emperors; a poor soldier would not rule for long. Rival candidates for the purple, put forward by different legions, fought each other for control of the Empire while the borderlands were left denuded of troops and invitingly open to barbarian or, in the east, Persian attack. For example, in 253 Valerian was forced to withdraw troops from the Rhine to fight a usurper and the Franks immediately launched an invasion of Gaul, which had been left defenceless. Even when one claimant emerged supreme for a time, he had to be ever watchful of his more successful and popular generals in case they should take the opportunity presented by a military crisis to attempt to usurp the Empire. As a consequence a general who felt the eye of imperial suspicion upon him often felt forced to revolt as the only means of self-defence against a treason charge and inevitable execution. At the same time the constant attempts of the emperors to buy the loyalty of the soldiers

---

[17] Myres, *op. cit.*; pp. 50–1, Schmidt, *op. cit.*, vol. 1, pp. 38–9. This continuity would seem to rule out the theory, discussed by Wenskus, *op. cit.*, pp. 543–4, that the Saxons were invaders of Scandinavian origin. For further references relevant to this subject see chapter 1, n. 71.

[18] Wenskus, *op. cit.*, p. 549; Schmidt, *op. cit.*, vol. 1, p. 39. The numerical superiority of the Chauci is probably indicated by the fact that by the fourth century the Weser had become, as it was to remain until the Frankish conquest, the power base of the Saxons.

[19] Schmidt, *op. cit.*, vol. 1, p. 38.

deepened the financial crisis of the Empire. To raise extra revenue the emperors progressively debased the coinage but this led in turn to disastrous inflation. Between the murder of Severus in 235 and the accession of Diocletian in 284, civil war was endemic. Of the 26 emperors who were recognised in Rome in this period, all but one died by violence, to say nothing of the numerous pretenders whose ambitions ended in their execution or assassination. For example Gallienus alone had to suppress 18 usurpers in his nine year reign (259–68) only to be murdered at the end by his officers. Under Gallienus the Empire came to the very brink of collapse under the double stresses of civil war and invasion but his reign also marks the turning point in the crisis of the Empire as his radical reform of the army to create a defence in depth based on field armies ensured its survival. The crisis is generally considered to have been ended by the almost complete restructuring of the Empire by Diocletian. By then, however, the barbarian confederations had been permanently welded together by years of warfare. The reorganised Empire survived but remained on the defensive against stronger and more united Germanic peoples than it had had to face at the beginning of the third century.

The weakness of the Empire was certainly the main general external cause of the increased barbarian pressure of the third century but it is one that applies equally to both land and sea raids and invasions. One specific factor which encouraged the upsurge in Germanic piracy in this period was the beginning, c. 230, of the Dunkirk II marine transgression which brought about great changes in the geography of the lower Rhine and the North Sea coast of Germany by the end of the third century[20]. The effects of this were not uniform as the transgression was caused by a combination of eustatic and isostatic effects. At the peak of the transgression in the fourth century, the absolute rise in sea level was probably between three and eight feet above modern levels; but in the southern North Sea subsidence of the land combined with this to produce an effective sea level rise of 12 to 14 feet in the lands around the Rhine mouths.[21] In the Low Countries this produced particularly drastic changes in the landscape, while the agricultural economy of the area was ruined by flooding, and severe depopulation followed.[22] A Roman poet of the late third century thought the

---

[20] See H. Porter, 'Environmental change in the third century', in A. King and M. Henig (eds), *The Roman West in the Third Century*, BAR IS 109 (Oxford, 1981), pp. 353–5, on the general effects of the transgression in north-western Europe.

[21] H. Thoen, 'The third-century Roman occupation in Belgium: the evidence of the coastal plain', in King and Henig (eds), *op. cit.*, pp. 41–2.

[22] The coastal plain of Belgica was almost totally depopulated by 268–70: Thoen, *ibid.*, p. 42. The Roman-occupied areas of the Netherlands were largely depopulated by the end of the third century: L. P. Louwe Kooijmans, 'Archaeology and coastal change in the Netherlands', in F. H. Thompson (ed.), *Archaeology and Coastal Change* (London, 1980), p. 129. The *civitas* of the Canninefates at Voorburg had been abandoned even before this, *c.* 250: A. van Doorselaer, 'De Romeinen in de Nederlanden', in D. P. Blok *et al.*, (eds) *Algemene Geschiedenis der Nederlander 1, Middeleeowen* (Haarlem, 1981), p. 98. Thoen suggests that Germanic piracy may have accelerated the process of depopulation in Belgica.

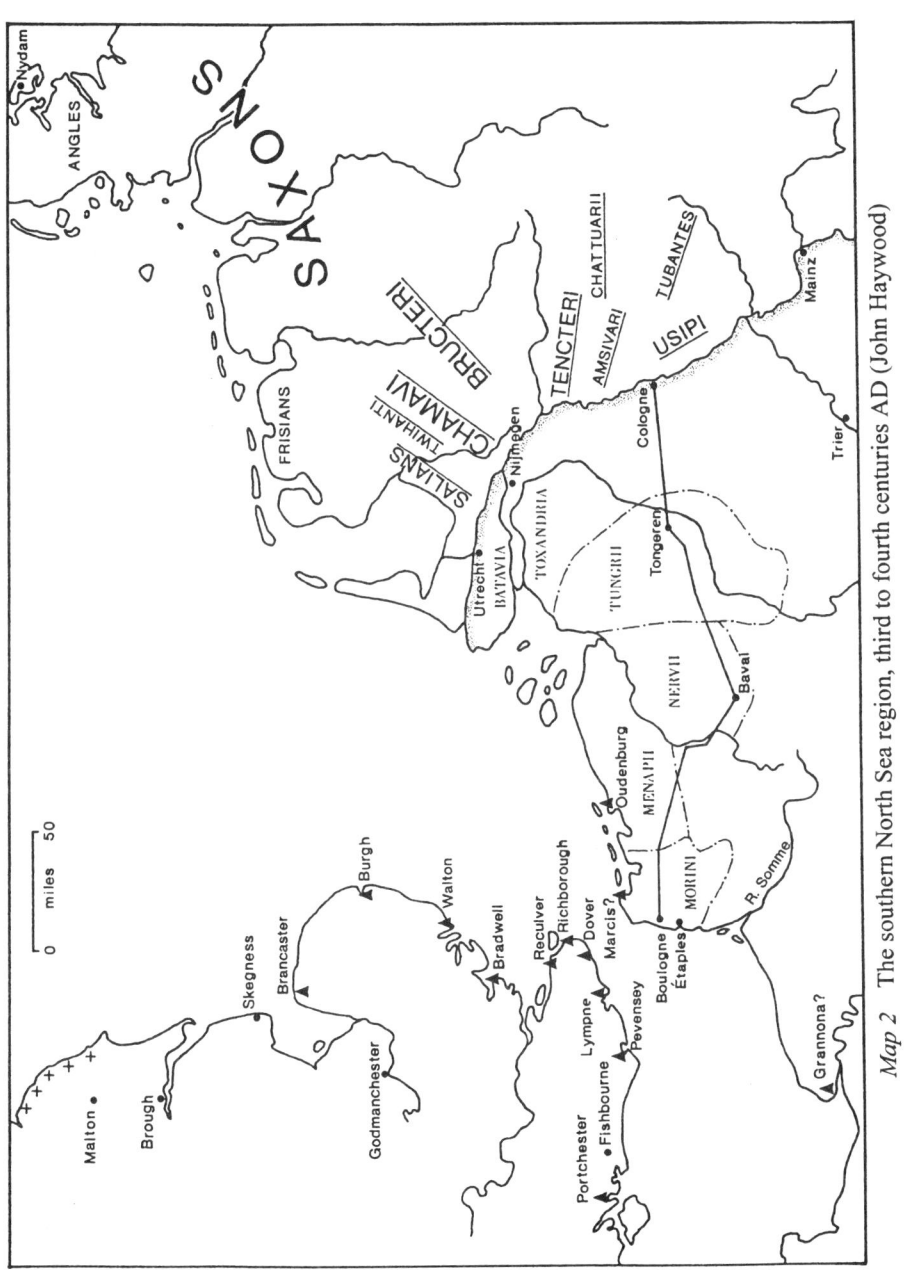

The 3rd and 4th Century Raids of the Franks and Saxons

Map 2 The southern North Sea region, third to fourth centuries AD (John Haywood)
Key: ▲ = military site, × = signal station, Frankish tribes underlined

area between the Scheldt and the Rhine so wet and swampy that it could not truthfully be described as a 'land' at all.[23] The depopulation of the Roman territories on the lower Rhine led the Romans gradually to reduce their military presence in much of the area which there was now little point in defending. Flooding caused the Roman fort at Valkenburg, covering the mouth of the Old Rhine, to be abandoned *c.* 240.[24] By *c.* 250 the Romans had withdrawn the garrisons of most of the forts on the Rhine between Nijmegen and the sea, and the main Roman defence line in the region was withdrawn to a series of fortifications along the Cologne to Bavai road.[25] Before the end of the century the fort at Aardenburg had also been abandoned.[26] Only at Utrecht was a significant Roman military presence maintained, though this too seems to have been abandoned by the mid-fourth century.[27] The Franks were quick to move into the vacuum thus created and for the first time gained easy access to the open sea. It is no coincidence, surely, that the first pirate raids soon followed.

For the North Sea coastal Germans the effects were rather different, though the results were the same. Particularly in the Chaucian area, the second century had seen the progressive reclamation of salt marsh for agriculture, indicating a steadily expanding population.[28] In the third century the marine transgression quickly destroyed these gains and population pressure on the remaining agricultural land must have become acute.[29] While the transgression brought to the Franks the opportunity to turn to piracy, to the inhabitants of the North Sea coastal plain, by now probably calling themselves Saxons, it brought the necessity. To the Frisians it must have brought near extinction as it is hard otherwise to account for their virtual absence from the sources in the third and fourth centuries.[30] They were as well placed as the Franks or Saxons to raid the Roman Empire by sea but if they did there were clearly never enough of them to make much of an impression.[31]

---

[23] *Incerti panegyricus Constantio Caesari dictus* (ed. and trans. E. Galletier in *Panégyriques Latins* (3 vols, Paris, 1949–55), vol. 1, pp. 82–100), VI. 1.

[24] J. Mertens, 'Oudenburg and the northern sector of the continental *litus Saxonicum*', in Johnston (ed.), *op. cit.*, p. 51; Demougeot, *op. cit.*, p. 489.

[25] Van Doorselaer, *op. cit.*, p. 98.

[26] Mertens, *op. cit.*, p. 53.

[27] Mertens, *op. cit.*, p. 53.

[28] Todd. *op. cit.*, pp. 87–8.

[29] *Ibid.*, and Myres, *op. cit.*, pp. 53–4.

[30] Louwe Kooijmans, *op. cit.*, p. 128, points to the modest number of finds from the Groningen district of Friesland from the period of the Dunkirk II transgression as an indication of the depopulation of the area. Wenskus, *op. cit.*, p. 550, goes further and concludes, from destruction layers in late Roman period settlements in Frisia, that the Frisians were conquered and effectively extinguished by the Saxons, who settled their lands. But the land continued to be called after its old inhabitants and in time the Saxon immigrants began to take their name from the land, thus giving the Frisians the appearance, but not the reality, of continuity. Wenskus supports his case by reference to the German settlers of Prussia, a Slavic area. See also in a similar vein Chadwick, *op. cit.*, pp. 87–97.

[31] It is possible that Frisian pirates were active at the end of the third century: see below, n. 89.

The effects of the transgression on navigating conditions will have been mixed. Certainly many inland areas will have become more vulnerable to attack from the sea as the coastline advanced. This was especially true of the Fens, where the coastline in places reached over 30 miles inland from the modern coast of the Wash,[32] and on the coastal plain of Belgica, where the coastline advanced over ten miles in places.[33] On the other hand conditions in some river estuaries, such as the Thames or Humber, may have become more difficult as the higher sea-level caused silt to be deposited further upstream than before, hindering access to inland ports like York and their hinterlands; though this may have hindered defenders as much as pirates as harbours silted up and increased coastal erosion destroyed defence works.[34]

All these factors worked to encourage the Franks and Saxons to turn to piracy. The main factors are identical to those which motivated other Germans to invade the Roman Empire by land: the desire for loot and the tempting weakness of the Empire, coupled inextricably with the growing strength of the Germans, which together promised greater success. On top of this the various effects of the marine transgression provided the coastal Germans with both increased opportunities and incentives for piracy.

The Earliest Frankish Pirate Raids

The earliest recorded Frankish pirate raids occurred *c.* 260 and *c.* 278. Both are quite exceptional events showing an opportunism and a confidence on the part of the Franks which suggests most strongly that they were not newcomers to piracy on the high seas.

The first of these, in *c.* 260, was a major invasion of Gaul by the Franks in the aftermath of Valerian's crushing defeat and capture by the Persians at Edessa.[35] The Frankish group swept through Gaul with grave consequences for the Roman Empire.[36] Probably prompted by the ineffective response of the imperial

---

[32] On the Roman coastline of the Wash see, B. B. Simmons, 'Iron Age and Roman coasts around the Wash', in Thompson, (ed.) *op. cit.*, pp. 65–67.

[33] H. Thoen, *De Belgische kustvlakte in de Romeinse tijd*, Verhandelungen van de Koninklijke Academie voor wettenschappen. Letteren en schone kunsten van Belgie. Klasse der Letteren, XL (1978), no. 88, fig. 27, p. 95, and map 8, p. 252.

[34] F. Ramm, *The Parisi*, (London, 1978), pp. 124–5.

[35] For the chronology of the events surrounding the German invasions and Postumus's usurpation I have accepted the compelling arguments of J. F. Drinkwater, *The Gallic Empire*, Historia Einzelschriften 52 (Stuttgart, 1987), pp. 22–7, 92–106, and I. König, *Die gallischen Usurpatoren von Postumus bis Tetricius* (Munich, 1981), pp. 36–42. For alternative interpretations which place the invasion before Postumus's usurpation see S. J. Keay, 'The *Conventus Tarraconensis* in the third century' in King and Henig (eds), *op. cit.*, p. 477, and A. Balil, 'Hispania en los años 260 a 300 D. D. J. C.' *Emerita* XXVII (1959), pp. 270–1, 295.

[36] Aurelius Victor, *De Caesaribus*, ed. Fr. Pichlmayr (Leipzig, 1970), XXXIII. 3, is alone in calling the invaders *Francorum gentes*. Elsewhere, as for example in Eutropius, IX. 8, they are called simply *Germani*.

authorities, Postumus, a senior army officer, seized control of Britain, Gaul and Spain to create a 'Gallic' empire which was not to be restored to central imperial control for 14 years. However, Postumus was also unable to stop the Frankish advance and, after unsuccessfully besieging Tours, the Franks crossed the Pyrenees and invaded Spain, where they took and sacked Tarragona, an important port and provincial capital.[37] The destruction caused must have been severe as, according to Orosius, the damage was still visible in the fifth century, though this has yet to be corroborated by any archaeological evidence.[38]

In the harbour of Tarragona some of the Franks seized a fleet of (merchant?) ships and sailed across the Mediterranean to raid the coast of North Africa,[39] over 300 miles distant at its closest point. Unfortunately the only source to mention this raid tells us nothing about the movements of the Frankish pirates after they reached the African coast, but it has been claimed, on archaeological evidence of very uncertain value – an undated Latin inscription refering the defeat of an unnamed group of barbarians – that Tetuán in Morocco was sacked by them.[40]

---

[37] Aurelius Victor, XXXIII. 3 (text below, n. 39), Eutropius, IX. 8, Orosius, VII. 22.7 and Jerome, *Chronicon*, ed. R. Helm, (Die Griechischen Christlichen Schriftsteller 47 = Eusebius Werke 7, *Die Chronik des Hieronymus* (Berlin, 1956)), *sub anno* 264. Derived from Jerome is Prosper Tironensis, *Epitoma Chronicon*, ed. T. Mommsen, *MGH. AA, Chronica Minora* 1 (Berlin, 1892), pp. 341–485, *sub anno* 879. Unfortunately none of our sources is contemporary. The earliest are Aurelius Victor and Eutropius who both wrote in the later fourth century. Both used an earlier 'Imperial History' as their main source, but this work is now lost: see Drinkwater, *op. cit.*, pp. 46–54, and P. Dufraigne in his edition of Aurelius Victor, *Livre des Césars* (Paris, 1975), pp. xv xvii. On the attack on Tarragona see Keay, *op. cit.*, pp. 472–8, and Zöllner, *op. cit.*, p. 8.

[38] Orosius, VII. 22.8–9: 'Extant adhuc per diversas provincias in magnarum urbium ruinis parvae et pauperes sedes, signa miseriarum, et nominum indicia servantes: ex quibus nos quoque in Hispania Tarraconem nostram ad consolationem miseriae recentis ostendimus.' See also Keay, *op. cit.*, p. 477.

[39] Aurelius Victor, XXXIII. 3: 'Francorum gentes direpta Gallia Hispaniam possiderent vastato ac paene direpto Tarraconensium oppido, nactisque in tempore navigiis pars in usque Africam permearet.'

[40] The inscription reads: 'MVI provinci[am in]troivit barbaros [T]amudam inrupe[ntes] fugavit et in pacem [re]stituto vic. Aug. sacr.' Text in R. Thouvenot, 'Une inscription latine du Maroc', *Revue des études latines* XVI (1938), p. 266. Despite the lack of a reliable dating context, Thouvenot rejects the possibility that the barbarians might be Moors or Vandals on the eminently shaky grounds that if the barbarians concerned were from these peoples it would be normal for them to be called by name on the inscription. This inscription is supposedly unique in that the barbarians are anonymous. He concludes that the barbarians were probably Frankish because these were the only other barbarians known to have reached Africa and that therefore the inscription is third century. This is a very hypothetical argument but it has not stopped O. Fiebiger, 'Frankeneinfall in Nordafrika', *Germania* XXIV (1940), pp. 145–6, from reconstructing the course of the supposed Frankish attack in absurd detail. Strangely, neither he nor Thouvenot considers the possibility that the raiders may have been the Franks who sailed through the Mediterranean in *c.* 278 (see below, p. 52). Both Fiebiger and Thouvenot are rightly criticised by A. Balil, 'Las invasiones germánicas en Hispania durante la segunda mitad del siglo III D. D. J. C.' *Cuadernos de Trabajos de la Escuela Española de Historia y Arqueología en Roma* IX (1957), p. 124 (n. 65), for taking their conclusions farther than the evidence permits.

However, archaeological excavations have shown that Tetuán did suffer serious damage by fire in the mid-third century.[41] Orosius says that the *Germani* remained in Spain for 12 years in this period, so it may be that Frankish piracy in the south-western Mediterranean was protracted.[42] The pirates may eventually have returned to their homes overland from Spain but, in view of later events discussed below, it is not impossible that they returned by sea in their stolen vessels, via the Atlantic and the Channel.

In 278 Gaul, by now reunited with the rest of the Roman Empire, once again suffered a major Frankish invasion. On this occasion, however, the Franks suffered a heavy defeat at the hands of the emperor Probus.[43] A great number were captured and these were resettled by Probus in Pontus on the Black Sea coast of Asia Minor.[44] The Black Sea and Aegean coasts of the Roman Empire had been suffering severely at the hands of Gothic and Herul pirates since 253; even major cities such as Athens, Nicomedia and Nicaea had been sacked.[45] Probus probably intended that the Frankish settlement would provide a defence for Pontus against these pirates. In the event, the settlement was a costly failure. Probably taking advantage of a civil war which had broken out in the Empire in 279, the Franks rebelled, seized a fleet of Roman ships, turned pirate themselves and embarked on an epic voyage which eventually returned them to their homes on the lower Rhine.[46] The Frankish pirate fleet was able to leave the Black Sea,

---

[41] See M. Tarradell, 'Marruecos antiguo: nuevas perspectivas', *Zephyrus* V (1954), pp. 129–31. Tarradell suggests that the barbarians of the inscription may have been responsible for the destruction but stops short of identifying them.

[42] Orosius, VII. 41.2.

[43] *SHA: Probus* XII. 3, and Zosimus, I. 68.1. The date is not absolutely secure: see Zöllner, *op. cit.*, pp. 10–11.

[44] *Incert. Pan. Constantio Caesari*, XVIII. 2 (see n. 45 below). *SHA: Probus*, XVIII. 2, refers to a group of Gepids, Greuthungi and Vandals, settled by Probus in Thrace, who rebelled and turned to piracy:

> sed cum et ex aliis gentibus plerosque pariter transtullisset, id est ex Gepidis, Greuthungis et Vandalis, illi omnes fidem fregerunt et occupato bellis tyrannicis Probo per totum paene orbem pedibus et navigando vagati sunt nec parum molestiae Romanae gloriae intulerunt.

The *SHA* is notoriously unreliable and this may be a confused reference to the Frankish rebellion or to a quite separate incident of piracy. It certainly should not be taken as evidence that the Franks were settled on the Danube rather than in Pontus, as it is by Demougeot, *op. cit.*, pp. 431, 471. Demougeot compounds his error by citing Zosimus, I. 71.1–2, in support. Zosimus does not in fact say where the Franks were settled. On the reliability of *Probus* see Barnes, *op. cit.*, p. 30.

[45] On the Gothic and Herul pirates in the Black Sea see above, n. 1.

[46] *Incert. pan. Constantio Caesari*, XVIII. 2:

> Recursabat quippe in animos illa sub divo Probo paucorum ex Francis captivorum incredibilis audacia et indigna felicitas, qui a Ponto usque correptis nauibus Graeciam Asiamque populari nec impune plerisque Libyae litoribus appulsi ipsas postremo navalibus quondam victoriis nobiles ceperant Syracusas et immenso itinere peruecti Oceanum qua terras inrumpit intrauerant, atque ita eventu temeritatis ostenderant nihil esse clausum piraticae desperationi, quo navigiis pateret accessus.

Also Zosimus, I. 71.2, who describes how the Franks raided Greece with a large fleet after rebelling and then went on to sack Syracuse, killing many of the inhabitants. After this they

apparently unopposed, passing through the Bosphorus into the Aegean Sea. It is a sign of the quality of Frankish seamanship that they were able to navigate the Bosphorus without apparent difficulty: on the first occasion that the Goths had attempted to navigate this waterway, some 20 years before, the treacherous currents had swept many of their ships to destruction with great loss of life.[47] The coasts of Greece and Asia Minor were pillaged before the fleet crossed the Mediterranean and attacked Cyrenaica. From here the Franks sailed to Sicily and sacked Syracuse, massacring many of the city's inhabitants, before returning to Africa, landing in Tunisia. Here they met their only documented opposition and were driven off by a Roman army sent out from Carthage. However, the defeat was not serious enough to prevent the Franks escaping to sail through the Straits of Gibraltar into the Atlantic. At no point in their journey through the Mediterranean were the Franks opposed by Roman naval forces, a sign of the degree to which Roman naval power there had been allowed to decay in the long years of peace that had followed the suppression of the Cilician pirates in the first century BC.[48] Eventually the Franks returned triumphantly to the Rhine, presumably following the coasts of Spain and Gaul. A distant memory of this remarkable voyage may have given rise to the belief held by the Franks in the seventh century that their race had a Trojan origin.[49]

The confident and daring opportunism which the Franks showed on this last voyage is quite breathtaking and is entirely comparable with the most spectacular voyages of the Vikings. The exploits of the Franks clearly shook the Romans, one author remarked that 'nowhere that could be reached by ships' was safe from them and complained of their 'incredible audacity'.[50] The triumphant success of this voyage is a certain sign that the Franks were already superb seamen and it can hardly be the case that these raids were their first. Despite this, it is by no means certain when Frankish piracy began. Incursions by the Franks overland were frequent after 253 [51] but their earliest recorded pirate raids in northern waters did not take place until the 280s (see below). There is persuasive archaeological evidence of widespread piracy in the northern seas by the 270s but this may not be exclusively the work of the Franks as by this time it is almost certain that the Saxons were also active. Coin hoards, evidence of depopulation and fortification in coastal areas of Britain and northern Gaul are all indicators of insecurity which may have been caused by piracy. However, this evidence does present problems of interpretation as it is certain that other factors played a part in causing insecurity in this period; this is especially important in interpreting the

---

landed in Africa but were driven off by Roman forces near Carthage. However,ced he concludes, the Franks were still able to return home, unharmed.

[47] Zosimus, I. 42.2.

[48] On which see H. A. Ormerod, *Piracy in the Ancient World* (Liverpool, 1969), pp. 248–60.

[49] S. Dill, *Roman Society in Gaul in the Merovingian Age* (London, 1926), p. 6.

[50] *Incert. pan. Constantio Caesari*, XVIII.2, quoted above n. 46.

[51] Zöllner, *op. cit.*, p. 8, suggests that the immediate cause of their raids was the withdrawal of Roman troops from the Rhine frontier by Valerian in 253 to fight in a civil war.

The 3rd and 4th Century Raids of the Franks and Saxons

coin hoard evidence. Another important limitation of even the best evidence is the impossibility of identifying the raiders or assessing the relative importance of the different groups who were involved.

Despite Demougeot's claims to the contrary, there is no marked distribution of coin hoards in the coastal areas of Britain or Gaul until the 270s.[52] By contrast the decade 270–80 does see a marked distribution of coin hoards on the south eastern coasts of Britain[53] and on the coast of Gaul from the Channel to Aquitaine, indicating insecurity in those areas, most credibly explained in terms of piracy.[54] Of course other factors may have had a significant effect on the frequency of coin hoarding in this period. In addition to barbarian invasions, this decade saw the collapse of the Gallic Empire in the face of central imperial counter attack; and the internal disturbances, debasement of the coinage and political instability which accompanied it are all likely to have encouraged hoarding.[55] However, Galliou has noted that in Brittany coin hoarding actually increased towards the end of the 270s, too late for it to have had anything to do with the fall of the Gallic Empire.[56] The same is true of coin hoards in Sussex in south-east England; these show a definite peak during the reign of Probus (276–82), which would also seem to rule out any connection with the fall of the Gallic Empire.[57] How else, then, can this pattern of coin hoarding be interpreted except as evidence of piracy?

Though it is wholly reasonable to conclude that the coin hoard distribution in the period c. 270 to c. 280 does reflect a threat to coastal areas from piracy, it is equally certainly quite unrealistic to use this kind of evidence to draw specific

---

[52] Demougeot, *op. cit.*, pp. 488–90, 501–2, 508. The total coin hoard evidence for piracy in the Channel in the 240s and 250s offered by Demougeot consists of seven hoards, from the coastal areas of Britain, Belgica and Germania combined, terminating with coins dating from between 243 and 256. It is quite clear from the coin hoard distribution map which he himself provides (map 18a) that coin hoards are far more common from inland areas of Belgica and Germania in this period. There is no doubt that this indicates that overland raids were a far greater threat than piracy in this period.

[53] A. S. Robertson, 'Romano-British coin hoards: their numismatic, archaeological and historical significance', in J. Casey and R. Reece (eds), *Coins and the Archaeologist* BAR 4 (Oxford, 1974), pp. 30–2 (fig. 4). Robertson notes the coastal distribution but prefers to account for the hoards in terms of imperial monetary policy in the wake of the defeat of Tetricius, the last Gallic emperor, by Aurelian and the reincorporation of Britain into the central empire. However, it is difficult to see why financial insecurity should have affected only the coastal districts of the south-east and not the whole country.

[54] Demougeot, *op. cit.*, p. 502 and map 18b. The coastal distribution is most marked in Brittany and Aquitaine; in Belgica and Germania there is no clear coastal bias, presumably because of the threat of overland raids. Drinkwater, *op. cit.*, pp. 201–2, thinks that the peak of coin hoards in the 270s is more likely to be a result of Aurelian's reconquest of the Gallic empire than of barbarian action.

[55] For divergent discussions of the relative significance of these factors see R. Reece, 'Coinage and currency in the third century' in King and Henig (eds), *op. cit.*, pp. 86–7, and Drinkwater, *op. cit.*, pp. 189–214.

[56] P. Galliou, 'Western Gaul in the third century', in King and Henig (eds), *op. cit.* p. 273.

[57] B. Cunliffe, *The Regni* (London, 1973), p. 30.

conclusions about the dates and locations of individual raids. For example, Demougeot claims that there was an outbreak of Frankish piracy in 268–9 on the basis of just two coin hoards from the Seine estuary area.[58] Balil claims that a Frankish pirate fleet from the Rhine ravaged the coast of Lusitania before passing through the Straits of Gibraltar and raiding Alicante in *c.* 262 on equally inconclusive coin hoard evidence.[59] Such a raid would clearly have been within the capabilities of the Franks, but Spanish coin hoards are poorly dated and distribution patterns show no marked bias towards coastal areas this period, one in which Spain was subjected to a major overland Frankish invasion. This invasion was itself accompanied by Frankish piracy, which could just as easily have produced this kind of distribution pattern.[60]

In an age of widespread and prolonged insecurity from many causes – invasion by land, political upheaval, peasant brigandage and debasement of the coinage, as well as piracy – precision cannot be expected from coin hoard evidence. The newest coin in a hoard may well give a rough idea of the date the hoard was deposited but when insecurity was prolonged, as it was in the period 250 to 280, this date and the date of the event which led to the owner's failure to recover the hoard could have been many years apart. Moreover, under these circumstances the original cause of a hoard's burial and the actual cause of its non-recovery could be quite unrelated.[61] In this period it seems far safer to think in terms of a long-term, gradually worsening, threat in coastal areas from small-scale hit-and-run pirate raids, which simply added to the other problems, rather than of a few massive seaborne invasions.

Further possible evidence for serious piracy comes from the disappearance of many rural settlements in the provinces of Belgica and Armorica in the late third century. In Brittany many coastal villas were abandoned in the period *c.* 270–280 and others survived only at a very reduced level. The agricultural economy appears to have suffered serious and long term damage as pollen samples from peat bogs in Finistère show a sharp decrease in cultivation and a corresponding

---

[58] Demougeot, *op. cit.*, pp. 507–8.

[59] Balil, 'Hispania en los años 260 a 300', pp. 270–1.

[60] Drinkwater, *op. cit.*, pp. 197, 215–7, doubts that Spanish coin hoard distributions have anything useful to tell us, not only because of their even pattern but because they are very imprecisely dated. He is particularly critical of Balil's undiscriminating use of the evidence.

[61] Reece, *op. cit.*, pp. 86–7, suggests that the main reason for the non recovery of coin hoards in this period was simply that the rapid debasement of the coinage had rendered the buried coins worthless, so making it not worth the owner's while to recover them. Drinkwater, *op. cit.*, pp. 189–214, in his discussion of the coin hoard evidence takes the more traditional view that the non recovery of a coin hoard is usually indicative of some major dislocation in the owner's life (i.e. death, capture or flight). He rightly dismisses Reece's view as being unrealistic on the grounds that in a materially poor society, as Roman society essentially was, a hoard of base metal coins would never become valueless; even if the coins could no longer be used as a means of exchange they could still have been bartered for their scrap value. Wightman, *Gallia Belgica* (Oxford, 1985), pp. 197–8, is also dismissive of Reece's line of argument on similar grounds and points out that the value of the currency cannot have been a factor in the non-recovery of several hoards of silver plate which are known from Belgica in this period.

encroachment of forest.[62] However, the villa economy throughout Gaul declined in the late third century as a direct result of barbarian destruction and, indirectly, from the general dislocation to the economy caused by the invasions.[63] It is impossible to say which of these two factors was the more important in the abandonment of the Breton villas.

The evidence from Belgica is more striking. Out of 87 archaeologically attested *vici* (large roadside villages), 31 failed to survive the late third century. Of the 56 which did survive, 22 had been fortified by *c.* 300 and most had reduced populations. Though a comparison with the pattern of survival or failure in neighbouring provinces is necessary before certain conclusions are drawn from this evidence, it does seem significant that the rate of failure is far higher in the coastal *civitates* than in inland ones. Of a total of 38 *vici* in the four coastal *civitates* of the Tungri, Nervii, Menapii and Morini, 22 failed to survive; by contrast, only two out of a total of 27 *vici* failed to survive in the two *civitates* which were furthest from the sea, those of the Treveri and Mediomatrici.[64] It is in northern Gaul in the period *c.* 280 that we first hear of the rural bandits called *bagaudae* and it may be that they are a sign that social order had broken down in this area under the strain of pirate attacks.[65]

A number of burnt sites from this period in Sussex, including the great palace at Fishbourne, may be evidence of Frankish or Saxon raids on the south coast of Britain.[66] In general, though, Britain escaped the widespread destruction which was typical of Gaul in the later third century; protected by the Channel, Britain was immune to the great Germanic invasions which overwhelmed Gaul.[67] The relative prosperity of Britain in this period suggests that the Frankish and Saxon pirate raids, which alone troubled Britain, were fairly small scale affairs, at least compared to the incursions by land on the continent.

The Roman Coastal Defences

The most certain indicator of the seriousness of the pirate threat faced by the Romans is the great extension of the system of coastal fortifications between *c.* 250 and *c.* 280 on both sides of the Channel. This chain of fortifications is now commonly known as the 'Saxon Shore' system after the cross Channel command

---

[62] Galliou, *op. cit.*, p. 274.

[63] J. Percival, *The Roman Villa* (London, 1976), pp. 42–45.

[64] E. Wightman, 'The fate of Gallo-Roman villages in the third century', in King and Henig (eds), *op. cit.*, pp. 236–41. Of the 22 *vici* which failed in the coastal *civitates* only one did so because of the effects of the marine transgression.

[65] Aurelius Victor, 39. 17; Eutropius, 9. 10. R. Van Dam, *Leadership and Community in Late Antique Gaul* (Berkeley, 1985), pp. 30–2, suggests that, due to the failure of the central authority at that time, the bands may originally have formed around local leaders for the purpose of forming a collective defence against pirate raids on northern Gaul.

[66] Cunliffe, *op. cit.*, p. 30, and S. S. Frere, *Britannia*. 3rd edn (London, 1987), p. 216, n. 63.

[67] P. Salway, *Roman Britain* (Oxford, 1981), pp. 276–81.

of the *Comes Litoris Saxonici* into which they had been organised by the late fourth century (discussed further in chapter 3) and, although there is no evidence that either the command or even the *Litus Saxonicum* name was current before the late fourth century, it will be used henceforward for the sake of convenience.

Completely new fortifications were built in the period 250–80 at the old *Classis Britannica* bases at Boulogne, Lympne and Dover.[68] The site of the old Claudian fort at Richborough was also reoccupied and a new fort was built within the boundaries of the old one,[69] while the fortifications at Oudenburg were rebuilt.[70] The fort named in the *Notitia Dignitatum* as *Locus Quartensis sive Hornensis*, generally thought to have been near either Étaples on the Canche or Cap Hornu on the Somme, may also have been built in this period. So also may the two continental *Litus Saxonicum* forts of *Marcis* and *Grannona* (probably at Marck and Le Havre), if in fact they had not been built earlier in the century.[71] On the East Anglian coast, the mouth of the Yare was protected by a fort at Burgh and the northern coast of the Thames estuary was defended by forts at Walton and Bradwell.[72] A Roman site now lost to coastal erosion at Skegness may have been a fort built at the same time to protect the Lincolnshire coast.[73] At Brough-on-Humber the earlier earthworks were replaced by stone walls shortly after 270.[74] The Solent area was protected by a fort at Portchester.[75] Though the omission seems inconsistent with a system which generally paid close attention to the protection of river mouths, there was apparently no fort to protect the

---

[68] On Boulogne see J. Y. Gosselin and C. Seillier, '*Gesoriacum Bononia*: de la ville du Haut-Empire à la ville du Bas-Empire', *Revue archéologique de Picardie*, III IV (1984 = 'Les villes de la Gaule Belgique au Haut-Empire', pp. 259–64. A coin of Tetricius from the foundation trench of the walls gives a *terminus post quem* of 274 for the reconstruction (pp. 261–3). See also C. Seillier, 'Boulogne and the coastal defences in the fourth and fifth centuries', in Johnston (ed.), *op. cit.*, p. 35, and S. Johnson, *The Roman Forts of the Saxon Shore* (London, 1976), p. 116. On Lympne see B. Cunliffe, 'Excavations at the Roman fort at Lympne, Kent 1976–78', *Britannia* XI (1980), pp. 227–88, and J. N. Hutchinson *et al*, 'Combined archaeological and geotechnical investigation of the Roman fort at Lympne, Kent', *Britannia* XVI (1985), pp. 209–36. These recent investigations have shown that the present irregular plan is the result of subsidence: the fort was originally square in plan. On Dover see Philp, 'Dover', in Johnston (ed.), *op. cit.*, pp. 20–1, and Johnson *Forts*, pp. 51–3. The Saxon Shore fort was built much nearer the harbour than the old *classis Britannica* fort had been.

[69] Johnson, *Forts*, pp. 48–50.

[70] See Mertens, *op. cit.*, pp. 57–60, and Thoen, *Belgische Kustvlakte*, *op. cit.*, pp. 129–33. Like the earlier third-century fort (see chapter 1, n. 56), this fort was built of earth and timber.

[71] See Johnson, *Forts*, pp. 90–2, 125.

[72] *Ibid.*, pp. 37–40 (Burgh); pp. 40–2 (Walton); pp. 40–4 (Bradwell).

[73] *Ibid.*, p. 20. Johnson believes that this site might possibly be even earlier and linked to the fort at Brancaster on the other side of the Wash. The site is known only from the records of sixteenth-century antiquarians: see M. Todd, *The Coritani* (London, 1973), p. 44.

[74] J. Crickmore, *Romano-British Urban Defences*, BAR BS 126 (Oxford, 1984), pp. 140–1.

[75] See B. Cunliffe, *Excavations at Portchester Castle*, vol. 1 (Roman), Reports of the Research Committee of the Society of Antiquaries of London 32 (London,1975). See also Johnson, *Forts*, pp. 59–62. This is the best preserved of the Saxon Shore forts, retaining its curtain wall and most of its towers to almost their full height.

mouth of the Scheldt, an omission which would seem to have left the heart of Belgica Secunda open to attack by pirates. The defensive measures taken in Gaul may well have been more considerable than this list suggests. To judge from the *Notitia Dignitatum*, the Romans seem to have based their defence of the Gallic coast on existing urban centres and since these generally still are important urban centres comprehensive evidence from excavations is hard to come by.[76] Much evidence will have been destroyed by later disturbance and still more may be deeply buried under existing buildings, as for example a fortified site of the third or fourth century which is known to exist at Brest but which cannot be excavated because it lies beneath a modern military base.[77] Also, because many inland Gallic towns were fortified against overland barbarian attack in the late third century, it cannot be concluded with certainty that a coastal town such as Nantes, which probably received its walls shortly after 275, was walled primarily against pirates.[78]

These fortifications, which have much in common with the new urban defences being built in Gaul and elsewhere at the same time,[79] show a pronounced departure from earlier Roman practice. Their most impressive characteristic is that semi-circular external bastion towers replace the old style of watch towers which were always built flush with the outside of the wall (as was still the case with the earlier Saxon Shore forts at Reculver and Brancaster). Together with thicker walls and more massive gatehouses, the change represents a shift towards a more defensive posture by the Romans. The earlier regular rectangular shaped forts were clearly not built in the expectation that they would have to be defended against a determined attack. The stronger defensive features of the Saxon Shore forts, especially the bastion towers which could defend the walls with enfilading fire, and which perhaps mounted heavy catapult weapons like the ballista,[80] were built to withstand a siege if necessary. The strength of the Saxon Shore forts has important implications for the Romans' perception of the Frankish and Saxon threat. The forts are far more substantial than would seem necessary if small scale piracy was the only problem and we must conclude that the Romans had enough respect for Frankish and Saxon naval power to believe them capable of mounting a major seaborne invasion of Britain. However, as was

---

[76] *Notitia Dignitatum*, ed. O. Seeck (Berlin, 1876), Occ. xxxvii-xxxviii. See also Johnson, *Forts*, p. 80.

[77] What little is known about this site is summarised by R. Sanquer, 'The *castellum* at Brest (Finistère)', in Johnston, *Saxon Shore*, pp. 45–50.

[78] The difficulty is well illustrated by the case of Brittany. The capitals of all five Armorican *civitates*, Nantes, Rennes, Vannes, Corseul and Carhaix, show signs of destruction in the 270s, yet two of them, Carhaix and Rennes, are well inland. All were subsequently fortified but Corseul, the *civitas* of the Coriosolites, which is about eight miles inland, was abandoned in favour of the heavily fortified, but coastal, site of Alet near St Malo. It does seem as if factors other than piracy must have been at work to produce this pattern: see Sanquer, *op. cit.*, pp. 49-50.

[79] See Johnson, *Forts*, pp. 115–6.

[80] Many of the bastion towers seem too small for the effective operation of catapult weapons and there is some doubt about their regular use in British forts: *ibid.*, pp. 118–20.

pointed out above, there is no evidence to indicate that these fears were realised in the third century.

Most of these forts seem to have been built as part of a single concerted programme which most probably started in the years immediately after the collapse of the Gallic Empire in 273, when a major fortification programme to defend the towns of Gaul was also put under way.[81] However, some defensive work may have been carried out under the Gallic emperors. Two of Postumus's coin types show maritime themes, a galley and a figure of Neptune, that may show a concern for naval defences,[82] and earthwork defences and a watch tower at Richborough, which were built shortly before the stone Saxon Shore fort, probably date from his reign.[83] So probably does the fort at Burgh which is certainly the earliest of the later third century forts. The bastion towers at Burgh were clearly added as an afterthought at a stage when construction was already quite advanced as they are not fully bonded to the fort's walls. Nor are the towers so well sited to give enfilading fire to cover the walls as are the towers of later forts.[84] The fort at Portchester was probably a late addition as it was not completed until the period 285–93.[85]

The main factor in determining the location of a fort was not the defensibility of the site but its suitability as a base for naval operations and, outside the Dover Straits, a commanding position over a vulnerable river mouth.[86] It has been noted that the sites were also well suited for use as strategic supply depots and there is evidence that industrial activities took place in many of the forts.[87] Each fort probably had its own naval detachment which would have been expected to work

---

[81] Johnson, *Forts*, pp. 94–113, argued plausibly, in 1976, that most of the Saxon Shore forts were begun as part of a single defence programme started by Probus, probably soon after the invasions of 276. Nothing which has been discovered since has done anything to undermine this attractive theory. B. Cunliffe, 'The Saxon Shore: some problems and misconceptions', in Johnston (ed.) *op. cit.*, p. 3, is less committed and claims only that the forts are roughly contemporary and probably belong to the 260s or 270s. The dating evidence is not strong enough to make a more precise estimate, he maintains. The theory, advanced by D. A. White, *Litus Saxonicum* (Madison, 1961), that the forts were built by Carausius as a defence against an attempt by the central imperial authorities to recover Britain finds favour with nobody.

[82] Drinkwater, *op. cit.*, pp. 163–5, thinks that the Neptune coins, issued between 260 and 265, may have been issued to celebrate a successful naval expedition, and that the galley coins, issued in 261, may have been an attempt to win over the garrison of Britain. O. Höckmann, 'Römische Schiffsverbände auf dem Ober- und Mittelrhein und die Verteidigung der Rheingrenze in der Spätantike', *JRGZM* XXXIII (1986), p. 381, sees the latter issue as showing a special concern for the Rhine fleet.

[83] Johnson, *Forts*, pp. 107–9, 114.

[84] *Ibid.*, pp. 96–8, and Cunliffe, 'The Saxon Shore', p. 5.

[85] Cunliffe, *Excavations at Portchester Castle*, pp. 419–31.

[86] The following discussion of the strategic thinking behind the Saxon Shore system is based largely on Johnson, *Forts*, pp. 114–131.

[87] J. Cotterill, 'Saxon Raiding and the Role of the Late Roman Coastal Forts in Britain', *Britannia* XXIV (1993), 227-39. Cotterill argues that this, rather than coastal defence, was the main function of the Saxon Shore forts. But the question must be asked, from whose attentions did the supplies need protecting?

in co-operation with a mobile military garrison.[88] The strategic plan behind the Roman defences was straightforward. The defences were concentrated in the Straits of Dover which formed a natural bottleneck through which the pirates had to go if they wished to raid the coasts of southern Britain, Gaul and beyond. There was no real attempt at defence in depth at this time (though the forts at Portchester and *Grannona* may have been intended as longstop measures), and the whole system must have been conceived of as a maritime extension to the Rhine *limes* in that it was intended to stop, or at least detect, would be raiders at the 'border', which was probably thought of as running across the Straits of Dover and north along Britain's east coast. The straits were probably the only point at which regular patrolling was possible; in the wider seas of the Channel beyond, the raiders could hold out to sea, out of sight of shore stations which could co-ordinate fleet manoeuvres. It would have been very difficult for a large fleet to evade detection but individual raiding ships must have found it relatively easy to slip through the defences unobserved at night or in conditions of poor visibility, especially as it would have been impossible for the Roman commanders to maintain a high standard of alertness in troops engaged in what must generally have been tedious and uneventful guard duty. However, once through, there was only one practical way back and as soon as the raiders landed in search of loot their presence would no longer be a secret. With the defences alerted there would probably be a far greater chance of the pirates' being intercepted on the way home than on the way in. The system offered little protection to the coast of Belgica and, despite its defences, the east coast of Britain must have remained vulnerable to raiders descending from the open sea.

Frankish and Saxon Pirate Raids in the Late 3rd and 4th Centuries

The system of forts was probably completed by 285 by which time the situation in the Channel was becoming increasingly serious. For the first time we have explicit reference to Saxon pirates raiding along with the Franks. According to Eutropius the coasts of Belgica and Armorica were infested with Frankish and Saxon pirates by the mid 280s.[89] The Franks and Saxons were also being joined

---

[88] Two units named in the *Notitia Dignitatum*, the *milites Anderetianorum* (*Occ.* vii. 100), and the *classis Anderetianorum* (*Occ.* xlii. 23), though at that time (the early fifth century) stationed at different locations, had apparently been raised to man the Saxon Shore fort at Pevensey (*Anderida*) and presumably to work in co-operation with each other. No doubt there were similar units at the other Saxon Shore forts in the late third/early fourth century: see Johnson, *Forts*, p. 125.

[89] Eutropius, IX. 21: 'Per haec tempora etiam Carausius [qui] vilissime natus strenuae militiae ordine famam egregiam fuerat consecutus, cum apud Bononiam per tractum Belgicae et Armorici pacandum mare accepisset, quod Franci et Saxones infestabant.' Similarly, Orosius, VII. 25. 3: 'deinde Carausius quidam... cum ad obseuranda Oceani litora, quae tunc Franci et Saxones infestabant.' In his account, Aurelius Victor, XXXIX. 20 (see text below n. 93) calls the raiders simply *Germani*.

by raiders from Scandinavia, for in *c.* 287 Maximian defeated a force of Heruls, then settled in Denmark, who had attacked the lower Rhine along with the *Chaibones*, probably the Saxon tribe of the Aviones.[90] It also seems likely that Frisian pirates were active around this time.[91] The situation must already have been grave in the mid 270s when the Saxon Shore fort building programme was begun, and no doubt the great Germanic invasions of 276 were accompanied by piracy on the coasts. Further raiding may also have been encouraged by the triumphant return of those Franks who had been transported to Pontus by Probus in 277.[92]

Impressive though the Saxon Shore defences still look even today, the system cannot have operated very efficiently to begin with because of the decline of Roman naval power. The signs are that both the *classis Britannica* and the *classis Germanica* had been allowed to decay in the troubled years of the middle of the century.[93] What was left of the Rhine fleet was apparently destroyed by barbarians, probably the Franks, while it was laid up for the winter in 280.[94] To restore Roman naval power Carausius, a Menapian with a maritime background, was appointed to what appears to have been a cross-Channel command at

---

[90] Mamertinus, *Panegyricus Maximiano Augusto dictus* (ed. E. Galletier in *Panégyriques Latins*, vol. 1, pp. 24–37), V, and Mamertinus, *Panegyricus Genethliacus Maximiano Augusto dictus*, (*ibid.* pp. 50–67), VII. 1. On the origins of the Heruls see A. Russchen, 'Warns, Heruli, Thuringians', *It Beaken* XXVI (1964), p. 302. On the *Chaibones* see Pauly-Wissowa, *Realenzyklopädie der klassischen Altertums-wissenschaft* (reprint, Stuttgart, 1958), vol. III. 2, cols 2022–3, and Lintzel, *op. cit.*, pp. 5–6.

[91] *Incert. Pan. Constantio Caes.* IX. 3, describes the Frisians as *praedatores*. Though it is not made clear whether they raided by land or by sea, the latter seems more likely because of their geographical location.

[92] As Edward Gibbon delightfully put it: 'The example of their success, instructing their countrymen to conceive the advantages and to despise the dangers of the sea, pointed out to their enterprising spirit a new road to wealth and glory': *The History of the Decline and Fall of the Roman Empire*, ed. J. B. Bury (8 vols, London, 1897), vol. 1, p. 334.

[93] The *classis Britannica* is not known of after the reign of Philip (243-49): see H. Cleere, 'The *classis Britannica*', in Johnston (ed.), *op. cit.*, p. 18. The end of the *classis Germanica* seems to have come sometime in the late third century. Fourth-century tile stamps of the *Legio XXII primigenia* found at Strasbourg show ships and other marine images such as tridents and dolphins which may be a sign that control of naval operations on the Rhine had been handed over to the army after the *classis Germanica* had been wound up. Such was certainly the case with the Roman fleet on the Danube, as the *classis Pannonica* had been broken up into smaller, more localised units under legionary control by the fourth century, see Höckmann, 'Römische Schiffsverbände', pp. 409–15. It must be likely that the same decentralisation occurred in the old *classis Britannica* area and is reflected in the organisation of the Saxon Shore system: see above, n. 86. This will have been a much more flexible system than that based on the old regional fleets. Larger fleets seem only to have been raised on an *ad hoc* basis in the Late Empire: see C. G. Starr, *The Influence of Sea Power on Ancient History* (New York, 1989), pp. 79–81.

[94] *SHA: Firmus Saturninus Proculus et Bonosus*, 15. 1. Höckmann, *op. cit.*, p. 407. thinks it most likely that the barbarians were able to destroy the whole fleet because the ships had been gathered together, probably at Cologne, for some reason such as winter maintenance.

Boulogne in 285.[95] Carausius built up the fleet and quickly brought the situation back under control by an active naval policy which aimed to intercept the raiders at sea.[96] Coming from the lower Rhine himself, Carausius was probably familiar with the ways of the Franks, and this knowledge will no doubt have been of considerable use to him in combating their raids. It was probably on account of Carausius' success that Diocletian adopted the title *Britannicus Maximus* in 285.[97] However, in the atmosphere of mutual distrust so typical of the third century, Carausius' success soon aroused the suspicion, or jealousy, of Diocletian's co-emperor Maximian. He accused Carausius of deliberately allowing the pirates through the defences, of only intercepting them on their way home, after they had plundered, and embezzling their booty for his own purposes rather than returning it to the provincials or handing it over to the emperor.[98] The first part of the charge, at least, was probably unjust; that was simply the way the defence system worked best. Learning that Maximian had ordered his execution, Carausius seized Britain and the north coastal area of Gaul and proclaimed himself emperor in 286.

Under Carausius and his successor Allectus, Britain was to remain independent until 296. There is reason to believe that Carausius maintained the efficiency of his defensive system as there seems to have been a decline in coin hoarding in Britain and no coastal distribution pattern is discernible during his reign.[99] Not only was Carausius a successful naval commander; he also allied with the Franks against the central Roman authority,[100] and both he and Allectus recruited barbarian mercenaries into the army, and probably the navy.[101] This in

---

[95] Aurelius Victor, XXXIX. 20: 'Quo bello Carausius, Menapiae ciuis, factis promptioribus enituit; eoque eum, simul quia gubernandi (quo officio adolescentiam mercede exercuerat) gnarus habebetur, parandae classi ac propulsandis Germanis maria infestantibus praefecere.' There are good narrative accounts of Carausius's career in Johnson, *Forts*, pp. 23–33, S. Williams, *Diocletian and the Roman recovery* (London, 1985), pp. 46–62, 71–2, and Salway, *op. cit.*, pp. 295–300, 304–5. For a detailed analysis of the source material for the reigns of Carausius and Allectus see N. Shiel, *The Episode of Carausius and Allectus: the Literary and Numismatic Evidence*, BAR 40 (Oxford, 1977), pp. 3–20.

[96] Aurelius Victor, XXXIX. 21; Eutropius, IX. 21. For the texts see below n. 96.

[97] Johnson, *Forts*, p. 26.

[98] Aurelius Victor, XXXIX. 21: 'Hoc eliator, cum barbarum multos opprimeret neque praedae omnia in aerarium referret, Herculii [Maximian] metu, a quo se caedi iussum compererat, Britanniam, hausto imperio, capessiuit.' Eutropius, IX. 21, is more explicit about the nature of the charge:

> Multis barbaris saepe captis nec praeda integra aut provincialibus reddita aut imperatoribus missa cum suspicio esse coepisset consulto ab eo admitti barbaros, ut transeuntes cum praeda exciperet atque hac se occasione ditaret, a Maximiano iussus occidi purpuram sumpsit et Brittanias occupavit.

Orosius, VII. 25.3–4, is essentially similar to Eutropius.

[99] Shiel, *op. cit.*, pp. 88–93, maps 1–6.

[100] *Incert. pan. Constantio Caes*. IX. See also the discussion in Williams, *op. cit.*, p. 51.

[101] Carausius's mercenaries are described simply as *barbari*: *Incert. pan. Constantio Caes*. XII. 1. In view of Carausius's alliance with the Franks it is most likely that they were the barbarians he

itself would have diverted many of the more restless barbarians away from piracy. It was probably because he employed barbarian sailors in his navy that Carausius was given the insulting title *pirata* by Maximian's panegyrist.[102]

Because of the barbarian involvement in the campaigns which were waged by the Romans to recover Britain, it is worth looking at these. The first campaign was waged by Maximian in 288–9 under unfavourable conditions. Because Carausius held the Channel coast of Gaul, Maximian had no direct access to the sea; nor did he have a fleet. Rather than tackle Carausius head on by invading his Gallic territories, Maximian's first move was to eliminate the usurper's Frankish allies in order to gain control over navigation on the Rhine.[103] It may be that the unsuccessful Herul and Saxon raid on the Rhine in 287 had been encouraged by Carausius to interfere with his rival's plans. Having gained control by exploiting inter-tribal rivalries, Maximian formed his fleet up at Trier, proceeded to the Rhine mouth and set sail for Britain.

What happened next has been a cause of much conjecture. Our main sources for the expedition are two panegyric poems dedicated to Maximian, and the way the poet has treated the expedition has aroused the suspicion that it was a disaster. The earlier panegyric was delivered just before the expedition set out from Trier and is full of optimism about Maximian's inevitable triumph over the 'pirate',[104] but the second, delivered two years later, passes over the outcome of the expedition in silence.[105] A later panegyric, delivered to Constantius, the eventual re-conquerer of Britain, refers briefly back to Maximian's expedition saying that it failed due to bad weather.[106] However, highly plausible as this explanation is (especially as it is certain that Maximian's crews were inexperienced),[107] it has almost universally been seen as face-saving propaganda. Carausius will, no doubt, have had warning of the fleet's approach well in advance, probably before it even reached the sea, giving him ample time to prepare his defences. Moreover, these defences were specifically designed to deal with attackers approaching Britain by sea from the direction of the Rhine. As a

---

recruited, but this does not rule out the likelihood that Saxons and Frisians were also involved. Allectus's mercenaries are described explicitly as *Franci* (ibid., XVI. 2). Gallo-Roman merchant seamen were also recruited by Carausius (ibid., XII. 1). Shiel, *op. cit.*, pp. 8–9, suggests, not unreasonably considering the nature of the panegyric medium, that Carausius's reliance on barbarian mercenaries may have been exaggerated to some degree to show him in the worst possible light.

[102] Mamertinus, *Pan. Maximian*, XII. 1. *Pan. Constantio Caes.* VI. 1, describes Carausius's garrison at Boulogne as *piratae*, though it does not follow from this that they were barbarians.

[103] Mamertinus, *Pan. Maximiano* VII. 2: 'domitis oppressa Francis bella piratica'. See also Williams, *op. cit.*, p. 51.

[104] Mamertinus, *Pan. Maximiano*, delivered on 21 April 289: on the date see Galletier, *Pan. Lat.* vol. 1, pp. 8–9.

[105] Mamertinus, *Pan. Geneth. Maximiano*, delivered in July 291: On the date see Galletier, *Pan. Lat.*, vol.1, pp. 9–12.

[106] *Incert. pan. Constantio Caes.* XII. 2.

[107] *Ibid.*, XII. 1, describes the crews as being 'in re maritima nouis'.

consequence it has been widely believed that Maximian's fleet was successfully opposed by Carausius' navy and forced to withdraw without landing, perhaps following a naval battle.[108] Though the evidence for this conclusion is entirely circumstantial it may well be the correct one. Maximian never attempted another naval expedition himself, which he surely could have done if his fleet had only withdrawn because of bad weather, while the second, successful, expedition against Britain resorted to a completely different strategy. It would be pleasingly ironic if a Roman fleet approaching Britain from the Rhine was driven off by the Saxon Shore defences manned, in part, by one time Germanic pirates.

The second expedition to recover Britain began in effect in 293 when Constantius seized Boulogne following a short siege. The failure to hold Boulogne cost Carausius his control over the Channel coast of Gaul and also his life. He was assassinated and replaced by Allectus, one of his ministers, who was heavily dependent on the support of barbarian, mainly Frankish, mercenaries.[109] It was to take Constantius three years to build a fleet strong enough for the invasion of Britain. The fleet was divided into two parts. One, under Asclepiodotus, was probably intended to decoy Allectus' fleet away from the Straits of Dover by making a direct crossing from the Seine, while Constantius sailed for London with the main force from Boulogne. Allectus's fleet waited in the Solent but to no avail; in conditions of poor visibility, Asclepiodotus evaded interception and landed unopposed, and it was his force which fought and won the decisive battle against Allectus.[110] Allectus' surviving Frankish mercenaries withdrew on London where they probably hoped to seize ships in which to escape back to their homelands.[111] Constantius got there first and the barbarians were rounded up and killed.

It is possible, but by no means certain, that Frankish pirates raided as far afield as Spain in this period.[112] If so, it may be that the raids were carried out

---

[108] For example, Williams, *op. cit.*, p. 55. Salway, *op. cit.*, p. 298. Johnson, *Forts*, p. 29.

[109] For an account of Allectus's career see Williams, *op. cit.*, pp. 71–4.

[110] *Incert. pan. Constantio Caes.* XV. The best discussion of the campaign is that by D. G. Eicholz, 'Constantius Chlorus' invasion of Britain', *Journal of Roman Studies* XLIII (1953), pp. 41–7. Also worth consulting are Williams, *op. cit.*, pp. 73–4, and Johnson, *Forts*, pp. 31–3, both of whom take a less flattering view of Constantius's personal contribution to the campaign than does Eicholz.

[111] *Incert. pan. Constantio Caes.* XVI. 2.

[112] Keay, *op. cit.*, p. 477. Keay's conclusion is based on *Incert. pan. Constantio Caes.* XVIII. 4–5, which describes how Constantius's victory over Allectus and his Frankish allies has not only liberated Britain but also freed Gaul, Spain, Italy and Africa from the fear of Frankish piracy:

> Itaque hac victoria uestra non Britannia solum seruitute est liberata, sed omnibus nationibus securitas restituta quae maritimo usu tantum in bello adire periculi poterant quantum in pace commodi consequentur. Nunc secura est, ut de latere Gallico taceam, quamuis paene conspicuis litoribus Hispania, nunc Italia, nunc Africa, nunc omnes usque ad Maeotias paludes perpetuis curis vacant gentes.

The problem with Keay's interpretation is that this passage is almost immediately preceded by an account of the homecoming voyage of the Franks who rebelled in Pontus *c.* 278 (XVIII. 2: see note 45 above for the text) and it is not at all clear how much of the passage is referring back

partly to support Allectus by diverting Constantius into time-consuming defensive measures. Constantius was clearly worried that the Franks might try to interfere with his plans as a campaign against them preceded his attack on Allectus.[113] With control of the Channel coasts divided between two warring Roman factions the chances for successful piracy will certainly have increased.

The half-century which followed the downfall of Allectus does not seem to have been marked by serious piracy. Both Carausius and Allectus paid close attention to naval defence and the non-barbarian part of their forces will have been re-incorporated into the central authority's forces after Constantius' brief campaign against Allectus. Thus the Roman defences were perhaps quickly restored to the high level of efficiency they had attained under Carausius, with the result that piracy was held down to acceptable levels. Though the economy of Gaul was slow to recover from the multiple devastations of the third century,[114] Britain, relatively safe behind its defences, entered into a period of remarkable prosperity. A notable indication of the sense of security felt in Britain is the fact the reviving villas were not fortified as they were on the continent. In fact the period *c.* 275–350 saw the villa system reach the peak of its prosperity in Britain. This was partly because its relative security made Britain an important source of supplies for the embattled Rhine garrisons, partly because there appears to have been an influx of refugee landowners from Gaul.[115]

However, piracy by no means died out. There was a serious outbreak of Frankish piracy which affected the Empire's Atlantic coast as far as Spain sometime between 306 and 313.[116] Britain too seems to have suffered at least one serious raid as the small town of Godmanchester suffered major deliberate fire damage at the end of the third century.[117] Scattered, disarticulated human bones,

---

to this account; the references to Italy and Africa must certainly be and the reference to lake Maeotis (the Sea of Azov) is clearly an exaggerated allusion to the Franks' activities in the Black Sea. From the context, it seems possible that the panegyrist has simply dredged up events of two decades before to increase the significance of Constantius's triumph. Keay dates these putative raids to 293–305, but as it seems certain that the panegyric was delivered on 1st March 297 (Galletier, *Pan. Lat.,* vol. 1, p. 73), the raids must have taken place in or before 296.

[113] *Incert. pan. Constantio Caes.* VIII IX.

[114] Percival, *op. cit.*, pp. 44–8, Galliou, *op. cit.*, p. 274.

[115] Salway, *op. cit.*, p. 329, Percival, *op. cit.*, pp. 48–9.

[116] Nazarius, *Panegyricus Constantino dictus* (ed. E. Galletier, *Pan Lat.,* vol. 2, pp. 166–98), XVII. 1: 'Franci ipsi praeter ceteros truces, quorum uis, cum ad bellum efferuesceret, ultra ipsum Oceanum aestu furoris euecta, Hispaniarum etiam oras armis infestas habebat.' Galletier, p. 152, dates the raids to 313, while Keay, 'The *Conventus Tarraconensis*', p. 477, dates them to between 306 and 312. The raids certainly took place before Constantine's campaign against the Franks in 314.

[117] H. J. M. Green, 'Roman Godmanchester', in W. Rodwell and T. Rowley, *The Small Towns of Roman Britain,* BAR 15 (Oxford, 1975), p. 206. The dating of the destruction is based on two hoards, one of jewellery and coins, the other of coins alone, which both terminate with coins of Allectus (293–6). The attack may have taken place during Constantius's campaign against Allectus or in the immediate aftermath of his defeat when the defences of Britain may have been disorganised. The town did not recover from the disaster until the mid fourth century. Green thinks it most likely that the town was sacked by Saxon pirates.

some of them gnawed by dogs or wolves, lying on top of third century deposits near the *mansio*, which was burned along with the bath house, suggest that the fires were accompanied by a massacre of some of the town's inhabitants. The fact that the bodies were subsequently attacked by animals shows that there was nobody left in the town to bury the dead after the catastrophe. It must be assumed that such of the population as had not either been killed or captured had taken flight and been afraid to return to the town in the immediate aftermath. Unquestionably the town suffered a violent and disastrous attack, most probably by pirates. Godmanchester lies on the river Ouse and would have been easily accessible to Saxon or Frankish pirates who had penetrated the Wash.

Frankish and Saxon pirates also continued to evade the defences in the Dover straits for there are signs of intense activity at Portchester in the first half of the fourth century.[118] There are also the first signs that the *limes* type approach to coastal defence was proving inadequate, as the Romans built a new Saxon Shore fort at Pevensey sometime after 335 to plug the long gap in the defences of the south coast of Britain between the Dover straits and Portchester.[119] The Saxon Shore fort at Lympne was abandoned c. 340 [120] and it is tempting to see the fort at Pevensey as a replacement for Lympne, intended to provide greater defence in depth without actually increasing the number of troops deployed. It may be that this change was a response to some emergency such as the one which brought the emperor Constans rushing to Britain in midwinter 343. Unfortunately, nothing is known about the nature of the crisis which prompted this visit.[121] The unfavourable navigating conditions prevalent in winter make it more likely that the emergency was on the northern, land, frontier but piracy should not be ruled out as the cause.

After c. 350 references to pirate raids become more frequent and it seems that the Roman defences were coming under increasing strain, especially from the Saxons who from now on become more prominent than the Franks. In addition to plundering, both the Saxons and the Franks found mercenary employment, in the same circumstances as they had done in the reigns of Carausius and Allectus. The usurper Magnentius, himself of German ancestry, easily recruited Frankish and

---

[118] Cunliffe, *Excavations at Portchester Castle*, p. 423.

[119] Cunliffe, *The Regni*, pp. 38–40, Johnson, *Forts*, pp. 56–9. There are fortifications at Bitterne, near Southampton, and at Carisbrooke, on the Isle of Wight, which may also date from this period. Both sites are poorly dated and have never been thoroughly excavated. Their relationship, if any, to the Saxon Shore system is poorly understood and neither appears in the *Notitia Dignitatum*. See Johnson, *ibid.*, pp. 141–3.

[120] Cunliffe, 'Excavations at the Roman fort at Lympne', pp. 84–5, and Hutchinson, *op. cit.*, p. 233.

[121] Ammianus Marcellinus, XXVII. 8.3, makes a tantalising reference back to his account of Constans's visit to Britain in one of the books of his history which have since been lost. For speculation on the purpose of the visit see Salway, *op. cit.*, p. 349, and Johnson, *Forts*, p. 144.

Saxon soldiers to support his bid for the purple in 353, men whom Julian (later emperor) described as the fiercest of the tribes who lived beyond the Rhine.[122]

In the mid-350s the Franks and Alamanni overran much of the Rhine frontier. The invasions were accompanied by Frankish piracy which effectively closed the Rhine to Roman shipping. One of the emperor Julian's priorities in his campaigns to restore the frontier was to regain control of navigation of the Rhine so that he could import supplies from Britain directly into the shattered frontier zone. He achieved this with a massive naval show of strength, involving 600 ships, in the lower Rhine area *c*. 358.[123] The overawed Franks agreed to peace terms with the Romans which involved their giving hostages as a guarantee that they would stop interfering with Roman shipping.[124]

According to Zosimus, Julian's campaigns beyond the Rhine alarmed the Saxons who ordered one of their tribes, given the otherwise unknown name of *Kouadoi* by Zosimus, to begin attacks on imperial territory.[125] It seems that the invasion was originally intended to go overland, but the Franks, Zosimus tells us, did not wish to provoke the Romans, and refused to give the *Kouadoi* access to Roman territory. Undeterred, the *Kouadoi* outflanked the main area of Frankish settlement by sea and seized the Batavian island (Betuwe) at the mouth of the Rhine, a nominally Roman territory which had recently been settled by the Salian Franks. Expelling its Salian inhabitants, they used the island as a base to launch nocturnal hit and run attacks on Roman territory which the emperor Julian was only able to suppress with great difficulty. This raid was very much a harbinger of things to come; seizing an island at the mouth of a major river to use as a secure raiding base was to become a favoured and successful tactic of both Saxons and Vikings in the future.

There are three possibilities as to the exact identity of the *Kouadoi*: the Quadi, the Chamavi or the Chauci.[126] The first of these possibilities can be dismissed on geographical grounds: the Quadi lived far away on the Danube so it is hardly likely that they can be meant. However the other two candidates, the Chamavi and the Chauci, both have strong arguments in their favour. It is known from other sources that Julian campaigned against the Chamavi on the lower Rhine in 358,[127] but none mentions the Chauci or the Saxons as being involved. On the

---

[122] Julian, *Panegyric in Honour of Constantius*, (ed. and trans. W. C. Wright, *The Works of the Emperor Julian*, Loeb Classical Library (3 vols, London, 1913), vol. 1, pp. 4–127), XXXIV (at pp. 89–91).

[123] Zosimus, III. 5.2. Eunapius (ed. and trans. R. C. Blockley, *The Fragmentary Classicising Historians of the Later Roman Empire*, ARCA Classical and Medieval Texts, Papers and Monographs 10 (Liverpool, 1983), vol. 2, pp. 2–127), fr. 18.6.

[124] Eunapius, fr. 18.6.. See also Zöllner, *op. cit.*, p. 20.

[125] Zosimus, III. 6.1–4.

[126] There is a clear, balanced and well referenced discussion of this problem by Paschoud in his edition of Zosimus (vol. 3, pp. 76–7, n. 15), in which he opts for the Chamavian solution.

[127] For example, Julian, *Letter to the Athenians* (ed. and trans. J. Bidez, *L'empereur Julien: oeuvres complètes*, vol. 1.i = *Discours de Julien César* (Paris, 1932), V, pp. 206–35), ch. 8. Also Ammianus Marcellinus, XVII. 8, and Eunapius, fr. 18.6.

other hand, Zosimus' account makes little sense if the Chamavi are meant by the *Kouadoi*. The Chamavi could not have been prevented from raiding Roman territory by the neighbouring Frankish tribes because they bordered directly on to Roman territory[128] and could have raided at will. Nor is there any reason to believe that the Chamavi were ever subject to the Saxons.

From Zosimus' account it seems that the *Kouadoi* must have lived to the north of the Franks, on the coast, and this would favour the Chauci. Though the Chauci were last heard of nearly 200 years before and are presumed to have been absorbed by the Saxons in the third century, it is possible that they still retained an individual identity within the grouping, as the Aviones appear still to have done at the end of the third century, and as the Salians and others were long to do within the Frankish confederation. It would also not be unprecedented if the Saxons had operated out of Frankish territory; they certainly did so in Valentinian's reign (see below, p. 79). A firm conclusion to the problem seems impossible, and though, in my opinion, the general context of Zosimus' account favours the Chaucian solution it is quite possible that he was confused about more than just the name. It seems safest to conclude no more from Zosimus than that Saxon or Frankish pirates were active on the lower Rhine in 358. The Salians whom the *Kouadoi* had driven out moved into Roman territory. Julian, who was preoccupied with other matters, was unable to expel them and he settled them in Toxandria, no doubt as a temporary expedient, intending to deal with them when other events permitted.[129] However, the Salians never were to be expelled by the Romans and this settlement marks the beginning of the slow Frankish expansion into northern Gaul.

It is clear that by the early 360s the defences of Britain were finding it increasingly difficult to cope with the raids of both the Saxons and the Franks and, according to Ammianus Marcellinus, by 364 the raids of the former were continuous.[130] The Roman defences were by this time being further stretched by the appearance off the western coasts of Britain of Scottish pirates operating from Ireland and south west Scotland and also by Pictish pirates on the east coast.[131] Saxon Shore-type forts at Lancaster and Cardiff and a fortified harbour at Holyhead (Caer Gybi) may have been part of defensive system against these raiders in the Irish Sea. The raids reached a climax in June 367 with the

---

[128] Schmidt, *op. cit.*, vol. 2, p. 206.

[129] Zöllner, *op. cit.*; p. 18. Wightman, *Gallia Belgica*, pp. 209, 253; James, *op. cit.*, p. 51.

[130] Ammianus Marcellinus, XXVI, 4.5: 'Picti, Saxonesque et Scotti, et Attacotti Britannos aerumnis vexavere continuis.'

[131] *Ibid*. The attacks of the Scots are first mentioned by Ammianus, XX, 1.1 (*c.* 360). On Scottish piracy generally, see N. K. Chadwick, *The British Heroic Age* (Cardiff, 1976), pp. 24–37, and G. J. Marcus, *The Conquest of the North Atlantic* (Woodbridge, 1980), pp. 8–9, On Roman defences on the west coast, see Johnson, *Forts*, pp. 132–6. There is no literary evidence of Pictish piracy in this period but Gildas, *De excidio et conquestu Britanniae*, ed. M. Winterbottom (London, 1978), I, 14, 16, 17. seems to lump the Scots and Picts together as sea-borne attackers who ravaged Britain in the declining years of Roman rule: 'alis remorum remigumque brachiis ac velis vento sinuatis vecti' (I. 16).

barbarica conspiratio, a concerted effort by a confederation of Picts, Scots, Attacotti, Saxons and Franks which led to the virtual extinction of Roman authority in Britain.[132] As in the third century, the barbarians had access to up to date intelligence of the Empire's problems; the spur to this attack seems to have been the political paralysis which followed when the emperor Valentinian was struck down by a critical illness for some months at Trier.[133] While the Picts, Scots and Attacotti overran Britain from the north and west, the main role of the Saxons and Franks in the conspiracy was to attack the coast of Gaul, no doubt with the intention of cutting off the garrison of Britain from reinforcements.[134] This formidable alliance of barbarian tribes, attacking by land and sea, overwhelmed the defences of Britain; the commander of the bulk of the Roman forces in Britain, Fullofaudes the *dux Britanniarum*, was somehow neutralised and the commander of the coast defences, Nectaridus the *Comes Maritimi Tractus*, was killed.[135] The countryside was everywhere overrun by plundering bands of barbarians but London held out against them and so did many of the other cities and fortresses. It has proved very difficult to find archaeological evidence of destruction which can be securely dated to the years of the barbarian conspiracy, however decapitated skeletons discovered at a burned late fourth century farm site at Sherston in Wiltshire may well be victims of the invaders.[136] Initial Roman attempts to relieve the situation were ineffective and it was not until early in 368 that an effective counter attack began under count Theodosius.

The situation which Theodosius found was one of confusion; most of the Roman garrison were scattered, many troops had deserted, others had gone over to the enemy.[137] Theodosius rebuilt the garrison by issuing a general amnesty to these troops while mounting a vigorous counter insurgency campaign against the

---

[132] Ammianus Marcellinus, XXVII, 8.1: 'nuntio percellitur gravi, qui Britannias indicabant barbarica conspiratione, ad ultimam vexatas inopiam'. Good accounts of the conspiracy and its aftermath are contained in Salway, *op. cit.*, pp. 374–84, and Frere, *op. cit.*, pp. 339–48. The Attacotti, who had a reputation for cannibalism, were probably a Scottish tribe from Ireland or the Hebrides: see Salway, *op. cit.*, p. 369. On the date of the conspiracy see R. C. Blockley, 'The date of the Barbarian Conspiracy', *Britannia*, XI (1980), pp. 223–5.

[133] Salway, *op. cit.* p. 374.

[134] Ammianus Marcellinus, XXVII, 8.5: 'Gallicanos vero tractus Franci et Saxones, eisdem confines, quo quisque erumpere potuit, terra vel mari, praedis acerbis incendiisque, et captivorum funeribus omnium violabat.'

[135] Ammianus Marcellinus, XXVII, 8.1: 'Nectaridumque comitem maritimi tractus occisum, et Fullofaudes ducem hostilibus insidiis circumventum.' S. Johnson, 'Channel commands in the *Notitia*' in R. Goodburn and P. Bartholomew (eds), *Aspects of the Notitia Dignitatum*, BAR Supp. Ser. 15 (Oxford, 1976), p. 89, argues that the *Comes Maritimi Tractus* is probably the *Comes Litoris Saxonici* of the *Notitia Dignitatum, Occ.* xxviii.

[136] The extent of the destruction wreaked by the barbarians in 367–9 has proved very difficult to determine archaeologically. It is not that there is a shortage of evidence of destruction and insecurity in the late fourth century; such evidence is considerable and still increasing. But evidence which allows close dating is generally lacking; for example, Percival, *op. cit.*, p. 168, observes that many villas continued to be occupied in the late fourth century and there is not one whose destruction can be confidently dated to 367–8.

[137] Ammianus Marcellinus, XXVII. 8. 9–10, XXVIII. 3.1, 3.8.

roving bands of barbarians in the countryside. It is clear that Saxon pirates had joined in the general plundering of Britain because Theodosius specifically ordered aggressive naval countermeasures against them.[138] To consolidate his victory, Theodosius ordered extensive rebuilding of damaged city defences and forts.[139] British town walls were strengthened by the addition of external bastion towers in the late fourth century and these have often, though not necessarily rightly, been attributed to Theodosius' programme of restoration.[140] Five late fourth-century signal stations are known from the north Yorkshire coast with a sixth, possibly, at Sunderland and it is probable that these were also part of Theodosius' programme of restoration. The five Yorkshire signal stations were dependent on the inland fort at Malton which housed a highly mobile garrison, the *supervenientes* ('surprise attackers'), who would intercept any raiding parties as they moved inland towards the vale of York.[141] The east coast of England has been subject to considerable erosion since Roman times and it is likely that other signal station sites have been lost to the sea. There is inconclusive evidence that there were signal stations on the East Anglian coast and the Thames estuary;[142] perhaps the Yorkshire sites are all that remains of a chain of stations which originally stretched from Hadrian's Wall to the Thames? According to the early sixth-century British writer Gildas, shortly before Britain was abandoned, the Romans built a chain of watchtowers to protect the British coast against the Picts.[143] It is generally thought therefore that the signal stations on the Yorkshire coast were a part of this chain, designed to give warning of Pictish raiders trying to outflank Hadrian's Wall by sea.[144] However, the very fact of the barbarian conspiracy shows that the Franks and Saxons were in direct sea contact with the north of Britain, so the Yorkshire coast would have been just as vulnerable to

---

[138] Pacatus, *Panegyricus Theodosio dictus* (ed. E. Galletier, *Pan Lat.*, vol. 3, pp. 68–114), V. 2: 'Saxo consumptus bellis naualibus offeretur'. Also Claudian, *Carmina*, ed. and trans. M. Platnauer, Loeb Classical Library (2 vols, London, 1922), VIII: *De quarto consulato Honorii Aug.*, ll. 30–2.

[139] Ammianus Marcellinus, XXVIII. 3.1.

[140] The extent of Theodosius's work is discussed by Crickmore, *op. cit.*, pp. 78–82. The dating evidence is poor but sufficient, she believes, to indicate that many, even most, of the bastion towers were built before 367. Frere, *Britannia*, pp. 247–8, 346, takes an almost exactly contrary view of the same evidence and concludes that most of the work could not have been begun before 360. Frere at least has the literary evidence on his side.

[141] See Ramm, *op. cit.*, pp. 125–9.

[142] Johnson, *Forts*, pp. 125–6.

[143] Gildas, *De excidio*, I. 18.3, describes a chain of *turres* which he believed the Romans had built to the south of Hadrian's wall against the Picts shortly before they left Britain for good: 'In litore quoque oceani ad meridianam plagam, quo naves eorum habebantur, turres per intervalla ad prospectum maris collocant.' However, Gildas's reliability is questionable on this point as his account in the same chapter of the origins of the two Roman walls across Britain is quite wrong.

[144] For example J. C. Mann, '*Duces* and *comites* in the fourth century' in Johnston (ed.), *op. cit.*, pp. 11–15, who styles the system the 'Pictish Shore' (p. 14), and L. Alcock, *Arthur's Britain* (London, 1971), p. 96. Ramm, *op.cit.*, p. 126, prefers the Saxons as the main threat.

Germanic pirates coming from directly across the North Sea as it was to the Picts.

Though there is no obvious reason to doubt that Ammianus knew what he was talking about, not everybody has been prepared to believe that the 'barbarian conspiracy' really was a conspiracy. Recently, E. A. Thompson has suggested that there was no conspiracy, that the apparent co-ordination of the barbarian attacks was due solely to coincidence.[145] This in itself is not impossible, but the main plank of Thompson's argument, that it would have taken an unusually persuasive barbarian diplomat, who was also 'an above average linguist into the bargain', to arrange the whole conspiracy, is hardly convincing.[146] All of the barbarian peoples involved in this attack had for long been in close contact with the Roman Empire, both in peace and war. There will have been men among all of them who could speak Latin; it would not have been necessary for the Franks or Saxons to learn Pictish. And as to persuasiveness: would it really have been so difficult to persuade a number of barbarian tribes, with a common interest in plunder, to unite to attack a vulnerable and isolated province at a time when political difficulties would have hampered the defence? Under the circumstances, it seems more realistic to see the conspiracy, and its success, as a sign of the increasing political maturity of the barbarians.[147]

The barbarian conspiracy marks an apparent turning point in the history of Germanic piracy in north west Europe; there is no recorded Frankish pirate activity after this date while Saxon pirate activity is recorded with increasing frequency. Because of this divergence the future development of Frankish and Saxon seafaring will be dealt with in separate chapters. Though both Franks and Saxons had very much the same level of seafaring ability and must have used much the same tactics on their raids, the ships which they used were probably built in very different traditions. The ships of the Saxons, about which we are relatively well informed, will be discussed in the following chapter. The ships of the Franks are discussed below.

The Ships of the Franks

Although we know nothing certain about Frankish warships, it is possible to make an intelligent guess that they were carvel-built vessels, propelled by oar and sail. Probably they were similar in many ways to the light late Roman

---

[145] E. A. Thompson, *Saint Germanus of Auxerre and the End of Roman Britain* (Woodbridge, 1984), p. 44. Another doubter is P. Bartholomew, 'Fourth-century Saxons', *Britannia* XV (1984), pp. 169–85, who, in an extended argument which is too contrived to be convincing, claims that the conspiracy was nothing more than 'a food riot' among the urban poor (p. 181).

[146] Thompson, *St Germanus*

[147] Salway, *op. cit.*, p. 376.

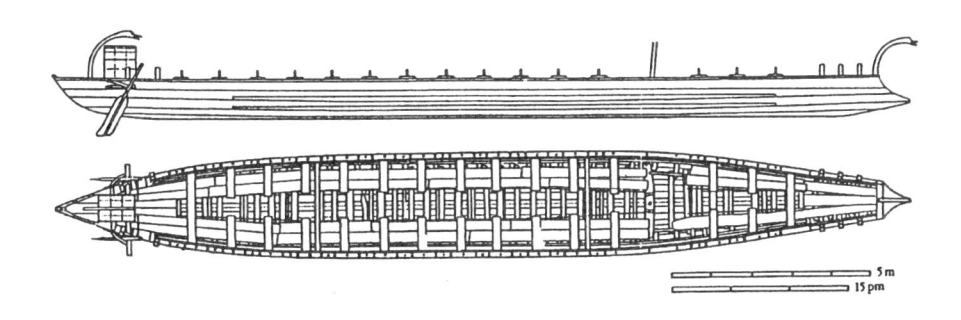

Figure 6 A reconstruction of a late Roman type-A warship ('lusoria') from Mainz
(O. Höckman, 'Late Roman Rhine Vessels from Mainz, Germany',
IJNA XXII (1993), fig. 6, p. 132).

warships discovered at Mainz in 1981–2, as these ships had much in common with the native, 'Celtic', shipbuilding methods of the Rhine area.[148]

A total of five wrecks were discovered in an old branch of the Rhine at Mainz, just outside the the walls of the Roman city. Traces of jetties show that the site had been a small harbour in late Roman times. Dendrochronological analysis shows that all the ships were constructed in the last decades of the fourth century. The ships had been stripped of their fittings, showing that they had simply been abandoned at the end of their serviceable lives, probably early in the fifth century. The finds have greatly increased our knowledge of late Roman shipbuilding in north west Europe. The wrecks represent two distinct types of vessel; type-A, a light galley type of warship, and type-B, a small, fast, military transport ship. The best preserved of the type-A ships, of which there are four, is the Mainz ship 9, the remains of which have formed the basis of Höckmann's detailed and convincing reconstruction of the type-A ships. The ship had a strong keel and was carvel-built, but the Romans had abandoned the immensely strong but time consuming Mediterranean method of shell building[149] in favour of an

---

[148] On the Mainz ships see the following works by O. Höckmann: 'Late Roman Rhine vessels from Mainz, Germany' in *IJNA* 22 (1993) pp. 125-35; 'Spätrömische Schiffsfunde in Mainz', in *Archaeologisches Korrespondenzblatt*, XII (1982), pp. 231–50; 'Zur Bauweise, Funktion und Typologie der Mainzer Schiffe', in G. Rupprecht (ed.), *Die Mainzer Römerschiffe*, 3rd edn (Mainz, 1984), pp. 44–77; *Antike Seefahrt* (Munich, 1985), pp. 133–4, 140–2; 'Römische Schiffsverbände', pp. 392–7.

[149] On this method of construction see P. Johnstone, *The Seacraft of Prehistory*, (London, 1980), pp. 72–5, and R. Unger, *The Ship in the Medieval Economy*, pp. 36–9. In the Mediterranean tradition the shell of the hull was built first and the internal frames were inserted afterwards. The planks of the hull were exactly shaped to fit each other and fastened with strong mortice and tenon joints. The completed hulls were immensely strong and so watertight that the seams often did not need caulking. Nordic, clinker-built ships were also built shell first, but Celtic ships were

adaptation of the Celtic frame first method of construction. The hull was built over a 'moulding frame', then the permanent frames were fitted and the moulding frame was removed (though not without leaving tell-tale traces on the hull). The planks were fastened to the permanent frames using the heavy iron clench nails typical of Celtic construction. The oak planks were not carefully shaped to fit each other closely as in the Mediterranean method and, as in Celtic ships, the hull relied heavily on caulking to make it watertight. However, the caulking material, Stockholm tar, followed Mediterranean practice rather than Celtic. The ship's main source of propulsion was its crew of 30 oarsmen but it also carried a mast and a light, possibly lateen, sail. The mast step, which is typical of both the Mainz type-A and the type-B ships, takes the form of a heavy transverse frame with a notch to hold the mast and shows striking similarities to those of the second century Bruges and Blackfriars boats[150] and also to that of the thirteenth century cog from Kollerup in Jutland.[151] The ship was long and sleek, about 60 feet long by about 10 feet broad, and had a very shallow draught, drawing only about 18 inches of water. The ship would have been stable, seaworthy, manoeuvrable and, with a full crew of oarsmen, capable of cruising at up to seven knots and reaching an estimated maximum speed of 10 knots for short distances.[152] Other notable features of Mainz ship 9 are that it had a small cargo capacity (presumably for military supplies), a fighting platform at the bow and, also at the bow, an unusual protruding forefoot which might have functioned as a short ram. One of the type-A ships also provided evidence for a shield rail around the sides of the ship. As in the later Viking ships, this would have provided both storage and protection to the oarsmen in battle.

Höckmann believes that the type-A ships are examples of the *lusoria*, a type of light, fast scoutship and warship which is often mentioned in late Roman sources but, unfortunately, never described in any detail.[153] However, the early fifth-century writer Vegetius does describe a type of fast, 20-oared, camouflaged warship used for scouting and interception called a *scafa exploratoria*.[154] This description certainly seems to fit the type-A ships: whether it is also to be equated to the *lusoria* is another matter as it is perhaps to be doubted that the

---

built frame first, the planks being fastened to the frames with large iron clench nails to form the hull.

[150] O. Crumlin-Pedersen, *From Viking Ships to Hanseatic Cogs*, The third Paul Johnstone Memorial Lecture (Greenwich, 1983), p. 18. Also, P. Marsden, 'A re-assessment of Blackfriars ship 1', in S. McGrail (ed.), *Maritime Celts, Frisians and Saxons*, CBA Research Report 71 (London, 1990) p. 73.

[151] Höckmann, *Antike Seefahrt*, 133–4; also Crumlin-Pedersen, *op. cit.*

[152] P. Marsden, 'A hydrostatic study of a reconstruction of Mainz Roman ship 9' in *IJNA* 22(1993), pp. 137-41.

[153] Höckmann, 'Late Roman Rhine vessels from Mainz, Germany', p. 131, and also his 'Römische Schiffsverbände', p. 396.

[154] Vegetius, *Epitoma rei militaris*, ed. C. Lang (reprint, Stuttgart, 1967), IV, 37. C. E. Dove, 'The first British navy', *Antiquity* XLV (1971), pp. 17–19, argues that the *scafae exploratoriae* should be equated with the *lusoria*.

The 3rd and 4th Century Raids of the Franks and Saxons

lusoria was quite such a definite type as Höckmann believes. Indeed, the very vagueness of the sources may be indicative that the Romans used the name indiscriminately of any light vessel in military service. For example, Ammianus Marcellinus describes an incident on the Rhine where 40 *lusoriae naves* were filled to capacity to transport a force of only 300 men, i.e. only seven to eight men per boat.[155] Even if Ammianus has not included the crews in this total, these boats must have been much smaller than the type-A ships. Contemporary illustrations of the type-A ship are perhaps to be found on many of the coin types of Carausius and Allectus and also on fourth-century legionary tile stamps from Mainz. These have many features in common with the Mainz type-A ships such as the straight gunwales, lack of ornamentation and vestigial ram. They do however seem to have a higher freeboard with oars being worked through oar holes instead of on thole pins, and small shelters at the stern.[156]

So far as we can tell from literary and iconographical evidence, in the first and second centuries the Romans used Mediterranean type warships, such as triremes and Liburnians, in their fleets on the Rhine and in the Channel. These ships were complex to build and required large crews, of 60 or more oarsmen, to operate them and they were probably neither very manoeuvrable for use on rivers nor very seaworthy for use in the rough waters of the Channel and the North Sea.[157] The Mainz type-A ship seems to have been developed as a response to the changed conditions of the third century. While the triremes and Liburnians were grossly wasteful of resources, the type-A warship was cheap and easy to build, it had a good performance and it required only one third of the crew of a Liburnian, allowing much more efficient use of increasingly scarce manpower.[158]

Höckmann has drawn attention to the similarities in size and performance potential between the Mainz type A ships and the Saxon or Anglian Nydam ship (see chapter 3, pp. 93–8) and this has led him to suggest that the Germans were influenced in their warship design by their experience in combat against the Roman ships.[159] This is of course not impossible. Moreover, Saxons and Franks had served in the Roman forces as well as fighting against them and, on at least two occasions, the Franks had used captured Roman ships for long pirate

---

[155] Ammianus Marcellinus, XVIII, 2.11–12.

[156] See Höckmann, 'Römische Schiffsverbände', p. 395, fig. 12, for the stamps. Dove, 'British navy', pp. 15–20, discusses the galley coins in detail, concluding that the galleys shown on them are Vegetius's *scafae exploratoriae* or *lusoriae*. Though Dove believes that these representations are true to life, the ships are probably stylised to some degree, especially as regards their length. According to Dove's own calculations, if the ships on the coins are portrayed accurately they would be less than half the length of the Mainz ship 9, in other words rather tub-like, seaworthy but too slow to be ideal warships. See also P. Marsden, 'Ships of the Roman period and after in Britain', in G. F. Bass (ed.), *A History of Seafaring Based on Underwater Archaeology* (London, 1972), p. 116.

[157] Höckmann, 'Römische Schiffsverbände', pp. 391–3.

[158] *Ibid*, pp. 392–3. According to Vegetius, IV. 37, Liburnians continued to be used alongside the *scafae exploratoriae* in British waters in the fourth century.

[159] Höckmann, *Antike Seefahrt*, pp. 118–21.

voyages. The Rhine Germans were quite receptive to Roman influences; in the fourth century some even built their houses in the Roman way.[160] In the first two centuries AD the influence was probably only one way; Roman to barbarian. However, the evidence of the influence of native shipbuilding techniques on the Mainz ships show that this was not the case by the third century, and it may even be that the Mainz type A ships were actually influenced by Germanic warship design. The Mainz warships represent a complete break with the warship types that the Romans had used before the third century. The high fighting platforms of the Mediterranean type galleys had been abandoned and if the protruding forefoot did function as a ram, it was plainly not intended to pierce the hull of an enemy vessel and could probably do no more than capsize a dugout canoe. Höckmann believes the protruding forefoot may merely have been retained to give the ship what Romans would have regarded as a true warship profile.[161]

Such a sharp break with tradition was probably as much due to the deficiencies of Mediterranean-type galleys in northern waters as it was to do with manpower shortages. If the barbarians were raiding in light, fast, seaworthy sailing ships, as indeed they must have been to enjoy such success and provoke such a costly defensive response from the Romans, the lumbering Liburnians would have been quite unable to cope. Certainly, in a sea battle a Liburnian would have been more than the equal of, say, a ship of the Nydam type, or of a Mainz type-A ship for that matter. The problem would have been bringing a pirate ship to battle in the first place. The Franks and Saxons were interested in plunder, not fighting, and they would have done their utmost to avoid combat on any but the most favourable terms. A Liburnian would have had a very poor chance of catching the pirates; what was needed was a ship that could catch them, in fact, something quite like the ships that the pirates used themselves. Roman history has an exact parallel to this situation in the Liburnian itself which was adopted by the Romans in the first century BC from the Liburnian pirates of Dalmatia who were threatening Adriatic shipping.[162]

The similarities of the Mainz ships to ships of the cog type has led Höckmann to suggest that among the ancestors of the cog were rowing longships.[163] This idea is supported by the fact that the earliest record of the cog name comes in references to warships in three charters of the late ninth, or early tenth century, from Utrecht.[164] Even stronger support comes from the use in eleventh-century German sources of the term *herikochun* ('war cog') to describe a kind of fast warship.[165] As these cogs were warships they were very probably fast oar propelled vessels, and Crumlin-Pedersen has suggested that they may have been

---

[160] Ammianus Marcellinus, XVII, 1.7.

[161] Höckmann, 'Römische Schiffsverbände', p. 395.

[162] Vegetius, IV.33. See also C. G. Starr, *The Roman Imperial Navy*, 2nd edn (Cambridge, 1960), p. 54, and Marsden, 'Ships of the Roman period', p. 116.

[163] Höckmann, *Antike Seefahrt*, p. 142.

[164] On these charters and their interpretation see Ellmers, *op. cit.*, pp. 70–1.

[165] *Ibid.*, p. 71.

The 3rd and 4th Century Raids of the Franks and Saxons

in some way related to the Mainz type-A ships.[166] It was suggested in the first chapter that the Rhine Germans built ships in the Celtic tradition and since many of these tribes were ancestral to the Franks this will have been the shipbuilding tradition which they inherited. Given the demonstrable interaction between Roman and Celtic shipbuilding traditions, it must be likely that seagoing Frankish warships were superficially similar to the Mainz warships. We should expect that constructional similarities included carvel-building and comparable mast step structures and similar size and draught. If the Frankish warships were built in the cog tradition they would probably have lacked the well-developed keel structure of the Mainz warships and this would rule out the possibility that they possessed rams.[167] This would not have been much of a disadvantage as it is difficult to see an important role for the ram in the kind of naval warfare that the Franks were engaged in.

For raiding Roman territory across the Rhine the Franks no doubt used simpler ships. Sherds of early fourth-century Samian pottery from Trier show what is evidently a Germanic, probably Frankish or Alamannic, warship.[168] The warship appears to be a plank-built boat, or an extended logboat, propelled by a large crew using paddles, so it is unlikely to be a seagoing ship. However, paddles still seem to have been in normal use among the Danube Germans in the later fourth century,[169] and the Trier potsherds suggest that the same was still the case among the Rhine Germans too. This should in no way be considered as a sign of backwardness. Rowing is far more energy efficient than paddling but over short distances, such as a river crossing, paddling does have many advantages, especially in warfare. As the Rhine Franks and other riverine German tribes were not engaged in long distance patrolling, as the Romans were, these advantages probably outweighed the advantages of the oar's energy efficiency.[170] Of primary importance is the ease of embarkation and disembarkation. On landing on a hostile and well-guarded shore men can leap out of a boat from a paddling position as soon as it grounds and be ready to fight instantly. Re-embarkation, when haste is even more necessary if there are pursuers, is equally easy; the crew can be in position to paddle as soon as they have climbed aboard. Getting large numbers of oarsmen in and out of a boat is a clumsy business in comparison. There are two further advantages; the paddling position is better for observation as the whole crew can see where they are going and watch for danger, and,

---

[166] Crumlin-Pedersen, *op. cit.*, p. 18.

[167] Höckmann, *Antike Seefahrt*, p. 121.

[168] D. Ellmers, 'Shipping on the Rhine in the Roman period: the pictorial evidence', in J. du Plat Taylor, *Roman Shipping and Trade: Britain and the Rhine Provinces*, CBA Research Report 24 (London, 1978), pp. 9–10. Ellmers suggests that they are Saxon warships, but I think that this is unlikely for the reasons given below.

[169] Ammianus Marcellinus, XVII, 13.17. Oars were in use on seagoing Germanic ships even in the Baltic by the fourth century: further in chapter 3, pp. 93 ff.

[170] McGrail, *Ancient Boats*, p. 206, points out that under special circumstances even boats that would normally be rowed were paddled. He cites the tenth century boat from Årby in Sweden as an example of a rowing boat that was also equipped with paddles.

important at night, paddling is generally quieter than rowing.[171] It is for exactly these reasons that the assault boats of modern armies are equipped with paddles rather than oars.

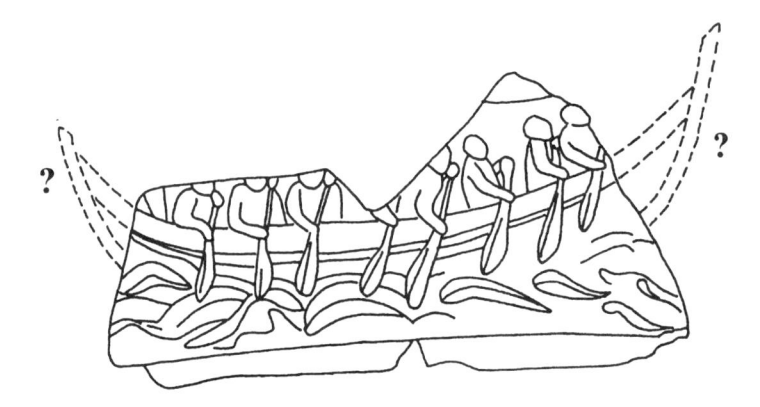

Figure 7 Barbarian warship from a Roman potsherd, Trier, early fourth century AD (after Ellmers, 'Shipping on the Rhine in the Roman Period' (1978))

---

[171] These advantages were very much appreciated by the Polynesians for night raiding or when making a landing through a reef or on a hostile shore. The relative inefficiency of paddling was unimportant as on open sea journeys the Polynesians relied on the sail for propulsion. See P. H. Buck, *Vikings of the Pacific*, (Chicago, 1959), pp. 35, 91. My conclusions are based also, in part, on personal practical experience of assault boat training in the Territorial Army.

3 Anglo-Saxon Piracy and the Migrations to Britain

Following the success of the 'barbarian conspiracy', Saxon piracy appears to have increased and was to remain endemic for the next two centuries. The period has been called 'a first Viking-age',[1] and indeed the parallels with the later activities of the Vikings are striking and not without implications for our assessment of the seafaring abilities of the Anglo-Saxons.

The Saxon Shore

Saxon raids continued to affect both sides of the Channel in the late fourth century and the basis of the Roman defence remained the chain of coastal fortifications which was by then certainly known as the *Litus Saxonicum*.[2] The exact significance of this title has been much debated: was the command area so called because it was the 'shore settled by the Saxons' or was it 'the shore attacked by the Saxons'?[3] The case for the first interpretation rests on two main points: the lack of any other Roman frontier named after the enemies who threatened it, and finds of so called Romano-Saxon pottery from eastern Britain, between the Thames and the Humber. This pottery, which was manufactured commercially, shows apparent stylistic similarities to continental Saxon pottery, and it has been claimed that it was intended to appeal to Saxons settled in Britain by the Romans as *laeti*.[4] However, Romano-Saxon pottery is of very uncertain value as evidence of Saxon settlement: the stylistic relationship with continental Saxon pottery is not proven, most of it is poorly dated and at least one piece carried a Latin inscription, making it probable that some Romano-Saxon pottery was manufactured not for Germanic but for Romano-British tastes. Groups of

---

[1] I. N. Wood, *The Merovingian North Sea*, Occasional Papers on Medieval Topics 1 (Alingsås, 1983), p. 5.

[2] The name is known only from the *Notitia Dignitatum (Occ.* xxviii), which was compiled in the late 390s: see J. C. Mann, 'What was the *Notitia Dignitatum* for?', in Goodburn and Bartholomew, p. 8. Mann's date is rather earlier than the date in the 420s given by Jones, *The Later Roman Empire*, vol. 3, p. 353, which has been widely accepted.

[3] The evidence for both cases is comprehensively summarised in S. Johnson, 'Late Roman defences and the *limes*', in D. E. Johnston (ed.), *The Saxon Shore*, CBA Research Report 18 (London, 1974) pp. 63–7 and in less detail in *idem*, 'Channel commands', p. 81–2.

[4] See on this pottery J. N. L. Myres, *Anglo-Saxon Pottery and the Settlement of England* (Oxford, 1969), pp. 66–73, *idem, The English Settlements*, (Oxford, 1986), pp. 89–96, and W. I. Roberts, *Romano Saxon Pottery*, BAR BS 106 (Oxford, 1982).

Alamanni, Burgundians, Marcomanni and Vandals were settled in Britain in the fourth century, while in the same period the regular army units stationed in Britain would have come to contain increasing numbers of barbarians serving alongside provincial troops; it is surely not necessary to postulate Saxon settlements to account for Germanic influences on Romano-British culture.[5]

As this pottery is the sole material evidence for Saxon settlement before the end of the fourth century, the case for 'the shore settled by Saxons' is weak. On the other hand, we can be certain that the coasts of Britain and Gaul were subject to attacks by Saxon pirates in the fourth century. The Romans did not normally guard a frontier with a unit raised from the enemy who threatened it and it is difficult to believe that in this case the Romans would have acted differently and settled Saxons in these areas to fend off the attacks of other Saxons.[6] In fact, the only Saxon unit which we know of in the Roman army in the fourth century was stationed in Phoenicia; just about as far from from the *litus Saxonicum* as it was possible to send it (see below). Therefore, it seems safer, at present, despite the uniqueness of the name, to prefer the second interpretation, that the *Litus Saxonicum* was so called because it was the shore attacked by the Saxons.

The name of the *Litus Saxonicum* certainly points to the Saxons being the largest and most prominent group of Germanic seafarers in the late fourth and early fifth centuries. This impression is reinforced by our other sources: between the barbarian conspiracy and the mid-fifth century no other Germanic tribes are recorded as being pirates in north-west Europe. It is most striking that we do not hear of the Angles, in a contemporary source, until the mid-sixth century,[7] yet they must have been active seafarers long before this, quite possibly even since the third century. The mid-sixth century is also the first time that we hear of the Jutes in a contemporary source.[8] However, we cannot doubt that both of these peoples were active as pirates alongside the Saxons from an early date because of the major role which Bede credits them with in the settlement of England (which is of course named after the Angles, not the Saxons). The complete absence of the Angles and Jutes from the fourth- and fifth-century sources is no doubt a result of the cultural similarity of the three Germanic tribes which must have made it difficult for the Romans to differentiate between them. Another possibility is that the Angles confined their activities largely to the east coast of Britain, where Bede says they made their main settlements[9] and, unlike the Saxons, rarely ventured onto the Channel coasts of Britain and Gaul.

---

[5] P. Salway, *Roman Britain* (Oxford, 1981), pp. 386–8, argues that most Germanic influences in late Roman Britain came via the regular army.

[6] E. A. Thompson, *St Germanus of Auxerre and the End of Roman Britain* (Woodbridge, 1984), pp. 97–8, argues this point well.

[7] Procopius, *History of the Wars*, ed. and trans. H. B. Dewing, Loeb Classical Library, (5 vols, London, 1913–28), VIII. xx. 1–41.

[8] Venantius Fortunatus, *Carmina*, ed. F. Leo, *MGH AA* 4 (Berlin, 1881), IX, 1, line 74.

[9] Bede, *Historia Ecclesiastica Gentis Anglorum*, ed. B. Colgrave and R. A. B. Mynors, *Bede's Ecclesiastical History of the English People* (Oxford, 1969), I. 15.

The first Saxon raid to be recorded after the barbarian conspiracy came in 370. A strong Saxon raiding party, 'having overcome the difficulties of the ocean', landed in Gaul and, brushing the initial Roman resistance aside, penetrated some way inland before it was stopped by stronger Roman forces. The two sides were presumably fairly evenly matched as the Saxons were able to negotiate with the Romans for a safe passage back to their ships in return for surrendering their loot and some of their number as recruits for the Roman army. However, the Romans negotiated in bad faith, a justifiable expedient in the opinion of Ammianus, and the retreating Saxons were ambushed and slaughtered after a bitter fight which the Romans came close to losing.[10] The defeat of a group of Saxons by the Romans in Frankish territory which is recorded by Jerome and Orosius, and dated by Jerome to 373, may or may not refer to the same incident.[11]

A letter of St Ambrose from 388 refers to Saxons serving in the army of the usurper Magnus Maximus in the Balkans[12] and the *Notitia Dignitatum* lists a unit of Saxons stationed in Phoenicia.[13] Both groups may have been mercenary units but it is equally likely that they were raised from prisoners of war taken after unsuccessful raids, such as that in 370 described above. A late fourth-century letter of the senator Symmachus makes reference to Saxon prisoners of war whose fate was less fortunate.[14] The emperor had promised to send Symmachus 29 Saxon prisoners to perform in a gladiatorial combat at the circus games he was organising. However, the Saxons rather spoiled the proceedings by unsportingly preferring to kill themselves before the games started rather than shed each other's blood for the entertainment of the crowds.

The depletion of the British garrison following the usurpation of Magnus Maximus in 383 probably led to an increase in pirate attacks by the Saxons, Picts and Scots upon the province, and parts of Wales were even colonised by the Scots.[15] Claudian's statement that the Saxons had even reached the Orkney Islands in this period might be thought to be exaggeration but for the fact that a Saxon attack on the islands in the mid-fifth century is also recorded by

---

[10] Ammianus Marcellinus, *Rerum gestarum libri*, ed. and trans. J. C. Rolfe, Loeb Classical Library (3 vols, London, 1935), XXVIII. 5.1–7.

[11] Jerome, *Chronicon, s.a.* 2389 (373): 'Saxones caesi Deusone in regione Francorum'. E. Zöllner, *Geschichte der Franken bis zur Mitte des sechsten Jahrunderts* (Munich, 1970), p. 22, suggests that Diessen, about 10 miles west of Eindhoven, is perhaps to be equated with *Deusone*. Orosius, *Historiarum adversum paganos libri VII*, ed. C. Zangmeister (leipzig, 1989) VII, 32.10: 'Valentinianus Saxones, gentem in oceani litoribus et paludibus inuiis sitam, uirtute atque agilitate terribilem, periculosam Romanis finibus eruptionem magna mole meditantes in ipsis Francorum finibus oppressit.'

[12] Ambrose, *Epistolae* (ed. J. P. Migne, *Patrologia Latina* XVI (Paris, 1866), cols 876 ff.), 40. 23 (cols 1156–7).

[13] *Notitia Dignitatum*, ed. O. Seeck (Berlin, 1876), *Oriens*, xxxii. 37.

[14] Symmachus, *Epistolae*, ed. O. Seeck, *MGH. AA* 6 (Berlin, 1883), II. 46.

[15] Frere, *Britannia*, p. 355.

Nennius.[16] Though Maximus' bid to win control of the western half of the empire was defeated in 388, it was not until 396–9 that the central Roman authority gave serious attention to the defence of Britain. An expedition was sent, and perhaps also commanded, by Stilicho which seems to have engaged in naval activity against the Saxons, Scots and Picts.[17]

It has been suggested that Stilicho organised the *Litus Saxonicum* defences into the form in which they are described in the *Notitia Dignitatum*.[18] If so, it is interesting to note that the *Comes Litoris Saxonici* had no naval forces at all under his command. In fact the *Notitia* lists only one naval unit on the Channel coast, the *classis Sambrica* at the *Locus Quartensis sive Hornensis* (at either Étaples or Cap Hornu), under the command of the *Dux Belgicae Secundae*, which must have maintained an essential link with Britain.[19] The only other naval unit in the area was the *classis Anderetianorum*, clearly originally from the Saxon Shore fort at Pevensey (*Anderida*) but now stationed at Paris under the *Magister Peditum per Gallias*.[20] The impression is that, though the Romans could raise a

---

[16] Claudian, *Carmina*, ed. and trans. M. Platnauer, Loeb Classical Library (2 vols, London, 1922), VIII: *De quarto consulatu Hon. Aug.*, lines 31–2, refers to the Saxons in the Orkneys in the aftermath of the barbarian conspiracy: 'maduerunt Saxone fuso / Orcades'; Nennius, *Historia Brittonum*, ed. J. Morris (London, 1980), ch. 38: 'Et [Hengist] jussit ut invitaret eos, et invitavit Octha et Ebissa cum quadraginta ciulis. At ipsi cum navigarent circa Pictos, vastaverunt Orcades insulas.' Morris, p. 4, believes that this section of Nennius's history is an extract from a British chronicle, probably dating from as early as the sixth century.

[17] The poems of Claudian are our only source for this campaign. See *Carmina*, XXII: *De consulatu Stilichonis II*, lines 250–5:

> me quoque vicinis pereuntem gentibus inquit
> munivit Stilicho, totam cum Scottus Hivernum
> movit et infesto spumavit remige Tethys.
> illius effectum curis, ne tela timerem
> Scottica, ne Pictum tremerem, ne litore toto
> prospicerem dubiis ventarum Saxona ventis

and *ibid.*, XVIII: *In Eutropium I*, ll. 392–3:

> ...domito Saxone Tethys
> mitior aut fracto secura Britannia Picta.

Claudian also refers to coastal defences against Saxons and Picts in a poem of 399; *ibid.*, XXV: *Epithalamium*, lines 89–91:

> ...quae Saxona frenat
> vel Scottum legio, quantae cinxere cohortes Oceanum.

On Stilicho's campaign in general see Frere, *op. cit.*, pp. 355–6, and Salway, *op. cit.*, pp. 419–22.

[18] *Ibid.*, p. 424. If so, Stilicho may have divided the command because two Gallic forts which are described in the *Notitia* as being *in litore Saxonico*, Marcis (Occ. xxxviii. 7) and Grannona (Occ. xxxxvii. 14), are not under the command of the *Comes Litoris Saxonici*, though the persistence of the name indicates that they once were.

[19] *Notitia Dignitatum*, Occ. xxxviii. 8. On the location see S. Johnson, *Roman Forts of the Saxon Shore* (London, 1976), pp. 90–2, 125. The likelihood is that the fleet had two bases, one on the Somme (hence the name) and the other at Étaples, where tiles stamped CLSA have been discovered: see Seiller, 'Boulogne and the coastal defences in the fourth and fifth centuries', in D. E. Johnston (ed.), the *Saxon Shore*, CBA Research Report 18 (London, 1977), p. 37.

[20] *Notitia Dignitatum*, Occ. xlii. 23.

fleet for a special purpose, such as Stilicho's expedition, they had effectively lost control of the seas to the Saxons and other pirates by the end of the fourth century.

How long the Saxon Shore forts continued to be part of a co-ordinated command system after Stilicho's expedition is uncertain. The normal indicator by which occupation of a fort is judged, coin sequences, is unreliable after 388 because there was no mint in Britain after Magnus Maximus' usurpation and thereafter coin supplies to Britain from the continent became intermittent.[21] Only Richborough has provided clear evidence of occupation in the early fifth century.[22] At some forts the garrisons may not have been withdrawn so much as abandoned to their own devices, as was the case later in the fifth century in the Danube province of Noricum where the soldiers carried on living in their forts for security but started farming for a living when their pay stopped turning up.[23] Pevensey may have been occupied by the descendants of such men when it was stormed by the Saxons in 491.[24] The chain of signal stations on the Yorkshire coast seem also to have fallen out of use by the early fifth century. At least two of them, Huntcliff and Goldsborough, were certainly violently destroyed by raiders, though the identity of these, Pictish, Saxon or other, cannot be ascertained.[25]

From Raiding to Settlement and Conquest; the 5th to 7th Centuries

If Stilicho's expedition brought security to Britain, it was short lived. The early fifth century saw further troop withdrawals from Britain[26] and in 410 a major Saxon attack caused the British provinces to expel the Roman administration (whether of Honorius or of the usurper Constantine is uncertain), and to arrange their own defences.[27] Thereafter Britain remained in a state of *de facto* independence from the Roman Empire.[28] Saxon raids on Britain continued,

---

[21] Salway, *op. cit.*, pp. 424–5, Frere, *op. cit.*, pp. 363–4.

[22] Johnson, *op. cit.*, p. 150. The first decade of the fifth century in fact appears to have been the period of the most intense activity in the history of the fort.

[23] Eugippius, *Vita S. Severini*, ed. T. Mommsen, *MGH. SSRG* 26 (Berlin, 1898), XXII. 4.

[24] *Anglo-Saxon Chronicle*, ed. B. Thorpe, Rolls Series 23 (2 vols, London, 1861), 491.

[25] Frere, *op. cit.*, p. 365, H. Ramm, *The Parisi*, (London, 1978), pp. 127–9. Bodies were thrown down the wells at both sites and at Goldsborough other bodies were found in the tower itself.

[26] Salway, *op. cit.*, pp. 422–7.

[27] *Chronica Gallica a CCCCLII*, ed. T. Mommsen, *MGH. AA 9 = Chronica Minora I*, pp. 646–664 (even numbered pages), 62: 'Britanniae Saxonum incursione devastatae'; Zosimus, *New History*, ed. and trans. F. Paschoud, *Zosime: Histoire Nouvelle*, Collection des universitiés de France (3 vols, Paris, 1971–9), VI. 5.2–3, VI. 10.2. On the dates of the British entries in the Gallic Chronicle see M. E. Jones and J. Casey, 'The Gallic Chronicle restored: A chronology for the Anglo-Saxon invasions and the end of Roman Britain', *Britannia* XIX (1988), pp. 379–97.

[28] Much has, of course, been written on the end of imperial rule in Britain. Salway, *op. cit.*, pp. 426–45, and Frere, *op. cit.*, pp. 353–77, both have judicious accounts. Contrasting views of

however. In 429 a combined Saxon and Pictish invasion was defeated at an unknown location by the Britons, supposedly led by St Germanus who taught them the famous Alleluia cry that so alarmed the raiders that they fled.[29] Despite this defeat, there is nothing to suggest that the raids ceased, and in 441 the almost contemporary *Gallic chronicle of AD 452* reports that Britain, after suffering many disasters, fell under Saxon domination.[30] This certainly does not mark a Saxon conquest of all of Britain, for the Britons appealed to Aetius for help not long after,[31] but there can equally be no doubt either that the Saxons did gain control of a significant part of the island in this year.

This brings us to the intractable problem of the point when Saxon, Anglian, Jutish and, perhaps, Frisian piracy turned into settlement and political conquest. It is a complex subject and what follows is necessarily simplified. The main problem is that the literary and the archaeological sources contradict each other: even if we exclude the questionable evidence for fourth-century settlement, it is still certain that the Anglo-Saxon settlements began before any of the dates which can be gleaned from the literary sources for the *adventus Saxonum*.[32] The archaeological evidence points to two phases of settlement. The first began in the early fifth century and was confined mainly to eastern Britain between the Humber and the Thames, but with a noticeable cluster in the upper Thames valley. The second phase, which saw the settlement of Kent and the south coast and the penetration of the Midlands from East Anglia, began around the middle of the fifth century and continued until the early sixth century and involved far greater numbers than the first phase.[33]

Britain's status *vis-à-vis* the empire are offered by H. W. Böhme, 'Das Ende der Römerherrschaft in Britannien und die angelsächsische Besiedlung Englands im 5. Jahrhundert', *JRGZM* XXXIII (1986), pp. 558–61, who argues for the effective survival of Roman authority in Britain until the 440s, and I. N. Wood, 'The fall of the western empire and the end of Roman Britain', *Britannia* XVIII (1987), pp. 251–62, who accepts that a pro-imperial faction may have survived in Britain after the events of 410, but not that any form of direct Roman authority did. E. A. Thompson, 'Britain, AD 406–10', *Britannia* VIII (1977), pp. 303–18, attempts to interpret the history of this period in terms of social revolution.

[29] Constantius, *Vita S. Germani*, ed. B. Krusch and W. Levison, *MGH. SSRM* 7 (Hanover, 1919-20), pp. 247–83, 17–18. St Germanus' first visit to Britain is the one datable point in his *Vita*: see Thompson, *St Germanus*, pp. 1–2. Thompson, *ibid.*, pp. 39–46, reconstructs this raid and its circumstances in far greater detail than the imprecise nature of the source material allows.

[30] *Chron. Gall. a CCCCLII*, 126: 'Britanniae usque ad hoc tempus variis cladibus eventibusque latae in dicionem Saxonum rediguntur.' Also, *Chronica Gallica a DXI*, ed. T. Mommsen, *MGH. AA 9* = *Chronica Minora I*, pp. 647–66 (odd-numbered pages), 602. On the date see Jones and Casey, *op. cit.*, pp. 394–5.

[31] Gildas, *De excidio et conquestu Britanniae*, ed. M. Winterbottom (London, 1978), 20.1. Though 446 is the generally accepted date for the appeal, the famous *gemitus Brittanorum*, it could have been addressed to Aetius at any time between that year, when he held his third consulship (from which the date is derived), and 454, when he held his fourth: Frere, *op. cit.*, p. 363.

[32] The phrase is from Gildas, 22.

[33] Böhme, *op. cit.*, pp. 532–59.

The exact nature of the settlements is obscure. The interpretation of the archaeological evidence is bedevilled by dating problems and until these are solved it will be impossible to understand the relationships, if any, of the early settlements to neighbouring sites of Romano-British settlement: the fact that an early Anglo-Saxon settlement is sited next to a Romano-British town need not be significant unless both sites were occupied at the same time. For literary evidence which is at all contemporary we are forced to rely on a notoriously difficult source, the Briton Gildas' *De excidio et conquestu Britanniae*, which was written in the first half of the sixth century.[34] Gildas tells us that after they became independent from Rome the Britons were unable to defend themselves against the Picts and Scots. They appealed to the Roman general Aetius, described as *ter consul*, for help but the Britons' request was refused. The Britons then turned for help to the Saxons, who were invited to Britain by someone he calls only *superbus tyrannus* and offered lands to settle in return for military service against the Picts and Scots. The initial contingent of three ships' crews was quickly reinforced and soon the Saxons began to demand of their hosts more and more pay for their services. Gildas uses the same technical terms, *annona*, *epimenia*, and *hospites*, as were used by the Romans in agreements to settle barbarians on imperial territory as federates, giving credibility to his account.[35] Gildas continues his account by telling us that when the Britons refused their demands, the Saxons rebelled and began to conquer the country for themselves.[36]

Gildas' chronology is exceptionally vague; and although he places the *adventus Saxonum* after the failure of the appeal to Aetius, it is plain that he did not know when this 'coming' was. Bede used Gildas as a source for his own account of the origins of the Anglo-Saxon settlements and tried to calculate a date for the *adventus*. Bede knew that Aetius had held his third consulship between 446 and 454 and he also knew, probably from Kentish sources, that a British king, Vortigern, had settled Jutes, who were said to have been led by Hengist and Horsa, in Kent during the joint reign of Marcian and Valentinian III (450–5). The coincidence of the dates led Bede to identify Vortigern with Gildas' tyrant, associate the events and condense the two accounts.[37] However, 450–5 is far too late to be reconcilable with the archaeological evidence. Even the Saxon conquest recorded in 441 in the *Gallic Chronicles* is too late in this respect. However, there is good archaeological evidence of Jutish settlement in Kent in

---

[34] On the value and limitations of Gildas see D. N. Dumville, 'The chronology of *De excidio Britanniae*, book 1', in M. Lapidge and D. N. Dumville (eds), *Gildas: New Approaches* (Woodbridge, 1984), pp. 61–84.

[35] Gildas, 23. On Gildas's use of these terms see Myres, *English Settlements*, p. 14. For a wider ranging examination of the methods used by the Romans to settle and provision barbarian federates on their territory see W. Goffart, *Barbarians and Romans: the Techniques of Accommodation* (Princeton, 1980), especially pp. 46–52, 143–88.

[36] Gildas, 24.

[37] Bede, I. 15. For this interpretation see Myres, *English Settlements*, p. 11. See also *ASC*, 449.

the mid-fifth century,[38] so it would seem that the story of the Jutish federate settlement has some basis in truth: Bede erred only in supposing it to have been the first English settlement. There was probably not one *adventus* but many. The literary sources may record individual settlements, some by invitation, such as those recorded by Gildas and Bede, some uninvited, such as that noted in the *Gallic Chronicle*, but none of them records the first.

It is difficult to be sure under what circumstances Anglo-Saxon federates would have been brought to Britain. However, the threat of Pictish or Scottish invasion cannot have been the main motive for settling Anglo-Saxon federates in Britain. If it had been, one would surely expect some evidence of early Anglo-Saxon settlement in the north and on the west coast, but there is none at all. Whatever the circumstances, it was a move that was fraught with danger as the Saxons had proved themselves to be just as dangerous an enemy of the Britons as had the Picts and Scots, with whom they had sometimes allied. By settling the Anglo-Saxons on the east coast the Britons gave them a stranglehold on the main river routes of southern Britain and had little chance of preventing further immigration. It is hard to believe that the Britons would voluntarily have settled Anglo-Saxons in these positions to keep out other Anglo-Saxons, though there may well have been rivalries between different groupings within the Anglian and Saxon peoples which the Britons were able to exploit to their own advantage.

One of the earliest known settlements, at Mucking in Essex, was certainly established in the early fifth century. Mucking was positioned strategically at the mouth of the Thames, dominating the river approaches to London, and so was in an ideal position to close the river to pirates. The site has produced a few pieces of military equipment and in its early phases the settlement was apparently not self-sufficient. Because of these factors a military origin has been postulated for the settlement. But this need not have been a federate military origin as has so far been assumed [39] the settlement could just as easily have been an unauthorised one as the position of Mucking is an ideal one for a band of pirates to seize with the intention of preying on shipping and riverside communities. This was a tactic used by the Saxons in Gaul (see below) and it was of course a favoured tactic of the Vikings in the ninth century. Nor would we expect a pirate settlement to show many signs of agricultural activity. We may, therefore, suspect that at least some Anglo-Saxons arrived uninvited in the troubled years of the early fifth century. If, later, the Britons found it impossible to dislodge the pirates, some of them may well have become federates. Under these circumstances, comparable to those faced by the Franks in Normandy with the Danes in 911, the Britons may have granted federate status to the settlers in the hopes that they would defend the territory against other pirates. If this was the case, the policy may have been

---

[38] See on the evidence H. Neumann, 'Jutish burials in the Roman Iron Age', in V. I. Evison (ed.), *Angles, Saxons and Jutes* (Oxford, 1981), pp. 1–10, and E. Bakka, 'Scandinavian type gold bracteates in Kentish and continental grave finds', in Evison (ed.), *op. cit.*, pp. 11–38. See also Myres, *Anglo-Saxon Pottery*, pp. 95–7, and *idem*, *English Settlements*, p. 115.

[39] M. U. Jones, 'Saxon Mucking: a post-excavation note', in S. C. Hawkes (ed.), *Anglo-Saxon Studies*, BAR BS 72 (Oxford, 1979), p. 27. Also Myres, *English Settlements*, p. 131.

successful in the short term, but in the long term it was certainly a disaster. Just as the Normans became in time too strong for the French kings to handle, the Anglo-Saxons, constantly reinforced from across the North Sea, eventually became strong enough to ignore their federate obligations.

The presence of infiltrators does not rule out the likelihood that there were also deliberately planned and executed federate settlements of Anglo-Saxons by British leaders; indeed it is hard to account for the settlements in the upper Thames valley in any other way. But we should not seek contexts which involve defences against Picts, Scots or other Anglo-Saxons. It is far more likely that Anglo-Saxon federates would have been settled by the leaders of one faction in a civil war.[40] Only under these circumstances would the enormous long term risks of the policy of seeking Anglo-Saxon support be decisively outweighed by its short-term benefits.

According to the *Anglo-Saxon Chronicle* the Anglo-Saxons who came to Britain after the mid-fifth century, such as Cerdic in Wessex or Aelle in Sussex, did not arrive as either pirates or federates but as seaborne conquerors, intent from the outset on seizing lands for themselves and their followers. These late fifth-century warbands cannot have numbered more than a few hundred men to begin with if the figures given by the Chronicle are accurate. Hengist and Horsa arrived with three ships, Aelle also arrived with three ships as did Stuf and Whitgar, Cerdic came with five and Port with just two.[41] Because of their smallness, the numbers have been considered to be more credible than the numbers given elsewhere in the chronicle for the size of Viking fleets,[42] but it is difficult to see a logical reason why this should be so. If we are to accept the small figures as credible, should we not also accept as credible the large figures which are given alongside them for example, 5000 Welsh killed in battle by Cerdic in 508[43] or do we reject them as exaggeration just because they are large? In fact, there are good reasons for regarding the chronicle's account of the settlements as being largely a mixture of traditional origin legend and folk etymology, and consequently no store can be set by any of the figures in this section, small or large.[44] However, whether it is historical or not, there is nothing inherently incredible in the pattern of the chronicle account, especially as Gildas also writes of the Saxons arriving in just three ships.[45] The first landings probably will have involved only small numbers of ships, but they will have been probing reconnaissance raids, searching out weak spots or potential settlement

---

[40] Salway, *op. cit.*, pp. 472–4, discusses both this possibility and the less credible possibility that the settlements were made by a British government which had reason to fear a Roman reoccupation of the province.

[41] *ASC*, 449; 477; 514; 495; 501.

[42] R. P. Abels, *Lordship and Military Obligation in Anglo-Saxon England* (Berkeley, 1988), p. 35.

[43] *ASC*, 508.

[44] B. Yorke, 'The Jutes of Hampshire and Wight and the origins of Wessex', in S. Basset (ed.), *The Origins of Anglo-Saxon Kingdoms* (London, 1989), pp. 84–8.

[45] Gildas, 23.

areas. Any successes will have been quickly reinforced, as, for example, Octha and Ebissa are said by Nennius to have reinforced Hengist with a force of 40 ships.[46]

The Saxons were also well established in Gaul by the mid-fifth century when a Saxon contingent fought alongside Romans, Visigoths, Franks and others against the Huns at the battle of the Catalaunian plains in 451.[47] The Roman coastal defence system had probably broken down long before this time, opening the area to settlement, though evidence is lacking on which to base an informed conclusion. The main area of settlement was in the Bessin (around Bayeux), in the area which was known in the ninth century as the *Otlingua Saxonica*, and another colony was formed on islands at the mouth of the Loire.[48] Both settlements were ideally situated for raiding inland along the river systems, and it is noteworthy that the Vikings also formed settlements in the same areas. A third Saxon settlement has been identified from place name and archaeological evidence in the Boulonnais. Saxon settlement began here early: one settlement at Vron dates from as early as the 370s and was abandoned *c.* 450, perhaps because its inhabitants decided to join in the settlement of Britain.[49]

Saxon pirates remained active in Gaul at least until the seventh century, though they were probably raiding from England or their bases in Gaul rather than from 'old' Saxony by the late fifth century. According to Sidonius, Saxon raids were a problem in Armorica *c.* 455; no doubt they had been encouraged by the assassination of Aetius.[50] The Saxons, led by Odovacer, took Angers in 463,

---

[46] Nennius, 38.

[47] Jordanes, *Getica* (ed. T. Mommsen, *MGH. AA* 5.i (Berlin, 1882), pp. 53–138), XXXVI. 191.

[48] On the Saxons of the Bessin see, A. Longnon, *Géographie de la Gaule au VIe siècle* (Paris, 1873), pp. 174–5, and C. Lorren, 'Des Saxons en Basse Normandie au VIe siècle?', *Studien zur Sachsenforschung* II (1980), pp. 231–59. On the Saxons on the Loire see Longnon, *op. cit.* pp. 173–4.

[49] See on the evidence R. Derolez, 'Cross Channel language ties', in P. Clemoes (ed.), *Anglo-Saxon England 3* (Cambridge, 1974), pp. 6–12, M. Rouche, 'Les Saxons et les origines de Quentovic', *Revue du Nord* LIX (1977), pp. 457–78, Seiller, *op. cit.*, p. 37, n. 1, and J. Morris, *The Age of Arthur* (London, 1973), pp. 286–92.

[50] Sidonius Apollinaris, *Carmina et Epistolae*, ed. and trans. W. B. Anderson, Loeb Classical Library (2 vols, London, 1936–65), *Carmina*, VII *(Panegyricus ... Avito Aug.)*, says that Saxon raids intensified after the assassination of Aetius in 454, only to cease when Avitus became emperor, ll. 369–71:

> quin et Aremoricus piratam Saxona tractus
> cui pelle salum sulcare Britannum ludus et
> assuto glaucum mare findere lembo.

ll. 388–90:

> Vt primum ingesti pondus suscepit honoris,
> ...Saxonis incursus cessat.

Wood, *op. cit.*, p. 5, thinks that Sidonius's statements are pure flattery. Given the nature of the medium and Sidonius's relationship to Avitus, this does not seem unreasonable, but the Saxons had taken the opportunity provided by instability in the Roman empire to step up their raids in the third and fourth centuries so it may in fact be the truth. The reference to the Saxons' use of hide boats suggests that Sidonius knew little about them at this time: later in his life he had direct contact with Saxons and Heruls at the Visigothic court.

and exercised control over the town and the surrounding countryside from island bases in the Loire until *c.* 469 when the Franks under Childeric drove them out.[51] At the same time the Romans and Franks captured the Saxons' island bases, inflicting heavy casualties on them.[52] However, they returned soon enough; Nantes was attacked in 481–511 and again in 570.[53] Pagans, probably Saxons from the Bessin, sacked Beauvais in 561, showing a Viking like preference for soft targets like churches and monasteries.[54] According to a later tradition St Helier was killed at his hermitage on Guernsey by pagan pirates in the sixth century.[55] The Saxons were also active around the Garonne: the village of Marsas was sacked by a large Saxon fleet in the reign either of the Visigothic king Theodoric I (419–51) or Theodoric II (453–66)[56] and in the 470s the Visigoths kept a fleet on the Garonne as a defence against Saxon raids which were much feared.[57] As this fleet was officered by Gallo-Romans it may be that

---

[51] Gregory of Tours, *Historiarum Libri X*, ed. W. Arndt and B. Krusch, *MGH. SSRM* 1 (Hanover, 1885), pp. 31–450, II. 18:

Igitur Childericus Aurilianis pugnas egit, Adovacrius vero cum Saxonibus Andecavo venit... Mortuus est autem Egidius et reliquit filium Syagrium nomine. Quo defuncto, Adovacrius de Andecavo vel aliis locis obsedes accepit... Veniente vero Adovacrio Andecavus, Childericus rex sequenti die advenit, interemptoque Paulo comite, civitatem obtinuit. Magnum ea die incendio domus aeclesiae concremata est.

Adovacrius seems to have taken Angers at the time of the battle of Orleans (463) and it seems that he still held the town in some sort of subjection, having taken hostages from it and other places after Aegidius' death in 465, when Childeric drove him out in 469. Adovacrius has been identified with Odovacer, who became king of Italy in 476: see J. Martindale, *The Prosopography of the Later Roman Empire. Volume 2, AD 395–527* (Cambridge, 1980), pp. 791–3.

[52] Gregory of Tours, *Hist.*, II. 19: 'His ita gestis, inter Saxones atque Romanos bellum gestum est; sed Saxonis terga vertentes, multos de suis, Romanis insequentibus, gladio reliquerent; insolae eorum cum multo populo interempto a Francis captae atque subversi sunt.'

[53] Gregory of Tours, *Liber in gloria martyrum*, ed. B. Krusch, *MGH. SSRM* 1, pp. 484–561, ch. 59: 'Igitur cum supra dicta civitas [Nantes] tempore Chlodovechi regi barbarica valleretur obsidione.' The fact that Gregory calls the attackers 'barbarians' makes it most likely that they were Saxons: Gregory would not have called the Franks or the Christian Bretons barbarians. Venantius Fortunatus, *Carmina*, III. 9, *Ad Felicem episcopum*, praises bishop Felix of Nantes for negotiating effectively with ferocious Saxon raiders in 570; ll. 103–4:

aspera gens, saxo vivens quasi more ferino:
te mediiante, sacer, belua reddit orem.

[54] Chilperic I, *Epistola*, ed. K. A. F. Pertz, *MGH. Diplomata* 1 (Hanover, 1872), 8 (at pp. 11–12): 'paganis irruentibus in terras Francorum, ecclesiae destructae et monasterio quam plurima depopulata atque vastata sunt.' Chilperic undertook to restore the church of SS Peter and Lucian which was destroyed in the attack.

[55] M. Mollat, *La vie quotidienne des gens der mer en Atlantique (IXe XVIe siècle)* (Paris, 1983), p. 20.

[56] *Vita Viviani*, ed, B. Krusch, *MGH. SSRM* 3 (Hanover, 1896), pp. 92–100, ch. 7: 'Accidit etiam quodam tempore, ut multitudo hostium Saxonum barbarorum cum plurimis navibus ad locum qui dicitur Marciacus amore depraedationis incumberet.'

[57] Sidonius, *Epp*, VIII. 6. To Namatius, 13–15: 'constanter asseveravit nuper vos classicum in classe cecinisse atque inter officia nunc nautae, modo militis litoribus Oceani curvis inerrare contra Saxonum pandos myoparones.'

the Visigoths had inherited it from the Romans when they were settled in the area earlier in the century. It may even be that the Visigoths had been settled in the area in the first place to help defend it against Saxon pirates.[58] Not all contacts between the Visigoths and Saxons were necessarily hostile, however, as Sidonius notes the presence of Saxons at king Euric's court.[59]

By 578 the Saxons of the Bessin seem to have been forced into some form of subservience to the Merovingian kings as in this year they served in the Frankish army which invaded Brittany.[60] In 591 these Saxons found themselves fighting alongside the Bretons on the orders of Queen Fredegund who was intent on sabotaging the military campaign of one of her many personal enemies.[61] It may be that the Saxons on the Loire still survived as a distinct community in the late sixth century. A certain Childeric the Saxon enjoyed a brief but colourful career in the Loire region between 584 and 590.[62] A merchant who was shipping wine on the Loire was killed by two Saxon slaves near Orleans c. 585 who may perhaps have originated with this group of Saxons rather than those in Saxony.[63] Though the Saxon settlement in the Boulonnais is not explicitly mentioned in the sources, it too may long have preserved a distinct identity as the population of this area was still pagan even in the seventh century.[64]

It is certain that Anglo-Saxons raided Gaul from England in this period. Clovis passed legislation towards the end of his reign concerning the recovery of *servi* who had been carried off 'trans mare', that is presumably to England.[65] Even as late as the reign of Dagobert (629–39), St Riquier went on a mission to 'Saxonica ultra mare' to redeem captives.[66] Some of these raids may have been quite ambitious if the strange tale, recorded by Procopius, of the jilted princess of the *Angiloi* has even a grain of truth in it.[67] Jilted by her betrothed, a king of the Warni of the lower Rhine, she is said to have revenged herself by raiding his lands with a fleet of 400 ships and 100,000 men. While the context of this story does not inspire confidence (see below), it may have its origin in the memory,

---

[58] J. M. Wallace-Hadrill, *The Long-Haired Kings* (London, 1962), pp. 28–9.

[59] Sidonius, *Epp*, VIII. 9.5, ll. 21–2:
> istic Saxona caerulum videmus
> assuetum ante salo solum timere.

[60] Gregory of Tours, *Hist.*, V. 26.

[61] *Ibid.*, X. 9.

[62] *Ibid.*, VII. 3, VIII. 18, X. 22. He first appears at Poitiers, spent some time under Gregory's protection at Tours, and was later made a *dux* in Gascony where he died at Auch in 590 after a bout of heavy drinking.

[63] *Ibid.*, VII. 46; Longnon, *op. cit.*, p. 174.

[64] Rouche, *op. cit.*, p. 461.

[65] *Pactus Legis Salicae*, ed. K. A. Eckhardt, *MGH. LL* 4. 1 (Hanover, 1962), 39.2. On the possible implications of this see Wood, *op. cit.*, pp. 12–13.

[66] *Vita Richarii*, ed. B. Krusch, *MGH. SSRM* 7 (Hanover, 1920), pp. 438–53, ch. 7: 'Mox ut ipse servus Dei conperuit, ut aliquid haberet, ut captivos redemere potuisset, sua cogitatione disposuit, ut ultra mare in Saxonia captivos redemere properaret.'

[67] Procopius, VIII. xx. 1–41.

much embroidered, of an actual cross-Channel raid. However, there is no other evidence, literary or archaeological, that the Warni were ever settled on the Rhine or North Sea coast. Before the Migration Period the Warni were settled on the Baltic coast of eastern Germany, a short sea crossing from the Anglian homeland in Jutland. Could it be that what Procopius has been told, without him realising it, is an ancient epic tale of the Anglian people?[68]

In the wake of the British recovery in the early sixth century which followed the battle of Mount Badon, it seems that some groups of Saxons left Britain to seek easier pickings on the continent, perhaps in much the same way that many Vikings left England for Francia following Alfred the Great's victories. One such group returned to Saxony and then found service with the Frankish king Theodoric (511–34).[69]

Another tribe which raided the continent in the fifth century was the Heruls. In 455–7 seven Herul ships carrying a force of about 400 men landed near Lugo on the north-western coast of Spain.[70] The local inhabitants gathered a force against the Heruls who were clearly interested only in plunder and had no stomach for a serious fight as they retreated to their ships after two of their number had been killed in a skirmish. Returning homewards, the raiders then plundered their way along the north coast of Spain towards Gascony. In 458–62 the Heruls returned to raid Lugo again before going on to raid along the coast as far south as Andalusia.[71] Though the Heruls were originally from Denmark or Sweden, it is unlikely that these particular raiders sailed directly to Spain from their homelands. The eastward course which the earlier group of raiders took for home suggests that they might actually have been part of the Saxon settlement on the Loire, an ideal base for voyages to Spain: certainly there were Herul seafarers

---

[68] H. M. Chadwick, *The Heroic Age* (Cambridge, 1912), pp. 97–9. A. Russchen, 'Warns, Heruli, Thuringians', *It Beaken* XXVI (1964), p. 302.

[69] *Translatio S. Alexandri auctoribus Ruodolfo et Meginharto*, ed. G. H. Pertz, *MGH. SS* 2 (Hanover, 1829), pp. 673–81, ch. 1

Saxonum gens, sicut tradit antiquas, ab Anglis Britanniae incolis egressa, per Oceanum navigans Germaniae litoribus studio et necessitate quaerendarum sedium appulsa est, in loco qui vocatur Haduloha [Hadeln], eo tempore quo Thiotricus rex Francorum contra Irminfridum generem suum, ducem Thuringorum, dimicans, terram eorum crudeliter ferro vastavit et igni.

Theodoric enlisted the aid of the Saxons in his war with Irminfred and gave them in return lands in Thuringia. F. M. Stenton, *Anglo-Saxon England*, 3rd edn (Oxford, 1971), p. 31, dates the landing to 531. Stenton believes that the story clearly has its origins in counter migration following the battle of Mount Badon. This event is also clearly the basis of Widukind's account of the Saxons' origins: *Res gestae Saxonicae*, I. 3–6.

[70] Hydatius, *Chronicon*, ed. A. Tranoy, *Hydace*, Sources Chrétiennes, 218 (2 vols, Paris, 1974), 171: 'De Erulorum gente septem nauibus in Lucensi litore aliquanti aduecti, uiri ferme CCCC expediti, superuentu multitudinis congregatae duobus tantum ex suo numero effugantur occisis: qui ad sedes proprias redeuntes Cantabriarum et Vardulliarum loca maritima crudelissime depraedati sunt.' *Vardullia* is the coast between the river Sella and the Pyrenees: vol. 2, p. 103. In general on these raids see E. A. Thompson, *Romans and Barbarians* (Madison, 1982), pp. 180–1.

[71] Hydatius, 194: 'Eruli maritima conuentus Lucensis loca nonnulla crudelissime inuadunt, ad Baeticam pertendentes.'

in Aquitaine in the 470s.[72] A Vandal raid on north-west Spain was also recorded in 445.[73] Though the Vandals were great pirates, this is their only recorded naval activity outside the Mediterranean and it has been suggested that these raiders were actually also Heruls.[74]

Anglo-Saxon expansion began again in the second half of the sixth century and the early seventh century saw the kingdom of Northumbria expand across Britain to the shores of the Irish Sea. Northumbrian fleets were soon active on that sea as Anglesey and the Isle of Man were conquered by Edwin.[75] How long the Northumbrians continued to rule the islands is unclear. Anglesey at least may have been retaken by the Welsh king Cadwallon in the short period of anarchy which followed Edwin's death in 632. Bede unfortunately gives no clue as to whether the islands were still under Northumbrian domination in his day, though the fact that he describes both islands in terms of their hidage suggests that they had been assessed for the payment of tribute. The largest Northumbrian naval expedition was an invasion of Ireland ordered by Ecgfrith in 684.[76] The raid, led by the ealdorman Beorht, appears to have been successful, taking captives and loot, but it earned the condemnation of Bede for burning churches. This was perhaps a punitive expedition intended to discourage the Irish from aiding

---

[72] Sidonius, *Epp.* VIII 9.5, ll. 31–3, notes the presence of Heruls at Euric's court in Bordeaux (along with Saxon seafarers: ll. 21–2):

> hic glaucis Herulus genis vagatur,
> imos Oceani colens recessus
> algoso prope concolor profundo.

Thompson, *Romans and Barbarians*, p. 181, suggests that Heruls were among the settlers of Britain and may have raided Spain from there.

[73] Hydatius, 131: 'Vandali nauibus Turonio in litore Gallaeciae repente aduecti familias capiunt plurimorum.'

[74] Tranoy, *op. cit.*, finds it difficult to accept that the Vandals, by this time settled around Carthage, would have much interest in raiding north west Spain and thinks it more likely that the raiders were Heruls. He believes that Hydatius did not actually know who the raiders were and has attributed the raid to the Vandals because they were well known at this time for their pirate activity in the Mediterranean, on which see: see H. J. Diesner, *Das Vandalenreich* (Stuttgart, 1966), pp. 53–74, 124–8, and C. Courtois, *Les Vandales et l'Afrique* (Paris, 1955), pp. 185–204.

[75] Bede, II. 5, II. 9.

[76] Bede, IV. 26: 'Anno Dominicae incarnationis dclxxxiiii, Ecgfrid rex Nordanhymbrorum, misso Hiberniam cum exercitu duce Bercto, vastavit misere gentem innoxiam et nationi Anglorum semper amicissimam, ita ut ne ecclesiis quidem aut monasteriis manus parceret hostilis.' In the *ASC*, 684, Beorht is given his Anglo-Saxon title *ealdorman*. The raid is also mentioned, though not under the same dates, in the Irish sources which identify the area attacked as Meath: see *Annals of Ulster*, ed. S. Mac Airt and G. Mac Niocaill (Dublin, 1983), *s.a.* 685. 2, and *Annals of the Kingdom of Ireland*, ed. J. O'Donovan (Dublin, 1856), 683, which adds that the Saxons took prisoners and that, in the following year, 684, Adomnan went to Northumbria and negotiated for the prisoners' release.

Ecgfrith's Scottish and British enemies in Dalriada (a Scottish kingdom comprising of Argyll and part of northern Ireland) and Strathclyde.[77]

That Dalriada itself was well organised for naval defence by *c.* 660 is evident from the *Senchus Fer n Alban*, a document which defines the army and navy service due from the different clans of the Scottish branch of the kingdom.[78] Two warships of 14 oarsmen were to be provided by every 20 households, giving the kingdom a theoretical naval strength of 177 ships.[79] These ships were small by Anglo-Saxon standards (see below) and it may be that the spirit of the *Senchus* was that every 20 households should raise 28 oarsmen rather than literally two ships.[80] The date of the *Senchus* has led to the suggestion that it was drawn up specifically as a response to the threat of Northumbrian expansion in the Irish Sea area.[81] Dalriada was involved in eight naval expeditions between 568 and 733 alone, including the earliest recorded naval battle (*bellum maritimum*) in British waters in 719, and there is ample evidence from Irish annals of a well developed tradition of naval warfare among the Irish-Scots and Picts in this period so it must be that other Celtic kingdoms also possessed strong warfleets.[82] It is certain, therefore, that the Northumbrian successes were won against peoples who had the means to oppose them at sea and so, despite the sparseness of the evidence, we should not underestimate Northumbrian naval strength.

It is interesting to note at this point that the development of Anglian and Saxon naval activity mirrors that of the Vikings. A phase of hit and run pirate raids (*c.* 280–450) is succeeded by a period when raiding colonies are formed (*c.* 430–60), and this in time is followed by a prolonged period of settlement and consolidation (*c.* 450–600). The seventh century sees a final phase of naval activity with clear political objectives under royal control. The parallel is not exact of course; the first and third stages of Anglo-Saxon activity are both much longer than the equivalent phases of Viking activity. On the other hand, the final phase was, so far as we can tell, very limited compared to the activities of Svein and Cnut. It is also noteworthy that the range of the raids of the Saxons and their associates, from Orkney to southern Spain, is almost identical to that of the Danish Vikings four or five centuries later.[83]

Of equal significance is the similarity of the tactics used by both the Saxons and the Vikings. Like the Vikings the Saxons were greatly feared by their victims

---

[77] Stenton, *op. cit.*, p. 88. A. P. Smyth, *Warlords and Holy Men* (London, 1984), p. 26, suggests that Ecgfrith also had a personal motive in that the Irish had given refuge to his exiled brother Aldfrith.

[78] J. Bannerman, *Studies in the History of Dalriada* (Edinburgh, 1974), p. 155, assumes that a similar document existed for the Irish branch of Dalriada.

[79] The *Senchus Fer n Alban*, ed. and trans. J. Bannerman in *idem, op. cit.*, pp. 41–9, lists a total of 1770 households.

[80] Bannerman, *op. cit.*, pp. 153–4.

[81] *Ibid.*, p. 155.

[82] Bannerman, *ibid.*, pp. 152–3.

[83] This similarity is noted but not examined by L. Musset, 'Deux invasions maritimes des Iles Britanniques: des Anglo-Saxons aux Vikings', in *Settimane* XXXII (Spoleto, 1986), p. 35.

because of their ability to strike from the sea without warning;[84] they even chose to raid in bad weather to increase the chances of surprise – surely a sign of confidence in the seaworthiness of their ships – and they were usually able to make good their escape before a counter attack was possible.[85] They also used rivers as routes to attack inland areas. The Saxons were also feared for their brutality and their practice of sacrificing a proportion of their captives in order to secure a fair passage home.[86] The Saxons preferred to hit a soft target and avoided combat when possible, but they would fight to the death if they had to and could even capture towns and fortresses. Yet the Saxons achieved this in the face of defences which, until the late fourth century at least, were far more formidable than those the Vikings generally had to face. On the basis of this comparison we might be justified in concluding that, in practical terms, the ships used by the Saxons, Angles and Heruls in the fourth and fifth centuries had a performance which was not greatly inferior to those used by the Vikings. However, the archaeological evidence for Anglo-Saxon shipbuilding does not, as it stands, support such a view.

---

[84] Ammianus Marcellinus, XXVIII. 2.12, compares the Maratocupreni, a tribe of desert raiders on the eastern frontier, to the Saxons: 'Nec quisquam adventum eorum[i.e. the Maratocupreni] cavere poterat inopinum, non destinata, sed varia petentium et longinqua, et quoquo ventus duxerat erumentum: quam ob causam prae ceteris hostibus Saxones timentur ut repentini.' The similarity between desert and ocean navigation is of course well known and, when it is remembered how readily the Arabs adapted to seafaring in the seventh century, Ammianus' comparison is a singularly appropriate one. This passage suggests that the Saxons used sailing ships: see below.

[85] Sidonius Apollinaris, *Epp.* VIII. 6.14:

'hostis est omni hoste truculentior. inprovisus aggreditur praevisus elabitur; spernit obiectos sternit incautos; si sequatur, intercipit, si fugiat, evadit. ad hoc exercent illos naufragia, non terrent. est eis quaedam cum discriminibus pelagi non notitia solum, sed familiaritas. nam quoniam ipsa si qua tempestas est huc securos efficit occupandos, huc prospici vetat occupaturos, in medio fluctuum scopulorumque confragosorum spe superventus laeti periclitantur.

This passage has actually been used by C. Green, *Sutton Hoo. The Excavation of a Royal Ship Burial* (London, 1963), p. 49, as evidence of the unseaworthiness of Saxon ships. It is more likely that it points to the opposite conclusion; if the Saxons deliberately set sail in poor weather, they must have had great confidence in their ships.

[86] Sidonius Apollinaris, *Epp..* VIII. 6.15:

praeterea, priusquam de continenti in patriam vela laxantes hostico mordaces anchoras vado vellant, mos est remeaturis decimum quemque captorum per aquales et cruciarias poenas plus ob hoc tristi quod superstitioso ritu necare superque collectam turbam periturorum mortis iniquitatem sortis aequitate dispergere.

The reference to human sacrifice rules out the possibility of confusion with the now largely Christian Britons or Irish.

The Ships of the Angles and Saxons

Compared with what we know about Frankish ships, we are relatively well informed about the ships used by the Angles, thanks to a number of major ship finds from Anglian settled areas of Britain and the continent. There have been no such finds from Saxon settled areas and we are dependent on literary sources alone for our knowledge of their ships. However, it is usually assumed that their ships were similar to those used by the Angles. While we know nothing from later Anglo-Saxon shipbuilding to suggest that this was not the case, it is as well to remember that the Saxons could have been influenced by the shipbuilding techniques of their western neighbours on the lower Rhine as easily as by those of their Anglian and Jutish neighbours to the north.

While the evidence from both literary and archaeological sources is comparatively good compared to earlier periods, it is still strictly limited and it does leave many questions unanswered. This must be borne in mind particularly with the ship finds; the sample group is still very small, so no matter how impressive an individual ship may be, the conclusions which can be drawn from it are true for that ship alone.

The earliest of the ship finds are the three ships from Nydam Moss on the southern Danish island of Als, discovered in the nineteenth century. The ships were deliberately sunk in the bog as votive offerings along with substantial quantities of weapons and other gear. Therefore it must be accepted that there is a possibility that none of the vessels is local in origin, as they may represent loot taken on a successful expedition abroad or the spoils from the defeat of an enemy raid. The largest of the vessels, the oak ship, was found in a remarkably good state of preservation. The second vessel, the pine ship, was less well preserved, but enough material survived for the characteristics of the ship to be reconstructed. The third vessel, evidently a small rowing boat, was very poorly preserved and is not discussed here.[87] Extensive re-excavation of Nydam Moss in the 1990s has recovered further ship fragments, including a beautifully preserved side rudder and ornamental wood carvings, belonging to the pine ship. It is clear that Nydam Moss still has much to reveal but its future is currently threatened by the progressive drying out of the acidic peat which has so far preserved the organic remains buried within it.

The oak ship was a large open rowing boat, over 70 feet long by 12 feet broad.[88] It was clinker-built with 5 broad strakes, each made from shorter lengths of plank scarfed together, to each side. The strakes were riveted together

---

[87] On this ship see Åkerlund, *Nydamskeppen*, p. 103.
[88] For details of the oak ship see *ibid., passim*, Greenhill and Morrison, *The Archaeology of Boats and Ships*, pp. 177-8.

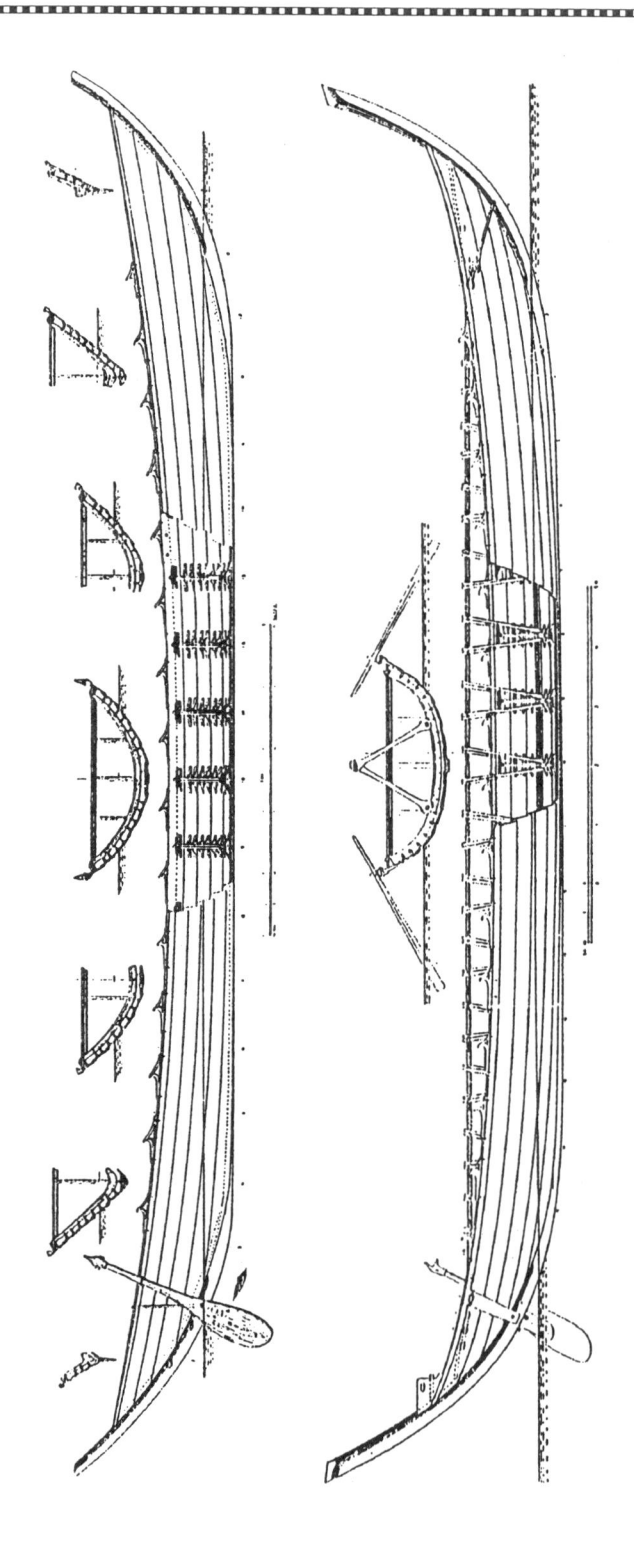

Figure 8 The Nydam Oak ship. Above, as it is currently preserved. Below, Åkerlund's reconstruction to allow for shrinkage of the wood, showing the controversial hogging truss. (Åkerlund: *Nydamskeppen*)

with iron clench nails, the earliest securely dated example of their use in north European shipbuilding yet discovered. However, lashings were used to fasten the internal strengthening frames to cleats on both to the strakes and to the broad flat keel plank. The long raking stems were fastened to the keel by scarf joints which have been considered to be rather weak. The boat had a crew of 30 oarsmen whose oars were held on rowlocks lashed to the gunwales and was steered by a large steering oar, though it is not at all clear how this was fastened to the ship. Since it was excavated in 1863, the ship has shrunk by some 14 per cent due to drying, with the result that it no longer presents a true appearance: the hull was originally broader and more stable than is now apparent.[89] The oak ship was originally dated to c. 350 on the basis of the style of brooches found in it. Dendrochronological analysis has since shown that the ship was built of timbers felled between AD 310 and 320.[90]

The keel structure of the Nydam oak ship is generally considered to have been too weak to support a mast and sail and perhaps too weak even for it to have been a true sea-going vessel. It was in the light of this belief that the Swedish archaeologist Harald Åkerlund interpreted a number of loose wooden objects found in the ship, including some shaped rather like 4½-feet-long ring spanners or 'eye-poles', as supports for a hogging truss, a rope tensioning device designed to give the ship extra longitudinal strength.[91] Greek and Roman galleys were often strengthened in a similar way and hogging trusses were normal on ancient Egyptian ships, which were structurally weak because of the difficulty in obtaining long lengths of building timber in the Egyptians' treeless country.[92] Åkerlund suggests that the structure was detachable and was set up only in rough seas. However much they might agree with him about the structural limitations of the oak ship, Åkerlund's theory has found little favour among maritime archaeologists, as his putative hogging truss would have taken up a great deal of room when in use. But despite their scepticism archaeologists have struggled to come up with an alternative explanation for the function of the eye-poles. The most credible suggestion made so far is that these mysterious objects are parts from a rather complicated frame tent, perhaps used as a shelter by the crew, either on or off the ship.[93] Early (AD 400–600) picture stones from Gotland do in fact show simple tent-like structures in some ships. It is, nevertheless, difficult to see how a tent constructed with these poles could stay up, so this is still not an entirely convincing explanation.

---

[89] Åkerlund, *op. cit.*, pp. 36, 43–4, 156.

[90] Greenhill and Morrison, *op. cit.*, p. 178.

[91] Åkerlund, *op. cit.*, pp. 63–73.

[92] On the use of hogging trusses on Greek and Roman ships see P. Johnstone, *Seacraft of Prehistory*, pp. 83–4; on Egyptian ships see L. Casson, *Ships and Seamanship*, pp. 17, 20–1.

[93] F. Rieck and E. Jørgensen, 'Non-military equipment from Nydam', in A. Nørgård Jørgensen and B. L. Clausen (eds), *Military aspects of Scandinavian society in a European persepective AD 1-1300*, Publications of the National Museum, Studies in Archaeology and History, vol. 2 (Copenhagen, 1997), 220-25, p. 222.

Figure 9 Rowing vessel with tent or ritual structure from a Gotland picture stone
c. AD 400–600

The main objection to Åkerlund's theory, however, is one that has not generally been appreciated by maritime archaeologists. The oak ship quite simply did not need a hogging truss: the use of iron rivets to fasten its overlapping strakes would have given the oak ship a very strong hull which could have supported the light keel structure unaided. The keel structure of the oak ship, therefore, was not in itself an obstacle to sea-going or to the adoption of a light sailing rig. A rare piece of iconographical evidence – a small inscribed stone discovered at Karlby on the east coast of Jutland in the 1980s – does suggest that at some point in their evolution similar vessels to the Nydam oak ship were adapted to carry a mast and sail. The stone carries a tiny picture of a ship with an identical profile to the oak ship carrying a mast and patterned square sail.[94] Atop the mast is a flag or weather vane. Unfortunately the stone was not found in a datable context, limiting its value as evidence, but it is thought to be seventh century on the basis of decorative animal ornament also carved on the stone. However, *if* a Nydam-type ship could carry mast and sail in the seventh century, there seems no obvious reason why they could not also have carried them much earlier.

A recent find from east Jutland has shown that the Nydam oak ship by no means represents the upper size limit for this type of ship. The Kongsgårde ship was built *c.* 600 and is known only from a single rib.[95] The ship had either five broad or nine narrow strakes a side and was built using the same techniques as the oak ship. The shaping of the frame, which had a span of 12½ feet, shows that it did not come from the midships area, so it can be safely concluded that the Kongsgårde ship had a maximum breadth of well over 13 feet compared to the

---

[94] F. Rieck and O. Crumlin-Pedersen, *Både fra Danmarks oldtid* (Roskilde, 1988), pp. 129, 133.

[95] *Ibid.*, p. 134. Also O. Crumlin-Pedersen, 'Boats and ships of the Angles and Jutes', in S. McGrail (ed.), *Maritime Celts, Frisians and Saxons*, CBA Research Report 71, (London, 1990), p. 111.

oak ship's 12 feet, that is, probably not much smaller than the Sutton Hoo ship. Though the oak ship itself was probably not intended to sail on the high seas, it is likely that larger ships built using similar techniques were used by Saxon and Anglian pirates in the fourth and fifth centuries. It is clear that the Heruls who raided Lugo in 455–7 (see above) also used large ships; no doubt built in the same tradition. The Herul ships had crews of about 55 men, more than the oak ship could have carried safely even on a short voyage in sheltered waters.

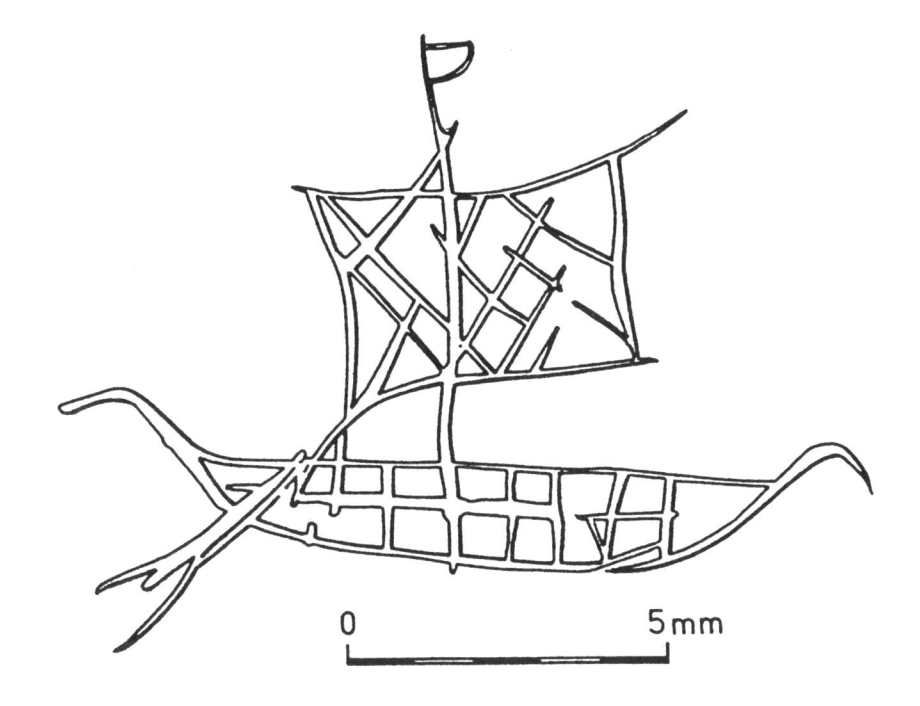

Figure 10 The Karlby ship-carving
(Drawing W. Karrasch, National Museum, Copenhagen)

The pine ship from Nydam was rather smaller than the oak ship; about 61 feet long by nearly 10 feet broad, with a crew of only 22 oarsmen and, like the oak ship, clinker-built but with seven strakes a side.[96] The scarf joints which fastened the stem and stern posts were of a stronger construction than the oak ship's, and the keel had a definite projection, making this the earliest known boat from northern Europe to have a 'T' shaped keel section. The pine ship was also equipped with a fully developed and highly efficient side rudder which was mounted on a boss on the side of the hull: it is the earliest known from northern Europe. Unlike the loosely attached steering oar of the oak ship, which could not have applied sufficient leverage, this would have been suitable for use in a sailing

---

[96] See Åkerlund, *op. cit.*, pp. 98–101, Greenhill and Morrison, *op. cit.*, p. 178.

ship. A replica has performed well in sea trials on a square rigged ship.[97] The ship was richly decorated and had an elegant profile, probably similar to the oared ships shown on the earliest types of the Gotland picture stones.[98] A shield found in the ship was made of wood felled in AD 296 while a runic inscription and decorative patterns carved on the ship itself point to a date of around 350.[99] The pine ship was therefore more or less contemporary with the oak ship. It is likely that the pine ship originated in Norway or Sweden because pine is not native to southern Denmark or the north German plain: close similarities between decorations on the boat and those on early picture stones from Gotland perhaps make a Swedish origin most likely.[100] On the other hand, there is no reason to believe that the oak ship originated far from the place it was found, and the likelihood is that it is an Anglian boat, though certainly not an example of the type ship used for the migrations to Britain. However, the differences between the techniques used in the construction of the two ships demonstrate that even in the fourth century there was marked diversity in north European shipbuilding and this should warn us against generalising too much on the basis of individual finds.

Probably the best-preserved north European ship from the pre-Viking period as regards shape is the Sutton Hoo ship. It was buried *c.* 625 in what may well be the grave mound of king Rædwald of East Anglia, sited on a low ridge overlooking the estuary of the river Deben in Suffolk. The ship was not new when it was buried as it had been repaired in several places and a date of construction of *c.* 600–10 has been suggested on these grounds.[101] As it was a royal ship, the Sutton Hoo ship is probably no more representative of the kind of ships used for the Anglo-Saxon migrations than is the Nydam oak ship.

The wood of the ship's hull had completely decayed in the burial mound but the shape of the ship's timbers was preserved as an impression in the earth, with the iron clench nails which had fastened the strakes still in their original positions, though heavily corroded, so making an accurate reconstruction possible. It was a very large vessel, *c.* 89 feet long, 14 feet broad and 4½ feet deep, yet despite its size it would have drawn only about 2 feet of water unladen.[102] The ship, which was probably built of oak, was clinker-built, with

---

[97] E. and J. Gifford, 'The sailing characteristics of Saxon ships as derived from half-scale working models with special reference to the Sutton Hoo ship', *IJNA* XXIV (1995), 121-31, p. 126. Also E. and J. Gifford 'The sailing performance of Anglo-Saxon ships as derived from the building and trials of half-scale models of the Sutton Hoo and Graveney ship finds', *Mariner's Mirror* LXXXII (1996), 131-53, p. 143.

[98] For illustrations of the relevant stones see E. Nylén, *Bildstenar*, 2nd edn (Visby, 1987), pp. 22-3, 29, 35, 155.

[99] E. Jørgensen and F. Rieck 'Mere fra Mosen' in *Skalk* 6 (1997), 5-9, p. 9.

[100] Åkerlund, *op. cit.*, pp. 121–2. F. Rieck, *Jernalderkrigernes Skibe. Nye og gamle udgravninger I Nydam Mose* (Roskilde, 1994), p. 62, 65.

[101] R. L. S. Bruce-Mitford, *The Sutton Hoo Ship Burial. Vol. 1. Excavation, Background, the Ship, Dating and Inventory* (London, 1975), pp. 350, 584–8, 678–82, 715–17.

[102] *Ibid.*, pp. 350–410, provides the fullest description of the ship available.

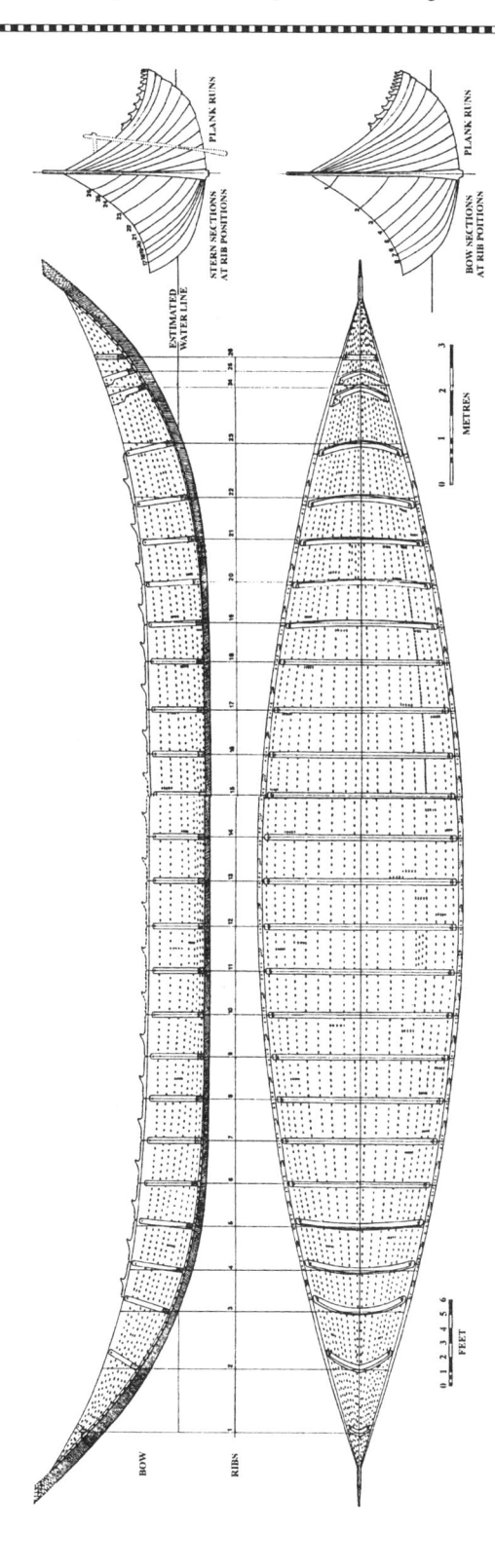

Anglo-Saxon Piracy and the Migrations to Britain

Figure 11 The Sutton Hoo ship (British Museum)

nine narrow strakes per side. Each of these strakes was built up from several shorter planks which were scarf-jointed together. The ship's stems were raked at angles similar to those of the Nydam oak ship and rose at least 12½ feet above the keel. Internal strengthening was provided by 26 frames which were probably fastened directly on to the strakes rather than being lashed to cleats, as was the case with the Nydam ships. There were additional frames in the stern, two of which had been reinforced on the starboard side to take a side rudder, though neither the rudder nor its fittings have survived; they were probably removed prior to burial. The keel was formed by a flat, heavy, plank which projected about 2 inches below the hull.

The ship had 14 pairs of rowlocks which were attached to the top of the gunwales with iron spikes. No traces of rowlocks were found in the midships section where there is space for a further six pairs of oars. Did the ship originally have 20 pairs of rowlocks and were those in the midships section removed to accommodate the burial chamber? The likelihood is that they were never there to begin with as the iron spikes which were used to fasten the rowlocks to the gunwale would have rusted into the wood. If the rowlocks had been removed, most of the iron would have been left behind to leave some trace in the earth.[103] This arrangement of oarsmen, with a gap amidships, is seen on pictures of Anglo-Saxon ships on the 11th century Bayeux Tapestry.[104] The ship was probably decked and the 28 oarsmen would have sat on sea chests, as was the arrangement on the Oseberg and Gokstad ships.[105]

No evidence for mast and sail has survived but this should not be considered as conclusive evidence that the ship was simply a large, open, rowing boat. The burial chamber was sited at the centre of the ship and the mast and mast step, if they existed, would have been removed to accommodate it.[106] The lack of any fittings for rigging need not be significant either; if they had been made of wood, as they were on the Oseberg ship, they would have decayed as completely as the hull. It is worth noting with regard to this that in the case of the tenth-century Ladby ship, which was preserved in an identical way to the Sutton Hoo ship, all trace of the mast and mast step had decayed; the ship was only recognised as a sailing ship by the survival of eight iron shroud rings.[107]

As with the Nydam oak ship, it is usually claimed that the Sutton Hoo ship's flat keel would have been too weak to support a mast and sail and would have given the ship a poor performance when attempting to sail to windward: clinker-built ships of the Nordic tradition, it is claimed, could only carry a mast and sail

---

[103] E. and J. Gifford, 'The sailing performance of Anglo-Saxon ships as derived from the building and trials of half-scale models of the Sutton Hoo and Graveney ship finds', p. 133.
[104] Bruce-Mitford, *op. cit.*, pp. 413-20.
[105] Bruce-Mitford, *loc. cit.*
[106] Bruce-Mitford, *op. cit.*, p. 422.
[107] K. Thorvildsen, *The Viking Ship of Ladby* (Copenhagen, 1961), p. 22.

after the perfection in eighth century Scandinavia of the projecting 'T' shaped keel, seen at its most spectacular in the tenth century Gokstad ship from Norway.[108] However, Edwin and Joyce Gifford have identified a great deal of evidence that suggests that the Sutton Hoo ship was designed and built as a sailing ship:[109]

- The flat bottom and round bilge of the midships section is well suited to carrying sail.
- Its waterline shape would have made the ship fast and generated lateral resistance to leeway in a side or head wind.
- The leaf-shaped plan of the ship is one generally associated with sailing ships: rowing galleys have nearly parallel sides designed to maximise the output of the oarsmen and minimise hull resistance (compare, for example, with the plan of the late Roman Mainz type-A warship, p. 71).
- The distribution of oars is associated with rowing and sailing ships shown on the Bayeux Tapestry rather than galleys.
- The additional frames in the stern were probably required to strengthen the hull against the heavy rudder loads of sailing: a rowing galley needs only a light steering oar and no special strengthening.
- The projection of the stem and sternposts was larger than needed for strength but would have been useful in creating resistance to leeway under sail.
- The closely spaced gunwale to gunwale frames would have given the hull sufficient strength to withstand the stresses and strains of sailing.

The Giffords have put these observations to the test with *Sæ Wylfing*, a half-scale sailing model of the Sutton Hoo ship. While the results of their sea trials do not prove that the Sutton Hoo ship was a sailing ship, they do prove beyond any doubt that the reasons usually given as to why it could not have been a sailing ship are quite false. *Sæ Wylfing* proved to be a highly effective sailing ship, fast, manoeuvrable and, despite its low freeboard, remarkably dry even in choppy seas. In smooth water the boat was able to make slow progress directly to windward and even in higher seas was able to hold station against the wind. The addition of a slightly projecting false keel, such as may have been used on the late Anglo-Saxon Graveney boat,[110] brought only a small improvement in windward sailing performance, confirming that the main resistance to leeway was generated

---

[108] For example by A. W. Brøgger and H. Shetelig, *The Viking Ships*, 2nd edn (Oslo and London, 1971), pp. 38–40. Their linking of the deep 'T'-shaped keel to the adoption of the sail in north European ships has been most influential and widely accepted.

[109] E. and J. Gifford, 'The sailing performance of Anglo-Saxon ships as derived from the building and trials of half-scale models of the Sutton Hoo and Graveney ship finds', pp. 132–3. E. and J. Gifford, 'The sailing characteristics of Saxon ships as derived from half-scale working models with special reference to the Sutton Hoo ship', p. 121.

[110] E. and J. Gifford, 'The sailing performance of Anglo-Saxon ships as derived from the building and trials of half-scale models of the Sutton Hoo and Graveney ship finds', p. 135. On the Graveney ship see V. Fenwick, *The Graveney Boat*, BAR BS 53 (National Maritime Museum, Archaeological Series 3, Greenwich, 1978), pp. 227, 251.

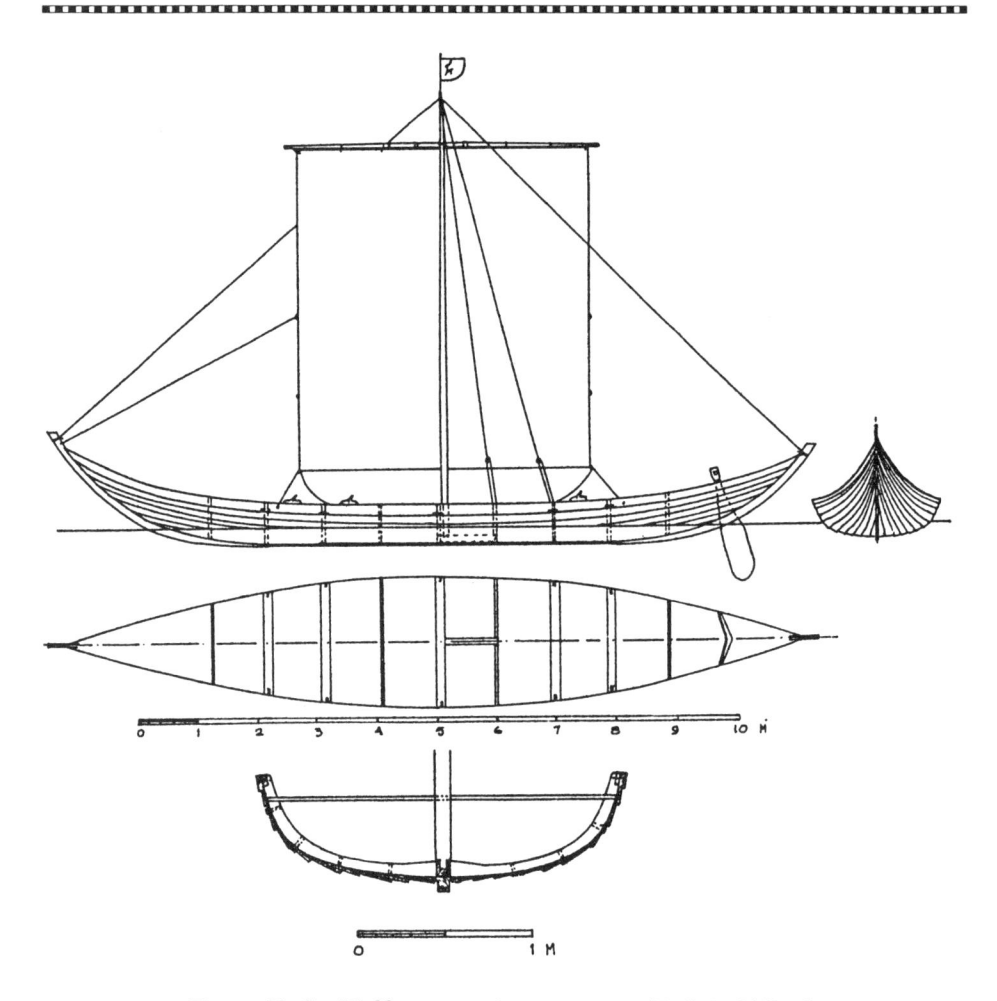

Figure 12 Sæ Wylfing general arrangement (E. & J. Gifford)

by the underwater shape of the hull. The hull of *Sæ Wylfing* proved more than strong enough to withstand the modest stresses of carrying a light mast and square sail. The shallow draught and flat bottom made the boat easy and safe to beach even when driven ashore hard under sail.[111]

By extrapolation, these results show that the Sutton Hoo ship would have been a most efficient sailing ship, scarcely inferior to Viking sailing ships. In a moderate wind the Sutton Hoo ship could have reached a speed of around 10 knots and had a theoretical maximum speed of about 12 knots. On a calm sea it could have made progress directly to windward at about 1.5 knots and held station even in a high wind – in this respect it would have had far superior

---

[111] E. and J. Gifford, 'The sailing performance of Anglo-Saxon ships as derived from the building and trials of half-scale models of the Sutton Hoo and Graveney ship finds', pp. 143-51. E. and J. Gifford, 'The sailing characteristics of Saxon ships as derived from half-scale working models with special reference to the Sutton Hoo ship', pp. 126-31.

performance to the later medieval sailing cogs. The lack of a 'T' shaped keel would not have made the ship too weak to carry a mast and sail. The strength of the keel would have been irrelevant if the mast step had been linked to one or more of the internal strengthening ribs. Perhaps the most important of the Giffords' conclusions is that the flat bottom and lack of projecting keel are not signs that the Sutton Hoo ship was an incompletely evolved Viking ship, they are completely evolved adaptations to the shallow shoaly seas of the southern North Sea. They enabled the ship to be sailed close inshore and far up rivers and to be beached safely even in a high surf. Once beached, the flat bottom meant that the ship stayed upright as the tide fell, making it easier to load and unload than a ship with a deep keel like the Gokstad ship which would fall on to its side. Indeed, the flat-bottomed hull remained the rule for ships built to operate in the southern North Sea until the end of the age of sail. It is probably relevant here to point out that the massively projecting keel of the Gokstad ship appears to be a specifically Norwegian feature, presumably an adaptation to deep Atlantic waters where the improved resistance to leeway would outweigh the greatly increased draught. The keels of Danish Viking ships, such as the Ladby ship and Skuldelev 5, intended for use in the shallow Baltic Sea do not have large projections.[112]

Sæ Wylfing, half-scale model of the Sutton Hoo ship under sail (E. & J. Gifford)

---

[112] See Greenhill and Morrison, *op. cit.* pp. 198-203.

There remain a number of related ship finds to be discussed. The first is the ship from Gredstedbro, on the south-west coast of Jutland, which, being radio-carbon dated to *c.* 610, is an exact contemporary of the Sutton Hoo ship.[113] The structure of the keel and the scarf joints which join the bow and stern posts to it are similar to those of the Sutton Hoo ship. The ship had eight narrow strakes to a side and its length has been estimated as 60 to 75 feet. The ribs had been shaped to fit the strakes closely and were fastened directly onto them with trenails. It is thought that the same method was used to fasten the ribs to the strakes in the Sutton Hoo ship.[114] This represented a more efficient use of timber and a considerable saving in building time compared to the method used in the Nydam ships, as well as the later Viking ships, where the strengthening ribs were lashed to cleats.[115] This may have been a fifth-century development, when the pressure of the migrations to Britain created an urgent need for large numbers of ships. There is as yet no evidence for the means of propulsion but this may eventually be discovered as the ship has not been fully excavated.

Two other Anglo-Saxon ships are known from East Anglia, neither of which has provided evidence for mast and sail. One of these was discovered in a burial mound at Sutton Hoo in 1938, and has recently been re-excavated by Professor Carver. No wood has survived and the remains were greatly disturbed. There has as yet been no definitive reconstruction but provisional conclusions suggest that the boat was 18 to 26 feet long, clinker-built with perhaps six strakes a side and a riveted construction. The keel had a projection of about 2 inches by 2 inches in section.[116] The other boat, from Snape, was excavated in the nineteenth century and not well recorded by modern standards. It probably dates from *c.* 600 on the evidence of the grave goods and like the Sutton Hoo finds was preserved only as an impression in the earth, marked by decomposed wood and iron clench nails. It was about 50 feet long, clinker-built, with eight or nine strakes a side. No evidence of the means of propulsion, either oar or sail, was recorded.[117]

Finally, there is the boat find from Ashby Dell near Lowestoft, which has been presumed to be an Anglo-Saxon boat. No date can be ascribed to the Ashby Dell boat with confidence, nor can it be said for certain that it was clinker-built, nor is the true context of the find known. Its most interesting feature is that though the ribs were lashed to the strakes, the cleats were not integral parts of the strakes, as on the Nydam boats, but were carved from separate pieces of wood and trenailed to the strakes. Typologically this would seem to place the ship somewhere between the Nydam oak ship and the Sutton Hoo ship, though in other respects no iron was used in its construction, for example it would seem to

---

[113] See the descriptions in McGrail, *Ancient Boats*, pp. 136–8, and Greenhill and Morrison, *op. cit.*, pp. 178-80.

[114] Bruce-Mitford, *op. cit.*, p. 426.

[115] Greenhill and Morrison, *op. cit.*, p. 179.

[116] M. O. H. Carver, personal communication, 24th October 1988.

[117] The Snape boat is discussed in R. L. S. Bruce-Mitford, *Aspects of Anglo-Saxon Archaeology* (London, 1974), pp. 119–22, and Green, *op. cit.*, pp. 57–60.

Anglo-Saxon Piracy and the Migrations to Britain

be more primitive than the Nydam ship. Other features, such as the shape of the stern post and the joint with which it was fastened to the keel, do not seem to be part of the north European tradition at all.[118] It would be dangerous to draw any conclusions on the basis of this particular find.

An important indirect source of evidence about the ships used in northern waters during the Migration Period comes from the study of late Iron Age boat houses in western Norway, which presumably reflected the size of the boats that were to be kept in them. These are commonly between 75 and 105 feet long and 15 to 20 feet wide, though some of over 120 feet in length are known.[119] The length to width ratios of the buildings show that they were used to store long narrow vessels, presumably warships: their size shows that even ships as large as that from Sutton Hoo were by no means unusual in the period.

The conversion of the Anglo-Saxons to Christianity in the seventh century brought an end to the practice of ship burial and, except for a scattering of fragments from cemeteries,[120] the ships discussed represent the sum total of archaeological evidence for the characteristics of Anglo-Saxon ships before the Viking-age. There is even less literary evidence. The most often cited author who has had anything to say about Anglo-Saxon ships is Procopius in his famous digression on Britain.[121] Procopius tells us, on the basis of what is presumed to have been the testimony of an Angle who had accompanied a Frankish delegation to Constantinople,[122] that the *Angiloi* did not use the sail on their ships but relied on oars alone.[123] Taken together with the lack of any archaeological evidence for the use of the sail, this passage has sometimes been taken as conclusive evidence that the Anglo-Saxons still had not adopted the sail in the sixth century.[124] However, this is not the conclusive evidence it seems, as the briefest consideration of its context shows. Procopius' informant also told him that Britain was a home to the souls of the dead, and even that there were no horses in Britain and never had been and that the inhabitants had never so much as seen a

---

[118] See Green, *op. cit.*, pp. 60–3, and Bruce-Mitford, *Sutton Hoo*, pp. 426–8.

[119] See B. Myhre, 'Boathouses and naval organization' in A. Nørgård Jørgensen and B. L. Clausen (eds), *Military aspects of Scandinavian society in a European persepective AD 1–1300*, Publications of the National Museum, Studies in Archaeology and History, vol. 2 (Copenhagen, 1997), pp. 169-83.

[120] See M. Carver, 'Boat burial in Britain: ancient custom or political signal?' in O. Crumlin-Pedersen and B. Munch Thye (eds), *The ship as symbol in prehistoric and medieval Scandinavia*, Publications of the National Museum, Studies in Archaeology and History, vol. 1 (Copenhagen, 1995), pp. 111-24.

[121] Procopius, VIII. xx. Procopius was unaware that the island he was writing about, which he called *Brittia*, was Britain as he had been confused by his informant's description of its location. On the causes of Procopius's confusion see A. R. Burn, 'Procopius and the island of ghosts', *English Historical Review* LXX (1955), pp. 258–9.

[122] Burn, *ibid.*, p. 261. Procopius, VIII. xx. 58, himself says that what he recorded was the testimony of the inhabitants of *Brittia*.

[123] Procopius, VIII. xx. 31.

[124] For example A. C. Leighton, *Transport and Communication in Early Medieval Europe* (Newton Abbot, 1972), p. 143.

picture of one.[125] A passage which contains such palpable nonsense can hardly be regarded as a reliable source about anything. The inescapable conclusion is that Procopius' informant was spinning a yarn or perhaps, as discussed above, relating a traditional tale of some antiquity. In fairness to Procopius, he himself makes plain his scepticism and says that he is only recording the stories for the sake of completeness.[126]

The evidence of Procopius is, in any case, contradicted by an earlier and far more credible source, a letter of Sidonius Apollinaris of *c.* 473 in which he expressly refers to the Saxons' use of sailing ships for their raids on the Gallic coast: They made human sacrifices, he tells us, 'when [they were] ready to unfurl their sails for the voyage home from the continent and to lift their gripping anchors from enemy waters.'[127] Sidonius had played an important role in Gallic politics for many years by this time, he had a close friend in the Visigothic fleet on the Garonne, had seen Saxon and Herul seamen at Bordeaux and elsewhere in his writings shows himself to have been a keen observer of barbarian ways.[128] Moreover, Sidonius' description in this passage of the Saxons' ships as 'curving pirate galleys' (*myoparones*) exactly describes the profile of a Nydam or Sutton Hoo type ship (see photo. p. 103), strongly suggesting that he had seen one for himself or, at the very least, been given an accurate description by someone who had. We might therefore reasonably prefer Sidonius' testimony on this subject to Procopius', yet this passage has only rarely been referred to by archaeologists and maritime historians.[129] A century earlier Ammianus had spoken of the Saxons going wherever the wind drove them,[130] the natural interpretation of this being that the Saxons were using sailing ships. If this passage was found in a poem we might readily dismiss it as a literary device, yet Ammianus was not a poet; he was a serious and generally precise historian, and if he talks about the Saxons using the wind there must be a strong presumption that it is because they raided in sailing ships in the fourth century.

There is also a very strong circumstantial case to be made for the use of the sail in the fourth century, and probably earlier, by the Saxons and other Germanic tribes settled along the North Sea coast. As was pointed out in the first chapter, the sail was already in use among some of the Germanic tribes in close contact with the Roman Empire in the first century AD, and there can be little doubt that the Franks used sailing ships from the outset of their raids *c.* 250. We know that in the following century the Franks and Saxons raided the same areas and

---

[125] Procopius, VIII. xx. 48–58, xx. 29.

[126] *Ibid.*, VIII. xx. 47.

[127] Sidonius Apollinaris, *Epp.* VIII. 6.15. The translation is Anderson's, from the Loeb edition, vol. 2, p. 431 (see n. 87 above for the Latin text).

[128] See for example his comments on Burgundian hair style, diet and music. *Carm.* XII. 1-19.

[129] Green, *op. cit.*, p. 51, cites Sidonius's reference in this letter, 6.13, to *remiges* as evidence that the Saxons did not use sails while inexplicably ignoring his later reference, cited above, to their use of sails.

[130] Ammianus Marcellinus, XXVIII, 2.12 (see text above, n. 85).

sometimes raided in alliance with each other: even if the use of the sail had not spread as far as the neck of the Jutland peninsula by 250, how long can we realistically expect the Saxon pirates to have sweated it out at their oars without realising the benefits of the sail when they had the Frankish, and Roman, example to learn from?

Even if the Saxon ships could only use their sails in a following wind, that would still have brought them great advantages on long distance raids. Rowing boats would have been very vulnerable to the Roman defences: they would have had to hug the coast, making them easier to detect and intercept; they would have needed to make frequent landfalls for supplies and to rest the crew, who would quickly have become exhausted; and at such times they would have been exposed to attack by Roman coastguards. Above all, rowing boats would have been slow. Assuming that crews could keep up a rowing speed of three knots for 12 hours a day, such a boat could only make 36 nautical miles a day in favourable conditions.[131] Against a headwind or in bad weather even less distance would be made. With a following wind even a primitive sailing vessel could have covered twice to three times the distance in a day without exhausting the crew and without having to make a landfall at night.[132] Such a vessel could easily have passed undetected through the Roman defences in the Straits of Dover in the course of a summer night and been within striking distance of any part of the Gallic coast in a couple of days. A rowing boat would take weeks of hard labour to cover the same ground, all the while hugging a hostile and defended coast. For short-range warfare, such as a raid on a neighbouring tribe, the advantages of the sail would have been less clear-cut. The wind could not be guaranteed to blow the right way whenever it was needed, a sail would make a ship more visible and, since a warship had to have a large crew of able-bodied men anyway, the oar may have continued to be preferred to the sail for centuries on ships built for this type of warfare. No doubt the Nydam ships are examples of such vessels. Because of the economic benefits of smaller crews, sails were probably first used on trading ships (which would be unlikely to find their way into the votive offerings or royal burials which have provided the bulk of ship finds), and only gradually adopted on warships as the range of raiding activity expanded.[133] However, it is perfectly clear that this process of adoption had begun several centuries earlier than the current orthodoxy would have it.

The question of the Anglo-Saxon use of the sail has important implications for our understanding of the settlement of England. If the first federate settlers and pirate-infiltrators came in rowing boats their communities will have been very

---

[131] McGrail, *Ancient Boats*, p. 282.

[132] *Ibid.*, p. 282. This figure assumes an average speed of 6 knots maintained over a 24-hour period.

[133] Lebecq, *Marchands et navigateurs*, vol. 1, pp. 177–81, argues, *vice versa*, that sails would have been adopted on warships before trading ships on the grounds that, at first, sails would have been too dangerous for merchants to have considered using them. But merchants were in a better position to await favourable sailing conditions than warriors and would probably have found that the economic benefits outweighed the initial risks.

isolated; several weeks of hard rowing lay between them and the support of their kinsmen. A request for help might not be answered for months and then only with limited numbers. If on the other hand sailing ships were available, communications with the Anglo-Saxon homelands will have been relatively quick and easy; in favourable conditions a crossing under sail from East Anglia to north Germany takes a few days only so a request for reinforcements might be answered in a few weeks. When the final rebellion against British authority happened, the Anglo-Saxons could have built up their numbers very quickly, overwhelming native resistance.

The archaeological evidence points conclusively to a massive population movement out of the area between the Weser and the Jutland peninsula in the second half of the fifth century: almost all the known settlements and cemeteries in this area had fallen out of use by *c.* 500.[134] Thus we can be quite certain that in its early stages the Anglo-Saxon settlement of Britain was the consequence of a mass folk migration, not of an aristocratic or political takeover (though much of the subsequent expansion clearly was). Unger has claimed that under such circumstances there would have been no incentive for the Anglo-Saxons to adopt the sail: with large numbers of people to move there would have been no shortage of manpower to row the ships.[135] However, there are a number of problems with Unger's theory. Firstly, it implies that each ship was used only once; it could not have made a return journey because its crew was busy tilling the land. This objection cannot be avoided by suggesting that there were crews of professional oarsmen; if this was the case, there would have been no room in the ships for a worthwhile number of passengers once the crew and their supplies were embarked. A second objection is that it cannot be assumed that the passengers of a ship were capable of rowing it effectively or piloting it safely. Able-bodied adult males will not have formed the majority of the emigrants; women, children and, no doubt, dependent old folk will have gone along. On top of this the settlers will have taken tools and farm implements, seed corn, supplies to last until the first harvest, some of the more valuable livestock, weapons and much else besides. It may be doubted that there was room in a ship for a full crew of oarsmen. It is far easier to account for the completeness of the Anglo-Saxon migration if we assume that the settlers came in sailing ships with small professional crews who could make several return journeys in a season, building

---

[134] Böhme, *op. cit.*, pp. 558–9. It is this evidence of the mass depopulation of the ancestral Anglo-Saxon homelands that is the strongest evidence for folk migration. Though the spread of Anglo-Saxon material culture in Britain could be explained, in isolation, by the influence exerted by a small conquering aristocracy, it is also difficult to account for the almost complete absence of Welsh loan-words in Old English except in terms of a mass migration.

[135] Unger, *The Ship in the Medieval Economy*, pp. 62–3. M. E. Jones, 'The logistics of the Anglo-Saxon invasions', in M. Daniel (ed.), *Papers of the Sixth Naval History Symposium held at the U. S. Naval Academy on 29–30 September 1983* (Wilmington, 1987), pp. 62–9, takes the opposite view and argues that the Anglo-Saxon settlements must have been an aristocratic takeover because a mass folk migration would have been impossible in the rowing boats which, he accepts, were all that were available to the Anglo-Saxons. The problem with this interpretation is that the settlement evidence is against it.

up the settlers' numbers rapidly. In fair weather, each voyage across the North Sea would have been measured in days rather than weeks and the risks would have been slight.[136] In terms of travelling time the 300-mile voyage between Jutland and the Thames estuary would have been no longer than a 60 mile-long journey overland. Of course, arguing that things would have been easier for the Anglo-Saxon settlers if they had used sailing ships does not prove that they did so. The settlements would, no doubt, still have been possible if the Anglo-Saxons had used only rowing boats. But the enterprise would have been incomparably more arduous, and it is difficult to believe that, after centuries of contact with sail-using peoples, the Anglo-Saxons would have chosen to continue doing things the hard way.

By the second half of the seventh century we can be quite certain that the sail was in everyday use by the Anglo-Saxons. Some of these sailing ships, such as the one which king Oswiu of Northumbria fitted out to take St Wilfred to Gaul in c. 664,[137] could be very large. On Wilfred's return journey a storm blew up and the ship was driven ashore on the coast of Sussex, which was at that time still pagan. The local Saxons tried to seize the ship and a skirmish broke out between them and the crew and passengers. Eddius goes on to say that things looked grim for the Christians because they were 'few in number', there being 'only' 120 of them.[138] However, they were well armed and held off the pagans until the tide came back in, when they refloated the ship and, driven by a south-west wind, escaped to Kent. The exact number of men in the ship may or may not be correct, but the important point here is that Eddius was a contemporary of Wilfred's, writing for a contemporary audience who would have known whether this was a realistic number to be on one ship: it is unlikely to be far wrong. From the size of its complement, we are justified in concluding that this ship was as large as, if not larger than, the Sutton Hoo ship which was buried less than 40 years before. According to Eddius, Wilfred also returned to England from Gaul in 658 in a sailing ship, but on this occasion we cannot be certain that it was an Anglo-Saxon ship.[139] In 678, Wilfred went into exile, again by sailing ship, making what seems to have been a direct crossing of the North Sea from the Humber to

---

[136] See M. O. H. Carver, 'Pre-Viking Traffic in the North Sea', in McGrail (ed.), *Maritime Celts, Frisians and Saxons*, 117-25, pp. 119-22.

[137] Eddius Stephanus, *Vita Wilfridi episcopi*, ed. J. Raine, *Historians of the Church of York*, 1, Rolls Series 71 (London, 1879), pp. 101–103, ch. 12. It is true that Eddius nowhere explicitly mentions a sail but his constant references to the state and direction of the wind in the following passages leave no doubt that sailing ships were being used.

[138] *Vita Wilfridi*, 13:

Ita et isti sodales sancti pontifici nostri, bene armati, viriles animo, pauci numero (erant enim centum et viginti viri in numero, Mosaicae aetatis), inito consilio et pacto ut nullus ab alio in fugam terga veteret, sed aut mortem cum laude, aut vitam cum triumpho (quod Deo utrumque facile est) habere mereventur.

[139] *Ibid.*, 7.

Frisia.[140] The works of Bede also provide a number of examples that demonstrate that the use of the sail was widespread among the Anglo-Saxons in the seventh century even on small boats, as for example that used by three monks to sail between the Farne Isles and Lindisfarne c. 683–695. Caught in a sudden storm the monks 'could make progress neither by sail nor oars' and were saved, they believed, only by the power of prayer.[141]

One final literary source which must be examined is the eighth-century Old English epic poem *Beowulf*.[142] This poem is rich in seafaring imagery and descriptions of what may have been typical small Anglo-Saxon warships of the eighth century. Beowulf's ship is broad beamed and high stemmed with ringed or spiralling figurehead carvings. It was sail driven – indeed, oars are never mentioned – and carried a crew of only 14 men.[143] So basic is the sail deemed to be to seafaring that the poet even describes the sea as the *seglrad* – the 'sail-road'.[144] A second sailing ship is described in the poem's account of the funeral of the Danish king Scyld Scefing: the king was laid to rest in the ship, surrounded by treasure, which was then set adrift on the open sea.[145] In appearance these ships must have looked very similar to the warships on the early ninth-century coins from Hedeby and the eighth-century picture stones from Gotland,[146] or the Norwegian Oseberg ship of c. 800.[147] However, it would be unjustifiable on the basis of this evidence alone to conclude that there was necessarily a close interaction between Anglo-Saxon and Scandinavian shipbuilding traditions in this period.

Anglo-Saxon Naval Power on the Eve of the Viking-Age

It is ironic that just at the point when we can be absolutely certain that the Anglo-Saxons had effective sailing ships, recorded Anglo-Saxon naval activity ceases.

---

[140] *Ibid.*, 26: 'secundum desiderium ejus flante Zephyro vento ab occidente temperanter, versis navium rostris, ad Orientem usque dum in Freis prospere cum omnibus pervenit.'

[141] Bede, V. 1: 'Et tanta ingruit tamque fera tempestati hiems, ut neque uelo neque remigio quicquam proficere.' See also III. 15 and V. 10.

[142] Despite some recent revisionism, much of it highly contrived, intended to show that *Beowulf* was written in Alfredian times or after, no one has yet bettered the arguments proposed for an eighth- or early ninth-century date presented by D. Whitelock, *The Audience of Beowulf* (Oxford, 1951), pp. 24–6, 57–64. For more recent discussions of this question, by no means all of which favour a post-Viking age date, see the articles in C. Chase (ed.), *The Dating of Beowulf*, Toronto Old English Series 6 (Toronto, 1981). See also R. D. Fulk, 'Dating *Beowulf* to the Viking age', *Philological Quarterly* LXI (1982), pp. 341–59, who effectively points out the many shortcomings of the revisionists' arguments.

[143] See the following descriptive passages: *Beowulf*, ed. C. L. Wrenn, revised edn (London, 1958), ll. 205–21, 293–8, 1896–1920.

[144] *Beowulf*, l. 1429.

[145] *Beowulf*, ll. 1–52.

[146] See Nylén, *op. cit.*, pp. 104–39, for a well illustrated discussion of these stones.

[147] For this ship see Brøgger and Shetelig, *op. cit.*, pp. 88 ff. and Greenhill, *op. cit.*, pp. 208–11.

There is no further evidence of Anglo-Saxon naval power after Ecgfrith's raid on Ireland in 684 until the mid-ninth century. Ecgfrith himself was killed by the Picts at Nechtansmere in 685; after this disaster Northumbrian power began to wane and the eighth century is marked by a stabilising of the borders between the Anglo-Saxon and Celtic kingdoms. Anglo-Saxon pirate attacks on Francia had probably died out in the course of the seventh century. It was no doubt the rulers of the Anglo-Saxon kingdoms who were responsible for this, rather than any improvements in the Frankish defences. As they converted to Christianity and consolidated their own authority in their kingdoms, the kings will have suppressed unruly elements in the interests of maintaining good relations with their Frankish neighbours.

While their naval power may have declined simply through a lack of need for it, there is ample evidence that seafaring remained of great importance to the Anglo-Saxons. Literary references to peaceful seafaring activity are common and archaeological evidence shows that ports such as Hamwih (near Southampton) and Ipswich flourished on trade with the continent.[148] In 794 Charlemagne even thought an embargo on Anglo-Saxon merchants an effective weapon in a dispute with the Mercian king Offa.[149] The sea was also the subject of scientific investigation: Bede wrote a treatise on the tides that was not to be much improved upon until Newton's time.[150] It is therefore surprising that this survey of Anglo-Saxon naval activity must end rather anticlimactically. While the Franks under Charlemagne and Louis the Pious mounted a vigorous naval response to the sudden outbreak of Viking piracy in the 790s, Anglo-Saxon measures against the early raids appear to have involved only defences on land, such as bridges to block rivers.[151] No Anglo-Saxon naval activity is recorded until 851 when a fleet commanded by king Athelstan of Kent and ealdorman Ealhhere fought and defeated a Viking fleet at Sandwich, capturing nine ships.[152] After this, it is the reign of Alfred the Great (871–99) before we again have evidence of Anglo-Saxon naval activity against the Vikings. In 875 Alfred took a fleet to sea, fought against 'seven ships' companies' (i.e. seven ships?), capturing one ship and putting the rest of the Vikings to flight. Alfred again took the fleet to sea in 882 when it defeated a force of four Danish ships, wiping out two ships' companies and capturing the rest [153]. Two years later the royal fleet destroyed a Danish fleet of 16 ships in the estuary of the river Stour in East Anglia but was

---

[148] See D. M. Wilson, 'England and the continent in the eighth century; an archaeological viewpoint', *Settimane* XXXII, pp. 219–44, and E. Sabbe, 'Les relations économiques entre Angleterre et le Continent au haut moyen age', *Le Moyen Age* LVI (1950), pp. 169–93.

[149] 149. Alcuin, *Epp.*, 100.

[150] For an account of Bede's research on the nature of the tides see W. M. Stevens, *Bede's Scientific Achievement*, Jarrow Lecture 1985 (Jarrow, 1985), pp. 13–18.

[151] N. Brooks, 'The development of military obligations in eighth and ninth century England' in P. Clemoes and K. Hughes (eds), *England before the Conquest* (Cambridge, 1971), 69—84, pp. 79-80.

[152] *ASC*, 851.

[153] *ASC*, 882.

itself soon after defeated by a larger Viking fleet.[154] In 896 Alfred had new, larger, warships built for the fleet and in the same year nine of these new vessels trapped six Danish ships in an estuary on the south coast, capturing two of them and causing heavy losses in the other ships.[155] Under Alfred's successors in the tenth century the Anglo-Saxon fleet developed into an efficient and powerful force; at its peak, under Athelstan, Edgar and Edward the Confessor, it was used effectively to create a loose Anglo-Saxon hegemony over the British Isles.[156] Yet as a defensive force the Anglo-Saxon fleet was ultimately a failure, being powerless to prevent the resurgence of Viking raiding in Aethelred's reign (978-1016) or the Norman invasion in 1066. This was a consequence of the limited seaworthiness of early medieval ships which meant that fleets could only be kept at sea for short periods. As a result, it was not possible for a defender to achieve more than a fleeting dominance over the seas around his own coasts: the initiative therefore lay usually with the attacker.

Despite these limitations to the effective use of naval power in defence, the lack of an early Anglo-Saxon naval response to the onset of Viking raiding is still puzzling: probably it was a consequence of the political fragmentation of England, of a resultant lack of political will for co-operative action and of a dissipation of the resources which were needed to build fleets strong enough to challenge the Vikings. Alfred did not have this problem as the Vikings had eliminated the other Anglo-Saxon monarchies and those parts of England which the Danes did not occupy were effectively absorbed into the kingdom of Wessex. With a united realm, Alfred was in a position to use the resources of England far more efficiently to provide effective defences against the Danes, including a reformed army and the system of fortified burghs which, in fact, played a far more important role in his success than the new fleet.

---

[154] *ASC*, 885 (884).

[155] *ASC*, 897 [896].

[156] On the later Anglo-Saxon navy see C. W. Hollister, *Anglo-Saxon Military Institutions on the Eve of the Norman Conquest* (Oxford, 1962), pp. 103–26, and Abels, *op. cit., passim*. For a brief discussion of later Anglo-Saxon warships see Cameron, *op. cit.*, pp. 325–6.

4 Frankish Naval Power from Clovis to Pippin III

The Decline of Frankish Piracy

After the 'barbarian conspiracy' of 367, Frankish piracy disappears, at least from the sources, and it is not until the reign of Charlemagne that there is again plentiful evidence for Frankish naval activity. It is impossible to be certain whether the disappearance of Frankish piracy from the surviving sources is a result of a decline in activity or simply an accident caused by a lack of literate observers in the critical areas at the critical times or by the loss at a later date of relevant source material. The problem is exacerbated by the fact that there is little evidence of hostile activity of any kind by the Salians, probably the main seafarers among the Franks, in the first half of the fifth century. Assuming that the decline in Frankish piracy was a real, rather than an apparent, phenomenon, it would probably have been a direct consequence of the gradual weakening of the Rhine frontier of the Roman empire from 400 onwards.

Even before 367, the Salian Franks had begun to settle the Roman territory of Toxandria (now north-eastern Belgium) and the emperor Julian, recognising that, because of commitments elsewhere, there was no immediate prospect of expelling them, granted the settlers official status as *foederati* in 358.[1] This in itself may have encouraged the Salians to end their pirate raids. Now that they had recognition of their settlements the Salians may have felt that they had too much to lose by provoking the Romans with pirate raids, especially as they were now more vulnerable to Roman reprisals than they had been when they were still settled north of the Rhine. As federates the Salians would have been expected to supply recruits to the Roman army, which might also have reduced piracy by siphoning off some of the more restless elements of the tribe. Perhaps they also had to supply the Romans with naval forces? As the empire weakened in the fifth century, the other Frankish tribes more and more turned their energies to raiding across the increasingly fluid land frontier and to the unobtrusive acquisition of new lands for settlement. Piracy may have declined naturally as the Franks availed themselves of easier pickings on land or settled down to consolidate new territories.

---

[1] E. Zöllner, *Geschichte der Franken bis zur Mitte des sechsten Jahrhunderts* (Munich, 1970), p. 18; E. Wightman, *Gallia Belgica* (London, 1985), pp. 209, 253; E. James, *The Franks* (Oxford, 1988), p. 51.

Compared to other barbarian peoples, such as the Vandals and the Visigoths, Frankish expansion was initially unspectacular, but by the time of Clovis' accession in 482 they had intensively occupied most of the area covered by the Roman provinces of Germania and Belgica. However, it is unlikely that Frankish seafaring ceased entirely in this period as there is some archaeological evidence of Frankish settlement or trade in south-eastern England which shows that Frankish seafarers may still have been active in the Channel.[2]

Under Clovis (482–511) the Franks were united and the last vestiges of Roman authority in Gaul were swept away. Major territorial expansion began and by the middle of the sixth century almost all of Gaul and large areas of Germany were under the control of the Merovingian kings. In the second half of the sixth century expansion ceased, and, as the internal problems of the kingdom multiplied in the seventh century, in some areas, such as on the lower Rhine, territory was actually lost. However, towards the year 700, the losses began to be recovered and expansion began anew as the weak Merovingian monarchy fell under the control of the line of capable Carolingian mayors; Pippin II, Charles Martel and finally Pippin III, who, in 751, deposed the last Merovingian king and took the crown for himself.

Though the nature of Frankish territorial expansion under the Merovingians was entirely continental, the Franks, especially in the old Salian homelands on the lower Rhine and the Scheldt, did not abandon naval warfare in this period as a number of incidents, some of them outstanding, show. Moreover, the Franks remained proud of their maritime heritage as the legend, current in the seventh century, of the descent of the Merovingian royal family from a Frankish princess and a sea monster surely shows.[3]

Hygelac's Raid and the 6th Century

The earliest evidence of Merovingian naval power is the defeat of a large Scandinavian fleet which attacked the Frankish lands on the lower Rhine at some time between 516 and 534. There can be no doubt that this was a major battle because it is recorded in four apparently independent sources.[4] The earliest and

---

[2] The case argued by V. I. Evison, *The Fifth Century Invasions South of the Thames* (London, 1965), is that southern England saw large-scale settlement by the Franks in the fifth century (summarised: pp. 79–87). Myres, *English Settlements*, pp. 127–8, is more cautious, arguing that the Frankish influences which Evison points out could be the result of trading contacts alone.

[3] I. N. Wood, 'The Channel from the 3rd to the 7th centuries AD', in S. McGrail, *Maritime Celts, Frisians and Saxons*, CBA Research Report 71 (London, 1990), p. 96. For the legend, see *Chronicarum quae dicuntur Fredegarii Scholastici libri IV*, ed. B. Krusch, *MGH. SSRM* 2, (Hanover, 1888), pp. 1–167, III. 9.

[4] On the independence of the sources see D. Whitelock, *The Audience of Beowulf* (Oxford, 1951), pp. 42–50. R. W. Chambers, *Beowulf: an Introduction*, 3rd edn (Cambridge, 1959), pp. 4–5. For a contrary view see W. Goffart, 'Hetware and Hugas: datable anachronisms in *Beowulf*', in C. Chase (ed.), *The Dating of Beowulf*, Toronto Old English Series 6 (Toronto, 1981), pp. 84-88.

fullest account of this event is that given by Gregory of Tours in his *Historiarum Libri X*, written between 575 and 594.[5] Gregory's account tells us that, at some unspecified time after the consecration of bishop Quintianus of Clermont, the Danes under their king Chlochilaic brought a fleet to Gaul and plundered one of the districts ruled by king Theodoric:

> The next thing that happened was that the Danes sent a fleet under their king Chlochilaic and invaded Gaul from the sea. They came ashore, laid waste one of the regions ruled by Theodoric and captured some of the inhabitants. They loaded their ships with what they had stolen and the men they had seized, and then set sail for home. Their king remained on the shore, waiting until the boats should have gained the open sea, when he planned to go on board. When Theodoric heard that his land had been invaded by foreigners, he sent his son Theudebert to those parts with a powerful army and all the necessary equipment. The Danish king was killed, the enemy fleet was beaten in a naval battle and all the booty was brought back on shore once more.[6]

Gregory's geographical horizons are not broad and it is an indication of the importance of this event that he has included it in his history. This passage also provides us with our best evidence for dating the raid. Gregory tells us that the raid took place after the consecration of bishop Quintianus, which was in 516, while it cannot have been later than 534, the year of Theodoric's death. A date sometime in the mid 520s seems the most likely.[7]

The raid is also referred to in a second Frankish source, the anonymous *Liber Historiae Francorum,* written *c.* 727.[8] The author clearly used Gregory of Tours'

---

[5] W. Goffart, *The Narrators of Barbarian History (AD 550–800): Jordanes, Gregory of Tours, Bede and Paul the Deacon* (Princeton, 1988), p. 124. The work was probably begun soon after the start of Gregory's episcopate in 575.

[6] Gregory of Tours, *Historiarum Libri X*, III. 3:

> His ita gestis, Dani cum rege suo nomine Chlocilaichum evectu navale per mare Gallias appentunt. Egressique ad terras, pagum unum de regno Theudorici devastant atque captivant, oneratisque navibus tam de captivis quam de reliquis spoliis, reverti ad patriam cupiunt; sed rex eorum in litus resedebat, donec navis alto mare conpraehenderent, ipse deinceps secuturus. Quod cum Theodorico nuntiatum fuisset, quod scilicet regio eius fuerit ab extraneis devastata, Theudobertum, filium suum, in illis partibus cum valido exercitu ac magno armorum apparatu direxit. Qui, interfecto rege, hostibus navali proelio superatis oppraemit omnemque rapinam terrae restituit.

Translation: L. Thorpe, *Gregory of Tours: The History of the Franks* (Penguin Classics, Harmondsworth, 1974), pp. 163–4.

[7] For a discussion of the date of the raid see G. Storms, 'The significance of Hygelac's raid', *Nottingham Medieval Studies* XIV (1970), pp. 9–10. Storms thinks that the raid probably did not take place until after *c.* 523 on the grounds that Theudebert would have been too young to lead an army much before that date. Also Chambers, *op. cit.*, pp. 381–7, who proposes a date between 520 and 531.

[8] For the date see R. A. Gerberding, *The Rise of the Carolingians and the Liber Historiae Francorum* (Oxford, 1987), p. 1.

account as one of his sources but he has also added information from another, unknown, source, which says that Chlocilaic was killed in a bloody battle and gives the *pagus Attoari* as the main target of the raid.[9] The *Attoarii*, or Chattuari, were a minor Frankish tribe settled, Storms argues convincingly on place name evidence, on the lower Rhine in the area around Nijmegen.[10] The *Liber* does not refer to a naval battle but it does mention that the Danish ships carrying the captives reached the sea, which at least tells us the naval battle referred to by Gregory did not take place in the *pagus Attoarii* which is 70 miles inland.

Finally, there are two Anglo-Saxon sources, the eighth-century Old English epic poem *Beowulf* and the Latin *Liber monstrorum de diversis generibus*, written in East Anglia around the year 800.[11] In the *Beowulf* account the raiders are called Geats rather than Danes and their king is called Hygelac, not Chlocilaic.[12] Despite the superficial dissimilarity between the names, Grundtvig demonstrated in the early nineteenth century that Hygelac and Chlocilaic refer to the same person.[13] The significance of the difference in the tribal names has been much debated but it remains uncertain whether *Beowulf* confirms or contradicts the Frankish sources at this point as the Geats may have been either Jutes from Denmark or Goths from Västergotland in Sweden.[14] On practical grounds it is perhaps more likely that the raiders originated from Jutland, only a short sailing distance from Frisia, so it seems acceptable to call them Danes after the Frankish sources rather than Geats after the Anglo-Saxon sources, though it is clearly not impossible that the raiders originated in western Sweden.

---

[9] *Liber Historiae Francorum*, ed. B. Krusch, *MGH. SSRM* 2 (Hanover, 1888), pp. 215–328, c. 19:

In illo tempore Dani cum rege suo nomine Chochilaico cum navale hoste per alto mare Gallias appetunt, Theuderico paygo Attoarios vel alios devastantes atque captivantes, plenas naves de captivis alto mare intrantes, rex eorum ad litus maris resedens. Quod cum Theuderico nuntiam fuisset, Theodobertum, filium suum, cum magno exercitu in illis partibus dirigens. Qui consequens eos, pugnavit cum eis caede magna atque prostravit, regem eorum interfecit, preda tullit et in terra sua restituit.

On the sources of the *Liber Historiae Francorum* see Gerberding, *op. cit.* pp. 38–41. Gerberding believes that the author, a Neustrian Frank, was able to draw on local written sources and oral traditions now lost. Gerberding's discussion provides an effective answer to Goffart's hypothesis, 'Hetware and Hugas', pp. 84–8, that the author invented much of his geographical information to lend credibility to his work. Also on the sources, though in less detail than Gerberding, see B. S. Bachrach, *Liber Historiae Francorum* (Lawrence, 1973), pp. 17–22.

[10] Storms, *op. cit.*, pp. 10–11. M. Gysseling, 'Germanisering en taalgrens', in D. P. Blok, *Algemene Geschiedenis der Nederlanden 1*, p. 109, locates the Hetware a further 15 miles upstream on the Rhine, around Cleves. The distance Hygelac would have had to cover would be about the same for both locations.

[11] On the date of *Beowulf*, see chapter 3, n. 135; on the *Liber monstrorum* see Whitelock, *op. cit.*, pp. 46–50.

[12] For example *Beowulf*, ed. C. L. Wrenn, rev. edn (London, 1958), l. 1202.

[13] N. F. S. Grundtvig, 'Om Bjovulfs Drape', *Dannevirke* II (1817), pp. 284–6, showed that *Chochilaic* is a corruption of *Kong Hilac* or *Got-Hilac*.

[14] See on the problem Whitelock, *op. cit.*, p. 42.

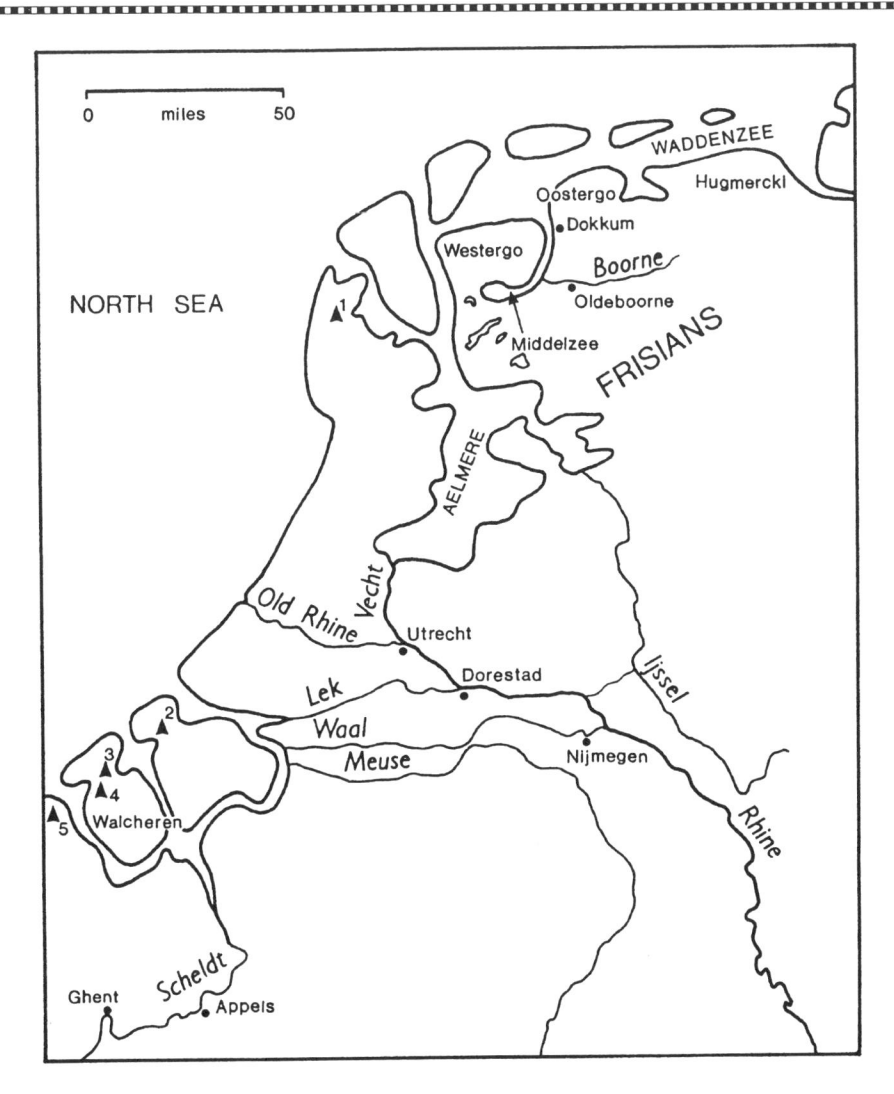

Map 3 The lower Rhine area in the early Middle Ages showing the Merovingian coastline. (John Haywood, outline based on Heidinga, *medieval Settlement and Economy North of the Lower Rhine*, p. 82, fig. 13)
Key: ▲ = Carolingian fortress: 1 Den Burgh on Texel; 2 Burgh on Schwouen; 3 Middelburg; 4 Oost Souberg; 5. Oostburg

The raid is mentioned in four passages of *Beowulf*. The first refers to the battle in which Hygelac met his death and to the booty taken by the Franks.[15] The second passage also refers to the same battle, which was fought on foot, naming the Hetware as the opponents and describing Beowulf's escape by swimming and solitary return home.[16] In the third passage Beowulf recalls how he killed

---

[15] *Beowulf,* lines 1202–1214a.
[16] *Beowulf,* lines 2354b–2368.

Dæghrefn, the champion of the Hugas.[17] It is usually accepted that the *Beowulf* poet used the name Hugas as a poetic name for the Franks,[18] yet the evidence for this, none of which dates from before 967, is extremely tenuousnd nowhere in the poem itself are the Hugas explicitly identified with the Franks.[19] It is far more likely that the Hugas were the inhabitants of the *Hugmercki*, that is modern Humsterland, the district around Groningen in Dutch Friesland,[20] and therefore almost certainly a Frisian people. The final passage describes how Hygelac's raid had earned the enmity of the Franks and the Frisians and explains his defeat in terms of the superior numbers of the Hetware.[21] The third passage seems to refer to a completely separate battle so the *Beowulf* account suggests that the raiders had successfully plundered in northern Frisia before moving on to the Frankish territory of the Hetware,[22] which, it is universally accepted, is to be identified with the *pagus Attoarii* of the *Liber Historiae Francorum*.

The *Liber monstrorum* is a collection of marvels in which Hygelac features because of his reputed giant stature. The book tells us nothing about the raid itself, merely noting that Hygelac's giant bones could still be seen on an island in

---

[17] *Beowulf*, lines 2497–2506a.

[18] For a recent exposition of this identification see Goffart, 'Hetware and Hugas', pp. 88–99. It is the norm for the standard critical editions of *Beowulf*, e.g., Wrenn, p. 314.

[19] The evidence comes from two Saxon works, the *Res gestae Saxonicae* by Widukind of Corvey, ed. G. Waitz and K. A. Kehr, rev. P. Hirsch, *MGH. SSRG* 60 (Hanover, 1935), I. 9, 'Post haec moritur Huga rex Francorum', and the *Annales Quedlinburgenses, pars prior,* ed G. H. Pertz, *MGH. SS* 3 (Hanover,1839), pp. 22–69 (p. 31), *sub anno* 532, 'Hugo Theodoricus iste dicitur, id est Francus, quia olim omnes Franci Hugones vocabantur a suo quodam duce Hugone'. Widukind's work dates from 967 (Goffart, 'Hetware and Hugas', p. 91), and Huga is used only as a personal name and appears to refer to Clovis (M. Lintzel, 'Zur Entstehungsgeschichte des sächsichen Stammes', *Sachsen und Anhalt* III (1927), p. 13). The Quedlinburg annals date from shortly after 1000, but the crucial statement, though explicit, is of doubtful value because it is an interpolation of unknown date (Lintzel, *ibid.*., p. 12). The name was almost certainly not used in any relation to the Franks before the tenth century, despite being used in relation to sixth-century events: see Goffart, 'Hetware and Hugas', pp. 94–7, and R. W. Chambers, *Widsith. A Study in Old English Heroic Legend* (Cambridge, 1912), p. 112. See also Zöllner, *op. cit.*, pp. 3–4, who dismisses the idea that the Hugas of *Beowulf* were Franks.

[20] The name first appears in the ninth-century *Vita S. Liudgeri*, ed. G. H. Pertz, *MGH. SS* 2 (Hanover, 1829), pp. 403–425, I. 19 (p. 410), in relation to mid-eighth-century events. The name *Hugmarki* is derived from 'Hugumarki', the march or border of the Hugas; see M. Gysseling, *Toponymisch Woordenboek van België, Nederland, Luxemburg, Noord-Frankrijk en West Duitsland* 1. Bouwestoffen en studiën voor de Geschiedenis en de Lexicografie van het Nederlands VI. 1 (Tongeren, 1960), pp. 524–5. Also his 'De oudste Friese toponymie', *Philologica Frisica Anno 1969* (Grins, 1970), p. 46. Also in support of the Hugas/Hugmerki connection see R. Wenskus, *Stammesbildung und Verfassung* (Cologne-Graz, 1961), pp. 527–30, and also his *Sächsicher Stammesadel und fränkischer Reichsadel*, Abhandlungen der Akademie der Wissenschaften in Göttingen, Philologisch-Historische Klasse: Folge 3: 93 (Göttingen, 1976), pp. 61–2. Wenskus, however, believes that the Hugas are to be identified with the Chauci rather than with the Frisians or Franks.

[21] *Beowulf*, lines 2913b–2921.

[22] A similar conclusion was reached by K. Müllenhoff, 'Die austrasische Dietrichssage', *Zeitschrift für deutsches Altertum* VI (1848), p. 438, who suggested that Hygelac fought two battles, one against the Frisians, which he won, and a second against the Franks, which he lost.

the Rhine.[23] These Anglo-Saxon sources are important not so much for the information they contain, for they add little that is concrete to our knowledge of the raid, but for the way they generally confirm the Frankish accounts and also demonstrate that the impact of the raid was both widespread and lasting.

As the only historically identifiable incident in Beowulf, the raid has attracted much discussion, though sometimes insufficient account has been taken of the considerable changes which the geography of the Low Countries has undergone since the sixth century.[24] The most significant of these from our present point of view is the change in the relative importance of the mouths of the Rhine. In the Roman period the main channel had been the Old Rhine but by the sixth century this had changed to the Vecht, which flowed into the Aelmere (the proto-Zuyder Zee) and which is now no longer navigable.[25]

After their successful preliminary strike against the Hugas in northern Frisia the raiders would have had a choice of two possible routes by which to penetrate Frankish territory. One possibility would have been to continue along the North Sea coast and enter the mouth of the Old Rhine, the Lek or the Waal. This would have been the longer route and the one most exposed to the elements, so it seems to me that this is the less likely of the possibilities. Alternatively the raiders could have entered the sheltered waters of the Aelmere to reach the Nijmegen district by sailing up either the Vecht or the Ijssel into the Rhine and eventually into the Waal, on which Nijmegen stands. The approach via the Vecht would have been the shorter and quicker route, requiring about four days of arduous upstream rowing, sailing and perhaps also towing, as opposed to five via the Ijssel.[26] Magoun considers that the Ijssel was the more likely route despite its greater length on the grounds that an approach via the Vecht would have taken the raiders past Dorestad, whose inhabitants, he believes, would have tried to prevent

---

[23] *Liber monstrorum de diversis generibus. De Hyglaco Getorum rege.* Latin text in Chambers, *Beowulf*, p. 4. The island is perhaps the Betuwe (Batavia), the strip of land that lies between the Rhine and Waal from their divergence to their entry into the sea.

[24] Storms, *op. cit.*, for example.

[25] Lebecq, *Marchands et navigateurs*, vol. 1, p. 124. For general accounts of the geography of the lower Rhine in the Middle Ages see A. M. Lambert, *The Making of the Dutch Landscape*, 2nd edn (London, 1985), pp. 114–122, and H. A. Heidinga, *Medieval Settlement and Economy North of the Lower Rhine* (Assen-Maastricht, 1987), *passim* (but see especially the topographical map, fig. 75, p. 176).

[26] F. P. Magoun, 'The geography of Hygelac's raid on the lands of the West Frisians and the Hætt-Ware, *c.* 530 AD', *English Studies* XXXIV (1953), pp. 160–3, estimates that the Ijssel route would have taken three to four days of rowing, the others perhaps less. This may be an underestimate; 15 miles a day was the average speed of merchant shipping sailing up the lower Rhine in the early Middle Ages (see D. Ellmers, *Frühmittelalterliche Handelsschiffahrt in Mittel- und Nordeuropa* (Neumunster, 1972), pp. 253–4) and the fleet would have had about 70 miles to cover to Nijmegen via the Vecht, 85 miles via the Ijssel. The Danish warships will have been faster than merchant ships, but not much faster. O. Höckmann ('Römische Schiffsverbände, pp. 393–4) estimates that the late Roman type-A warships from Mainz (see chapter 2), which were propelled by about 20 oarsmen and a sail, would have been capable of only about 1.5 knots upstream, even with the wind. Thus it seems appropriate to increase Magoun's estimate by one to two days.

their passage.[27] However, there is no evidence to indicate that Dorestad was a place of any importance before the early seventh century so there is no reason to think that at the time of the raid it would have proved to be an obstacle to Hygelac's fleet.[28]

This was certainly no mere hit-and-run raid.[29] Hygelac's force had penetrated deep into hostile territory and was some 70 miles from the relative safety of the open sea by the shortest route, which was down the Waal. Hygelac must have known that each day that passed increased the chances of interception by a Frankish army, yet he appears to have been in no hurry. The Franks had time to gather a large and well equipped army of infantry,[30] put a fleet to sea, and get both to the lower Rhine in time to bring the raiders to battle. Such a delay on Hygelac's part can only be explained if he was sure of his strength, in other words, if his fleet and army were large. Unfortunately for him, the Franks caught him with his forces divided.

For reasons which are quite unclear, the ships carrying the booty and the captives had sailed but Hygelac had remained on land. Perhaps the fleet had sailed downstream, carrying the captives for greater security, while Hygelac, with part of his force, marched overland with the intention of rendezvousing with the fleet on the coast. However, the Frankish royal army, probably assisted by the Frisians and local Hetware, overtook the raiders and defeated them in a bloody infantry battle in which Hygelac and most of his warriors were killed. Hygelac's fleet had probably withdrawn down the Waal as this would have been the quickest way to reach the open sea. Once there the fleet would have been effectively safe from interception, so the Frankish fleet must have caught the Danes near the mouth of the Waal. The most likely centre of Frankish naval power in this period was the area settled by the Salians around the Scheldt: Clovis possibly had a fleet stationed there at the beginning of the sixth century[31]

---

[27] Magoun, *op. cit.*, p. 162.

[28] Lebecq, *op. cit.*, vol. 1, pp. 150–2. Another factor which would be decisive, but which I am reluctant to make much of because of the uncertainty surrounding it, is the navigability of the channel which now links the Ijssel and the Rhine. Heidinga, *op. cit.*, p. 217, thinks that the Ijssel may only have functioned as a branch of the Rhine from the Carolingian period on. If so, an approach to the *pagus Attoarii* via the Ijssel would have been impossible in the early sixth century.

[29] Storms, *op. cit.*, pp. 12–16, argues that the raid had been incited by Theodoric the Great as a diversionary tactic in his struggles with the Franks, but there is no evidence to support this, as I. N. Wood, *The Merovingian North Sea*, Occasional papers on Medieval Topics I (Alingsås, 1983), p. 7, points out.

[30] *Beowulf*, lines 2364 and 2919, makes it clear that the Franks were also foot soldiers. Note also the emphasis on the size of the Frankish army in the three main sources: 'valido exercitu ac magno armorum' (*Hist.*, III. 2), 'magno exercitu' (*LHF*, 19), and *Beowulf*, lines 2916–19a. See Zöllner, *op. cit.*, p. 152, for a discussion of the battle in the context of other sources for Frankish warfare.

[31] Gregory of Tours, *Hist.* II. 40. Clovis was on board a ship in the Scheldt estuary when king Sigibert of the Ripuarian Franks was murdered at Cologne at his instigation. Unfortunately, Gregory does not tell us the ostensible reason for Clovis's presence there as he is concerned only with Clovis's actual reason, which was to provide himself with an alibi. We may

and warships' figureheads of probable Frankish origin dating from the fourth to seventh centuries have been recovered from the river.[32] A fleet based on the Scheldt would have been in a good position to intercept the raiders as they tried to escape; it had only to move to the mouth of the Waal and wait to force them to battle. The defeat of the Danish fleet seems to have been as total as that of their army on land. All the booty and prisoners are said, by Gregory of Tours, to have been recovered, so it would appear as if very few, if any, of the Danish ships escaped. It is, therefore, not surprising that this raid became a part of the heroic tradition epitomised by Beowulf, for the Franks had inflicted a crushing and decisive defeat on the Danes both by land and by sea.

That this raid penetrated deeply into Frankish territory has been challenged by Goffart.[33] He considers it unlikely that the Danes would have penetrated so far inland on what was, he believes, a first raid, his argument being that the Vikings did not begin to penetrate the river systems of the Frankish territories for over 30 years after the start of their raids. But the two cases are not directly comparable. Under Charlemagne and Louis the Pious the Frankish empire possessed an efficient system of coastal defence which successfully prevented the Vikings from penetrating inland until it began to break down due to the empire's internal problems in the 830s. Though the Merovingian kingdom plainly did possess some coastal defences (the fleet, for instance), it had nothing to compare with the Carolingian system based on fleets, fortifications and beacon chains (see chapter 5). Moreover, the Carolingians controlled all the entrances to the Rhine river system. Because of expansion along the coast south of the old Roman frontier on the Old Rhine by the Frisians in the fifth century,[34] it is probable that the Merovingians lacked direct control over several of these strategic gateways to their territory and so could not have adopted a defence system of the Carolingian type, if, indeed, their administrative abilities had been equal to the task.

More to the point, this may not have been a first raid and it was certainly not the last one before the coming of the Vikings. Sometime between 565 and 575 a Danish invasion of the region around the river Boorne in northern Frisia was

---

reasonably suspect that Clovis's alibi was that he had gone to inspect his fleet. The *Epistula ad Waldebertum et Bobolenum* by Jonas, ed. B. Krusch in *Ionae Vitae Sanctorum Columbani, Vedastis, Iohannis. MGH. SSRG* 37 (Hanover-Leipzig, 1905), pp. 144–8, refers to the river's plentiful shipping in the seventh century. The Scheldt was certainly a base for Frankish naval power in Charlemagne's reign: *Annales Regni Francorum* (henceforth *ARF*), ed. F. Kurze, *MGH. SSRG* 6 (Hanover, 1895), 811. Storms, *op. cit.*, p.14, suggests the Scheldt as the base of the Frankish fleet because the area had long been settled by the Salians.

[32] See below, pp. 132-3.

[33] Goffart, 'Hetware and Hugas', p. 86.

[34] On the ethnic expansion of the Frisians see Lebecq, *op. cit.*, vol. 1, pp. 107–10, and Heidinga *op. cit.*, pp. 178–80. The exact southern boundary of Frisian expansion is unknown, though it certainly extended south of the Old Rhine and probably to many of the islands in the Rhine estuary. To the east their expansion extended to the Ems and to the North Frisian islands and Heligoland, at that time considerably larger than it is now, which was shared with the Danes.

repulsed by a Frankish army led by duke Lupus.[35] Like Hygelac's raid, this was no hit-and-run attack, for the Franks will not quickly have been able to amass a force and advance to so remote an area. We must therefore assume that this was a raid of considerable strength settled on the area for some time. These two major incidents suggest that small scale hit and run raids by Danish pirates on Frisia may have been quite common in the sixth century, a conclusion which is supported to some extent by the Finn episode in *Beowulf*. Finn is a king of the Frisians who becomes involved in the feuds of the family of his Danish wife. The Danes kill Finn in his own home and carry his wife and treasure back to their ships. While little store can be set by this as an historical incident, the story doubtless has its origin in actual Danish raids on Frisia in the early Middle Ages.[36] The absence of evidence of raiding in the sparse Frankish sources is not significant. Such minor incidents in a remote pagan province would easily have passed unnoticed and unremarked in Francia.

It has not been widely accepted that the fleet which defeated Hygelac's Danes was actually Frankish in origin. Frisian, Saxon and Roman origins have all been suggested. However, in some cases, these claims are manifestly based on preconception rather than evidence, direct or indirect. Chambers believed that the fleet was Frisian and justified his view solely by the unsupported statement that: 'The Franks were of course a land power'.[37] As Gregory of Tours nowhere explicitly says that the fleet was Frankish, the Frisians may seem a likely

---

[35] Venantius Fortunatus, *Carmina*, ed. F. Leo, *MGH. AA* 4 (Berlin, 1881), VII. 7, *De Lupo Duco*, ll. 49–58:

> quae tibi sit virtus cum prosperitate superna,
> Saxonis et Dani gens cito victa probat.
>
> Bordaa quo fluvius sinuoso gurgite currit,
> hic adversa acies te duce caesa ruit.
>
> dimidium vestris iussis tunc paruit agmen;
> quam merito vincit qui tua iussa facit!
>
> ferratae tunicae sudasti pondere victor
> et sub pulverea nube coruscas eras,
>
> tamque diu pugnax acie fugiente secutus,
> Laugona dum vitreis terminus esset aquis.

The mistaken identification of the *Laugona* with the *Bordaa* by Venantius's editor, F. Leo, p. 160, is misleading as it makes the passage read as if Lupus fought the Saxons and Danes together at the same place. However, Venantius is actually referring to two quite separate battles; as the *Orbis Latinus*, ed. H. Plechl *et al.* (Brunswick, 1972), shows, the *Laugona* is actually the river Lahn in Hesse, then near the borders of Saxon territory and the scene also of later Saxon raids (see *ARF*, 778, and Eigil, *Vita S. Sturmi*, ed. G. H. Pertz, *MGH. SS* 2, pp. 366-77, chapter 23).

[36] *Beowulf*, lines 1068–1159. It is probable that the fragmentary *Finnsburg*, ed. A. J. Wyatt and R. W. Chambers in *Beowulf and the Finnsburg Fragment* (Cambridge, 1925), pp. 158–62, refers to the same incident. The possible historical context of the episode is discussed by A. Russchen, 'Jutes and Frisians', *It Beaken* XXVI (1964), pp. 33–5.

[37] Chambers, *Beowulf*, p. 341

candidate but there is in fact no evidence earlier than the late seventh century to suggest that they were an important seafaring people. Bachrach also justifies his view that the fleet was not Frankish by an unsupported statement, one which is highly inaccurate into the bargain: 'there is no record... of the Franks as an ethnic group taking part in any noteworthy naval activity either before or after this event [i.e. Hygelac's raid]'.[38] He proposes instead that the fleet was Roman in origin, a remnant of the Channel fleet, maintained by the Merovingians for coastal defence. This does not seem likely. The latest evidence which we have for the presence of a Roman fleet in the Channel is the appearance of the *classis Sambrica* in the *Notitia Dignitatum*.[39] As the Notitia was compiled in its basic form in the late 390s and was thereafter revised only in a haphazard fashion up to c. 408,[40] it is quite impossible to be certain that the fleet was still in existence even in the early fifth century, let alone in the early sixth. The presence of Saxon settlements on the Channel coast of Gaul after the mid-fifth century suggests that there was probably no Roman naval presence in the Channel for the Franks to take over by that time.[41]

The Saxons are themselves another possibility and, as we have seen, they certainly did perform military service for the Franks on land at times.[42] But though there were Saxons settled in the Boulonnais, their main settlement in Gaul was in the area of Bayeux,[43] too far from the scene of the battle to have made any intervention on their part likely. Also, Gregory of Tours was very aware of the military and other activities of the Saxons;[44] had they played an important role in this battle we might expect that he would have mentioned it.

In short, there is no obvious reason to conclude that the fleet which routed the Danes was not Frankish and the onus of proof clearly lies with those who would have it otherwise. The Franks had for long lived around the mouths of the Rhine and, as we have seen, had certainly performed many noteworthy naval exploits in the past. This incident should therefore be considered as important evidence pointing to a continuing naval tradition among the Franks in the sixth century.

Though the defeat of Hygelac provides the only direct evidence of Frankish naval power in this period, the effectiveness of the fleet shows that the crews

---

[38] B. S. Bachrach, *Merovingian Military Organisation, 481–751* (Minneapolis, 1972), p. 34.

[39] *Notitia Dignitatum*, ed. O. Seeck (Berlin, 1876), Occ. xxxviii.8. The fleet was probably based on the Somme and/or Étaples, on the Canche.

[40] J. C. Mann, 'What was the *Notitia Dignitatum* for?', in R. Goodburn and P. Bartholomew (eds), *Aspects of the Notitia Dignitatum*, BAR Supp. Ser. 15 (Oxford, 1976), p. 8.

[41] Our understanding of the extent of Roman control over the Channel coast of Gaul in the fifth century is hampered by a lack of archaeological evidence from which to date the abandonment of Roman coastal fortifications: C. Seillier, 'Boulogne and the coastal defences in the fourth and fifth centuries', in D. C. Johnston (ed.), *The Saxon Shore*, CBA Research Report 18 (London, 1977), p. 36.

[42] James, *op. cit.*, p. 104. James cites the fleet as probable evidence of Frankish naval power but reserves the possibility that it may have been provided by Frisian or Saxon allies.

[43] See chapter 3, n. 48, on the Saxon settlement in the Bessin.

[44] Gregory of Tours *Hist.*, II. 18–19, V. 15, 26, VII. 46, X. 9.

were no novices. This effectiveness was probably the result of experience gained in clashes with Anglo-Saxon pirates who, rather than the Danes, would have been the Frankish fleet's most likely opponents. While Frankish piracy seems to have died away by the fifth century, the piracy of the Saxons, joined now by Angles and Heruls, had intensified and begun to develop in a way comparable to ninth century Viking piracy. The raids of the Angles and Saxons on the Channel and Atlantic coasts of Gaul were to continue into the seventh century, ceasing only when recognisable kingdoms, concerned about their relations with neighbouring states and able to control the behaviour of their subjects, began to be consolidated in England.

Frankish naval power seems never to have been sufficient to drive the Anglo-Saxon pirates from the seas but there were times when it certainly was sufficient to enforce some kind of authority on the English side of the Channel. The Franks would have had a natural interest in achieving this state of affairs, as it would have given them the means at least to reduce piracy and increase the security of their northern coasts.[45] In its legislation for the return of servi who had been carried off 'trans mare' (i.e. to England), the *Pactus Legis Salicae* from the end of Clovis' reign provides evidence not only for the existence of Anglo-Saxon piracy but also for the exercise of Frankish authority in England.[46] For the code lays down the procedure to be followed in the foreign court to secure the return of the servi to their original lords. This would have been pointless unless Clovis's authority was recognised trans mare[47] and only the possession of effective naval power could have brought this situation about.

Later in the same century, Frankish ambassadors to the eastern Roman emperor Justinian at Constantinople claimed that their kings held sovereignty over Britain.[48] Despite the probability of limited Frankish settlement in south-eastern England in the fifth century, this claim almost certainly reflected Frankish aspirations rather than reality. Even so, it would be surprising if the Frankish claim had no basis in reality whatsoever. The most likely context for the claim, which Justinian did not accept, is that the influential position achieved by Clovis had been maintained but the Franks were hoping to use the prestige of the empire to strengthen their position in England. If so, the least that the Frankish claim to sovereignty indicates is that Clovis' immediate successors had maintained an effective fleet with which they could at least contemplate an attack on England to enforce their authority if necessary. Even at the end of the sixth century it is clear that the Frankish kings regarded Kent, at least, as being part of their sphere of

---

[45] James, *op. cit.*, p. 103.

[46] *Pactus Legis Salicae*, ed. K. A. Eckhardt, *MGH. LL* 4.1 (Hanover, 1962), 39.2.

[47] On the possible nature and extent of the Frankish hegemony over southern England see Wood, *op. cit.*, pp. 12–15.

[48] Procopius, *History of the Wars*, ed. and trans. H. B. Dewing, Loeb Classical Library (5 vols, London, 1913–28), VIII. xx. 8–10. For a helpful discussion of the Frankish embassy see A. R. Burn, 'Procopius and the island of ghosts', *English Historical Review* LXX (1955), p. 259.

influence while the marked concentration in Kent of gold coins from Frankish mints also speaks of close relations.[49] Whether these coins found their way to Kent as a result of trade or were paid to the kings of Kent as a subsidy in return for submission to the Merovingians is not known. Frankish naval power is also implied by the panegyric poem which Venantius Fortunatus addressed to king Chilperic (561–84) in which he claims that the Danes and Euthians (probably the Jutes) were within the Merovingians' sphere of influence.[50]

It is also possible that Frankish ships were active around the coast of Brittany in the sixth century. In 556, king Lothar's son Chramn rebelled and allied with the Bretons. Lothar sent an army against him and Chramn was defeated. However, Chramn had a number of ships at his disposal on the coast against such an eventuality, kept in readiness to put to sea as soon as they were required.[51] If they were to have provided a sure means of escape, Chramn's ships would probably have been oared warships which did not have to wait on a suitable wind. In the event Chramn lost time trying to save his family and was captured and killed. Since Chramn's allies, the Bretons, were themselves great seafarers, it is possible, however, that these ships were not Frankish but Breton.

It should be said in passing that the Franks would have been in no way exceptional among the barbarian successor states in maintaining naval forces. During their wars with the emperor Justinian in the sixth century, the Ostrogoths engaged in an ambitious naval shipbuilding programme.[52] The Visigothic kingdom appears to have controlled naval forces throughout most of its existence: a fleet was maintained on the Garonne in the 470s [53]; in 583 the river Guadalquivir was blockaded to force the surrender of Seville[54]; King Sisebut used a fleet to transport an army to northern Spain for a campaign against the Basques in 613[55] and Isidore of Seville refers in glowing terms to Sisebut's achievement in building up Visigothic naval power[56]. Wamba (r. 672–80) led a naval expedition against Nîmes [57] and according to a late and unverifiable source, during his reign the Visigoths destroyed a Saracen fleet of 270 ships

---

[49] Wood, *op. cit.*, pp. 12–13.

[50] Venantius Fortunatus, *Carmina*, IX, 1, ll. 73–6.

[51] Gregory of Tours, *Hist.*, IV. 20: 'naves in mare paratus habens'.

[52] Cassiodorus, *Variae*, ed. T. Mommsen, *MGH. AA* XII (Berlin, 1894), V. 16-20.

[53] Sidonius, *Epp.*, VIII. 6. To Namatius, 13-15.

[54] John of Biclar, *Chronica*, ed. T. Mommsen, *MGH. AA* 11, *Chronica Minora* II (Berlin,, 1894), pp. 207-23, ch. 66 (it is possible from the context that a physical obstruction of the river is meant, rather than a naval blockade).

[55] *Epistulae Sisebuti regis Gothorum*, ed J. Fontaine in *idem*, *Isidore de Séville: traité de la nature* (Bordeaux, 1960), pp. 329–35, ll. 7–8.

[56] Isidore of Seville, *Historia Gothorum*, ed. T. Mommsen, *MGH. AA* 11, *Chronica Minora* II (Berlin, 1894), pp. 268-95, ch. 70.

[57] Julian of Toledo, *Historia Wamba regis*, ed. B. Krusch and W. Levison, *MGH. SSRM 5* (Hanover, 1910), pp. 501-26, chs 12-13.

which attacked the coast of Spain.[58] However, this source does not explicitly say that Visigothic naval forces were responsible – the fleet is perhaps more likely to have been captured and burned when beached. The Vandal kingdom of Carthage also maintained a strong navy which inflicted humiliating defeats on Roman fleets in 460 and 468 and even sacked Rome itself in 455. It also enabled them to build a maritime empire including the Balearic Islands, Corsica, Sardinia and part of Sicily.[59] The Germanic barbarians, it seems, were never slow to appreciate the value of naval power.

Frankish Naval Activity in the Later Merovingian Period

The next known area of Frankish naval operations is Frisia, towards the end of the Merovingian period. The Frisians have a very low profile in the sources before the late seventh century and it is difficult to be certain what their status was in the early Merovingian period, though by the early seventh century we can be sure that they were in some kind of official subjection to the Franks, while the Frisian settled areas south of the Old Rhine, along with the whole course of the lower Rhine, came under direct Frankish rule.[60] Soon after 650, however, the Frisians achieved full independence, the Franks lost control over the mouths of the Rhine and the Frisians extended their territory inland to the town of Dorestad. Dorestad had by this time begun to develop as a major trading emporium and was important enough to be the seat of a Frankish mint between 630 and 650.[61] The disappearance of the mint *c.* 650 in all probability marks the start of Frisian independence.[62] Possession of Dorestad gave the Frisians control over one of northern Europe's most important trade routes, that between the North Sea and Mediterranean Europe via the Rhine, and for this reason the town must quickly have become a centre of Frisian power.

---

[58] *Crónica de Alfonso III*, cited in P. D. King, *Law and Society in the Visigothic Kingdom* (Cambridge, 1972), p. 198.

[59] Wood, *op. cit.* p. 7, points to their appearance in the *Lex Ribuaria* ,of Dagobert's reign (623–39) where they are accorded the same wergilds as other Merovingian subjects such as the Burgundians, Alamans, Bavarians and Saxons. See also Russchen, *op. cit.*, p. 33.

[60] See H. J. Diesner, *Das Vandalenreich*, pp.53–74, 124–8, and C. Courtois, *Les Vandales et l'Afrique*, pp. 185–204.

[61] Lebecq, *op. cit.*, vol. 1. p. 150. W. A. van Es and W. J. H. Verwers, *Excavations at Dorestad 1. The harbour: Hoogstraat 1* (Amersfoort, 1980), pp. 294–9; D. Jellema, 'Frisian trade in the Dark Ages', *Speculum* XXX (1955), p. 17. The town reached its apogee in the period 675–850.

[62] The Ravenna Cosmographer lists both Dorestad and the mouth of the Rhine as being in Frisian territory (*Ravennatis Anonymi Cosmographia*, ed. J. Schnetz in *Itineraria Romana* II (Leipzig, 1940), pp. 1–110, I. 11 and IV. 24). According to Lebecq, *op. cit.*, vol. 1, p. 205, the Frisians must have become independent sometime between *c.* 650, when the mint ceased, and 667–70, when the *Cosmographia* was written.

Around this time also, the Frisians acquired a reputation as pirates, according to a geographical poem of the seventh century.[63] This piracy cannot have approached Saxon or Viking piracy in seriousness for no other contemporary source mentions it.[64] It may be that the piracy was not very wide ranging but preyed primarily on ships plying the sheltered but confined waters of the Aelmere and the Waddensee between Francia and Scandinavia.

The loss of Dorestad and the dues which would have been levied on trade there must have been a serious blow to the Frankish kingdom,[65] and the recovery of the town was the first objective of the reconquest of Frisia begun by the Austrasian Mayor, Pippin II, in the 680s. After two preliminary campaigns,[66] Pippin marched on Dorestad in c. 689.[67] Dorestad was defended by an army under the Frisian *dux*, Radbod, which met the Frankish army in battle outside the town. The Frisian battle line broke under the Frankish assault and Radbod was forced to flee to avoid capture.[68] Though described as a *castrum* in the sources, archaeological evidence indicates that Dorestad was probably not fortified at this

---

[63] *Versus de Asia et de Universi Mundi Rota*, anonymously edited in *Corpus Christianorum, series Latina CLXXV, Itineraria et alia geographica* (Turnhout, 1965), pp. 435–54, xxiii, lines 67–9:

> Interfuso Ociano   ibi manent Saxones,
> Agiles et cor durati   et in armis validi,
> Scridifinni et Frisones   valentque piratici.

D. Norberg, *La poésie latine rythmique du haut moyen âge*, Studia Latina Holmiensis 2 (Stockholm, 1954), pp. 82–6, argues that the poem was written in Provence or Spain in the late seventh century. The *Scridifinni* who appear in line 69 are probably the 'ski Finns' i.e. Lapps.

[64] There is, however, one reference in the twelfth-century *Gesta Danorum* by Saxo Grammaticus to a Frisian warrior called Ubbo who was defeated by the Danes while raiding on the coast of Jutland (Saxo Grammaticus, *Gesta Danorum*, eds J. Olrik and H. Raeder (2 vols, Copenhagen, 1831), VII. x. 9 (vol. 1, p. 208)). If this incident has a historical basis it could have taken place at any time between the mid-sixth and early eighth centuries. K. Malone, 'Ubbo Fresicus at Bravellir', *Classica et Mediaevalia*, VIII (1946), pp. 116–120, prefers the earlier dating on literary evidence. G. Jones, *A History of the Vikings* (Oxford, 1973), p. 54, proposes a date at the beginning of the eighth century on a possibly more reliable 'dead reckoning' approach.

[65] J. M. Wallace-Hadrill, *The Barbarian West, 400–1000*, 3rd edn (London, 1967), p. 79.

[66] *Annales Mettenses priores*, ed. B. Von Simson, *MGH. SSRG* 10 (Hanover-Leipzig, 1905), 691, 692. The chronology of the *Annales Mettenses priores* is often unreliable, but their historical value, once considered to be doubtful, has now been established. See F. L. Ganshof, 'L'historiographie dans la monarchie franque sous les Mérovingiens et les Carolingiens', *Settimane XVII, La storiografia altomedievale* (Spoleto, 1970), vol. 2 pp. 677–9. Also Lebecq, *op. cit.*, vol. 2, p. 327, citing I. Haselbach, *Aufstieg und Herrschaft der Karolinger in der Darstellung der sogennanten Annales Mettenses Priores* (Lübeck-Hamburg, 1970). The actual date of these two campaigns cannot be determined but they seem likely to have taken place in the 680s rather than the 690s.

[67] *Chronicarum Fredegarii continuationes*, ed. B. Krusch, *MGH. SSRM* 2 (Hanover, 1888), pp. 168–93, chapter 6, *Annales Mettenses priores*, 697. All that can be said with certainty about the date of this campaign is that it must have taken place before the start of St Willibrord's Frisian mission in 695. Less helpful on this question than might be expected is Lebecq, *op. cit.* vol. 1, pp. 111–17, who discusses the conquest in general terms only

[68] *Chron. Fred. cont.*, chapter 6.

Dark Age Naval Power

time and could not have withstood a siege.[69] After the battle, which was perhaps forced on Radbod by the town's lack of defences, Dorestad fell once again into Frankish hands along with all the Frisian territory south of the Old Rhine.[70] Frisian power was not broken, however, and the Frisians continued to be able to challenge Frankish control of the Rhine, to judge from the occasion in 716, when Radbod took a fleet up the Rhine as far as Cologne, causing great damage and inflicting heavy losses on a Frankish counter attack.[71]

The geography of Frisia in the early Middle Ages was very favourable for defence since the low-lying marshy terrain, broken up by swamps, fens, tidal creeks, rivers and lakes, would have made progress arduous for a land army and would have been ideal for guerrilla warfare.[72] It is therefore not surprising that the Frisians were not finally subjugated until, in 734, Charles Martel led a naval expedition against them, which, judged by its results, must be considered one of the outstanding naval campaigns of the early Middle Ages. Thanks largely to the account of Fredegar's continuator we are relatively well informed about the course of this decisive campaign.[73] After Pippin II's successful campaign of 689, it was Utrecht, strategically positioned at the divergence of the Rhine and the Vecht, rather than Dorestad, which had become the main Frankish military and ecclesiastical centre for the conquest and conversion of the Frisians,[74] and it was probably here that Charles gathered his fleet and army. From there the fleet

---

[69] For example by Fredegar's continuator, chapter 6. No archaeological evidence of fortifications has yet been discovered: see Lebecq, *op. cit.* vol. 1, p. 151.

[70] Bede, *Historia Ecclesiastica Gentis Anglorum*, ed. B. Colgrave and R. A. B. Mynors, *Bede's Eccliastical History of the English People* (Oxford, 1969), V. 10.

[71] *Gesta Abbatum Fontanellensium*, ed. S. Loewenfeld, *MGH. SSRG* 28 (Hanover, 1886), chapter 3: 'Eodem denique anno venit Radbodus, dux Frisonum, navali ordine usque Coloniam urbem'. Also *Chron. Fred. cont.* chapter 9, and *Adonis archiepiscopi Viennensis chronico*, ed. G. H. Pertz, *MGH. SS* 2 (Hanover, 1829), pp. 315–23, *sub anno* 715. Both the *Annales Petaviani*, ed. G. H. Pertz, *MGH. SS* 1 (Hanover, 1826), pp. 7–18, s.a. 716, and the *Annales Mosellani*, ed J. M. Lappenberg, *MGH. SS* 16 (Hanover, 1859), pp. 494–9, 716, mention the unsuccessful counter-attack.

[72] In the eleventh century the area was described thus: 'Fresio regio est maritima, inviis inaccessa paludibus' (Adam of Bremen, *Gesta Hammaburgensis ecclesiae pontificum*, ed. B. Schmeidler, *MGH. SSRG* 2 (Hanover, 1917), I. 12, schol. 3 (p. 15). On the geography of this area in the early Middle Ages see Lambert, *op. cit.*, pp. 77–89.

[73] *Chron. Fred. cont.*, chapter 17:

Itemque, quod superius praetermissus, gentem dirissimam maritimam Frigionum nimis crudeliter rebellantam, praefatus princeps audacter navale evectione praeparat; certatim alto mare ingressus, navium copia adunata, Unistrachia [Westergo] et Austrachia [Oostergo] insulas Frigionum penetravit, super Bordine fluvio [R. Boorne] castra ponens. Bubonem gentilem ducem illorum fraodolentum consiliarium interfecit, exercitum Frigionum prostravit, fana eorum idolatria contrivit atque conbussit igne; cum magna spolia et praeda victor reversus est in regnum Francorum.

See also *Annales S. Amandi*, ed. G. H. Pertz, *MGH. SS* 1, (Hanover, 1826), pp. 6–14, 734, and *Annales Petaviani*, 734.

[74] Lebecq, *op. cit.*, vol. 1, pp. 147-8.

would have sailed down the Vecht and through the Aelmere to the open sea.[75] After reaching the open sea the fleet sailed east, ravaging Westergo as it went, before entering the Middelzee. Though the Middelzee has now been totally reclaimed from the sea, at that time it penetrated some 30 miles inland between Westergo and Oostergo. Though Fredegar's continuator describes Westergo and Oostergo as *insulae*, they were probably even then not true islands but were nevertheless isolated from the rest of Frisia by creeks, lakes and fens[76] and so could only effectively be attacked by using a fleet. After sailing the length of the Middelzee, and presumably ravaging both shores, the fleet attacked the area around the river Boorne, which was probably the centre of Frisian power. From the Frankish point of view, the campaign was a triumphant success. The resistance of the Frisians was completely overwhelmed, their army was crushed, their *dux* was killed and their lands were plundered. The Frankish victory also represented a victory for Christianity over paganism and the shrines of the Frisians' native gods were destroyed by fire. The Franks must have left an occupying force behind to hold the area in subjection, for a fort was built in the heart of Frisian territory, on the river Boorne, perhaps at Oldeboorn.[77]

The conquest did not result in the immediate and full incorporation Frisia into the Frankish kingdom. There was still a *rex Frigionum* in 747, when Pippin III had to call on Frisian aid against the Saxons,[78] and Frisian resistance to Christianity remained strong in the second half of the eighth century. Even as late as Charlemagne's reign the Frisians were capable of rebelling, but they never again came close to regaining their independence.

This spectacular and decisive success may not have been Charles Martel's only naval campaign against the Frisians. The *Annales S. Amandi* record that Charles had also campaigned in Westergo in 733.[79] This 733 campaign is recorded in the *Annales Mettenses priores* under the year 734, the second campaign, i.e. that of 734, being recorded under 736. Given the difficulties of the terrain and the inaccessibility of Westergo by land, it would probably be correct to conclude that this campaign, like its successor, involved a naval expedition.[80]

---

[75] This was the route taken by St Boniface to reach the same area on his final mission to the Frisians in 754, that which ended in his martyrdom: *Vita Bonifatii auctore Willebaldo presbytero*, (*Vitae Sancti Bonifatii archiepiscopi Moguntini*, ed. W. Levison *MGH. SSRG* 57 (Hanover Leipzig, 1905), pp. 1–58), chapter 8 (p. 47).

[76] See Lambert, *op. cit.*, pp. 77–89.

[77] Oldeboorn has been identified with *Bordonchar*, one of only three *civitates* listed by the Ravenna Cosmographer as being in Frisian territory (IV. 23) see Lebecq, *op. cit.*, vol. 2, p. 206. It would not be surprising if Charles sited the fort where it could dominate one of the Frisians' few urban centres. The two other *civitates* are *Dorostates* (I. 11) and *Nocdac* (IV. 23). Lebecq, *ibid.*, identifies *Nocdac* with Dokkum.

[78] *Chron. Fred. cont.* chapter 31.

[79] *Annales. S. Amandi*, 733: 'Karlus cum exercitu venit in Wistragou'.

[80] This conclusion is also drawn by W. Vogel, *Geschichte der deutschen Seeschiffsfahrt*, (Berlin, 1915), p. 75.

In his account of the campaign of 734, Fredegar's continuator describes the Frisians as the 'most fearsome maritime race',[81] and it is as seafarers that the Frisians are best known in the early Middle Ages. It is noteworthy, therefore, that the Franks seem to have faced no Frisian naval opposition on the decisive campaign of 734.[82] In fact, despite their prominence as merchant seafarers, evidence that the Frisians were a naval power is surprisingly lacking. This is significant because it has often been claimed that the Frankish conquest of the Frisians was a factor contributing to the success of the Viking raids which began later in the century since it destroyed the only naval power which could have stopped them.[83] But even if the Frisians were a strong naval power, this conclusion does not stand up to examination: if the Frisians could not defeat the Franks at sea, they could hardly have defeated the Vikings either. Frisian mercantile shipping was undeniably important and, if anything, the Frankish conquest stimulated rather than impaired its development. The failure of the Frisians, therefore, to develop any noteworthy naval power, either independently or, later, within the Carolingian military system, is curious and not obviously explicable;[84] perhaps there were simply too few of them.

On the inland waterways, the early Merovingians appear to have been impotent, if the supposedly sixth-century *Vita Genovefae* is to be believed, as Clovis was unable to prevent Paris from being supplied by boat after he had defeated Syagrius in 486.[85] However, by the early seventh century the Merovingian kings do appear to have had numbers of ships at their disposal on the major rivers of the kingdom. After being expelled from his monastery at Luxeuil by king Theuderic in 609, St Columbanus was sent under guard on a journey into exile which involved a voyage of several days down the Loire in a small flotilla of river craft, propelled by crews of oarsmen and carrying, as well as him and his guards, tents and provisions. At Nantes he was put on a ship to Ireland but he landed back in Gaul and took refuge with king Theudebert who provided him with boats and an escort to take him up the Rhine on his way to Italy.[86]

---

[81] *Chron. Fred. cont.* chapter 17: 'gentem dirissimam maritimam Frigionum'.

[82] If there had been effective naval opposition, then Charles's expedition would have failed. If there had been unsuccessful naval opposition, then Fredegar's continuator would surely have reported the defeat of the Frisian fleet along with the other achievements of the expedition.

[83] For example, F. M. Stenton, *Anglo-Saxon England*, 3rd edn (Oxford, 1971), p. 240, Chadwick, *The Origins of the English Nation*, (Cambridge, 1907), p. 88, n. 2, and G. Duby, *The Early Growth of the European Economy* (London, 1974), p. 113. In a similar vein is Wallace-Hadrill, *op. cit.*, p. 96 (though with the emphasis on Charlemagne's conquest of the east Frisians).

[84] Only at the end of the ninth century do Frisians appear at all prominently in naval warfare, in the service of king Alfred: see *ASC*, 897 (A version). The Frisians also defeated a Viking fleet in a naval battle on the Rhine in 885: see *Annales Fuldenses*, ed. G. H. Pertz, *MGH. SS* 1, (Hanover, 1926), pp. 343–415, *s.a.* 885.

[85] *Vita Genovefae*, ed. B. Krusch, *MGH. SSRM* 3 (Hanover, 1896), pp. 204–38, chapters, 35, 39.

[86] *Vita Columbani, Liber I*, ed. B. Krusch, *MGH. SSRG* 37, (Hanover-leipzig, 1905), pp. 148–224, chapters 20–23, 27.

It would be interesting to know if Merovingian armies ever used boats for building pontoon bridges on campaign, as the Carolingian armies were to do later. On at least one occasion a Merovingian army did build bridges while on campaign. Around the year 590 the Frankish army campaigning in Brittany built bridges over the river Oust.[87] This is not a major river and bridging it would not have posed the same problems as bridging the Elbe or Danube as Charlemagne's armies were able to do (see chapter 5). Nevertheless, pontoon bridges were known in the sixth century and used as substitutes for more lasting structures. Gregory of Tours gives an example of a bridge over the Loire which was supported on two boats.[88] However, the bridge had been replaced by a ferry by the time Gregory was writing. Though easy to build, pontoon bridges require a lot of maintenance if they are not to be washed away;[89] perhaps this one did not get it.

From the end of the Merovingian period, there are two examples of the Franks using ships on inland waterways in military operations. In 737 a Saracen invasion force was heavily defeated by Charles Martel in the valley of Corbières near Narbonne. The survivors fled towards the sea, trying to escape across the coastal lagoons near Narbonne, some in boats, some desperately swimming. But the pursuing Franks also took to boats, caught the Saracens and made short work of them, killing many with sword and spear and drowning others.[90] In 749 Pippin III prepared a naval force to launch an assault on Bavarian rebels who had taken up a defensive position beyond the river Enns. In the event, however, Pippin did not need to use his fleet because the rebels observed his preparations and decided to surrender.[91] These incidents are precursors of the ambitious and imaginative use of river fleets by the Franks in the reign of Pippin's son and successor, Charlemagne.

Merovingian Warships

Evidence for the characteristics of the warships which the Franks used in the Merovingian period is in very short supply: there is no major find of a seagoing ship from the Frankish area which dates to this period and iconographical

---

[87] Gregory of Tours, *Hist.*, X. 9: 'pontes desuper statuunt sicque exercitus omnis transivis'.

[88] *Ibid.*, V. 49.

[89] D. Hill, *A History of Engineering in Classical and Medieval Times* (London, 1984), p. 65.

[90] *Chron. Fred. cont.* chapter 20:

> illisque mutuo confligentibus, Sarraceni devicti atque prostrati, cernentes regem eorum interfectum, in fugam lapsi terga verterunt, qui evaserant cupientes navali evectione evadere, in stagno maris natantes, namque sibimet mutuo conatu insiliunt. Franci cum navibus et iaculis armatoriis super eos insiliunt suffocantesque in aquis interimunt.

> *Annales Fuldenses*, 734, surely describes the same incident. According to J. M. Wallace-Hadrill, *The Fourth Book of the Chronicle of Fredegar* (London, 1960), p. 95, n. 1, the lagoon was probably the Etang de Leucate.

[91] *Chron. Fred. cont.* chapter 32.

Figure 13 Figureheads from the River Scheldt, (a) Zele, (b) Appels, (c) Moerzeke
(Ellmers, *Frümittelalterliche Handelsschiffahrt*)

evidence is almost non existent. The main evidence for Frankish warships comes from the two, possibly three, ships' figureheads which have been dredged from the river Scheldt near Antwerp.[92] The finest of these, from Appels, is a fierce beaked monster, about 4½ feet tall and carved from oak. At its base it has a perforated tenon by which it could be slotted into the stem or deck of a ship. It has been radiocarbon dated to AD 400±150. The other heads, which are both

---

[92] See R. L. S. Bruce-Mitford, *The Sutton Hoo Ship Burial. Vol. 1. Excavation, Background, the Ship, Dating and Inventory* (London, 1975), pp. 382–4, 434, and *idem, Aspects of Anglo-Saxon Archaeology*, (London, 1974), pp. 175–87. See also H. E. F. Vierck, 'The origin and date of the ship's figurehead from Moerzeke Mariekerke, Antwerp', *Helinium* X (1970), pp. 139–49. S. J. de Laet, 'Wooden animal heads of Carolingian times found in the river Scheldt (Belgium)', *Acta Archaeologica* XXVII (1956), pp. 127–37, contains worthwhile descriptive material but his dating has been rendered obsolete by subsequent radiocarbon dating.

broken off at the neck, from Moerzeke and Zele are radiocarbon dated to AD 350±70 and 69±180 respectively. It should be remembered that the radiocarbon date gives only the age of the wood; in each case the date of deposition may have been considerably later. The Zele head is only just over two feet tall and it is thought possible that it is from a large piece of furniture or a cart, rather than a ship.[93] All are thought to be Frankish but they can tell us very little about the ships they may have adorned. At best it can be said, on the evidence of the substantial tenon at the base of the Appels figurehead, that the particular ship which this figurehead comes from was not built in the same way as the more or less contemporary Anglo-Saxon ships from Nydam and Sutton Hoo. Such a massive tenon could not have been fitted to the narrow, raking stems of these ships.[94] If it is true that the Frankish pirates of the third and fourth centuries used ships which were closely related to Romano-Celtic types, as proposed in chapter 2, then the Merovingians probably continued to use ship types based on them. The Appels head could certainly have been fitted prominently to the bow or stern of a warship like the late Roman ships from Mainz.

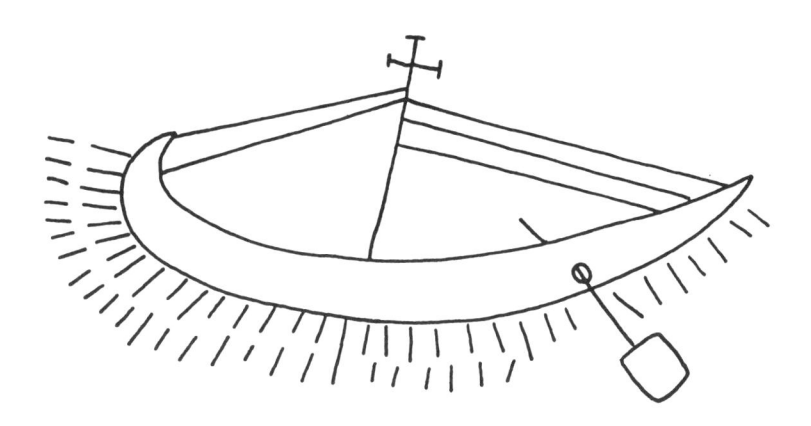

Figure 14 A ship from a Merovingian strap end found in northern France.

A metal strap end from a seventh-century Merovingian cemetery in northern France bears an engraving of a ship with a bow which is taller and steeper than the stern.[95] The ship carries a mast and standing rigging, so was presumably a sailing ship, and has a large side rudder near the stern. A series of hatched marks running along the whole length of the bottom of the hull might be representations of oars, in which case the ship is probably a warship. However, as one would not expect to find rowing oars positioned behind the side rudder, or running right up

---

[93] Bruce-Mitford, *Anglo Saxon Archaeology*, p. 179.
[94] Bruce-Mitford, *Sutton Hoo*, pp. 382–4.
[95] Bruce-Mitford, *ibid.*, p. 423.

to the bow, the marks may be stylised waves. The shape of this ship bears some resemblance to the ships featured on early ninth-century coins from Dorestad and Quentovic which are discussed in more detail in the following chapter. (p. 179)

It would probably be a mistake to look for a specifically Frankish shipbuilding tradition; Germanic, Roman and Celtic influences might all have played a part in its development. The evidence as it stands is far too slight for any more definite conclusions to be reached.

Before moving on to the reign of Charlemagne, it is worth stressing once again that, though evidence for Frankish naval power in the Merovingian period is scarce, such evidence, direct and indirect, as we do possess points convincingly to the maintenance of a tradition of naval warfare by the Franks throughout the period. The main area of Frankish naval activity in this period, the Channel and the Low Countries, coincides with one of the areas longest and most densely settled by the Franks. There can have been no shortage of men in this area engaged in seafaring for trade, fishing and, maybe, even piracy; and the skills of these men and of the shipwrights who supplied them, will have formed the basis of Frankish naval power in the region. There is no reason to believe that the Merovingians possessed a professional navy, and service in the fleet may well have been levied on seamen in lieu of taxes or service in the army.[96] Such a system does not preclude the possibility that other ethnic groups with seafaring experience, such as the Frisians or Saxons, who were subject to the Franks also performed naval service on similar conditions. But the core of Merovingian naval power must always have been ethnically Frankish.

Some historians have difficulty crediting the Franks with any naval prowess whatsoever.[97] However, nothing which has been described here is at all out of character with either the earlier or the later history of the Franks. Though the Merovingian Franks may not have been the equals of the Anglo-Saxons as seafarers, we should have no hesitation in concluding that they were one of the most important naval powers of northern Europe at the time – certainly, on the evidence, more important than their neighbours, the Frisians, and than the Danes.

---

[96] Procopius, VIII. xx. 49, tells us that the fishermen of northern Gaul had had the burden of tribute remitted by the Franks in return for performing the duty of ferrying dead souls across the Channel to Britain. While the substance of the tale is plainly fantastic, the notion of service being performed in lieu of tribute is quite credible. See also Wood, *op. cit.*, p. 6.

[97] H. Sproemberg, 'Die Seepolitik Karls des Grossen' in *idem, Beiträge zur belgische-niederländischen Geschichte*, Forschungen zur mittelalterlichen Geschichte 3 (Berlin, 1959), pp. 6–7, takes an extreme view and denies that the Frankish kingdom possessed any basis whatsoever for naval power. R. Latouche, *The Birth of Western Economy* (London, 1961), p. 134, takes an equally dim view of Merovingian sea power concluding that 'the Frankish kings who preceded Charlemagne made no attempt at all to protect the seaboard'.

5 Frankish Naval Power under Charlemagne and Louis the Pious

The reign of Charlemagne (768–814) was one of almost continuous military activity. Within two years of gaining the throne Charlemagne had begun a series of remarkable expansionist campaigns against the Saxons, the Lombards, the Slavs, the Avars and the Moors that were to lead to an enormous extension of the Frankish realm over the next 30 years. Naval forces played only a modest role in this expansion, which was almost entirely continental, but on the occasions when they were used it was always effectively and imaginatively. It was the final 14 years of Charlemagne's reign, however, that saw the greatest use of naval forces. Following Charlemagne's imperial coronation in 800, the pace of expansion slowed and, though it did not cease entirely, the empire increasingly found itself on the defensive as it became prey to Viking and Moslem pirates. Ultimately, the Frankish defence against these attackers was to fail and it has been commonly assumed that this was because the Franks of the Carolingian period had no understanding of the use of naval power and had completely turned their backs on the sea. For example, Pirenne in his influential work *Mohammed and Charlemagne* has described the Carolingian empire as 'purely an inland power',[1] while Latouche has written of 'the Frankish indifference to things of the sea' in this period.[2]

This image of the land-bound Carolingian has only rarely been questioned by historians.[3] Only one wide ranging study of Frankish naval power under Charlemagne has ever been attempted and this, by Sproemberg, starts from an *a priori* assumption that Charlemagne's naval policy was a failure.[4] Perfunctory treatment is the norm even among maritime historians[5] and in a recent textbook

---

[1] H. Pirenne, *Mohammed and Charlemagne* (London, 1939), p. 184; see also pp. 159–62, 166, 177–8, 248–9.

[2] R. Latouche, *The Birth of Western Economy* (London, 1961), p. 222.

[3] Two who have questioned it are D. Bullough, *The Age of Charlemagne* (London, 1965), p. 196, and P. D. King, *Charlemagne* (London, 1986), p. 46.

[4] Sproemberg, 'Die Seepolitik Karls des Großen'. Though sympathetic in approach, Sproemberg nevertheless sets out to discuss why, rather than whether, Charlemagne's naval policy was a failure.

[5] For example W. Vogel, *Geschichte der deutschen Seeschiffsfahrt* 1 (Berlin, 1915), p. 89, scarcely touches the subject. Only slightly less superficial is A. R. Lewis, *The Northern Seas* (Princeton, 1958), pp. 238–40, and more recently *idem*, with T. J. Runyan, *European Naval and Maritime History, 300–1500* (Bloomington, 1985), p. 92. M. Mollat, 'Les marins et la guerre sur mer dans le nord et l'ouest de l'Europe (jusque'au XIIe siècle)', *Settimane XV, Ordinamenti militari in occidente nell'alto medioevo* (Spoleto, 1967), vol. 2, pp. 1011–18, is emphatic about the

on Carolingian history Charlemagne's naval activities did not even rate a mention. A reappraisal is overdue, for an examination of the evidence shows conclusively that the prevailing dismissive view is wholly unjustified. Indeed, Charlemagne and his commanders were never slow to realize the potential of naval power for both offensive and defensive purposes, and their achievements, at sea and on the great rivers of Europe, were often impressive.

Charlemagne's Use of Fleets on Inland Waterways

It was on inland waterways that Charlemagne first used naval forces, his purpose being the support of his armies on campaigns against the Slavs, Saxons and Avars. These fleets performed a wide variety of duties; supply, transport and raiding were the main ones, though more unusual uses were also found for the ships.

The earliest of these campaigns was in 789 against the Wiltzites, a major Slav tribe settled between the Elbe and the Baltic.[6] It was a set-piece campaign that demonstrates Charlemagne's mastery of the pincer movement, one of his favourite and most successful campaign strategies.[7] The main body of the Frankish army, under Charlemagne himself, built two bridges across the Elbe, probably in the area of Magdeburg,[8] and invaded from the west. At the same time a fleet carrying Frankish and Frisian troops sailed down the Elbe and into its tributary, the Havel, which loops deep into Wiltzite territory, and eventually linked up with the army.[9] Further support came from Charlemagne's Slav allies, the Abodrites, who invaded from the north, and the Sorbs, who invaded from the south. The strength of this combination of converging forces was overwhelming and Dragowit, the leading Wiltzite *regulus,* submitted as soon as Charlemagne and the Frankish army appeared outside his *civitas*. The location of

---

'impuissance maritime des Carolingiens', and *idem, La vie quotidienne des gens de mer en Atlantique,* (IXe–XVIe siècle) (Paris, 1993), pp. 28–9, paints a picture of the Franks as complete landlubbers. C. de la Roncière, 'Charlemagne et la civilisation maritime au IXe siècle', *Le Moyen Age* X (1897), pp. 201–23, lacks all direction and fails to address the question of success or failure.

[6] *ARF,* 789. *Annales qui dicuntur Einhardi* (Reviser), ed. F. Kurze, *MGH. SSRG* 6 (Hanover, 1895), pp. 27–115 (odd-numbered pages), *s.a.* 789. *Annales Laureshamenses,* ed. G. H. Pertz, *MGH. SS* 1, (Hanover, 1826), pp. 22–39, *s.a.* 789. *Fragmentum annalium Chesnii,* ed. *idem, MGH. SS.* 1 (Hanover, 1826), pp. 33–4, *s.a.* 789.

[7] On Charlemagne's use of this strategy, used also against the Avars, Lombards, Bohemians and Bavarians, see J. F. Verbruggen, 'L'armée et la stratégie de Charlemagne', in W. Braunfels (ed.), *Karl der Grosse: Lebenswerk und Nachleben* 1 (ed. H. Beumann): *Persönlichkeit und Geschichte,* 3rd edn (Düsseldorf, 1967), pp. 433–5.

[8] On the location of the crossing see L. Dralle, *Slaven an Havel und Spree* (Berlin, 1981), pp. 94–5.

[9] *ARF,* 789: 'Et fuerunt cum eo in eodem exercitu Franci, Saxones; Frisiones autem navigio per Habola fluvium cum quibusdam Francis ad eum coniunxerunt.'

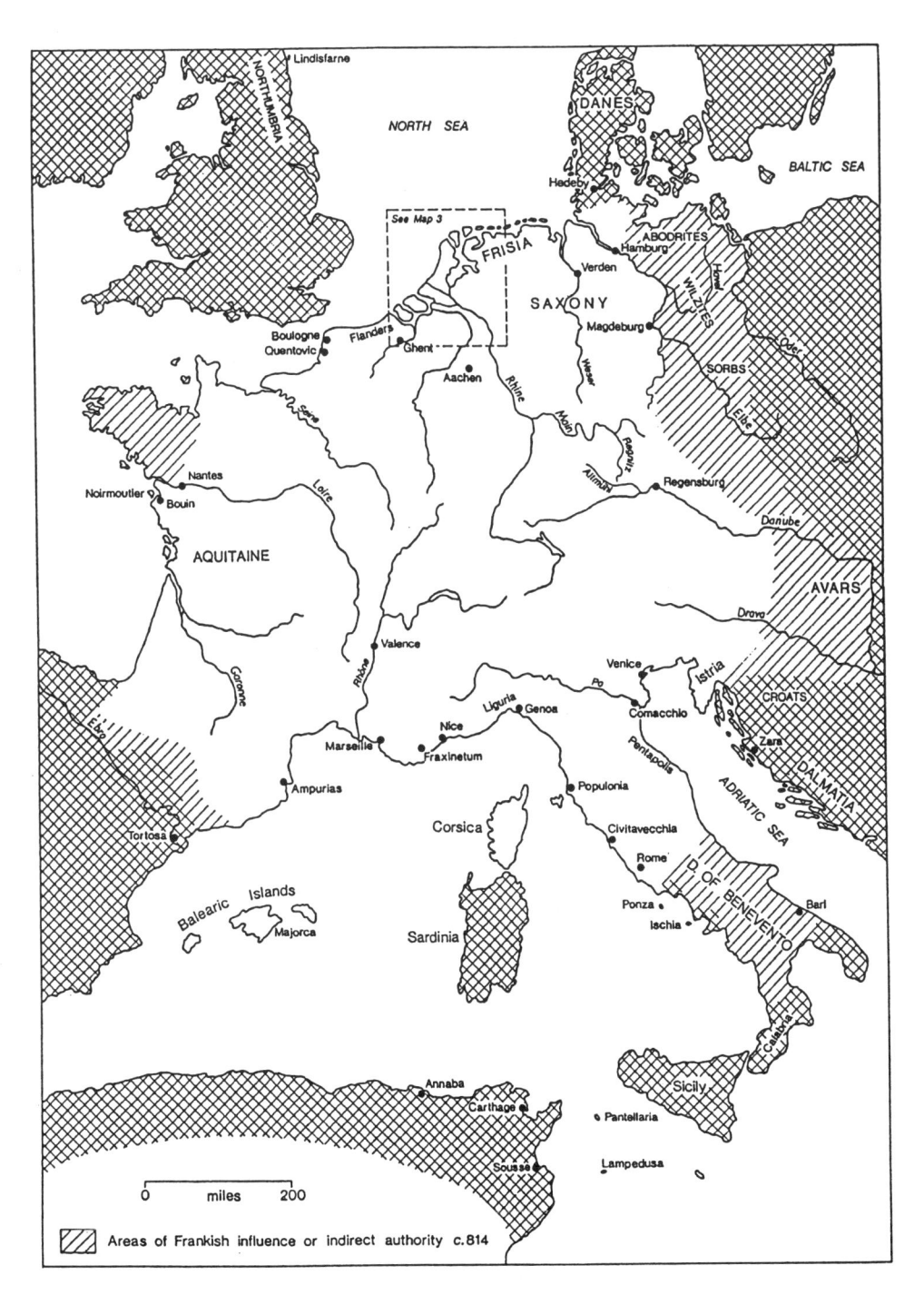

Frankish Naval Power under Charlemagne and Louis the Pious

Map 4 The Carolingian Empire

this *civitas* is unknown but has plausibly been identified with that of Brandenburg which was at this time a fortified island in the Havel and is known to have been a centre of Wiltzite power in the tenth century.[10] If this identification is correct the fleet may have been brought primarily to enable the army to storm the *civitas*, had an attack proved necessary, and thus its presence may have been a significant factor in the Wiltzites' swift submission. In addition the fleet must also have carried supplies, and no doubt it raided Wiltzite settlements along the river. It is worth noting the Frisian involvement in this campaign: remarkably, in view of the prominence of Frisian seafarers in early medieval sources, this is the only evidence we have for the involvement of Frisians in naval activity in Charlemagne's reign.

In 805 a fleet was again used in a campaign against the Slavs. For this campaign the fleet carried an army up the Elbe as far as Magdeburg, which was perhaps used as an advance base, before going on to ravage the district of *Genewana*, probably the Werinofeld which would then have been Sorb territory.[11] The major expedition of that year was a massive three pronged assault on the Bohemian Slavs[12] and the naval campaign was probably intended to protect that expedition's northern flank by tying down the Sorbs.

The Saxons too felt the weight of a Frankish fleet, in 797.[13] The target of Charlemagne's campaign in this year was Hadeln, a low, marshy coastal region between the Weser and the Elbe. Campaigning conditions in this area must have been very similar to those met by Charles Martel in Frisia, and ships would have been invaluable for transport duties alone. The ships were dragged overland where sailing was impossible, at which times they must have served as rather unwieldy baggage sledges. But transport, important as it must have been, was not the most notable purpose served by these ships, for they were apparently not ordinary ships. The Wolfenbüttel annalist describes them as 'naves magna' so we can probably assume that they were unusually large ships. The annalist says that 'he [Charlemagne] used these as a *castellum*' – that is as a fortress;[14] perhaps the

---

[10] Dralle, *op. cit.*, pp. 94–5.

[11] *Chronicon Moissiacense*, ed. G. H. Pertz, *MGH. SS* 1, pp. 282–313, *s.a.* 805: 'Quartus vero exercitus cum classe magna navium perrexit in Albia, et pervenit ad Magedoburg, et ibi vastaverunt regionem Genewana, postea reversi sunt in patriam suam.' On the location see P. D. King, *Charlemagne: Translated Sources* (Lambrigg, 1987), p. 146.

[12] *ARF*, 805; *Chron. Moissiacense*, 805; *Annales Mettenses priores*, ed. B. von Simson, *MGH, SSRG* 10, (Hanover-Leipzig, 1905), 805.

[13] *Annales Guelferbytani*, ed. G. H. Pertz, *MGH. SS* 1, (Hanover, 1826), pp. 23–31, 40–6, *s.a.* 797: 'Karolus rex iterum in Saxonia cum naves magna per terra tractas et per aquas, et in ipsias fecit castellum, et constrinxit Saxones nimis.'

[14] *Ibid.*: 'in ipsias fecit castellum' (translation: King, *Translated sources*, p. 161). An alternative interpretation might be that the ships were broken up and their timbers then used to build the fort (though if this had been the case we might expect the source to read *ex ipsis fecit castellum*). But this seems unlikely as the re-using of ships' timbers as building materials would have seemed commonplace to a contemporary and thus hardly worth noting: for early medieval examples see D. Ellmers, *Frühmittelalterliche Handelsschiffahrt*, p. 277 (from London); *idem*, 'Nautical archaeology in Germany II', *IJNA* IV (1975), p. 338 (from Schleswig-Holstein); F. Rieck and

ships were hauled ashore and drawn around the camp after the fashion of a wagon laager. To have provided practicable fighting platforms ashore these ships must have been flat-bottomed and fairly high-sided, requirements which could have been answered by the early cogs which were being used along the North Sea coast by this time.[15]

The most impressive example of a fleet being used in support of the army is found in the great campaign of 791 against the Avars, a Hunnish nation settled in Pannonia (roughly modern Hungary). The rapid collapse of the Avars in the face of Frankish attack suggests that they were already far gone in decline but their fearsome reputation, fully earned during the preceding centuries, was sufficient to ensure that this was one of Charlemagne's most meticulously prepared and powerful expeditions. In the opinion of Charlemagne's biographer Einhard, the Avar campaign was second only to the Saxon campaigns in the amount of effort and determination which Charlemagne devoted to it.[16] The three days of prayer and fasting observed by the army on the frontier of Avar territory are ample evidence of the almost superstitious awe in which they were held by the Franks.[17] Charlemagne used his favoured strategy and divided his forces for the campaign; a fast moving *scara* invaded Avar territory from Italy while the main army, which gathered at Regensburg to invade along the river Danube, was itself divided into two forces. On the north bank of the river marched the contingents of Saxons, Frisians, Thuringians and Ripuarian Franks under the command of Count Theodoric and Meginfred the Chamberlain. On the south bank marched an army of Franks and Alamanni under the command of Charlemagne himself. Between them on the river sailed a fleet. Part of its function was to carry the army's supplies but its most important role was to transfer troops from one bank to the other if one of the columns needed reinforcing 'so that the king could wield the power of his own army on either bank'.[18] Charlemagne was thus able to enjoy the advantages of dividing his forces without the disadvantages. In addition to giving him the mobility and flexibility to concentrate his forces whenever he wished, the fleet also enabled Charlemagne to deny the same freedom to the Avars who, in the sixth and seventh centuries with their Slav

---

O. Crumlin-Pedersen, *Både fra Danmarks Oldtid* (Roskilde, 1988), pp. 135–6 (from Jutland); S. McGrail, *Ancient Boats in North-West Europe*, (London, 1987), pp. 41 (from Dublin).

[15] The earliest evidence of their use in northern Germany comes from Hessens, near Wilhelmshaven, where a slipway of the seventh century has been excavated which was clearly built for a similar, flat-bottomed, broad-beamed boat: see Ellmers, *Handelsschiffahrt*, pp. 63–5, 130. See further on the cog below pp. 179-87 and, on its origins, above ch. 1, p. 36.

[16] Einhard, *Vita Karoli Imperatoris*, ed. R. Rau, *Quellen zur karolingischen Reichsgeschichte*, vol. 1 (Darmstadt, 1974), pp. 163–211, ch. 13.

[17] *ARF*, 791; *Rev.*, 791; *Ann. Mettenses priores*, 791. Also *Epistolae variorum Carolo Magno regnante scriptae*, ed. E. Duemmler, *MGH. Epp.* 4 (Berlin, 1895), pp. 494–567, no. 20 (pp. 528–9).

[18] *Ann. Laureshamenses*, 791: 'sed et navalis hostis per Danovium, ut ex utraque ripa rex potestatem habere potuisset cum exercitu suo' (translation: King, *Translated sources*, p. 139).

tributaries, had used naval forces both on the Danube and at sea and who must still have possessed boats suitable for transport and warfare.[19] Furthermore it would also have enabled him to outflank any Avar defensive positions along the river, such as the one which they built at the confluence of the river Kamp with the Danube,[20] and make the crossing of tributaries easier.

The Avars themselves probably realised very quickly the decisive tactical advantage which the fleet gave to the Franks for, in the event, they did not even attempt to defend their positions[21] and gave their western territories up to nearly eight weeks of devastation without a fight. The Frankish army reached the river Rába, some 180 miles inside the Avar frontier, before turning for home. The Franks' most serious loss was in livestock: a serious epidemic killed most of the army's horses. The fleet's control of the river guaranteed Charlemagne secure communications with his starting base at Regensburg and this too must have played a considerable part in his success.[22] In view of the results of the campaign there can be little doubt that Charlemagne's grasp of the tactical and strategic potential of the fleet was absolute.

---

[19] Though the Avars had certainly engaged in naval warfare in the past, their ships appear to have been supplied by allies or tributary peoples. In 576 a group of Avars seized ships on the Greek coast and used them to raid Thrace (John of Biclar, *Chronica* (ed. T. Mommsen, *MGH. AA* 11 = *Chronica Minora* II (Berlin, 1894), pp. 207–23), p. 214) and in 595 the Avars forced the Slavs to build them a fleet for use on the Danube: O. Pritsak, 'The Slavs and the Avars', in *Settimane* XXX, *Gli Slavi occidentale e meridionale nell'alto medioevo* (Spoleto, 1983), vol. 2, p. 410. In 602 the Lombards sent shipwrights to the Avars to assist them in a campaign in the Aegean (Paul the Deacon, *Historia Langobardorum*, ed. L. Bethmann and G. Waitz, *MGH. SSRL* 3 (Hanover, 1878), IV. 20) and in 626 Slav tributaries provided the Avars with a fleet of light warships during the siege of Constantinople (G. Vernadsky, *Ancient Russia* (New Haven, 1943), p. 198). Slav naval power on the Danube could be considerable and the Byzantines had developed advanced tactics to deal with it; see Maurice, *Strategikon*, trans. G. T. Dennis (Philadelphia, 1984), XII. 3 (pp. 157–8). In 592 a Slav fleet on the Danube was reported to be 150 vessels strong (Vernadsky, *op.cit.*, p. 187). Slav ships, though no match for Byzantine warships, were seaworthy and Slavic piracy was a serious problem in the mid-seventh century in the Aegean (*ibid.*, p. 247) and on the Italian coast (Paul the Deacon, IV. 44). The Bulgars, who filled the power vacuum left by the collapse of the Avars, also raided on the Danube and its tributaries; in 827 they sent a fleet up the Drava to attack Pannonia (*ARF*, 827). See also on Slav piracy before the ninth century, E. Eickhoff, *Seekrieg und Seepolitik zwischen Islam und Abendland: Das Mittelmeer unter byzantinischer und arabischer Hegemonie 650–1040* (Berlin, 1966), pp. 53–4.

[20] *ARF*, 791. Rev., 791.

[21] *ARF*, 791: 'Avari enim cum vidissent utrasque ripas exercitum continentes et navigia per medium fluvium venientes, a Domino eis terror pervenit: dereliquerunt eorum loca munita, ...firmitatesque eorum vel machinationes dimiserunt fuga lapsi.'

[22] See *Epp...Carolo Magno regnante*, no. 20 (n. 17 above), which was sent by Charlemagne to his wife as the army was on the point of entering Avar territory or very shortly after it had actually done so and shows plainly that he expected to be able to receive letters from his wife in reply while on campaign. Clearly some arrangements had been made for regular communications with Regensburg along the Danube, either a courier service by land or regular supply ships on the river.

Unfortunately, little is known about the fleet itself; how it was organised, who commanded it or what kind of ships comprised it are questions which cannot be answered.[23] Even who provided the fleet is open to question because of contradictory sources. The *Annales Fuldenses* say that it was Frisian, whereas the revised version of the *Annales regni Francorum* states that the fleet was Bavarian and also tell us that the Frisian contingent in the army returned home overland through Bohemia with the Saxons.[24] The question is an important one, considering the predominance which has been claimed for Frisian shipping in this period, and should be pursued.

As regards the authority of the sources, the case in favour of the revised royal annals is certainly the stronger. As the revision was carried out in the early years of the reign of Louis the Pious they are certainly closer to the events than the Fulda annals, which were not begun until the 830's.[25] More significantly, the Reviser himself is notably well-informed about events in the east and clearly had good sources, if, indeed, he was not, as seems likely, an easterner himself.[26]

The case for the version of the Fulda annals has recently been argued by Lebecq.[27] He believes that a Frisian fleet sailed up the Rhine to reach Regensburg via the Main and the Regnitz and a short portage overland into the Altmühl, a tributary of the Danube. Certainly, had a Frisian fleet been sent this would have been the only practicable route and just as certainly the strategic potential of that route for transporting troops and supplies by boat from the north to the eastern frontier was fully understood by Charlemagne and his advisers. Indeed they were soon to attempt to link the Regnitz and the Altmühl with a canal; and that the portage was practicable is proved by the fact that the king had his own ships carried between the two rivers after the canal project itself failed (see below).

Plausible though this is, against it must be set the fact that of the sources which mention the Frisian involvement with this campaign only the Fulda annals do so in connection with the fleet. The other sources which mention the Frisians agree that they formed part of the army that marched on the north bank of the Danube under the command of Theodoric and Meginfred.[28] The weight of the

---

[23] M. Deanesly, *A History of Early Medieval Europe from 476 to 911* (London, 1956), p. 370, suggests that the fleet was commanded by Gerold, the *praefectus* of the Bavarians.

[24] *Annales Fuldenses*, ed. G. H. Pertz, *MGH. SS.* 1 (Hanover, 1826), 791: 'Frisonibus vero et qui cum ipsis deputati sunt navali evectione per alveum euntibus'. Rev., 791: 'Baioriis cum commeatibus exercitus, qui navibus devehabantur, per Danubium secunda aqua descendere iussis.... Saxones autem et Frisones cum Theodorico et Meginfredo per Beehaimos, ut iussum erat, domum regressi sunt.'

[25] B. W. Scholz and B. Rogers, *Carolingian Chronicles* (Ann Arbor, 1972), pp. 7–8; Pertz, *MGH. SS* 1, p. 337.

[26] King, *Translated Sources*, p. 18.

[27] S. Lebecq, *Marchands et navigateurs frisons du haut moyen âge* (2 vols, Lille, 1983), vol. 1, pp. 212, 216–7, fig. 49.

[28] *Ann. Laureshamenses*, 791: 'sed et de alia parte Danovii alius exercitus Ribuariorum et Fresionum et Saxonorum cum Toringos.' *ARF*, 791, also places the Frisians with the army on

evidence clearly favours the Reviser's account and the Fulda annals must be considered to be in error on this point; the Frisian contingent on this campaign was purely military and reached Regensburg by land, probably via Saxony. The Danube was an important artery of trade and transport and we can safely assume that Charlemagne had no need to call on the Frisians for ships as the Bavarians would have been quite capable of supplying sufficient of their own to support the campaign.[29]

Lebecq has surely overestimated the importance of Frisian naval forces in this period. Apart from their role in the Wiltzite campaign of 789 no other activity is known. They played no apparent role, and therefore were probably not prominent, in Charlemagne's naval defences against the Vikings, nor do they seem to have possessed any naval forces of their own with which to oppose the Danish attack on the Frisian islands in 810.[30] So far from being prominent as *mercenaires de la mer*[31] they are not even known in that capacity in Charlemagne's reign.

For the follow up campaign against the Avars which was planned for 792, Charlemagne refined his arrangements for transferring troops across the Danube and for crossing tributaries by ordering the construction of a pontoon bridge from ferry-boats.[32] These boats were held together by ropes and anchors in such a way that the bridge could be dismantled and moved to another site after use. Skilled boatmen would have been needed to manoeuvre the pontoon boats into position before the bridge could be completed by laying a roadway out across the tops of their gunwales. Even transporting the pontoon boats overland would have been straightforward; if the boats were at all comparable to the light dug-out boats which the Romans used for the same purpose, several could have been carried on a single wagon.[33] The planning and resources devoted to the construction of the

---

the north bank without specifying who manned the fleet: 'Saxones autem cum quibusdam Francis et maxime plurima Frisonum de aquilonale parte Danubii similiter iter peragentes.' The other sources which mention the Frisians on this campaign, the *Ann. Mettenses priores* and *Poeta Saxo*, ed. Pertz, *MGH. SS* 1, (Hanover, 1826), pp. 225–79, are both derived from the *ARF*.

[29] See A. C. Leighton, *Transport and Communication in Early Medieval Europe* (Newton Abbot, 1972), p. 41, on water transport on the Danube in the Carolingian period.

[30] *ARF*, 810, *Chron. Moissiacensec*, 810.

[31] Lebecq, *op. cit.*, vol. 1, pp. 211–13.

[32] *ARF*, 792: 'Pons super navigia flumina transeuntia factus est, anchoris et funibus ita coherens, ut iungi et dissolvi possit.' See also Rev., 792.

[33] Vegetius, *Epitoma Rei Militaris*, II. 25, III. 7. The Franks would have found an adaptable model in the 'paved' boats which were used widely as ferries in Germany throughout the Middle Ages and up to the present century. These were composite boats made up, usually, of two linked dugouts or simple plank boats with a deck laid across the top to carry vehicles and animals. See S. McGrail, *Log Boats of England and Wales*, BAR BS 51 (Oxford, 1978), pp. 49–50, fig. 159. The Deutsches Schiffahrtsmuseum in Bremerhaven has an early medieval example made with two dug-outs from the Weser at Minden. Each boat had a matching line of holes through the hull below the gunwales which held lashings to hold the boats together, side by side, and to fasten down the plank deck onto the hulls. Lateral rigidity was increased with wooden spars which linked the ends of the boats together. Large numbers of such boats could have been linked together for bridge building without further modification and a roadway lashed on top of them.

bridge must have been considerable but so far as is known it was never used: due to a Saxon rebellion, the campaign was cancelled and the fate of the pontoon bridge is unknown. This is the only occasion on which a pontoon bridge is mentioned in the sources but it does not follow from this that the bridge was unique. A number of bridges were built on other campaigns over major rivers and the likelihood is that these were also pontoon bridges; indeed, on one or more of the later occasions it is not impossible that the bridge built in 792 was being re used. The Elbe was bridged at least twice on campaigns against the Slavs: in 789 to attack the Wiltzites and in 808 for the unsuccessful campaign against the Smeldingi and Linones.[34] In 796 the lower Weser was bridged in the course of a campaign against the Saxons of Wihmodia at *Alisni*, a location which has yet to be identified convincingly.[35] It has also been suggested that the ships which accompanied the army into Hadeln in the following year may have been used for bridge building in addition to their other functions.[36]

Both the Weser and the Elbe are several hundred yards wide in the areas where they must have been bridged on these campaigns, and it is inconceivable that bridging could have been achieved in the time available without using pontoons.[37] Major rivers could not be bridged quickly by conventional means even if wood was the only material used. The 500-yard-long bridge which Charlemagne built over the Rhine at Mainz was constructed only of wood and took ten years to complete.[38] The bridge built at *Alisni* might have been considerably longer than this and each of the other bridges must have been at least 200–300 yards long, yet very little time can have been available to complete

---

[34] *ARF*, 789; Rev., 789; *ARF*, 808; *Annales Laurissenses minores*, ed. G. H. Pertz, *MGH. SS* 1, (Hanover, 1826), pp. 114–23, *s.a.* 808; *Ann. Fuldenses*, 808.

[35] *Annales Petaviani*, ed. G. H. Pertz, *MGH. SS* 1, (Hanover, 1826), 796: 'Feceruntque Franci pontem super amne Wisera, in loco cuius vocabulum est Alisni'. Two locations have been proposed for *Alisni*. S. Abel and B. Simson, *Jahrbücher des fränkisches Reiches unter Karl dem Grossen* (2 vols, Leipzig, 1888, 1883: reprint Berlin-Munich, 1969), vol. 2, p. 120, n. 6, suggest Elsfleth, about 20 miles downstream from Bremen. L. Halphen, *Etudes critiques sur l'histoire de Charlemagne* (Paris, 1921), p. 195, n. 5, rejects this on linguistic and practical grounds, suggesting Alsen, about seven miles upstream of Elsfleth, where the Weser is narrowed by an island. Both locations seem unlikely on practical grounds since even at Alsen the river is nearly 1000 yards wide and the considerable tidal range would pose further problems still. It seems more realistic to suppose that the bridge was built upstream of the tidal limit, perhaps at Etelsen, ten miles south of Bremen, where the river is less than half as wide as it is at Alsen.

[36] Verbruggen, *op. cit.*, p. 432.

[37] The second-century historian Arrian uses exactly this argument to justify his conclusion, in the *Anabasis Alexandri*, ed. and trans. P. A Brunt, Loeb Classical Library (2 vols, London, 1976–83) V. 7, that Alexander the Great built a pontoon bridge to cross the Indus in 326 BC.

[38] Einhard, *V. Karoli*, 17, 32. See also F. Vercauteren, 'Comment s'est on défendu, au IXe siècle dans l'empire franc contre les invasions normandes?', *Annales du XXXe Congrès de la Fédération Archéologique de Belgique* (1936), pp. 123–4, and J. M. Hassal and D. Hill, 'Ponte de l'Arche: Frankish influence on the Anglo Saxon burh', *Archaeological Journal* CXXVII (1970), pp. 192–4, on the construction of a 400-yard-long fortified bridge of wood and stone over the Seine at Pîtres by Charles the Bald as a defence against the Vikings. Despite considerable urgency and close royal supervision, the work took six years to complete.

them in. Even a delay of a week would have been enough to lose the element of strategic surprise that a rapid and unexpected river crossing could secure. Even today, the pontoon bridge remains the only method suitable for bridging rivers more than about 50 yards wide during military operations.[39] Pontoons must surely have been used on all these occasions, though they would not necessarily have been made of boats built for this purpose. Boats could have been adapted on an *ad hoc* basis or the pontoons might have been constructed by lashing groups of barrels together as was the practice in the later Middle Ages. Whichever method was employed, a major river could easily be bridged in the space of a single day using pontoons. The Romans and Byzantines could do this using boats and, in the fifteenth century, so could the Turks and Burgundians using barrels.[40] Charlemagne certainly had able engineers at his disposal, so there seems no reason why his armies could not have bridged rivers with equal efficiency.

Though the Huns (and perhaps other barbarian peoples) carried rafts with them on wagons to use as ferries,[41] Charlemagne is apparently unique in the early medieval west in using pontoon bridges. However, it may be that further research will provide other examples of bridge building where pontoons must have been used. Though the details given in the sources are sparse, one striking parallel with late Roman practice raises the intriguing possibility that Charlemagne drew his inspiration from a classical source. On the Wiltzite campaign of 789 mentioned above, one of the two bridges which were built was fortified at each end with a wood and earth *castellum* in which a garrison was installed.[42] This accords exactly with the instructions given by the late fourth-century Roman

---

[39] D. Hill, *A History of Engineering in Classical and Medieval Times* (London, 1984), , p. 65.

[40] Vegetius, II. 25, III. 7, Arrian, *Anabasis Alexandri*, V. 7, and Maurice, *Strategikon*, XI. 4, XII. 21, give detailed accounts of Roman and Byzantine methods. Also of interest is a coin of Severus of c. 209 which carries a representation of a bridge of boats: see A. S. Robertson, 'The bridges on the Severan coins of AD 208 and 209', in W. S. Hanson and L. J. F. Keppie (eds), *Roman Frontier Studies 1979*, BAR IS 71 (3 vols, Oxford, 1980), vol. 1, pp. 131–9. For examples of the speed with which major rivers like the Rhine, Danube and Euphrates could be bridged by the Romans see Ammianus Marcellinus, *Rerum gestarum libri*, ed. and trans. J. C. Rolfe, Loeb Classical Library (3 vols, London, 1935), XIV. 10.6, XVI. 11.8, XVII. 1.2 and 12.4, XVIII, 7.2 (Persian army), XXIII. 2.7 and 5.4, XXVII. 5.2–6. See further Philippe de Commynes, *Mémoires*, trans. M. Jones (Harmondsworth, 1972), I. 6. i (pp. 85–6), which describes how the Burgundians used a few small boats and a large number of barrels to bridge the Seine near Étampes in a morning in 1464 (this included the time taken to assemble the barrels out of cartloads of staves). For the Turks' use of this method, S. Runciman, *The Fall of Constantinople, 1453* (Cambridge, 1965), pp. 110–11.

[41] Priscus, ed. and trans. R. C. Blockley in *The Fragmentary Classicising Historians of the Later Roman Empire*, vol. 2, ARCA Classical and Medieval Texts, Papers and Monographs 10 (Liverpool, 1983), pp. 222–400, fragment 11.2. The Huns bridged the river Nischava when they besieged Nish in Yugoslavia in 442 (Priscus fr. 6.2), though the bridge itself was probably built by captured Roman engineers; see R. C. Blockley, *The Fragmentary Classicising Historians of the Later Roman Empire*, vol 1, ARCA Classical and Medieval Texts, Papers and Monographs 6 (Liverpool, 1981), p. 54.

[42] *ARF*, 789: 'usque ad Albiam fluvium venit ibique duos pontes construxit, quorum uno ex utroque capite castellum ex ligno et terra aedificavit.' Also Rev., 789.

military writer Vegetius in his *Epitoma Rei Militaris* for constructing and guarding a pontoon bridge in hostile territory if it was intended to return by the same route, as in fact Charlemagne did on this occasion:

> As the enemy generally endeavour to fall upon an army at the passage of a river either by surprise or ambuscade, it is necessary to secure both sides thereof by strong detachments so that the troops may not be attacked and defeated while separated by the channel of the river. But it is still safer to palisade both the posts since this will enable you to sustain any attempt without much loss. If the bridge is wanted, not only for the present transportation of the troops but also for their return and for convoys, it will be proper to throw up works with ditch and rampart to cover each head of the bridge, with a sufficient number of men to defend them as long as the circumstances of affairs require.[43]

Vegetius's work was certainly well known in Francia by the first half of the ninth century, significantly, in lay as well as clerical circles: a manuscript of the *Epitoma* is listed in the will of Count Everard of Friuli c. 837 and Charles the Bald was given a copy by Freculph, bishop of Lisieux, sometime before 853.[44] It is certain that Vegetius was already known in England at the beginning of the eighth century for the *Epitoma* is quoted in two of Bede's works; *De Temporum Ratione* and the *Historia Ecclesiastica*.[45] Intellectual contacts between England and Francia were very close throughout the eighth century and it is likely that the *Epitoma*, like many other classical works, first found its way to Francia in this period from England.[46] However that may be, there is some reason to believe that Charlemagne had a first hand knowledge of the *Epitoma* and may have tried to turn some of its teaching into practice.

---

[43] Vegetius, III. 7:

> Festinantur adversarii ad transitus fluminum insidias vel superventus facere consueuerunt. Ob quam necessitatem in utraque ripa conlocantur armata praesidia, ne alveo interveniente divisi obprimantur ab hostibus. Cautius tamen est sudes ex utraque parte praefigere ac sine detrimento, si qua vis inlata fuerit, sustinere. Quod si pons non tantum ad transitam sed etiam ad recursum et commeatus necessarius fuerit, tunc in utroque capite percussis latioribus fossis aggereque constructo defensores milites debet accipere, a quibus tamdiu teneatur, quamdiu locorum necessitas postulat.

(Translation, J. Clarke, 'Vegetius, The military institutions of the Romans', in T. R. Phillips (ed.), *The Roots of Strategy* (Harrisburg, 1944), p. 73.

[44] R. McKitterick, *The Carolingians and the Written Word* (Cambridge, 1989), p. 246; M. L. W. Laistner, *Thought and Letters in Western Europe. AD 500–900* (London, 1931), p. 218.

[45] C. W. Jones, 'Bede and Vegetius', *The Classical Review* XLVI (1932), pp. 248–9. Laistner, *op. cit.* p. 202, points out that Vegetius was probably also known in Ireland in the eighth century.

[46] On the transmission of classical works to Francia from England in the eighth century see W. Levison, *England and the Continent in the Eighth Century* (Oxford, 1946), pp. 140–4. Among the classical authors whose works first reached Francia from England in this period are Tacitus, Ammianus Marcellinus, Suetonius, Livy and Vitruvius.

Dark Age Naval Power

The Franks also used what can only be described as prefabricated assault boats on at least one occasion, on campaign against the Moors in Spain in 803.[47] The army was divided into two forces to approach the objective, Tortosa, from converging directions. The main force advanced along the Mediterranean coast from Barcelona, while a smaller force was sent inland to cross the river Ebro in secrecy to mount a surprise attack on the enemy. Presumably so that this force could avoid recognised crossing points which were likely to be guarded, it was equipped with light boats to act as ferries. As the force had to travel in secrecy, there could have been no question of carrying the boats on lumbering wagons so each was divided into four sections, each one of which could be carried between two horses or mules. Once the river was reached the boats could be easily reassembled using hammers and nails, and the joints were to be caulked with pitch, wax and tow which were prepared in advance for the purpose.[48] Waterproofed hide would have been the lightest material available for boats and it was certainly used by the army in large quantities for other purposes,[49] though from the Astronomer's account it seems more likely that the boats were built from wood. After four days travelling only at night the force reached the Ebro, reassembled the boats and crossed the river. The horses were left to swim across and this, surprisingly, led to the expedition's discovery despite the Franks' technical ingenuity and caution. Dung from one of the horses or mules floated downstream where it was spotted by an alert Moorish soldier who was swimming. Identifying it by smell as coming from an animal fed on barley (the Franks could have had no time to graze their animals and so must have carried grain for them) the Moor concluded, rightly, that the Franks had crossed the river upstream and were planning an ambush. The alarm was raised and the Franks had to fight their way out of trouble.

Though the Frankish plan failed in this last example, it does serve to underline the notable flexibility which the Franks showed in warfare on the inland waterways. Rivers and wetlands are considered as weak points in the enemy's defences, to be exploited to maximum advantage, rather than as obstacles. In this appreciation Charlemagne could have learned nothing from the Vikings.

---

[47] Astronomer, *Vita Hludowici imperatoris* (Rau, *op. cit.* vol. 1, pp. 215–53), ch. 15. The dating here, as often with the Astronomer, is tentative; see King, *Translated Sources*, pp. 21–2.

[48] Astronomer, ch. 15:

scilicet ut naves transvectorias fabricantes, unamquamque earum in quaternas partirentur partes, quatinus pars quaterna cuiusque duobus equis vel mulis vehi posset, et praeparatis clavis et marculis facile coaptari valerent; pice vero et cera ac stuppa praeparatis, mox ut ad flumen veniretur, conpagum iuncturae obcludi possent.

[49] *Capitulare de villis*, in *Capitularia regum Francorum 1* = *MGH. LL* 2, ed. A. Boretius (Hanover, 1883), no. 32, *c.* 64.

The Regnitz-Altmühl Canal

Charlemagne also understood the strategic importance of water transport to military operations. Supplies, armies and the king himself travelled by ship on the inland waterways of the kingdom.[50] The capitularies emphasise the importance of water transport to the army; the counts were ordered to ensure that they had sound boats at their disposal for the use of the army[51] and the double capitulary of Thionville of 806 exempted military supplies from the exaction of tolls.[52] The importance of water transport to the kingdom in general is shown by the frequent legislation against illegal tolls.[53]

But Charlemagne's strategic vision went far beyond this. In 792 he started a project to open up direct navigation between the Rhine and Danube river systems by building a canal to link the headwaters of the Regnitz (known as the river Rezat), a tributary of the Main, with the river Altmühl, a tributary of the Danube.[54] Had the project been completed successfully the internal communications of the kingdom would have been greatly enhanced; trade would certainly have benefited but this would have been incidental to the canal's main purpose which was military. In the years 792–3, Charlemagne faced a serious military and political crisis. Famine, internal conspiracy and, later, Saracen invasion all played their part, but the greatest problems were a major Saxon rebellion in the north coupled with the threat of what was expected to be a devastating Avar counter-attack in the east. Charlemagne had no reason to expect that either could be dealt with easily and so was faced with the prospect of a two-front war which might have been prolonged. The need to be able to transfer troops and supplies efficiently and speedily between the two fronts was obvious, the more so when the great losses of horses from disease in 791 are considered, and the canal would have brought immense strategic benefits in the short term had his worst fears been realized. There were potential long-term benefits too, as the improved communications might have aided Frankish expansion to the east.

The decision to build the canal was taken late in 792 according to the *Annales Alemannici*.[55] Though some of our other sources give the impression that Charlemagne only gave the order to build the canal in the summer of 793,[56] this

---

[50] *Annales Mosellani*, ed. J. M. Lappenberg, *MGH, SS.* 16 (Hanover, 1859), 791 (error for 792). *ARF*, 793. Rev., 790. *Ann. Laureshamenses*, 793; cf. *ARF*, 821 (Louis the Pious).

[51] *Capitulare Aquisgranense, MGH. LL* 2, no. 77, c. 10: 'Et unusquisque comis duas partes de herba in suo comitatu defendat ad opus illius hostis, ut habeat pontes bonos, naves bonas.'

[52] *Capitulare missorum in Theodonis villa datum secundum generale* (806), *MGH. LL* 2, no. 44, c. 13.

[53] See *MGH. LL* 2, nos 20 (c. 18), 32 (c. 62), 44 (c. 13), 57 (c. 7), and 58 (c. 6).

[54] *ARF*, 793, Rev., 793, *Ann. Laureshamenses* 793. *Ann. Guelferbytani*, 793. *Ann. Mosellani*, 792 (error for 793).

[55] *Annales Alamannici*, ed. G. H. Pertz *MGH. SS* 1, (Hanover, 1826), 792: 'Et fossatum iussit facere'.

[56] Rev., 793, *Ann. Laureshamenses* 793.

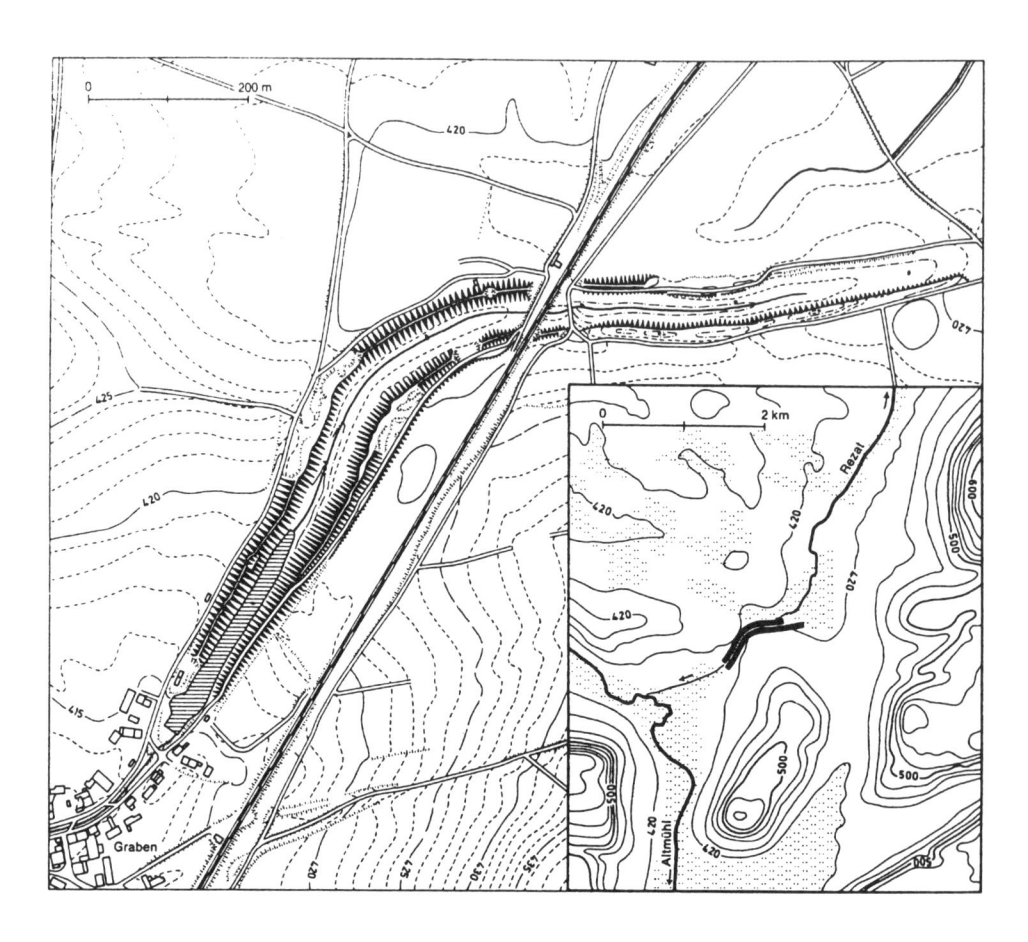

Map 5 The Fossa Carolina (Ellmers, *Frühmittelalterliche Handelsschiffahrt*)

is not a sufficient reason to doubt the reliability of the *Annales Alemannici* on this point because such a vast undertaking as the canal project could not have been organised on the spur of the moment. Many months of advance planning must have been required to raise the necessary workforce, supplies and materials. Work probably began in the late spring or early summer of 793 and was certainly well under way, and perhaps already running into difficulties, when Charlemagne visited the site at the end of the summer or in the early autumn of that year.[57] He remained there, supervising the work until just before Christmas, when work was abandoned, the Reviser says, because of bad weather and ground so waterlogged that no matter how much was dug out during the day, an equal amount slumped

---

[57] The *Ann. Mosellani*, 793, make it clear that work had begun before Charlemagne arrived at the site: 'circa tempus autumni ad quendam aquaeductum, quem inter Danuvium fluvium et Radantiam alveum facere caeperat.' The pluperfect should be noted.

down to replace it overnight.[58] The ships in which Charlemagne had travelled from Regensburg were dragged overland into the Regnitz down which he sailed to the monastery of St Kilian at Würzburg where he spent Christmas and New Year. Work was never restarted; presumably because either the impossibility of the task or the total collapse of Avar power had become apparent.

Even incomplete, the canal must rank as one of the major engineering projects of the early Middle Ages and its earthworks have survived substantially intact to this day. The site must have appeared ideal to Charlemagne's engineers as they surveyed it. The distance between the Rezat and the Altmühl at this point is not great, only 1,500–1,800 yards between navigable waters, and the watershed is low, less than 30 feet above the level of the Altmühl.[59] It is difficult to reconstruct fully the plan used by Charlemagne's engineers because the remains give us no clue as to how they intended to solve the problems caused by the slightly different altitudes of the two rivers. This meant that the waters of the two rivers could not have been allowed to join as this would simply have led to the Altmühl, which was the lower river, capturing the headwaters of the Rezat. This would have deprived the Regnitz of its source and caused it to dry up below the point where it was joined by the canal. As the chamber lock was unknown in Europe before the fifteenth century,[60] a dam would have had to be retained in the canal to prevent this happening.[61] If the dam had been properly graded, vessels could have been hauled over it with a minimum of difficulty using a winch or simply animal (or man) power. The canal itself need only have had a breadth of about four yards and a depth of about two feet to have made it navigable to most of the river boats of that period.[62]

Work started initially on excavating a cutting through the watershed to draw a navigable channel from the Altmühl towards the Rezat. At first work obviously went well for the southern section of the canal still holds water today and gives a good idea of how the engineers envisaged the whole scheme would turn out.[63] But after a cutting about 1,200 yards long by 50–80 yards wide had been excavated,[64] the project ran into geological problems which have been explained by modern investigation of the site, which confirms also the accuracy of the

---

[58] Rev. 793: 'Nam propter iuges pluvias et terram quae palustris erat, nimio humore naturaliter infectam opus, quod fiebat, consistere non potuit; sed quantum interdiu terrae a fossoribus fuerat egestum, tantum noctibus, humo iterum in locum suum relabente, subsidebat.'

[59] H. H. Hofmann, '*Fossa Carolina*: Versuch einer Zusammenschau', in Braunfels, (ed.), *op. cit.*, p. 441.

[60] The earliest known use of the chamber lock was in China *c.* AD 825; it was unknown in the west before 1452. The matter is discussed by C. Singer, 'East and west in retrospect', in C. Singer and E. J. Holmroyd (eds), *The Oxford History of Technology*, vol. 2, *Mediterranean Civilizations and the Middle Ages* (Oxford, 1979), p. 771.

[61] Hofmann, *op. cit.*, p. 442.

[62] Ellmers, *Handelsschiffahrt*, p. 232.

[63] See the photographs in Bullough, *op. cit.*, p. 68, fig. 18.

[64] The Reviser's estimate of the size of the excavation as 2,000 paces long by 300 feet wide (Rev. 793) is an overestimate.

Reviser's explanation of the canal's failure. What happened was that the excavation had cut down through the clay topsoil, which was ideal for the purpose of carrying a canal, into a layer of waterlogged quicksand in the subsoil. The weight of the heavy clay soil above will have squeezed the quicksand out through the sides of the cutting in a steady and unstoppable flow which will have continually replaced whatever had been dug out from the bed of the canal.[65] This must have baffled the engineers and it is not surprising that a later annalist explained the canal's failure in terms of supernatural intervention.[66] It seems that an attempt was then made to divert the course of the canal to join the Rezat further downstream but this also ran into quicksand and swampy ground. Progress was plainly impossible and the canal was abandoned. The heavy rains mentioned by the Reviser were probably not a major factor in the canal's failure though they may have sapped the morale of the workforce. The geological problems, however, were as insuperable to the technology of the age as they had been unforeseeable. Neither Charlemagne nor his engineers can fairly be accused of bad judgement on this score.

The importance which Charlemagne attached to the canal can easily be gauged by the immense resources of manpower, supplies and money which were devoted to its construction in a year of severe famine.[67] Hofmann has produced an estimate of the size of the workforce, based on the methods used by German engineers in the early nineteenth century for calculating the manpower needed for major manual excavations.[68] He suggests that about 6,000 labourers and about 1,500 support and supply workers would have been needed, plus many hundreds of draught animals. This is probably an overestimate as it is based on the assumption that work began only when Charlemagne arrived at the site at the end of the summer and so could have continued only for about ten weeks. But work was certainly well under way by then; we should consider that in all the work lasted for at least 20 weeks. The number of man-days required to complete the task remains the same, of course, so Hofmann's estimate should probably be halved. The population of the area was sparse so most of the labour must have been imported. A late source tells us that it was made up of a great number of Franks, Swabians and Avars.[69] The last will no doubt have been prisoners of war

---

[65] Hofmann, *op. cit.*, p. 442

[66] *Annalium Salisburgensium additamentum*, ed. W. Wattenbach, *MGH. SS* 13 (Hanover, 1881), pp. 236–41, 793: 'Set nec prudencia nec concilium est contra Dominum. Postmodum circa easdem fossas per singulis noctes audite sunt voces mugiencium, set et ludencium et garriencium confusi strepitus.' The annals were compiled in the twelfth century. The superstition of this product of the twelfth-century renaissance is in stark contrast to the rationalism of the Reviser's account from the Carolingian renaissance.

[67] *Ann. Mosellani*, 792 (error for 793). Cf. also *Ann. Laureshamenses*, 793. *Chron. Moissiacense*, 793.

[68] Hofmann, *op. cit.*, pp. 446–7.

[69] *Ann. Salisburgensium add.*, 793: 'Eodem anno ingens opus iussu inutiliter fiebat a Wavarorum et Francorum et Swevorum multitudine.'

taken during the 791 campaign.[70] The labour force could not have lived off the land and the famine must have exacerbated supply problems. Men engaged on heavy manual work need a high daily calorific intake if they are to remain effective, so enormous quantities of provisions would have been needed. Hofmann has used typical eighteenth-century German army rations to form the basis of an estimate of the probable supply needs of the canal project's workforce.[71] Over the whole period of work some 1,200–1,500 tons of provisions and approximately 50,000 gallons of beer would have been required together with over 1,000 oxen and about 3,500 pigs. Again, Hofmann's calculations are based on the assumption that work continued for only ten weeks but in this case we can accept his figures unadjusted as a smaller labour force working for twice as long will have had the same total provisioning requirements. If these supplies had to be bought at famine prices the cost would have been enormous.[72] On top of this there may also have been wages to pay to most of the workers. In fact, the resources which were committed to the project make it comparable to a military campaign.

Despite all efforts, however, the canal was an expensive and very public failure. Could it have worked if the geological conditions had not been so unfavourable? Hofmann believes that the project was essentially well conceived but stresses that the answer depends entirely upon the accuracy of the engineers' understanding of the problem of the different river levels.[73] It is certain, however, that had the problem not been understood, the canal could not have worked.

The canal project has been discussed at some length because it is only with an understanding of the magnitude of the task that the seriousness of Charlemagne's purpose can be appreciated. It is inconceivable that it would have been attempted unless the strategic benefits were fully understood. No further confirmation of the soundness of Charlemagne's strategic vision is needed than the renewed interest shown in the canal in the Napoleonic period when the French military considered

---

[70] Many Avars were taken prisoner by Charlemagne according to the *Ann. Laureshamenses*, 791.

[71] Hofmann, *op. cit.*, pp. 449–51.

[72] A rough idea of the cost of provisioning the work force can be gained from the price-fixing legislation of the Synod of Frankfurt in 794. Twelve 2 pound wheat loaves were to be sold for 1 *denarius*. The price of barley loaves was fixed at 40 per cent less, oat loaves at 50 per cent less. According to Hofmann, each man would have required one 2 pound loaf per day giving a total daily requirement for the whole workforce of about 3,750 loaves per day. Depending on the type of grain used, these would have cost between 150 and 300 *denarii* at the fixed market prices exclusive of the costs of transportation. Any grain bought from royal storehouses would have cost 25 per cent less than this (*Synodus Franconofurtensis, MGH. LL* 2, no. 28, c. 4). On these figures, assuming that work continued for 20 weeks, the minimum cost of bread supplies alone would have been around 1,300 *solidi*. Some idea of the cost of meat comes from the *Capitulare Saxonicum* of 797 (*MGH. LL* 2, no. 29, c. 11) which gives the price of a yearling ox as one *solidus*. The total cost will have been considerably more than the tribute of 100 pounds of silver extracted from the Frisians by the Danes in 810 (*ARF*, 810).

[73] Hofmann, *op. cit.*, p. 444.

completing it to speed their own troop movements, though they too discovered, on examination, that the geological conditions made success impossible.[74]

The Frankish-Byzantine Naval Conflict in the Adriatic

At sea, the Franks were even more active during Charlemagne's reign than they were on the inland waterways. Charlemagne's conquests considerably increased the coastline of the Frankish kingdom and by c. 800, it extended, in the north and the west, from the Elbe to the Gulf of Gascony, and in the western Mediterranean, from Barcelona to Rome, including the Balearic Islands and Corsica, as well as a considerable part of the northern Adriatic coastline. In all there were considerably more than 3,000 miles of coastline to be defended. However, the period from c. 740 to c. 790 had been a peaceful one at sea everywhere and the Frankish kingdom seems not to have had any formal measures for coastal defence in the north or in the Mediterranean. Compared to land frontiers, coasts seemed to provide secure borders and if piracy existed, it was not serious enough to attract the attentions of contemporary annalists.

This happy state of affairs began to change as the century drew to its close. Viking piracy (which will be discussed in detail later in this chapter, pp. 163–71) broke out in the North Sea quite suddenly in the early 790s and became an increasingly serious problem after 800. At the same time, Moslem pirates, from Spain and North Africa, again became active in the Mediterranean after a break of half a century. In the Adriatic, Frankish-Byzantine tension about sovereignty over Venice and Dalmatia meant that the Franks also had to come to terms with the threat of Byzantine naval power. In each case, Charlemagne and his advisers formed rapid and accurate appreciations of the nature of the threat and took effective countermeasures. Although defensive considerations dominated Frankish naval countermeasures, in all three theatres, the Franks could, and did, take effective offensive naval action, especially in the Mediterranean where they were notably successful.

The first campaign to be considered is the short naval war with the Byzantine empire in the Adriatic between 806 and 810. This war was a part of the wider Frankish Byzantine hostilities which had broken out in 788. The causes were complex: a broken marriage alliance, religious issues and the status of the Lombard duchies in southern Italy were all factors in the outbreak of the war, which was not to be formally ended until 815. Early hostilities had gone badly for the Byzantines; an invasion of Benevento had been heavily defeated by Frankish and Lombard forces and by 791 the Franks had seized the Byzantine province of Istria.[75] After this the conflict settled down into a 'cold' war,

---

[74] Hofmann, *ibid.*, p. 441; Bullough, *op. cit.*, p. 68. The Regnitz and the Altmühl were eventually linked in the nineteenth century by the 50-mile-long Ludwigs canal which has over 100 locks and follows a very different course.

[75] King, *Translated Sources*, pp. 56–7.

conducted through diplomacy and theology, to which Charlemagne's assumption of the imperial title in 800 merely added another twist.

It may be that the Byzantine invasion of 788, despite its failure, had provided a spur to the development of Frankish naval power in the Mediterranean by demonstrating the vulnerability of Italy to seaborne attack. At any rate, Charlemagne certainly possessed considerable naval strength in the Mediterranean by 799 when a Frankish force, sent to aid the Balearic islanders, won a notable victory over Moslem pirates.[76] Another sign of Frankish naval power is that in 800 Charlemagne had planned an invasion of Sicily and had been in diplomatic contact with the Byzantine governor of the island, no doubt to ascertain if he was a potential ally in the enterprise.[77] Perhaps the reply was unfavourable as, in the event, nothing came of the scheme. In the following year Charlemagne sent a fleet from Liguria to Africa to collect an elephant and other gifts that the caliph Harun al Raschid had sent from Baghdad.[78]

When open hostilities broke out again in 806 it was over Charlemagne's assumption of sovereignty over the nominally Byzantine territories of Venice and Dalmatia. There were good reasons why Venice should seek closer relations with the Franks. At the outbreak of hostilities with the Byzantine Empire in 788, Charlemagne had ordered the expulsion of Venetian merchants from Ravenna and the Pentapolis[79] and the continuing hostilities will have done nothing to improve business. Opinion among the Venetians as to the best course of action seems to have been divided into distinct pro-Frankish and pro-Byzantine factions. In 803 the pro-Byzantine party appears to have had the upper hand when the pro-Frankish patriarch of Grado was driven out. By 805 the pro-Frankish party was in control of Venice and the two *duces*, Obelerius and Beatus, together with the *dux* and bishop of the Dalmatian city of Zara, came to Charlemagne and transferred their allegiance to him at Christmas 805.[80]

The Byzantine response was swift and before the end of 806 the emperor Nicephorus had despatched a fleet under the patrician Nicetas to recover Dalmatia and Venice.[81] It seems that the fleet settled down to a not very effective

---

[76] *ARF*, 799. Rev., 799.

[77] Theophanes, *Chronographia,* trans. H. Turtledove, *The Chronicle of Theophanes* (Philadelphia, 1982), *s.a.* 6293 (800–1). Both *ARF*, 799, and Rev., 799, mention that a legate from the governor of Sicily met Charles in Saxony but do not explain the purpose of his mission. King, *Charlemagne*, p. 40, suggests that the legate may have been sent in response to soundings as to the governor's attitude to Charlemagne's possible elevation to the imperial dignity. *ARF*, 811, mentions a *spatharius*, Leo, from Sicily who had been in exile with Charlemagne since 800; King, *Translated Sources*, p. 65, suggests that Leo may have been a supporter of Charlemagne's.

[78] *ARF*, 801: 'Tum illi misit Ercanbaldum notarium in Liguriam ad classem parandam qua elefans et ea, qua cum eo deferebantur, subveherentur.'

[79] *Codex Carolinus,* ed. W. Gundlach, *MGH Epp.* 3 (Berlin, 1892), pp. 476–653, no. 86.

[80] *ARF*, 806.

[81] *ARF*, 806. John the Deacon, *Chronicon Venetum,* ed. G. H. Pertz, *MGH. SS* VII (Hanover, 1846), p. 14.

blockade of Venice; Frankish legates returning by sea from a mission to Baghdad were able to slip through the Byzantine fleet unnoticed to reach Treviso.[82] By 807, however, Venice was back in Byzantine hands: Nicetas signed a truce with Pippin, Charlemagne's son and king of Italy, and departed.[83]

In 809 another fleet was despatched from Constantinople, first to Dalmatia, then to Venice. From there a section of the fleet launched an attack on Comacchio but was decisively repulsed by the garrison.[84] In the early Middle Ages the course of the Po ran far to the south of its present course and Comacchio had a commanding position on an island near its mouth. As a consequence, it was then the most important port in the northern Adriatic[85] and as such the most likely centre of Frankish naval power in the region. Following the failure of this attack, which was no doubt intended to eliminate Frankish naval power in the area, the commander of the Byzantine fleet, the *dux* Paul, tried to negotiate a peace with Pippin but found himself thwarted at every turn by Beatus and Obelerius. It soon became apparent that they were playing a double game and, fearing treachery, Paul withdrew the fleet, leaving the Venetians exposed to the revenge of the now angry Pippin.[86] It may be that a Greek attack on Populonia on the Tuscan coast in this year was intended as a diversionary attack to support the campaign to regain Venice.[87]

The next year Pippin laid siege to Venice, overrunning all the city's mainland possessions and blockading it tightly by land and sea.[88] The Franks launched attacks by boat on the island of Malamocco, then the seat of the Venetian government, but it was well defended by barriers of spars driven into the bottom of the shallow lagoon, behind which the Venetians manned boats, and the Franks were repulsed. According to a late source, the defenders bombarded the Franks

---

[82] *ARF*, 806:,
Classis a Niciforo imperatore, cui Niceta patricius praeerat, ad reciperandum Dalmatiam mittitur; et legati qui dudum ante quattuor fere annos ad regem Persarum missi sunt, per ipsas Grecarum navium stationes transvecti ad Tarvisiani portus receptaculum nullo adversariorum sentiente regressi sunt.

[83] *ARF*, 807: 'Niceta patricius qui cum classe Constantinopolita sedebat in Venetia, pace facta cum Pippino rege et indutiis usque ad mensem Augustum constitutis statione soluta Constantinopolim regressus est.'

[84] *ARF*, 809: 'Classis de Constantinopoli missa primo Dalmatiam, deinde Venetiam appulit; cumque ibi hiemaret, pars eius Comiaclum insulam accessit commissoque proelio contra praesidium, quod in ea dispositum erat, victa atque fugata Venetiam recessit.'

[85] P. Longworth, *The Rise and Fall of Venice* (London, 1974), p. 11: throughout the eighth century Comacchio had enjoyed a virtual monopoly of trade along the Po and was the main entrepôt for imports from the east.

[86] *ARF*, 809.

[87] *ARF*, 809: 'In Tuscia Populonium civitas maritima a Grecis qui Orobiotae vocantur, depraedatata est'.

[88] *ARF*, 810: 'Interea Pippinus rex perfidia ducum Veneticorum incitatus Venetiam bello terraque marique iussit appetere.'

with loaves to show them that their blockade was not hurting them.[89] However, the blockade was eventually effective and the Venetians submitted after a siege of six months.[90] Pippin then sent the fleet to ravage the Dalmatian coast but, when a Byzantine fleet from Cephalonia approached under the command of Paul, the Frankish fleet withdrew.[91]

Shortly after this Pippin died and the war came to a rapid end. Venice was immediately restored to the Byzantines and in 812 terms for a lasting peace were agreed, though it would be another three years before this would be officially ratified. The Byzantine emperor recognised Charlemagne's imperial title and his sovereignty over Istria and the Croats. In return Charlemagne surrendered Venetia and Dalmatia.[92] In addition Venice would pay a considerable tribute to the ruler of Italy, and in fact continued to do so for at least the next century and a half.[93] Venetian ships would also have to serve with the Frankish fleet on naval expeditions against the Slavs, whose piracy was a problem in the Adriatic for much of the ninth century.[94] It was by no means an unfavourable agreement from Charlemagne's point of view. The Venetians also got what they wanted; they preserved their semi-autonomous position in the Byzantine empire and gained, at a price, secure access to the markets of the Frankish empire without submitting to Frankish domination.

---

[89] Constantine VII Porphyrogenitus, *De administrando imperio,* ed. and trans. G. Moravcsik and R. J. H. Jenkins, *Corpus Fontium Historiae Byzantinae* I (Washington, 1967), chapter 28. This detail is also mentioned by Andreas Danduli (*Chronicon Venetum,* ed. L. A. Muratori, *Rerum Italicarum Scriptores* XII.i (Bologna, 1938–47), pp. 1–405), VII, xiv.23. This thirteenth-century account is by far the fullest which exists but it includes improbable details and Dandolo, who was a doge of Venice, also neglects to mention that the Venetians did actually submit to Pippin in the end. The short account by John the Deacon, pp. 14–15, says simply that Pippin's assaults failed.

[90] Constantine Porphyrogenitus, 28.

[91] *ARF*, 810: 'subiectaque Venetia ac ducibus eius in deditionem acceptis eandem classem ad Dalmatiae litora vastanda misit. Sed cum Paulus Cefalaniae praefectus cum orientali classe ad auxilium Dalmatis ferendum adventaret, regia classis ad propria regreditur.'

[92] Bullough, *op. cit.,* pp. 196–7.

[93] Constantine Porphyrogenitus, 28, says that the tribute of 36 pounds of uncoined silver was still being paid to the king of Italy at the time when he wrote (948–52). Though it had been considered a heavy tribute at the time of its imposition, its value had since been very much reduced by inflation.

[94] It is believed that the *Pactum Hlotharii I, MGH. LL* 2, no. 233, of 840 reproduces the terms of the peace treaty of 812 (Bullough, *op. cit.,* p. 196). Cap. 7 concerns the naval obligations which were imposed on Venice:

> Et hoc statuimus ut, quandocumque mandatum domini imperatoris Lotharii clarissimi augusti vel missorum eius nobis nuntiatum fuerit, inter utrasque partes ad vestrum solatium navalem exercitum contra generationes Sclavorum, inimicos silicet vestros, in quo potuerimus, solatium prestare debeamus absque ulla occasione.

The treaty was renewed on exactly the same terms in 888: see *Pactum Berengarii I, MGH. LL* 2, no. 238. On Slavic piracy in the Adriatic in the ninth century see H. F. Brown, *Venice; An Historical Sketch* (London, 1893), pp. 48–50.

Though the Frankish fleet may not have been a match for a Byzantine fleet, the Byzantine position was weakened by the remoteness of the northern Adriatic from the main centres of Byzantine naval power. The Venetians themselves clearly did not welcome the permanent presence of Byzantine forces on their territory, so the Byzantine fleet could achieve only temporary dominance of the Adriatic; when the fleet withdrew, there was nothing to prevent the Franks once again enforcing their stranglehold on Venice. There can be little doubt then that the favourable peace terms offered by the Byzantine empire were, in part, a consequence of Frankish naval strength in the Adriatic.

It has been suggested that Charlemagne's motive in assuming sovereignty over Venice had been the acquisition of the city's naval power.[95] Though the peace treaty of 812 gave Charlemagne a measure of control over the Venetian fleet, it seems unlikely that this could have been the main motive. Events, particularly the Venetians' inability to break the Frankish naval blockade in 810, show that in the early ninth century Venice was not a major naval power. However, Venetian naval power developed rapidly in the ninth century and by the time the Frankish-Venetian treaty of 812 was renewed in 840, Venice was capable of putting to sea a fleet of 60 warships for a campaign against the Muslims.[96] This was nevertheless still considerably smaller than the fleet of 80 40-oared galleys and 100 smaller vessels the Croats could raise around this time.[97]

The Frankish-Moslem Naval War in the Mediterranean

Though the Frankish fleet had been used effectively in the Adriatic it seems to have seen little serious combat. Things were different in the western Mediterranean where the Franks waged a determined naval war against Moslem pirates from Spain and Africa. This conflict has received scant attention from historians and it has been described as 'the forgotten war of the ninth century'.[98] It does not deserve this obscurity for, if it is true that the Franks did lose control of the western Mediterranean in the long run, their opposition to the Moslem pirates was to be highly effective for at least 30 years after the first raids.

Moslem piracy had been a problem in the western Mediterranean following the Arab conquest of North Africa in 698, but this had finally petered out by the middle of the eighth century in the face of strong Byzantine naval opposition.[99]

---

[95] Pirenne, *op. cit.*, p. 177. A. R. Lewis, *Naval Power and Trade in the Mediterranean AD 500-1100* (Princeton, 1951), p. 106.

[96] For the treaty see *Pactum Hlotharii I*, for the naval expedition, which was a failure see John the Deacon, p. 17.

[97] Constantine Porphyrogenitus, 31.

[98] King, *Translated Sources*, p. 68.

[99] J. B. Bury, 'The naval policy of the Roman empire in relation to the western provinces from the 7th to the 9th century', in *Centenario della nascita di Michele Amari II* (Palermo, 1910), p. 26. A. M. Fahmy, *Muslim Sea Power in the Eastern Mediterranean from the Seventh to the Tenth*

The half-century of peace which followed was ended in 798 when Spanish Moors raided the Balearic Islands, which were under nominal Byzantine rule.[100] The islanders must have doubted the ability of the Byzantines to defend them effectively as they sent legates to Charlemagne to ask for his protection and offer their submission. The islanders will have been well pleased with their decision; Frankish help was immediately forthcoming and troops were despatched in time to meet the pirates when they returned in 799. The pirates were heavily defeated by the Franks and their captured standards were taken to Aachen in triumph and presented to Charlemagne.[101] It was 813 before pirates are known to have returned to the Balearics, and the islands were not finally to be occupied by the Moors until 902.[102] Despite their exposed position, possession of the Balearics gave the Frankish defence important strategic benefits as they lay across the sea routes from Spain to Corsica, Sardinia, Italy and Provence, providing a base from which Moslem shipping could be harassed, so limiting the freedom of movement of pirates operating in the western Mediterranean.[103]

Charlemagne's reaction to the Moslem sea-raids was to order his son Louis to build a fleet to protect the mouth of the Rhône,[104] which was the only important navigable river on the empire's Mediterranean coast. Probably at the same time, he ordered the construction of fortifications at ports along the coast from Narbonne to Rome.[105] Sometime before 812 Charlemagne also instructed Leo III to organise defences in the papal states.[106] As we have seen, Charlemagne must already have had warships available at some of these ports and no doubt these

---

Century AD (Cairo, 1966), p. 122, prefers to emphasise the internal problems of the caliphate as the main cause for the cessation of raids. The raids themselves are comprehensively summarised in A. Ahmad, *A History of Islamic Sicily* (Edinburgh, 1975), pp. 3–4.

[100] *ARF*, 798. Rev., 798.

[101] *ARF*, 799:

Insulae Baleares quae a Mauris et Sarracenis anno priore depraedatae sunt, postulato atque accepto a nostris auxilio nobis se dediderunt et cum Dei auxilio a nostris a praedonum incursione defensi sunt. Signa quoque Maurorum in pugna sublata et domno regi praesentata sunt.

Also, but in less detail, Rev., 799. The terms *Mauri* and *Sarraceni* are used rather indiscriminately in the sources to describe Moslems of whatever origin. For the sake of clarity, I refer to Spanish Moslems as Moors, North Africans as Arabs. The term Moslem is used only when the origin of the pirates cannot be determined from the sources.

[102] J. H. Pryor, *Geography, Technology and War. Studies in the Maritime History of the Mediterranean, 649–1571* (Cambridge, 1988), p. 91. Though 902 marks the definitive occupation of the Balearics by the Moors, they had been an Omayyad protectorate since 849.

[103] Deanesly, *op. cit.*, p. 376. This was also the islands' strategic importance in the war against the Moslem corsairs after the Aragonese seized the islands in 1229: see Pryor, *op. cit.*

[104] Astronomer, 15: see text below n. 143.

[105] Einhard, *V. Karoli*, 17: 'Fecit idem a parte meridiana in litore Narbonensis ac Septimaniae, toto etiam Italiae litore usque Romam contra Mauros nuper pyraticam exercere adgressos.'

[106] Leo III, *Epistolae*, X.6 (812), ed. K. Hampe, *MGH. Epp.* 5, p. 97: 'A quo enim de illorum adventu vestra nos exhortavit serenitas, semper postera et litoraria ordinata habuimus et habemus custodias.'

flotillas were strengthened to meet the increased threat. Genoa will certainly have been an important centre of Frankish naval power[107] and a fleet seems also to have been stationed at or near Ampurias on the Spanish coast.[108]

The Franks were remarkably successful in bringing the pirates to battle, always the most difficult task for defenders in this period, whether the enemy was Moslem or Viking. In 806 a Frankish force was sent to Corsica against the Moors who were ravaging the island. The pirates had made off before the Franks arrived, but one of the Frankish commanders, Hadumar, the count of Genoa, gave chase and intercepted them. His effort was in vain as his force was defeated and Hadumar was killed.[109] The next year the Franks were luckier. The Moors had already suffered a serious defeat on Sardinia when they attacked Corsica. Here their fleet was intercepted in harbour by a Frankish fleet under Burchard, the count of the stables, and heavily defeated, losing 13 ships.[110] In 809, 810 and 812 the Spanish Moors raided Corsica and (Sardinia, mainly for slaves, meeting nothing but local resistance.[111] However, in 813 an expedition under Irmingar, count of Ampurias in northern Spain, caught and defeated a pirate fleet returning to Spain from a raid on Corsica, off Majorca. Eight of the Moorish ships were captured, and 500 Corsican prisoners were found in them.[112] In retaliation, the Moors attacked the mainland of the empire for the first and only time in Charlemagne's reign. Nice and Civitavecchia were sacked but when the pirates raided Sardinia on their way home they received another serious beating from local forces.[113] The Moors suffered a lesser reverse on the seas between Africa

---

[107] The fleet which was sent to collect the elephant from Africa was Ligurian, so probably from Genoa (*ARF*, 801) and the count of Genoa was killed on an expedition to Corsica in 806 (*ARF*, 806).

[108] *ARF*, 813.

[109] *ARF*, 806:

Eodem anno in Corsicam insulam contra Mauros, qui eam vastabant, classis de Italia a Pippino missa est, cuius adventum Mauri non expectantes abscesserunt; unus tamen nostrorum, Hadumarus comes civitatis Genuae, inprudenter contra eos dimicans occisus est.

[110] *ARF*, 807: 'Ibi iterum in quodam portu eiusdem insulae cum classe cui Burchardus praeerat, proelio decertaverunt victique ac fugati sunt, amissis tredecim navibus et plurimis suorum interfectis.' The status of Sardinia in the early ninth century is unclear. Relations with the Franks were close (see *ARF*, 815, 828) but the island was probably still at least nominally within the Byzantine empire: E. Besta, *La Sardegna Medioevale* (2 vols, Palermo, 1908), vol. 1, pp. 32–8.

[111] *ARF*, 809 (it is clear that this was primarily a slave-raid; only the old and infirm, i.e. the unsaleable, were left by the Moors); *ARF*, 810; *ARF*, 812.

[112] *ARF*, 813: 'Mauris de Corsica ad Hispaniam cum multa praeda redeuntibus Irmingarius comes Emporitanus in Maiorica insidias posuit et octo naves eorum cepit in quibus quingentos et eo amplius Corsos captivos invenit.' There is no reason to believe that the whole Moorish fleet was captured and the large number of captives recovered in just eight ships is an indication of the devastating scale of the raids. Moorish ships must have been large: there was an average of 62 to 63 prisoners in each of the captured ships.

[113] *ARF*, 813: 'Hoc Mauri vindicare volentes Centumcellas Tusciae civitatem et Niceam provinciae Narbonensis vastaverunt. Sardiniam quoque adgressi commissoque cum Sardis proelio pulsi ac victi et multis suorum amissis recesserunt. Cf. Einhard, *V. Karoli*, 17, who states that only Civitavecchia was attacked and adds that it was taken as a result of treachery.

and Sicily when two Spanish ships were burned by Venetian ships.[114] These setbacks seem to have discouraged further Moorish piracy and nothing is heard of further raids from Moslem Spain until 838 when Marseilles was attacked.[115]

This success, significant as it was, was matched by Byzantine successes against the North African Arabs who were also becoming active in piracy. In 812, for the first time, pirates from North Africa joined in the raids on Corsica and Sardinia,[116] and in the same year an Arab fleet of 40 ships raided the islands of Ischia and Ponza while 13 others attacked Lampedusa.[117] Though the attacks on Ponza and Ischia were very destructive, the fleet which raided Lampedusa was completely annihilated by a Byzantine fleet. In 813 the Arabs suffered another reverse; a major fleet, said to have been over 100 strong, was destroyed by a storm at sea off Sardinia, though a smaller force successfully attacked Calabria.[118] These twin disasters must have seriously diminished Arab naval power, leaving Africa exposed to Byzantine retaliation. No doubt it was to head this off that the emir negotiated a ten-year truce with Gregory, the governor of Sicily, who, however, was frankly sceptical of the Arabs' good faith, pointing to breaches of two earlier treaties.[119] The end of 813 saw the Christians in complete control of the western Mediterranean. While the Byzantines had certainly borne the brunt of the Arab raids, the defeat of the Spanish Moors had been largely the achievement of Frankish forces.[120]

Gregory's doubts about Arab good faith were justified. In 819–20 raids on Sicily began again and intensified until, in 827, the Arabs took advantage of a civil war to begin their slow conquest of the island, a conquest which was not finally completed until 963. If it was the Byzantines who again bore the brunt of the Arab raids, the Franks were certainly not unaffected. It may have been a Frankish fleet which was defeated by the Arabs off Sardinia in 820.[121] It is also probable that Corsica was heavily raided for in February 825 Lothar ordered the

---

[114] Leo III, *Epp.* X.7 (813), p. 98: 'Ipsi vero missi Sarracenorum in navigiis Beneticorum venerunt, et sic veniendo combusserunt igne duo navigia, quae de Spania veniebant.'

[115] *Annales Bertiniani*, ed. R. Rau, *Quellen zur karolingischen Reichsgeschichte*, vol. 2 (Darmstadt, 1972), pp. 11–288, s.a. 838.

[116] *ARF*, 812.

[117] Leo III, *Epp.* X.6. pp. 96–7. This letter also contains evidence of the emerging naval power of the nominally Byzantine cities of Naples, Gaeta and Amalfi.

[118] Leo III, *Epp.* X.7, p. 98.

[119] *Ibid.*, p. 98. The Moors of Spain were specifically excluded from this truce.

[120] Einhard's assertion, *V. Karoli*, 17, that Charlemagne's measures were effective in preventing the Moors from doing serious damage seems to be much nearer the truth than the assessments of some modern historians. For example, Pirenne's assertions, *op. cit.*, pp. 248–9, that Charlemagne had no fleet on the Mediterranean and that he was 'incapable of assuring the safety of the seas' fly in the face of the evidence.

[121] *ARF*, 820: 'In Italico mari octo naves negotiatorum de Sardinia ad Italiam revertentium a piratis captae ac dimersae sunt.' Though the annalist does not give the nationality of the ships, which he describes as merchantmen, Arab sources report that in this year a Frankish fleet was beaten off Sardinia with the loss of eight ships: Scholz and Rogers, *op. cit.*, p. 197. There can at least be little doubt about the accuracy of the figure.

preparation of an expedition to Corsica.[122] Unfortunately, absolutely nothing else is known about this expedition, even whether it actually took place.

The Frankish response was certainly not entirely defensive. In 828 a fleet under count Boniface, the *praefectus* of Corsica, and his brother Berhard took a small fleet around the island to search for pirates. Finding none they moved on to Sardinia which also proved to be clear of pirates. Here they took on board local pilots who guided the fleet across to Africa where they landed between Utica and Carthage. The Arabs had well-organised coast defences and local forces were quickly alerted. The Franks fought and won five battles but were forced to withdraw to their ships after a defeat by coastguards and local Bedouin near Sousse.[123] It has been suggested that this raid was carried out in alliance with the Byzantines to divert the Arabs away from their attack on Sicily.[124] However, the Frankish sources seem to indicate that the raid was purely opportunistic and it might be more correct to say that the Franks took advantage of the Arab involvement in Sicily to raid Africa. This remarkable incident was in fact the only naval attack by the Latin West on Moslem Africa before the Pisans sacked Annaba (Bône) in 1034.[125]

Frankish naval power in the Mediterranean seems to have survived the civil wars of Louis' reign which were to have such a serious effect on the coast defences in the north as in 839 the Byzantine emperor sent an embassy to Louis to ask for a fleet to be sent to assist him against the Moslems.[126] Nevertheless, Louis' later years do seem to have witnessed a decline in the effectiveness of the Frankish defences as Moorish and Arab raids became more frequent. The raid on Marseilles in 838 was followed by raids on Arles in 842 and 850, Rome in 846,

---

[122] *Capitula de expeditione Corsica, MGH. LL* 2, no. 162.

[123] The fullest account is Astronomer, 42:

> Bonifatius comes, ab imperatore Corsicae praefectus insulae, cum fratre Berhardo aliisque adiunctis sibi conscensa parva classe, dum pyratas maria pervagando requirit et non invenit, sibi Sardorum insulam amicorum appulit: indeque aliquos gnaros itineris marini sibi assumens, in Affricam transvectus inter Uticam atque Kartaginem. Contra quem multitudo conveniens Afrorum, quinquies conflixit, totiens victa succubuit, et innumerabilem suorum multitudinem amisit; inter quos et quosdam contigit oppetere nostrorum, quos aut multa alacritas, aut inconsulta levitas ad nimis audendum impulit. Bonifatius tamen sotiis receptis ad naves se collegit, patriam repetivit, inexpertumque atque inauditum metum prius Afris reliquit.

> The account in *ARF*, 828, is not as full but supports the Astronomer's account in most respects. The main difference is that the *ARF* give the impression that the expedition suffered heavier casualties than does the Astronomer's account. The expedition is also recorded in Arabic sources which give an account of its defeat near Sousse: Eickhoff, *op. cit.*, p. 74.

[124] Lewis, *op. cit.*, pp. 132–3.

[125] Ahmad, *op. cit.*, p. 35.

[126] Genesius, *Regum Libri Quattuor*, ed. A. Lesmueller-Werner and I. Thurn, *Corpus Fontium Historiae Byzantinae* XIV (Berlin-New York, 1978), III.16. The *Ann. Bertiniani*, 839, record the arrival of this mission at Ingelheim but say nothing of its purpose. Louis did not in fact send a fleet but this is not necessarily an indication that he no longer possessed one; it could simply have been fully committed in the west. Fahmy, *op. cit.*, p. 106, suggests that the Byzantines were planning to attack Syria or Egypt which had often been the targets of naval expeditions in the past.

and Marseilles again in 848. In 840 the Arabs seized Bari as a permanent base on the Adriatic and in 860, mirroring Viking tactics, the Moors established their first permanent raiding base at the mouth of the Rhône and raided upstream as far as Valence and beyond into the heart of Burgundy. By the end of the ninth century they had established a base at Fraxinetum, near St Tropez, from which they raided the Alpine passes between Gaul and Italy. Provence was not to be freed of a Moorish presence until as late as 973.[127] The Balearic islands probably began to slip away from Frankish control in the 830s and had become a protectorate of the Omayyad caliphate of Cordova by 849,[128] a clear sign of the decline of Frankish naval power in the Mediterranean. This must have left the coast of Gaul dangerously exposed as, under the terms of the treaty with the caliphate, the Balearic islanders were forced to stop interfering with Moorish shipping. This decline, which is also evident in the north, was no doubt a consequence of the outbreaks of civil war in 829–34 and 841–43 and the decline of royal authority which resulted from them.

Despite its long coastline, Italy suffered less severely than might be imagined as its lack of navigable rivers and mountainous terrain made rapid forays inland difficult. Because of this, the Franks were generally able to hold the Moslem raiders at bay and in 871 an alliance between Louis II, Venice and Byzantium recaptured Bari.[129] The developing naval power of Italian cities such as Naples, Amalfi and Venice and the continued presence of Byzantine fleets in Italian waters must also have added to the security of the kingdom of Italy. It is likely that royal authority remained strong enough in Italy under the competent rule of Louis II (844–75) to ensure that some kind of royal fleet was maintained. In 846 Lothar raised a fleet from the Pentapolis and Venice against the Arabs who had attacked Benevento,[130] and in 850 Louis II issued a capitulary which ordered the repair of old warships.[131] Louis II left no heir and after his death royal authority decayed under his weak successors, not to be restored until the time of the German emperor Otto I. In the intervening period the control and development of Italian naval power passed definitively to the coastal trading cities

There is no concrete evidence for the characteristics of the warships used in the Frankish fleets in the Mediterranean. However, because of the strength of Byzantine influence in Italy, and especially in the Adriatic, there is good reason to believe that they were similar to Byzantine warships.[132] The most common Byzantine warship appears to have been the dromon, a fast galley with a single or double bank of oars. Dromons seem first to have been built in the late fifth century and were perhaps a development of the Liburnian. Unlike Mediterranean

---

[127] In general on the Moslem raids in the western Mediterranean in this period see Eickhoff, *op. cit.*, pp. 173–94, 297–8, 315–18, 370.

[128] *Ibid.*, p. 198.

[129] On Louis II and the campaigns against the emirate of Bari see Eickhoff, *op. cit.*, pp. 211–18.

[130] *Hlotharii capitulare de expeditione contra Sarracenos facienda*, MGH. LL 2, no. 203, c. 12.

[131] *Capitula comitibus papiae ab Hludowico II proposita*, MGH. LL 2, no. 212, c. 6.

[132] Eickhoff, *op. cit.*, p. 151.

Figure 15 A dromon from an early medieval graffito at Malaga, Spain

galleys of the classical period, such as the Liburnian, the dromon placed little reliance on the ram as a weapon. Another feature which distinguished the dromon from its predecessors was the use of the lateen sail, which brought great improvements in manoeuverability over the square sail.[133] From the seventh century on, the dromon could be armed with Greek fire projectors which gave the Byzantine fleet a formidable advantage over its enemies.[134] However this weapon was not suitable for use on the open sea and was only rarely used outside the Constantinopolitan area. Following their conquest of Egypt and the Levant in the seventh century, the Arabs had taken over intact the Byzantine shipyards of the area and as a consequence the warships of the Moslem fleets were very similar to contemporary Byzantine warships such as the dromon.[135] The fact that the Moslems could be beaten at sea by the Frankish fleets is an indication that,

---

[133] On the dromon see F. van Doorninck, 'Byzantium, mistress of the sea', in C. F. Bass (ed.), *A History of Seafaring Based on Underwater Archaeology* (London, 1972), pp. 134–5, and Unger, *The Ship in the Medieval Economy*, pp. 43–5.

[134] On Greek fire see J. Haldon and M. Byrne, 'A possible solution to the problem of Greek fire', *Byzantinische Zeitschrift* LXX (1977), pp. 91–9, whose conclusions have been tested by practical experimentation. Greek fire was simply crude oil, perhaps with a resin added to improve its adhesion to the target; the secret lay in the projector in which the oil was pre-heated under pressure before firing.

[135] Eickhoff, *op. cit.*, p. 152.

whatever their actual characteristics, Frankish warships were not inferior in battleworthiness to dromons.

While there can be little doubt that Frankish warships in the Mediterranean were built by local craftsmen using Mediterranean techniques and crewed by local sailors, the commanders seem mostly to have been Frankish. Of the six naval commanders whose names we know, Ercanbald, Hadumar, Burchard, Irmingard, Boniface and Berhard,[136] only the last two were certainly not Frankish; they were Bavarian.[137] To this list perhaps should be added Wala, a high ranking Frankish noble who had already served against the Danes, sent by Charlemagne to Italy in 812 to help meet the threat of a Moslem invasion.[138]

The Defence of the Northern Coasts against the Vikings

In the north, the Franks faced the threat of Viking piracy. In the long term this was to prove far more destructive than the Moslem raids, but initially the Vikings' raids were probably on a smaller scale. The earliest securely dated Viking raid occurred in 793 when the Northumbrian monastery on Lindisfarne was sacked by Norwegian pirates.[139] The raids which succeeded this were directed at the rich and vulnerable monasteries on the coasts of the British Isles and it was not until early in 799 that the first raid on Francia was recorded. The islands off the coast of Aquitaine were ravaged by a Viking fleet but, though serious damage was done, the raid was not a great success; some of the Vikings' ships were wrecked and 105 of the pirates were killed by the Franks.[140]

There is no doubt that Charlemagne was well aware of the activities of the Vikings in Britain and it can have come as little surprise that they had now turned their attention to Francia. Charlemagne reacted with his usual energy and in mid March 800 he left Aachen for the Channel coast where he ordered the formation of a fleet, perhaps at Boulogne, and other unspecified defensive measures.[141]

---

[136] *ARF*, 801; *ARF*, 806; *ARF*, 807 (Burchard was later also involved with the Danes *ARF*, 811); *ARF*, 813; *ARF*, 828. Astronomer, 42.

[137] E. Hlawitschka, *Franken, Alemannen, Bayern und Burgunder in Oberitalien (774–962)*, Forschungen zur oberrheinischen Landesgeschichte 8 (Freiburg, 1960), p. 47.

[138] *ARF*, 811, 812.

[139] Unlike the raid recorded in the *ASC* under 787 (i.e. 789), which is in any case dated only to the reign of king Beorhtric (786–802), we possess immediately contemporary accounts of the raid on Lindisfarne: see Alcuin, *Epp.*, nos 16–21.

[140] Alcuin, *Epp.* no. 184: 'Paganae vero naves, ut audistis, multa mala fecerunt per insulas oceani partibus Aquitaniae. Pars tamen ex illis periit; et occisi sunt in litore quasi centum quinque viri ex illis praedatoribus.'

[141] *ARF*, 800: 'Ipse medio mense Martio Aquisgrani palatio digrediens, litus oceani Gallici perlustravit, in ipso mari, quod tunc piratis infestum erat, classem instituit, praesidia disposuit, pascha in Centulo apud sanctum Richarium celebravit. Indeque iterum per litus oceani Ratumagum civitatem profectus est.' The Reviser for this year is almost identical, adding, perhaps with the benefit of hindsight, that the pirates were *Nordmanni*. A fleet was certainly

Charlemagne's concern for the defence of the coast is shown by frequent legislation in the years which followed. Capitularies ordering the construction of ships for the fleet were issued in 802, 808, and 810,[142] and in 810 fleets were ordered to be stationed on all of the empire's navigable rivers, including the Loire and the Garonne.[143] The fleet was first mobilised in 810 as a response to a Danish attack on Frisia but it did not engage the enemy.[144] This attack no doubt served to emphasise the vulnerability of the coast and in the following year Charlemagne attended to the naval defences in person, inspecting the fleets at Ghent and Boulogne, where he also ordered the restoration of the old Roman lighthouse as an aid to navigation.[145] At the same time Charlemagne issued a capitulary which ordered the lords to equip themselves for fighting at sea,[146] no doubt in anticipation of further Danish attacks.

Defences against the Vikings were also arranged on land. An Aquitainian capitulary of 802 laid down a tariff of fines for inhabitants of coastal districts, free and unlike alike, who failed to respond when called upon for assistance,[147]

---

stationed at Boulogne in 811: *ARF*, 811. According to the *Annales S. Amandi*, 800 (ed. G. H. Pertz, *MGH*, *SS* 1 (Hanover, 1826)), Charlemagne had gone to the coast for the fishing.

[142] *Capitularia missorum specialia, MGH. LL* 2, no. 34, c. 13a: 'De navigia praeparando circa littoralia maris'; *Capitula cum primis conferenda, ibid.*, no. 51, c. 10: 'De navibus quas facere iussimus'; *Capitulare missorum Aquisgranense primum, ibid.*, no. 64, c. 16: 'De materia ad naves faciendas'.

[143] Astronomer, 15: 'Praeceperat namque tunc temporis fabricari naves contra Nordomanicas incursiones in omnibus fluminibus quae mari influebant. Quam curam etiam filio iniunxit super Hrodanum et Garonnam et Silidam' (*leg.* Ligerim; King, *Translated Sources*, p. 175). Although King, *ibid.*, p. 22, dates the events of this chapter to 803, he has recently informed me that, following a reassessment of the evidence, he now believes them to date to 810. Mollat, *op. cit.*, p. 1013–14, doubts that Louis carried out his father's orders to build these fleets but there is no evidence to justify this conclusion. Also on the coastal defences see Einhard, *V. Karoli*, 17: see text below, n. 154.

[144] *ARF*, 810: 'Qui nuntius adeo imperatorem concitavit, ut missis in omnes circumquaque regiones ad congredandum exercitum nuntiis ipse sine mora palatio exiens primo quidem classi occurrere, deinde transmisso Rheno flumine in loco, qui Lippeham vocatur, copias, quae nondum convenerant, statuit operiri.'

[145] *ARF*, 811:

'Ipse autem interea propter classem, quam anno superiore fieri imperavit, videndam ad Bononiam civitatem maritimam, ubi eaedem naves congregatae erant, accessit farumque ibi ad navigantium cursus dirigendos antiqus constitutam restauravit et in summitate eius nocturnum ignem accendit. Inde ad Scaldium fluvium veniens in loco, qui Gand vocatur, naves ad eandem classem aedificatas aspexit et circa medium Novembrium Aquas venit.

This entry is confusing as it says that Charlemagne had gone to inspect the fleet which he had ordered to be built the previous year. But it is clear from the reference for 810 (see above) that Charlemagne already had a fleet in service by that year and, as we saw above, the first orders to build a fleet had gone out in 800. The annals must be referring to an order to reinforce the fleet, perhaps by creating a new flotilla, not a new initiative.

[146] *Capitulare Bononiensis, MGH. LL* 2, no. 74, c. 11: 'Ut quandocumque navigium mittere volumus, ipsi seniores in ipsis navibus pergant, et ad hoc sint praeparati.'

[147] *Capitularia missorum specialia, MGH. LL* 2, no. 34, c. 13b:

and in 808 the question of coastal defence was on the agenda for a meeting of Charlemagne and the *primi*.[148] Fortifications were constructed at ports and at the mouths of navigable rivers[149] and a chain of warning beacons was probably established along the coast.[150] Professional coastguard units were perhaps also formed.[151] The locations of Charlemagne's forts are not known with any certainty. A chain of eight early medieval forts are known on the North Sea coast between Flanders and Texel but there have been no extensive excavations and none of the sites are precisely dated. One, Oost-Souburg on Walcheren, has been dated to the early ninth century but this date is not precise enough to ascribe it confidently to Charlemagne's reign; it could equally well have been built by Louis.[152] The fort at Oost-Souburg, like the other forts, was round with four equally spaced gateways. The fort, which had regularly laid out internal roads and buildings, had a diameter of about 130 yards and was surrounded by a wide moat. The shape and layout of these forts has led to speculation that they were the model for the tenth-century round forts in Denmark of the Trelleborg-type.[153]

For a man who is rarely credited with an understanding of naval power, Charlemagne had, as Einhard makes quite clear in the *Vita Karoli*, come swiftly to an accurate understanding both of the nature of the threat facing the empire and of the appropriate countermeasures:

> De liberis hominibus qui circa maritima loca habitant: si nuntius venerit ut ad succurendum debeant venire, et hoc neglexerint, unusquisque solidos viginti conponat, mediaetatem in dominico, mediaetatem ad populum. Si litus fuerit, solidos quindecim conponat ad populum et fredo dominico in dorso iaccipiat. Si servus fuerit, solidos X ad populum et fredo dorsum.

[148] *Capitula cum primis conferenda, MGH. LL* 2, no. 51, c. 9: 'De marcha nostra custodienda terra marique'.

[149] Einhard, *V. Karoli*, 17; Astronomer, 15. See n. 143 above for texts.

[150] Nithard, *Historiarum libri IIII*, (ed. Rau, *op. cit.*, vol. 1, pp. 383–461), III. 3, refers to use of a beacon chain, like those used on the sea coast, on the banks of the Seine by Charles the Bald to provide warning of the approach of his half brother Lothar: 'Et ut perfacile dinosceretur, quo in loco adiutorium praeberi deberet, more maritimo signa in locis congruis atque custodias deputavit.' This incident took place in 841 and so proves only that beacon chains were in use at that time, but this is such a basic system that it would surely have been one of Charlemagne's first measures.

[151] Presumably the *excubitores* who were stationed at the river mouths (Einhard, *V. Karoli*, 17) would have been professional soldiers able to mount permanent guard. The speed of the reaction to the Viking attack of 820 (see below, p. 168) also suggests the presence of at least some standing troops in the coastal areas. *Ann. Bertiniani*, 867, mentions troops called *Cokingi* in action against the Vikings, and Ellmers, *Handelsschiffahrt*, p. 71, concludes, on the basis of charter evidence, that as these troops were paid out of tolls and taxation they were professionals. He suggests that they had their origin in Charlemagne's coastguard system.

[152] On these forts in general see P. H. Sawyer, *Kings and Vikings* (London, 1982), pp. 82–3 and H. Van Werveke, 'De oudste Burchten aan de Vlaamse en de Zeeuwse Kust', *Mededelingen van de Koninklijke Vlaamse Academie voor Wetenschappen, Letteren en Schone Kunsten van Belgie, Klasse der Letteren*, XXVII.1 (1965) pp. 3-22. On Oost-Souburg in particular see J. H. F. Bloemers *et al. Verleden Land* (Amsterdam, 1981), pp. 138–9.

[153] E. Roesdahl, *Viking Age Denmark* (London, 1982), p. 144.

> He undertook the building of a fleet to wage war against the Northmen and ships for this purpose were built on the rivers of Gaul and Germany which flow into the northern ocean. And because the Northmen were ravaging the coasts of Gaul and Germany with constant attacks, he provided fortifications and guard posts at every harbour and at the mouth of every river which was considered to be navigable by ships, and by such defensive measures prevented any enemy from being able to escape.[154]

It was impossible to protect the whole coastline and there was, in practical terms, nothing that could be done to defend isolated areas such as the Frisian islands; to have tried would have been uselessly to dissipate the defensive effort. But disastrous as these raids must have been for the victims, attacks on the periphery of the empire were a supportable burden. In fact there were few places of any importance on the open coastline; even the major ports, such as Quentovic and Dorestad, were situated inland on navigable rivers as were many rich monasteries. These rivers, especially the Rhine, Scheldt, Seine, Loire and Garonne, were the key to the effective defence of the empire against the Viking raiders. If the raiders penetrated these river systems they could roam at will in the rich heartlands of the empire, as indeed they were to do for decades after the death of Louis the Pious. Charlemagne's decision to concentrate the defences on the river mouths shows complete mastery of the strategic and tactical situation. The fleets and fortifications at these points could with luck prevent the Vikings getting into the empire in the first place, but even if they failed in this they could still block the raiders' escape back to the sea and bring them to battle. Charlemagne showed similar tactical sense in stationing a fleet at Boulogne to cover the Dover Straits; this was the only point on the coastline at which patrolling might offer a chance of intercepting the raiders at sea.

The parallels with the Roman defences of the third and fourth centuries are obvious and it is difficult to see what more Charlemagne could have done to combat the Vikings. Nevertheless, he laboured under certain disadvantages which had not applied to the Romans. Most obviously, he did not control both shores of the Channel and there is no evidence of defensive co-operation with the Anglo-Saxons which might have made good this lack. Possibly a greater disadvantage than this was the fact that by the 790s Norwegian Vikings had settled in Shetland, Orkney and Caithness and from there had raided the west coasts of Scotland, Ireland and Wales. It was perhaps also from there that the Vikings who had raided Aquitaine in 799 had come, as, indeed, they were to do later in the ninth century. Thus the Channel was no longer the bottleneck for

---

[154] Einhard, *V. Karoli*, 17:

> Molitus est et classem contra bellum Nordmannicum, aedificatis ad hoc navibus iuxta flumina, quae et de Gallia et de Germania septentrionalem influunt oceanum. Et quia Nordmanni Gallicum litus atque Germanicum assidua infestatione vastabant, per omnes portus et ostia fluminum, qua naves recipi posse videbantur, stationibus et excubiis dispositis, ne qua hostis exire potuisset, tali munitione prohibuit.

pirate ships that it had been in Roman times and the chances of getting early warning of attacks were reduced accordingly. Another limitation was the lack of a large standing army suitable for permanent guard and garrison duty. The Frankish army was a crushingly powerful offensive weapon but its soldiers served in fulfilment of a legal obligation, not for pay, and were motivated by the chance of plunder.[155] Defensive warfare carried similar risks to offensive warfare but none of the opportunities for profit and it is no surprise that Charlemagne sometimes had problems in mobilising troops for his later campaigns which were often defensive in purpose.[156]

A further disadvantage was that the Frankish host took time to gather for a campaign, time in which a highly mobile Viking fleet would be able to plunder and make off, as indeed happened in 810 when the fleet was mobilised for the first time. A large Danish fleet, of 200 ships according to the Royal Annals, devastated the Frisian islands, then landed on the mainland, defeated the Frisians and imposed tribute on them. Charlemagne reacted quickly, mobilising both the fleet and the army. The fleet was ordered to link up with the army for what was obviously intended to be a combined operation. However, almost at once the factors which would time and again cripple the Frankish (and also the Anglo-Saxon) defence against the Vikings in the following years began to tell. First, Charlemagne was delayed at the Rhine crossing, waiting for his forces to gather. Then having marched rapidly to the Weser, where he probably intended to link up with the fleet, and having set up camp at Verden, he could only wait on events since he did not know where the Danes would strike next. Meanwhile the Danish fleet had set sail and escaped unmolested and unchallenged.[157] Charlemagne no doubt realised that, because of these limitations, effective defence against the Vikings rested on local forces, not only because they were on the spot, but because they would be motivated by immediate self interest. It was perhaps with coastguard duties in mind that Charlemagne re emphasised the traditional watch duties in a capitulary of 811.[158] However, the problem of motivating men to fight in defence of others when they stood to gain nothing by it was not solved and it remained the weakest point of Charlemagne's defensive system and was probably the main long term cause of its failure.[159]

---

[155] For a discussion of the importance of plunder to the efficiency of the Carolingian military machine see, T. Reuter, 'Plunder and tribute in the Carolingian empire', *TRHS*, 5th Series, XXXV (1985), pp. 75–94.

[156] Reuter, *ibid.*, p. 90, makes this point with specific reference to coastguard duties.

[157] *ARF*, 810; *Ann. S. Amandi*, 810.

[158] *Cap. Bononiense*, c. 2; L. Halphen, *Charlemagne and the Carolingian Empire* (Amsterdam-New York Oxford, 1977), p. 68. I have doubts about Halphen's interpretation, for the *capitula* actually seems more concerned about misappropriation of *haribannus* by the counts than with the performance of guard-duty.

[159] Sproemberg, *op. cit.*, p. 27, rightly identifies this factor as a major cause of the failure of the coast defences, though he seriously underestimates the effectiveness of Charlemagne's coast defences.

Despite these limitations, Charlemagne's defences against the Vikings were highly efficient and would not be rivalled until the end of the ninth century. Though the seas were said to be infested with pirates by 800,[160] the Frankish empire was relatively untroubled by the Vikings for the remainder of Charlemagne's reign.[161] Apart from the Danish attack on Frisia in 810, and an Irish victory over Viking raiders in 812,[162] only two incidents are recorded in the Frankish sources. In 809 a ship sailing between Northumbria and Francia was intercepted by pirates and one of its passengers, a papal legate called Ealdwulf, was taken prisoner and held to ransom.[163] The only recorded attack on the empire itself was a serious raid on Frisia in 813.[164]

Far from being allowed to decay after Charlemagne's death, it is evident that the coastal defences continued to be maintained at an efficient level by Louis the Pious. Indeed, one of his earliest concerns as emperor was to attend to the coastal defences, sending garrisons out to vulnerable coastal areas in 814 and 815.[165] However, apart from sporadic outbreaks of trouble on the northern border with the Danes, none of which amounted to much (see below p.176), no Viking activity is recorded until 820. The incident which then occurred is a striking demonstration of both the strengths and the limitations of the Carolingian defence system:

> Thirteen pirate ships set out from *Nordmannia* and, first, tried to plunder on the coast of Flanders, but were repulsed by those who were on guard. However, because of the carelessness of the defenders, some worthless huts were burned down and a few cattle driven off. The Northmen made similar attempts on the mouth of the river Seine. The coast guards fought back and, five of their number having been killed, the pirates retreated empty handed. Finally, on the coast of Aquitaine they met with success, put a village called Bouin to the sack and then returned home with immense booty
>
> (*ARF*, 820)[166]

---

[160] Alcuin, *Epistolae*. no. 184 (ed. E. Duemmler, *MGH, Epp.* 4 (Berlin, 1895)); *ARF*, 800; Rev., 800.

[161] Hardly the mediocre achievement that F. L. Ganshof, *The Frankish Institutions Under Charlemagne* (New York, 1970), p. 64, would have it.

[162] *ARF*, 812.

[163] *ARF*, 809:

> Postquam Ardulfus rex Nordhanhumbrorum reductus est in regnum suum et legati imperatoris atque pontificis reversi sunt, unus ex eis, Aldulfus diaconus, a piratis captus est, ceteris sine periculo traicientibus, ductusque ab eis in Brittaniam a quodam Coenulfi regis homine redemptus est Romamque reversus.

[164] *Chron. Moissiacense*, 813: 'Exierunt autem Nortmanni cum navibus suis in Frisia, et fecerunt ibi grande malum, capuerunt viros, mulieres et praedam magnam.'

[165] *Chron. Moissiacense*, 814: 'nam et praesidia posuit in litore maris ubi necesse fuit'. The action seems to have been taken late in the year and was perhaps a response to a specific incident. Also *ibid.*, 815: 'Misit scaras suas ubi necesse fuit per marchas, et praesidia per litora maris'.

[166] *ARF*, 820:

The Vikings apparently did not try to enter the Loire, no doubt they expected to be met with the same determined opposition that had greeted them earlier in Flanders and on the Seine. However, efficient though the coastal defences plainly were, it is clear that they could not protect the whole coastline; a patient enemy who was prepared to keep probing would eventually find a weak spot.

The 13 Viking ships would probably have carried over 400 men,[167] a considerable force, yet the coastguard units twice drove the raiders off with ease. This must be taken as an indication that the organisation of the maritime marches was efficient enough to mobilise relatively large bodies of troops (i.e. as large as, or larger than, the Viking bands) in a very short time indeed. Nevertheless, even raids, such as that on Flanders, which were rapidly repulsed, must have been very damaging to the coastal communities directly affected, even if they were mere pinpricks as far as the empire as a whole was concerned. They may have been more common than is apparent from the sources as in 821 Louis acted to suppress peasant bands which were appearing in the coastal areas,[168] probably to provide better local defence. The vulnerability of isolated areas to attack may have been remedied to a limited extent by the provision of local fortifications; for example, the abbot of St Philibert on Noirmoutier was permitted to build a *castrum* near the abbey as a refuge in 830.[169] It is interesting that there is no record of bridge building to block rivers against Viking incursions from this period in Francia: in England it was already common practice.[170] Presumably the fleets and coastguards were effective enough to make this unnecessary.

In 821 Louis legislated to improve the administration of justice in the maritime marches; apparently their coastguard duties had led the counts to

---

De Nordmannia vero tredecim piraticae naves egressae primo in Flandrensi litore praedari molientes ab his, qui in praesidio erant, repulsi sunt; ubi tamen ab eis propter custodum incuriam aliquot casae viles incensae et parvus pecoris numeris abactus est. In ostio Sequanae similia temptantes resistentibus sibi litoris custodibus, quinque suorum interfectis inritae recesserunt. Tandem in Aquitanico litore prosperis usae successibus vico quodam, qui vocatur Buyn, ad integrum depopulato cum ingenti praeda ad propria reversae sunt.

[167] This estimate is based on the assumption that Viking ships rarely had crews of more than about 30: P. H. Sawyer, *The Age of the Vikings*, 2nd edn (London, 1971), pp. 126–7. It is, in my opinion, a conservative estimate because a ship like the Gokstad ship which had 32 oars could actually have carried many supernumerary crew members as well.

[168] *Capitula missorum*, MGH. LL 2, no. 148, c. 7: 'De coniurationibus servorum quae fiunt in Flandris et Menpisco et in caeteris maritimis locis volumus ut per missos nostros indicetur dominis servorum illorum, ut constringant eos, ne ultra tales coniurationes facere praesumant. Cf. the *bagaudae* in third-century Gaul: chapter 2, n. 65.

[169] F. Vercauteren, 'Comment s'est-on défendu au IXe siècle dans l'empire franc contre les invasions normandes', *Annales du XXXe Congrès de la Fédération Archéologique de Belgique* (1936), p. 121.

[170] See N. Brooks, 'The development of military obligations in eighth- and ninth-century England', in P. Clemoes and K. Hughes (eds), *England Before the Conquest* (Cambridge, 1971), pp. 72, 79–80.

neglect their other duties.[171] Further legislation in 829 requiring the counts to maintain a state of battle readiness for 40 days after an attack in case of a recurrence will no doubt have applied equally to marine and overland invaders.[172] But at some point after this date the defensive system began to break down.

This probably occurred between 830, when Louis' sons rose in open rebellion against the shape of his plans to divide the empire between them on his death, and 834, when the Vikings for the first time penetrated the empire's river systems and raided the major port of Dorestad.[173] Peace was restored in 834 but the problem of dividing the empire in a way which was satisfactory to all Louis' sons remained unsolved. It continued to preoccupy Louis for the rest of his reign and on his death civil war broke out again. The dispute was not finally resolved until the treaty of Verdun in 843. Louis, however, did not neglect the coastal defences in this last period of his reign. In 835 he ordered the coastal defences to be strengthened[174] and in 837 he held a general assembly at Nijmegen, which had perhaps now been fortified as a forward operational base, to investigate the failure of the coastal defences.[175] More fortifications were ordered and measures were taken to make the fleet more effective.[176] The following year Louis went to Nijmegen in May to attend to the defences and to await the expected attack.[177] It never came; the Viking fleet was caught in a storm and almost totally destroyed.[178] Louis also paid close attention to diplomatic measures to combat the Vikings in this period and was notably successful (see below pp. 175–8).

Despite this attention to the defences, the Vikings had raided Noirmoutier, Rhé, Antwerp, Witla (on the Meuse), Utrecht, Frisia (twice) and Dorestad (four

---

[171] *Capitula missorum*, c. 5: 'Volumus, ut comites qui ad custodiam maritimam deputati sunt, quicumque ex eis in suo ministerio residet, de iustitia facienda se non excuset propter illam custodiam, sed si ibi secum suos scabineos habuerit, ibi placitum teneat et iustitiam.'

[172] *Capitula missorum Wormatiense, MGH. LL* 2, no. 192, c. 13.

[173] *Ann. Bertiniani*, 834; *Annales Xantenses*, ed. R. Rau, *op. cit.*, vol. 2, pp. 339–71, *s.a.* 834.

[174] *Ann. Bertiniani*, 835: 'Imperator autem graviter ferens, Aquis perveniens, disposita omni maritima custodia'.

[175] Ann. Bertiniani, 837:

Imperator vero, generali conventu habito, publice cum his quaestionem habuit, quos principes ad eandem custodiam delegaverat. Qua discussione patuit, partim inpossibilitate, partim quorundam inoboedientia eos inimicos non potuisse resistere. Unde et ad Frisionum inoboedientiam strenui abbates ac comites directi sunt.

The fact that Nijmegen is from now on referred to as a *castrum* in the *Ann. Bertiniani* suggests the possibility of its fortification.

[176] Thegan, *Vita Hludowici imperatoris*, ed. R. Rau, *op. cit.*, vol. 1, pp. 215–53, *s.a.* 24: 'et statuit sediciones in nonnullis locis contra Danaos'; *Ann. Bertiniani*, 837: 'Verum ut deinceps illorum incursionibus facilius obsisti queat, classis quaquaversum diligentius parari iussa

[177] *Ann. Bertiniani*, 838: 'Nam illo iuxta condictum imperator progredi disponebat, quatenus sui praesentia dampnum, quod annis praeteritis pyratarum inportunitate nostrorumque desidia contigerat, vitaretur; habituoque conventu fidelium, copiosus circa maritima apparatus distributus est.'

[178] *Ibid.*

times) by the time Louis died in 840.[179] There seem to be two main factors in the failure of the defences to keep the Vikings out. First, the civil wars had seriously impaired Louis' authority in the empire and those men responsible for the defence of the coast were simply not obeying his orders. The assembly in 837 had found that the main obstacle to an effective defence had come from the disobedience of the Frisians. Frisia had borne the brunt of the Viking attacks and it would not be surprising if some of the Frisians had begun to reach an accommodation with the Vikings, perhaps by giving them unhindered passage into the Rhine in return for local immunity from attack. Louis made strenuous efforts to reinforce his authority in the area, both by sending out trusted counts and abbots to draw the Frisians back into line and by his prolonged presence at Nijmegen in 838.[180] The second factor is that the Vikings were now raiding in much greater strength than they had been before. Figures are not available for Francia but Anglo-Saxon sources suggest that a typical Viking fleet at this time consisted of 30 to 35 ships,[181] with potentially well over a thousand men, compared to the 13 ships and *c.* 400 men of the raid of 820. Whatever the actual strength of these raids, the Vikings clearly outnumbered the Frankish coastguard forces by a considerable margin as in 837 the Danes stormed a fort on Walcheren, killing a very large number of the defenders and capturing two dukes and many of the emperor's *optimates*.[182] The high rank of these prisoners shows how seriously Louis took coastal defence; this must have been a major force and its loss was a serious blow, causing Louis to abandon plans to visit Rome.[183] Louis' exertions, however, may have bought Francia a brief respite from Viking attack. There was no major raid from 838 until after Louis' death while the output of Dorestad's mints reached their peak in 838–40, clearly demonstrating the port's continuing prosperity.[184]

---

[179] See F. D. Logan, *The Vikings in History* (London, 1983), pp. 114–16, and Sawyer, *Kings and Vikings*, pp. 81–3.

[180] *Ann. Bertiniani*, 837, 838, 839.

[181] Sawyer, *Age of the Vikings*, p. 124.

[182] Thegan, 24:

> Illi vero Danai nave venientes ad unam sedictionem, et interfecerunt ibi innumerabilem multitudinem christ ianorum; et ibi cecidit Hemminch qui erat ex stirpe Danorum, dux christianissimus, et Eccihardus alius dux, et multi optimates imperatoris; et aliqui comprehensi sunt et postea redempti.

> The fort was probably on Walcheren as the *Ann. Bertiniani*, 837, state that the Vikings attacked the island that year before raiding Dorestad. There were two forts on Walcheren, at Souburg and Middelburg: Sawyer, *Kings and Vikings*, p. 124. The raid of this year is also mentioned by Einhard in a letter to Louis; he believed it to have been presaged by the appearance of a comet: Einhard, *Epistolae*, ed. K. Hampe, *MGH. Epp* 5 (Berlin, 1899), pp. 105–45, no. 40.

[183] Thegan, 24, *Ann. Bertiniani*, 837.

[184] J. L. Nelson, 'The Last Years of Louis the Pious' in P. Godman and R. Collins, *Charlemagne's Heir* (Oxford, 1990), 147-59, p. 158.

Diplomacy and War in Frankish-Danish Relations

Though military activities dominated the Frankish defence against the Vikings, there was also an important diplomatic element. This had been present from the very beginning of Viking activity when Charlemagne was asked to arrange for the ransoming of some of the monks who had been carried off by the Vikings who raided Lindisfarne in 793.[185] These measures were at their most sophisticated and effective in the reign of Louis the Pious but they have their origins in Charlemagne's attempts to stabilise his northern border with the emergent kingdom of Denmark. The tensions on this border exacerbated the problems of achieving security on the northern coasts. If these tensions boiled over into open war there was always the danger that the northern coasts would be subject to potentially destructive large scale invasion by Danish royal fleets. Diplomatic activity to defuse this threat took two forms, negotiation over the border itself and the destabilisation of the Danish monarchy by exploiting internal dissent. These methods were highly successful and only rarely was it necessary to reinforce diplomacy with military action.

Even though there is no evidence that Charlemagne ever contemplated the conquest of Denmark, the Danes must have watched him extend Frankish power towards their borders with mounting apprehension. The Danes had probably never enjoyed easy relations with their southern neighbours, the Saxons, and it was probably to create a barrier against them that a rampart, known as the *Danevirke*, was built across the neck of the Jutland peninsula between the Schlei and the Treene c. 737.[186] However, the powerful and expansionist Franks would have made a far more dangerous enemy and throughout Charlemagne's Saxon wars, the Danes readily gave refuge to dissident Saxon leaders, such as Widukind, who fled to the protection of the Danish king Sigfred in 777.[187]

Because of the prolonged resistance of the Saxons to Frankish domination, it was the early ninth century before the Danes and Franks actually came face to face across a land frontier. In 804 Charlemagne finally subjugated the Saxon tribes north of the Elbe and ensured that there would be no more rebellions by resorting to the drastic expedient of deporting the entire population.[188] This move must have caused great alarm to the new Danish king Godfred and it was perhaps

---

[185] Alcuin, *Epp.*. 20. Charlemagne also showed concern for prisoners taken by Moslem pirates; in 807 he ransomed monks who had been captured on the island of Pantellaria and sold as slaves in Spain: *ARF*, 807.

[186] The *Danevirke* is a complex series of earthworks with a total length of 18½ miles. The system was rebuilt and extended many times between the eighth and thirteenth centuries and was last used by the Danes as a defence line in the 1864 war with Prussia and Austria. The earliest section of the wall so far dated was built with logs from trees that were felled in 737. See Roesdahl, *op. cit.*, pp. 141–6. See also on the *Danevirke*, H. Jankuhn, *Haithabu. Ein Handelsplatz der Wikingerzeit*, 5th edn (Neumünster, 1972), pp. 69–74.

[187] *ARF*, 777; Rev., 777. See also *ARF*, 782, 804, and Rev., 782, for other occasions when the Danes gave refuge to Saxon rebels.

[188] *ARF*, 804; Einhard, *V. Karoli*, 7.

to allay his fears that a Frankish invasion was imminent that Charlemagne gave the vacated lands to his allies, the Abodrites, rather than settling Franks on them.[189] If this was the intention, Godfred was not convinced. A conference was arranged between the two rulers and Godfred gathered his fleet and army at *Sliesthorp*, which is certainly to be identified with Hedeby at the neck of the Jutland peninsula, on the Schlei, but was afraid to meet the emperor and came no further.[190] Charlemagne was keen to discuss the return of Saxon fugitives and it may be that Godfred still had hopes that the Saxons could be stirred up to rebellion once again and so deliberately dodged the issue.[191]

Relations between Godfred and Charlemagne deteriorated rapidly in the following years. In 808 Godfred allied with the Wiltzites and launched a fierce attack on Charlemagne's Slav allies, the Abodrites.[192] The Abodrites suffered severely in this attack; many of their *castella* were taken, one of their *duces* was captured and hanged and another fled to the Franks. Yet they fought back vigorously enough to cause the Danes very severe casualties. Godfred's final act on this campaign was to destroy a trading town in Abodrite territory called Reric and remove its merchants, probably to Hedeby.[193] Reric, whose exact location is unknown,[194] was under some kind of Danish control and paid considerable dues to Godfred; that he chose to burn the town is surely a sign that his attack had misfired. On reaching Hedeby, Godfred ordered the refurbishment, or extension,

---

[189] King, *Translated Sources*, p. 71. H. Jankuhn, 'Karl der Grosse und der Norden', in Braunfels (ed.), *op. cit.*, p. 700, believes that Charlemagne's intention was that the Abodrites would defend the northern border against the Danes.

[190] *ARF*, 804. On this and the later diplomatic contacts between Charlemagne and Godfred see H. Neifeind, *Verträge zwischen Normannen und Franken im neunten und zehnten Jahrhundert* (Heidelberg, 1971), pp. 142–45. Also worthwhile is the short, but informative, account in F. L. Ganshof, *The Carolingians and the Frankish Monarchy* (London, 1971), pp. 165–6. *Sliesthorp* is simply a Danish equivalent of Schleswig but there is no evidence of any settlement on the site of the modern town of that name at that time. However, there was a settlement at nearby Hedeby (the Südsiedlung, a few hundred yards to the south of the fortified settlement of the Viking period) from *c.* 750, so presumably it is this that *Sliesthorp* refers to. See Roesdahl, *op. cit.*, p. 73. On Hedeby in general see Jankuhn, *op. cit.*.

[191] *ARF*, 804.

[192] *ARF*, 808; *Chron. Moissiacense*, 808.

[193] *ARF*, 808: 'Godofridus vero priusquam reverteretur, distructo emporio, quod in oceani litore constitutum lingua Danorum Reric dicebatur et magnam regno illius commoditatem vectigalium persolutione praestabat, translatisque inde negotiatoribus, soluta classe ad portum, qui Sliesthorp dicitur, cum universo exercitu venit.' The *ARF* do not actually say that Godfred transported the merchants to Hedeby, though this seems to be a reasonable inference from the context.

[194] Alt Lübeck is a commonly cited possibility but excavations have shown that the site was uninhabited before 817: see H. Andersen, 'Det bjerg der kaldes Gamle Lybæk', *Skalk* II (1979), p. 12. A more likely location for Reric is Mecklenburg. Numerous finds of Arab coins point to this site having been a trading centre in the early ninth century: J. Herrmann, 'The northern Slavs' in, D. M. Wilson (ed.), *The Northern World* (London, 1980), p. 199.

of the *Danevirke* as a barrier to protect his frontier area,[195] no doubt in expectation of Frankish reprisals.

Charlemagne was in fact very reluctant to become involved in campaigns against the Danes and the weight of the (initially unsuccessful) Frankish counter-attack fell on those Slav tribes, the Wilzi and the Smeldingi, who had supported the Danish attack.[196] Negotiations with Godfred to find a solution proved fruitless but the sole Frankish measure against the Danes was that Charlemagne ordered the construction of a fort north of the Elbe, presumably both for defence and as a forward base from which to conduct future campaigns. A suitable site was selected at Itzehoe, on the Stör, and work began in March 810.[197] Probably because negotiations had proved fruitless, Charlemagne contemplated a campaign against Godfred in 810, but Godfred attacked first, sending a large fleet to attack Frisia. By the time that the news of the attack reached Charlemagne the Frisians had submitted to the Danes and paid them 100 pounds of silver in tribute, an enormous sum by the standards of the time.[198] Godfred was said to be claiming the right to rule both Frisia and Saxony and to be boasting that he intended to march on Aachen. The success of the attack on Frisia showed that Godfred had to be taken seriously, but although Charlemagne reacted quickly, the Danish fleet had sailed for home before the Franks could bring them to battle. Fortunately, the situation was defused when Godfred was murdered by one of his retainers. He was succeeded by his nephew, Hemming, who immediately made peace.[199]

---

[195] *ARF*, 808, rather exaggerates Godfred's role in the construction of the *Danevirke*, as well as its actual extent:

> Ibi per aliquot dies moratus limitem regni sui, qui Saxoniam respicit, vallo munire constituit, eo modo, ut ab orientali maris sinu, quem illi Ostarsalt [Baltic] dicunt, usque ad occidentalem oceanum totam Egidorae [Eider] fluminis aquilonalem ripam munimentum valli praeteraret, una tantum porta dimissa, per quam carra et equites emitti et recepi potuissent.

So far as is known, there were no fortifications at all on the Eider; the surviving earthworks stop at Hollingstedt on the Treene, a tributary of the Eider. Godfred was certainly not the originator of the *Danevirke* (see n. 186 above), and in fact no part of the system can at present be dated with any certainty to his reign. The *Kovirke*, a four mile long rampart running to the south of Hedeby, may be the best candidate for Godfred's wall as it contains the only gate so far known in the *Danevirke*: see Roesdahl, *op. cit.*, p. 144, and Jankuhn, *op. cit.*, pp. 69–74.

[196] *ARF*, 808, *Chron. Moissiacense*, 808, *Ann. Laurissenses min.*, 808. These three accounts vary considerably in their estimates of the success of the campaign. The semi-official *ARF* claim it as a complete success, the Moissac chronicle acknowledges that the Franks suffered some casualties, while the Lorsch chronicle candidly admits that the campaign was a costly failure.

[197] *ARF*, 809. The decision to build the fort appears to have been taken late in the year, in November at the earliest, after negotiations had failed to produce a solution.

[198] *ARF*, 810, where note the use of the term *vectigalis* by the annalist, used also to describe the tribute which Godfred received from Reric (see n. 193 above), which may point to a formal acceptance by the Frisians of Danish lordship; they were certainly not simply buying off their attackers. The tribute was heavy; three times greater than that which the Franks imposed on Venice in 812.

[199] *ARF*, 810, 811; Einhard, *V. Karoli*, 14.

What had provoked this violent turn of events? Was it simply aggressive over confidence on Godfred's part as the Frankish sources claim, or was there some other factor? It is possible that the provisions for channelling trade with the Slavs and Avars through nine official customs posts, set out in the Double Capitulary of Thionville in 806, may have had something to do with it.[200] Though they were clearly intended to increase imperial control over trade, these measures do not seem to have been an act of conscious economic imperialism in the sense that they were intended to destroy Danish trade but it must have looked very much that way to Godfred. Godfred had two trading centres under his control, Hedeby and Reric. Hedeby may have seemed to be under threat from Frankish expansion north of the Elbe and the two most northerly Frankish customs posts at Scheesel and Bardowick must have seemed to be intended to channel trade between Francia and the Baltic through the territory of the Abodrites. Had this happened, it might well have been to the benefit of Reric but Godfred's hold on the town was not secure and the Abodrites may have been on the point of seizing it when he attacked them. If Godfred's attack of 808 was intended to secure his hold on Reric, it was a failure. Godfred's decision to destroy the town was probably determined by his heavy casualties and his failure to break Abodrite power. However, he also failed to destroy Reric completely as the town seems to have been in the hands of the Abodrites in the following year when their *dux* Thrasco was murdered there.[201] Godfred's removal of the merchants from Reric may nevertheless have been decisive in the long term as the town disappears from the sources. It can be shown from archaeological evidence that very shortly after Godfred's death Hedeby began to expand and the town was to become one of the Baltic's most important trading centres.[202] If Godfred did indeed settle the merchants from Reric at Hedeby, his action could well have provided the decisive spur to the town's rapid development.

The failure of the Franks to mount an effective naval response to the Danish attacks was not the result of any failure on Charlemagne's part to understand the use of naval power. The Frisian islands themselves were too exposed to be defensible by any means. As for offensive action, the Danes were actually in a very strong position. No doubt naval attacks on the west coast of Jutland would have been possible but they would have been less effective than a land invasion which could have been made in greater strength and with less risk. The large and fertile islands of Fyn, Sjælland and Lolland could, obviously, be attacked only by a naval force, but to make such an attack the Franks first needed a secure base on the Baltic. In the event, the death of Godfred made a counter-attack unnecessary. The succession to Godfred was disputed between his sons and nephews for the next 30 years. Charlemagne and Louis the Pious were able to use these rivalries to keep the peace on the border and to suppress Danish raiding far more

---

[200] *Duplex capitulare missorum in Theodonis Villa datum*, MGH. LL 2, nos 43–4, c. 23.

[201] *ARF*, 809.

[202] No structure so far discovered in the main fortified settlement at Hedeby dates from before 811: Roesdahl, *op. cit.*, p. 74.

effectively than military action alone could have done. Louis only found it necessary to invade Denmark once, in 815.[203] The attack was successful; southern Jutland was ravaged and hostages were taken. However, the Danish army itself, supported by a large fleet, simply withdrew in front of the advancing Frankish army and took refuge on an island, probably Fyn, off the Baltic coast of Jutland;[204] lacking the support of a fleet, the Franks could not bring the Danes to battle. Nevertheless, this display of military might certainly demonstrated the vulnerability of Jutland to Frankish invasion.

Godfred's successor, his nephew Hemming, died in 812 and was succeeded in the kingship by the brothers Heriold (Harald) and Reginfred after a brief struggle which left two other rival claimants dead.[205] Their brother Hemming was sent to join them on the throne from the Frankish court where he had become a vassal of Charlemagne's. However, Hemming's arrival seems to have provoked an anti-Frankish reaction and the brothers were driven out of the kingdom by Godfred's four sons in 813.[206] They found refuge with the Abodrites and sought the support of the Franks to help them regain their kingdom. It was clearly in the Frankish interest to restore Heriold and his brothers to the throne and aid was duly promised.[207] The following year Heriold, Reginfred and Hemming unsuccessfully attempted to win back their kingdom; Reginfred was slain and Heriold fled into exile with Louis the Pious and became his *fidelis*.[208] Hemming also survived and went on to serve Louis as a commander in the coastguard forces.[209] Heriold was promised aid and received it in 815 in the Frankish expedition into Denmark mentioned above. Heriold, from his base in Saxony continued to cause trouble for Godfred's sons. In 817 Godfred's sons sent legates to Louis to ask for peace but their request was rejected: later in the same year they invaded Saxony, perhaps in an attempt to persuade Louis to end his support for Heriold, but were easily repulsed.[210]

When, in 819, Godfred's sons fell out among themselves the party which prevailed was the one which won Louis' support by taking Heriold into joint

---

[203] *ARF*, 815; Astronomer, 25; *Chron. Moissiacense* 815.

[204] Scholz and Rogers, *op. cit.*, p. 195.

[205] *ARF*, 812.

[206] *Chron. Moissiacense*, 813; *ARF*, 813.

[207] *Chron. Moissiacense*, 813. This entry clearly telescopes events of 813 and 814 together: *cf. ARF*, 813, 814.

[208] *ARF*, 814: 'Quo facto Herioldus rebus suis diffidens ad imperatorem venit et se in manus illius commendavit.' According to Ermoldus Nigellus, *In honorem Hludovici Caesaris Augusti libri IIII* (ed. G. H. Pertz, *MGH. SS* 2 (Hanover, 1829), pp. 466–516), bk IV, lines 601ff., Heriold also became Louis's *fidelis* in 826. See C. E. Odegaard, *Vassi and Fideles in the Carolingian Empire* (New York, 1972), pp. 56–7. On Louis's relations with Heriold and Godfred's sons see Neifeind, *op. cit.*, pp. 145–8, and Ganshof, *Frankish Monarchy*, pp. 171–3.

[209] I assume here that the *dux* of Danish extraction called Hemming who was killed by the Danes in 837 (Thegan, 24) was Heriold's brother. See n. 182 above.

[210] *ARF*, 817.

kingship with them.[211] However, the Danish kingdom did not gain in unity by this because there was constant tension between Louis' vassal Heriold and Godfred's sons and from 822 both he and they were sending separate delegations to the Frankish assembly.[212] So fine was the balance of power which Louis had created in the Danish kingdom that he could intervene directly in the disputes between the rival parties to the same extent as he could in the disputes of officially subject tribes such as the Abodrites and the Wiltzites.[213]

The high point of Louis' direct influence in Denmark came in 823 when he sent a delegation to investigate a dispute between Heriold and Godfred's sons.[214] Heriold's support in Denmark, however, was probably beginning to wane and in 826 Heriold, with his followers, sought baptism, no doubt as a means of bolstering Louis' support for him.[215] At the same time, Louis granted him the county of Rüstringen, on the North Sea coast, as a refuge in case it proved necessary for him to flee his kingdom. This Heriold was forced to do in the following year and in 828 Louis sent a delegation to the Danish border to discuss the dispute. Perhaps because he feared that Louis' support was now only lukewarm, Heriold invaded Denmark on his own account and wrecked the negotiations. In retaliation Godfred's sons led an army across the border and forced the unsuspecting Frankish delegation to flee; but they were quick to sue for peace on Louis' terms.[216] Heriold disappears from the sources after this incident, but the Danish kings continued to maintain friendly relations with Louis and it is probable that Heriold remained in Frisia as a potentially still useful tool in imperial diplomacy.[217]

When Viking piracy increased in the wake of the civil war of 830–4, diplomacy took on a new importance. Louis appears to have been satisfied that the Danish king Horic, the last survivor of Godfred's sons, had not incited the raids; and Horic was still wary of the strength of the empire and anxious to

---

[211] *ARF*, 819.

[212] *ARF*, 822, 823, 825, 826.

[213] See R. McKitterick, *The Frankish Kingdoms Under the Carolingians, 751–987* (London, 1983), pp. 127–9, on Louis' relationships with these two peoples. Ganshof, *Frankish Monarchy*, p. 173, suggests that Louis's intention was to turn Denmark into a Frankish protectorate.

[214] *ARF*, 823.

[215] *ARF*, 826; Astronomer, 40. The baptism is central to bk IV of Ermoldus Nigellus's *In honorem Hludovici Caesaris Augusti* who plainly regarded it as one of the great events of Louis's reign.

[216] *ARF*, 827, 828.

[217] The Danish pirate chief called Heriold who, according to the *Ann. Bertiniani*, was granted Walcheren as a *beneficium* in 841 was probably not the same man as he was a pagan: king Heriold was a Christian.

preserve good relations.[218] In 836 and 838, Horic even captured and executed pirate leaders who had raided Francia.[219]

Louis' emphasis on the use of diplomacy to counter Danish expansionism was not a consequence of weakness at sea; as we have seen the coastal defences initiated by Charlemagne were maintained by Louis and, at least until the 830s, continued to provide as effective a defence as the technology of the time allowed. Even in the 830s the reliance on diplomacy to suppress Danish pirates should not be seen as a last resort but as a successful continuation of an established policy. As modern governments have also found with terrorists, Louis no doubt understood that, even at the best of times, it was impossible to prevent pirates from penetrating the defences somewhere and that it was therefore necessary to try to stop them at source. It was not the policy of the Danish kings to encourage piracy, and overt military retaliation against them by the Franks, by land or sea, would therefore have been likely to result in more rather than fewer raids as the Danish kings in turn sought revenge. There was far more to be gained by manipulating the political situation within Denmark, by supporting dissidents, promoting civil war and exploiting rivalries, to keep the Danes occupied at home. This was a policy of strength, not of weakness, as is demonstrated by the fact that Louis was able to force an unpopular vassal king on the Danes for eight years. It is no doubt a measure of Louis' success that western Europe was little troubled by Danish pirates until the 830s and that even at the end of his reign he retained enough prestige to win the co-operation of the Danish king in suppressing piracy.

The Ships of the Northern Coast-Defence Fleets

As for all other periods of Frankish maritime history, we are poorly informed as to the characteristics of the ships which made up the Carolingian fleets in northern waters. As no Carolingian ships have been discovered (the Utrecht ship, long thought to have dated from *c.* 800, is now known to be twelfth century[220]) we are entirely dependent of iconographical evidence which is often highly stylised and difficult to interpret.

Ships with a curved 'banana-shaped' profile appear on coins minted at Quentovic and Dorestad during the reigns of Charlemagne and Louis the Pious. These ships have a single mast and a prominent broad bladed side rudder at the

---

[218] *Ann. Bertiniani*, 836: 'Eodem tempore Nordmanni Dorestadum et Frisiam rursum depopulati sunt. Sed et Horich rex Danorum per legatos suos in eodem placito amicitiae atque odoedientiae conditiones mandans, se nullatenus eorum inportunitatibus adsensum prebuisse testatus.'

[219] *Ann. Bertiniani*, 836: 'Ubi etiam missi eiusdem Horich venerunt, quaerentes summam eorum quos ipse captos ex his interfici fecerat qui in nostros fines talia iam dudum moliti sunt.' *Ann. Bertiniani*, 838: 'Ubi etiam missi Horich venientes, pyratarum in nostros fines dudum irruentium maximos a se ob imperatoris fidelitatem captos atque interfici iussos retulerunt, petentes insuper dari sibi Frisianos atque Abodritos.' Note that Horic professes his loyalty (*fidelitas*) to Louis.

[220] See Greenhill and Morrison, *Archaeology of Boats and Ships*, p. 183.

Figure 16 Early ninth-century coins from Dorestad (top) and Hedeby (middle & lower)
(Ellmers, *Frühmittelalterliche Handelsschiffahrt*)

stern, and, in some cases, the ships appear to have figureheads. The ships also have dashed marks around the base of the hull which have been interpreted as representations of oars.[221] However, as in some cases the putative oars are even shown astern of the steering oar which would hardly be likely in a real ship, it seems more likely that the dash markings are simply stylised waves. Another major source of iconographical evidence is the Utrecht Psalter which was made *c.* 820 at Rheims. This contains many elegant drawings of ships, sometimes with sails, though more often without, which also have a similar shape to those on the coins from Quentovic and Dorestad. Although the value of this iconographical evidence is very limited because of its extreme stylisation, and firm conclusions cannot be drawn from it, none of these ships is obviously a warship. It is possible that these ships were early versions of the hulk, a common type of merchant ship in northern waters during the central Middle Ages which appears in contemporary iconography with a similar curved profile.[222]

---

[221] R. Hodges, *Dark Age Economics* (London, 1982), p. 96.
[222] Unger, *The Ship in the Medieval Economy*, p. 59.

Also relevant here are the coins minted at Hedeby in Denmark in the early ninth century in imitation of the Carolingian coins from Quentovic and Dorestad.[223] These coins show two types of ship, one a Viking longship and the other a stocky ship with steep straight stems, a flat bottom and a single mast and square sail. The last ship-type has generally been considered to represent a trading cog. Similar ships were certainly in use in northern waters before this time and we may well be justified in concluding that this coin-type shows representations of a typical Carolingian long-distance trader.[224] Transport was one of the main duties of Charlemagne's fleets and it is likely that trading cogs, hulks and, no doubt, river barges were pressed into service in this role on rivers and along the coast.

Figures 17 Warships from Carolingian manuscripts. Left from the *First Bible of Charles the Bald* (c. 845–6). Right from the *San Paolo Bible* (c.846)

There are a few illustrations of warships in Carolingian manuscripts. One, from the *First Bible of Charles the Bald* (also known as the *Vivian Bible*) made at Tours *c.* 845–6, shows a 26-oared galley of rather Classical appearance under sail.[225] Even though medieval illustrators tended to draw and paint what they knew from personal experience and observation,[226] it is difficult to believe that this type of galley, which looks dated even by late Roman standards, was still being built in the Frankish realms in the ninth century. It is certainly the latest known representation of such a galley so it seems more likely that it was copied from a Classical original.[227] Another illustration, from the *San Paolo Bible*, made at Rheims shortly after 846 shows a 24-oared galley in the process of setting sail.[228] This has a high prow and stern and possibly also a protruding forefoot or

---

[223] On the origin of these coins see K. Bendixen, *Denmark's Money* (Copenhagen, 1967), pp. 12–13.

[224] Greenhill and Morrison, *Archaeology of Boats and Ships,* pp. 188–9.

[225] H. L. Kessler, *The Illustrated Bibles from Tours*, Studies in Manuscript Illumination 7 (Princeton, 1977), plate 130. See also L. V. Mott, *The Development of the Rudder* (London, 1997), p. 24, fig. 2.3.

[226] Professor R. McKitterick, personal communication.

[227] Mott, *op. cit.*, p. 24.

[228] Kessler, *op. cit.*, plate 131.

ram like those found on the late Roman warships from Mainz. Neither side rudder nor steersman are shown at the stern, probably because there was no room to paint them, all the available space being taken up by a crew member who is welcoming a passenger (St Jerome) on board. The large oar at the bow is probably a bow-sweep. These were often used on medieval vessels as an aid to tacking.[229] This ship looks far less archaic than that in the *Vivian Bible* and clearly represents a lighter and simpler vessel. It seems most likely that, in this case, the artist has painted a type of ship which was familiar to him so this may well represent the type of warship used by the Carolingians in northern waters.

Another clue to the characteristics of Carolingian warships comes from the existence in the later ninth century of coastguard troops called *Cokingi* whose name may have been derived from the use of the cog as a warship in the coast defence fleets.[230] There are also three charters from Utrecht from *c.* 900 where the cog-name appears in contexts which suggest that it was being used to describe warships.[231] In the eleventh century the term *herikochun* was being used in German sources to describe a kind of fast warship which may have been the type of ship from which the *Cokingi* derived their name.[232] The similarities between the Mainz Roman ships and later medieval cogs were noted in chapter 2, where it was suggested that Frankish warships of the third and fourth centuries may have shared many characteristics with late Roman warships such as those from Mainz. If this hypothesis is correct, we might expect that the Franks should have continued to use developments of these in Merovingian and Carolingian times and that the ninth-century 'war-cog' was an oar and sail-powered ship, not unlike that shown in the *San Paolo Bible*.

Because the evidence for the characteristics of Carolingian warships is so slight it is not possible to compare them with the Viking ships they opposed. It is certainly not safe to assume, as some have done, for example, that Carolingian warships were inferior in seaworthiness to the Vikings' ships.[233] Though we do know that the Vikings' ships were excellent, it does not necessarily follow from this that they were superior.

The Fate of the Coast Defences after Louis the Pious

The dispute between Louis' three sons over the division of the empire, which had festered unsolved during the last six years of Louis' reign, once again broke out into civil war on his death. With the outbreak of civil war, the raids recommenced with a vengeance. In 841 the Seine was penetrated and Rouen was

---

[229] Mott, *op. cit.*, pp. 67–9.
[230] *Ann. Bertiniani*, 867. On this interpretation of the entry see Ellmers, *Handelsschiffahrt*, p. 71.
[231] Ellmers, *op. cit.*, p. 70.
[232] *Ibid.*, p. 71.
[233] Sproemberg, *op. cit.*, p. 24.

sacked; in 842 Quentovic (near Étaples) and Nantes were sacked.[234] The sack of Nantes shows graphically how the disunity of the empire undermined its defences. A rebel count, seeing the Vikings as the means to seize the town for himself while Louis' heirs fought each other, guided the raiders upriver to take the town by surprise. The attack was notable for its savagery, but the Vikings got a rich haul of booty and the count got his town.[235] Even the Frankish rulers were not above this game; the emperor Lothar himself was accused of encouraging the Vikings to plunder his brothers' territories during the civil war.[236] The Vikings may indeed have been a welcome complication to those Franks who had political ambitions but it is unlikely that these sentiments were shared by the ordinary people who were the pawns in these power games. Worse still for the Franks, the raiders who had sacked Nantes in 842 did not return home; instead they took their booty-laden ships to Noirmoutier and wintered on the island, using it as a base from which to plunder the Loire and Garonne at leisure.[237] With these developments Viking activity entered a new and more destructive phase and it can be assumed that Charlemagne's defence system had by then effectively collapsed. Though a lasting peace between the brothers was settled by the Treaty of Verdun in 843, the effectiveness of the coastal defences was not restored: the civil wars had dealt the royal authority on which they depended a blow from which it did not fully recover

Nowhere is the loss of royal authority and prestige more obvious than in the diplomatic sphere. The civil wars in Francia enabled Horic to follow a more assertive policy towards the Franks, culminating in 845 with the sack of Hamburg.[238] When in 847 Danish pirates attacked Dorestad, Brittany and Aquitaine, Lothar, Louis II and Charles the Bald, no doubt hoping to continue Louis the Pious' successful policy, sent legates to Horic, threatening him with war if he did not act to prevent his subjects attacking Francia.[239] However, this time the Frankish demands went unheeded. Horic was apparently now confident that the Franks would not take united action against him and so could afford to ignore them. This is not to say that Horic pursued a provocative policy towards the Franks; in general he still sought good relations.[240] But the obviously unequal relations of Louis' reign were now a thing of the past.

Despite this picture of general collapse, it is probable that some elements of the coastal defences survived the civil wars. Beacon chains on the coast were

---

[234] *Ann. Bertiniani*, 841, 842, 843.

[235] *Ibid.*, 843. See also G. Jones, *History of the Vikings*, p. 211.

[236] Nithard, IV. 2.

[237] *Ann. Bertiniani*, 843. See also G. Jones, *op. cit.*, p. 211.

[238] Rimbert, *Vita S. Anskarii*, ed. D. C. F. Dahlmann, *MGH. SS* 2 (Hanover, 1829), pp. 683–725, chapter 16, probably has the fullest account of the attack. The *Ann. Bertiniani*, 845, make it clear that peace was restored very quickly afterwards by negotiation.

[239] *Ann. Bertiniani*, 847.

[240] Neifeind, *op. cit.*, p. 150.

used in the 840s.[241] Charles the Bald passed legislation concerning the defence of coastal areas in 854 and coastguard units may still have been in existence in 867 when local troops described as *cokingi* (see above) drove the Viking chief Roric out of Frisia.[242] Though there were evidently no warships on the Seine by 841,[243] vestiges of the fleets may have survived elsewhere as in 864 Charles fitted out ships in preparation for an attack on Vikings on the Rhine, and in 885 a Frisian fleet defeated a Viking fleet on the Waal.[244] However, there is no evidence of a co-ordinated system of coastal defence and by the late ninth century the Franks looked back on Charlemagne's firm defence with longing and held it up to their rulers as an example to emulate.[245] But the Frankish recovery, when it came, was to owe little to the Carolingian monarchs or to naval power, being based on local initiatives which were at the same time a symptom and a consequence of processes that were changing the shape of Frankish society.

---

[241] Nithard, III. 3. See note 150 above.

[242] *Capitulare missorum Attiniacense, MGH. LL* 2, no. 261, c. 2; *Ann. Bertiniani*, 867.

[243] Nithard, II. 6, relates that when Charles the Bald wanted to transport troops up the Seine in March 841 he had to requisition merchant ships which had been washed upstream from the mouth of the river by a flood tide.

[244] *Ann. Xantenses*, 864; *Ann. Fuldenses*, 885.

[245] The colourful stories told by Notker the Stammerer, *Gesta Karoli Magni*, ed. R. Rau, *op. cit.*, vol. 3, pp. 322–427, II. 13–14, of Charlemagne's eagerness to fight the Northmen can be best interpreted as an exhortation to Charles the Fat, to whom the work was presented, to do likewise.

Conclusions

Our knowledge of the shipbuilding techniques of the Germanic barbarians in north-western Europe before the ninth century is slight and the ship finds on which our knowledge is based cannot be regarded as a representative sample. Any generalised conclusions about the seafaring capabilities of these peoples are unlikely to be valid if they are based on the evidence of maritime archaeology alone: it is of vital importance that the historical context of barbarian seafaring activity is also taken into account. The clearest demonstration of this comes from the history of Saxon piracy in the third to the fifth centuries and the subsequent Anglo-Saxon settlement of England. While maritime archaeologists tell us that the Anglo-Saxons and their immediate ancestors were restricted to the use of relatively unseaworthy rowing boats, the literary sources, supported by other archaeological evidence, show that the range of their seafaring activity mirrored that of the Danish Vikings in the ninth and tenth centuries. The discrepancy between what the Anglo-Saxons actually achieved and what they could have achieved had the ships which we know of from archaeology been the best available to them is simply too great to be reconciled. The Anglo-Saxons must have had a much more sophisticated seafaring capacity than is presently assumed and the ships used, for example, for the Anglo-Saxon migration to Britain, have yet to be discovered.

The widespread belief that the keels of early Anglo-Saxon ships were both too weak and the wrong shape to bear mast and sail also appears to be ill founded in the light of the performance under sail of *Sæ Wylfing*, a half-scale model of the Sutton Hoo ship. We now know that such ships did not rely primarily on their keels for longitudinal strength but on their hull planks and internal strengthening frames. It is certain that the strength of the keel cannot have been the obstacle to the adoption of the sail that it is so often made out to be. The projecting 'T' shaped keel is an important feature of Viking Age shipbuilding in Scandinavia but the present fixation on its development as *the* key to the development of sailing ships in northern Europe is surely misplaced.

These conclusions have specific implications for the question of the diffusion of the sail in north-west Europe. Certainly any idea that the sail was not adopted by the Anglo-Saxons before the end of the seventh century can be dismissed out of hand. Contemporary literary evidence points to the sail being in widespread use on Anglo-Saxon vessels well before AD 700. It follows from this that there is no basis whatsoever for the widely held belief that the Anglo-Saxons adopted the sail as a result of Viking influence. The date at which the sail was first adopted by the Germanic barbarians, probably from contacts with the Romans or the Celts, cannot be ascertained but we can be sure, on the basis of the evidence of

Tacitus' *Histories*, that at least one of the Germanic tribes on the lower Rhine had begun to use sailing ships by the middle of the first century AD. Though we should expect that the diffusion of the sail along the North Sea coast was rapid, we do not have explicit literary confirmation that it was in use by the Saxons until c. 473 (which, however, is early enough for us to conclude that the Anglo-Saxon settlers did not arrive in Britain in rowing boats). Nevertheless, the literary and archaeological evidence which we possess for the nature and range of the Saxon raids points to their possession of effective sailing ships even at the time of their earliest recorded attacks on Gaul in the late third century. The Saxons' raids were preceded by those of the Chauci. The earliest Chaucian raids, in the first century AD, were limited in range but Chaucian raids in the later second century show marked similarities with those of the Saxons, indicating a much improved seafaring capability, and this suggests that the diffusion of the sail as far as the Elbe took place in the first half of the second century at the latest.

Little attention has been paid to the seafaring activities of the Franks by either maritime or medieval historians but this neglect is not justified by an examination of the evidence. In the third and fourth centuries the range of Frankish pirate raiding equalled, and even exceeded, that of Saxon piracy. Though there appears to have been a reduction in Frankish naval activity after the late fourth century, the Franks continued to be active at sea until the mid-ninth century. Indeed, they should be recognised as one of the major seafaring peoples of early medieval Europe. Certainly the Franks were a more important naval power in this period than the Frisians, whose reputation is inflated. In fact, there is no reason to believe that the Frisians were ever an independent naval power of any importance.

Archaeological evidence of Frankish shipbuilding techniques is, unfortunately, entirely lacking but it is suggested, on the basis of similarities between Celtic ships of the Roman period from the Rhine and the Low Countries and later medieval ships from the same area, such as the cog, that the Franks may have built ships by Celtic methods rather than in the clinker-building tradition favoured by the Anglo-Saxons and the Scandinavians. It is my belief that Frankish warships may have shared many of the characteristics of the late Roman Mainz type-A warships which were also strongly influenced by Celtic shipbuilding traditions.

Under Charlemagne and Louis the Pious, the Franks mounted a spirited and effective defence against Viking and Moslem pirate raids and although, in the long run, this defence failed, it was not as a result of any inherent Frankish lack of understanding of naval power or reluctance to go to sea. Charlemagne in particular has never received the credit which is due to him for his understanding of the use and importance of naval power both at sea and on inland waterways. Nor does Louis the Pious deserve his present poor reputation; he tackled the problems of defending the empire's northern coasts with an energy and resolve that compares favourably with that shown by his great father. The coastal defence system which Charlemagne bequeathed to his empire was as effective as the technology of the time allowed. The Frankish defence failed not because the Vikings were superior seamen but because of the failure, following the death of Louis the Pious, of the strong royal authority on which it was based.

Glossary

The definitions given here are based primarily on those to be found in P. Kemp *The Oxford Companion to Ships and the Sea* (Oxford, 1976), and V. Fenwick, *The Graveney Boat*, BAR BS 5–3 (National Maritime Museum, Archaeology Series 3, Greenwich, 1978), pp. 331–8.

CARVEL-BUILT Technique in which the side planks of the vessel are all flush, the edges laid close and caulked to make a smooth finish.

CAULKING Material forced between the seams of the hull after assembly to make it watertight.

CLEAT A wooden wedge used to hold lashings

CLENCH-NAIL A nail whose end has been bent over to prevent it working loose.

CLINKER-BUILT Technique in which the strakes are laid so that they overlap.

FRAME Transverse assembly of timbers forming the internal skeleton of a vessel. Called a rib when in one piece.

FREEBOARD The distance from the waterline to the gunwale measured at the middle of the ship.

GUNWALE The upper edge of the side of the vessel.

HOGGING TRUSS A vessel is said to be hogged when the bow and stern have drooped. A hogging truss is a rope tensioning device used to support the ends of a vessel to prevent, or remedy, this.

KEEL The main longitudinal strength member

KEEL-PLANK A plank used in the keel position.

MAST-STEP Wooden fitting to hold the base of the mast.

RIB Transverse strength member in one piece.

SCARF JOINT Method of joining two timbers by bevelling off the edges so that the same thickness is maintained throughout the length of the joint. Used to fasten the stem posts to the keel.

SHELL The part of the hull that keeps out the water, i.e. keel, stemposts and planking.

SHROUD Standing rigging of a sailing ship used to support the mast.

STEMS In a double-ended ship, the foremost and aftermost timbers of the hull, forming the bow and stern. They are joined at the bottom to the keel.

STOCKHOLM TAR Softwood tar made from carbonised resinous root stumps.

STRAKE A single plank or combination of shorter lengths of planks stretching the length of the vessel.

THOLE PIN Wooden pin inserted or fastened to the gunwale to provide a fulcrum for an oar.

THWART Transverse member used as a seat.

TRENAIL Wooden peg or through-fastening.

WASH STRAKE A strake fixed above the gunwale to increase the freeboard.

Bibliography of Works Cited

Primary Sources

Adam of Bremen, *Gesta Hammaburgensis ecclesiae pontificum,* ed. B. Schmeidler, *MGH. SSRG 2* (Hanover, 1917).

Adonis archiepiscopi Viennensis chronico, ed. G. H. Pertz, *MGH. SS* 2 (Hanover, 1829), pp. 315–23.

Alcuin, *Epistolae*, ed. E. Duemmler, *MGH. Epp.* 4 (Berlin, 1895), pp. 18–481.

Ambrose, *Epistolae*, ed. J. P. Migne, *Patrologia latina* XVI (Paris, 1866), cols 876ff.

Ammianus Marcellinus, *Rerum gestarum libri*, ed. and trans. J. C. Rolfe, Loeb Classical Library (3 vols, London, 1935).

Andreas Danduli, *Chronicon Venetum,* ed. L. A. Muratori, *Rerum Italicarum Scriptores* XII. i (Bologna, 1938–47), pp. 1–405.

Anglo-Saxon Chronicle, ed. B. Thorpe, Rolls Series 23 (2 vols, London, 1861).

Annales Alamannici, ed. G. H. Pertz, *MGH. SS* 1 (Hanover, 1826), pp. 22–30, 40–4, 47–56.

Annales Bertiniani, in R. Rau (ed.), *Quellen zur karolingischen Reichsgeschichte*, (Darmstadt, 1974), vol. 2, pp. 11–287.

Annales Fuldenses, ed. G. H. Pertz, *MGH. SS* 1 (Hanover, 1826), pp. 343–415.

Annales Guelferbytani, ed. G. H. Pertz, *MGH. SS* 1 (Hanover, 1826), pp. 23–31, 40–6.

Annales Laureshamenses, ed. G. H. Pertz, *MGH. SS* 1 (Hanover, 1826), pp. 22-39.

Annales Laurissenses minores, ed. G. H. Pertz, *MGH. SS* 1 (Hanover, 1826), pp. 114–23.

Annales Mettenses priores, ed. B. von Simson, *MGH. SSRG* 10 (Hanover Leipzig, 1905).

Annales Mosellani, ed. J. M. Lappenberg, *MGH. SS* 16 (Hanover, 1859), pp. 494–9.

Annales Petaviani, ed. G. H. Pertz, *MGH. SS* 1 (Hanover, 1826), pp. 7–18.

Annales Quedlinburgenses, pars prior, ed G. H. Pertz, *MGH. SS* 3 (Hanover, 1839), pp. 22–69.

Annales qui dicuntur Einhardi (Reviser), ed. F. Kurze, *MGH. SSRG* 6 (Hanover, 1895), pp. 27–115 (odd-numbered pages).

Annales Regni Francorum, ed. F. Kurze, *MGH. SSRG* 6 (Hanover, 1895).

Annales S. Amandi, ed. G. H. Pertz, *MGH. SS* I (Hanover, 1826), pp. 6–14.

Annales Xantenses, in R. Rau (ed.), *Quellen zur karolingischen Reichsgeschichte*, (Darmstadt, 1974), vol. 2, pp. 339–71.

Annalium Salisburgensium additamentum, ed. W. Wattenbach, *MGH. SS* 13 (Hanover, 1881), pp. 236–41.

Annals of the Kingdom of Ireland, ed. J. O'Donovan (Dublin, 1856).

Annals of Ulster, ed. S. Mac Airt and G. Mac Niocaill (Dublin, 1983).

Arrian, *Anabasis Alexandri*, ed. and trans. P. A. Brunt, Loeb Classical Library (2 vols, London, 1976–83).

Astronomer, *Vita Hludowici imperatoris*, in R. Rau (ed.), *Quellen zur karolingischen Reichsgeschichte*, (Darmstadt, 1974), vol. 1, pp. 215–53.

Aurelius Victor, *De Caesaribus*, ed. Fr. Pichlmayr (Leipzig, 1970).

Bede, *Historia Ecclesiastica Gentis Anglorum*, ed. B. Colgrave and R. A. B. Mynors, *Bede's Ecclesiastical History of the English People* (Oxford, 1969).

Beowulf, ed. C. L. Wrenn, revised edn (London, 1958).

Caesar, *The Gallic War*, ed. and trans. H. J. Edwards, Loeb Classical Library (London, 1917).

Capitularia regum Francorum I = MGH. LL 2, ed. A. Boretius (Hanover, 1883).

Cassiodorus, *Variae*, ed. T. Mommsen, *MGH. AA* XII (Berlin, 1894),

Cassius Dio, *Histories*, ed. and trans. E. Cary, Loeb Classical Library (9 vols, London, 1960–1).

Chilperic I, *Epistola*, ed. K. A. F. Pertz, *MGH. Diplomata* 1 (Hanover, 1872), 8, at pp. 11–12.

Chronica Gallica a CCCCLII, ed. T. Mommsen, *MGH. AA* 9 = *Chronica Minora* I (Berlin, 1892), pp. 646–64 (even-numbered pages).

Chronica Gallica a DXI, ed. T. Mommsen, *MGH. AA* 9 = *Chronica Minora* I (Berlin, 1892), pp. 647–66 (odd numbered pages).

Chronicarum Fredegarii continuationes, ed. B. Krusch, *MGH. SSRM* 2 (Hanover, 1888), pp. 168–93.

Chronicarum quae dicuntur Fredegarii Scholastici libri IV, ed. B. Krusch, *MGH. SSRM* 2 (Hanover, 1888), pp. 1–167.

Chronicon Moissiacense, ed. G. H. Pertz *MGH. SS* 1, pp. 282–313.

Claudian, *Carmina*, ed. and trans. M. Platnauer, Loeb Classical Library (2 vols, London, 1922).

Codex Carolinus, ed. W. Gundlach, *MGH. Epp.* 3 (Berlin, 1892), pp. 476–653.

Constantine VII Porphyrogenitus, *De administrando imperio*, ed. and trans. G. Moravcsik and R. J. H. Jenkins, *Corpus Fontium Historiae Byzantinae* I (Washington, 1967).

Constantius, *Vita S. Germani*, ed. B. Krusch and W. Levison, *MGH. SSRM* 7 (Hanover, 1919–20), pp. 247–83.

Eddius Stephanus, *Vita Wilfridi episcopi*, ed. J. Raine, *Historians of the Church of York*, 1, Rolls Series 71 (London, 1879), pp. 1–103.

Eigil, *Vita S. Sturmi*, ed. G. H. Pertz, *MGH. SS* 2 (Hanover, 1829), pp. 366–77.

Einhard, *Epistolae*, ed. K. Hampe, *MGH. Epp.* 5 (Berlin, 1899), pp. 105–45.

—*Vita Karoli Imperatoris,* in R. Rau (ed.), *Quellen zur karolingischen Reichsgeschichte,* (Darmstadt, 1974), vol. 1, pp. 163–211.

Epistolae variorum Carolo Magno regnante scriptae, ed. E. Duemmler, *MGH. Epp.* 4 (Berlin, 1895), pp. 494–567.

Epistula Sisebuti regis Gothorum, ed. J. Fontaine in *idem, Isidore de Séville: traité de la nature* (Bordeaux, 1960), pp. 329–35.

Ermoldus Nigellus, *In honorem Hludowici Caesaris Augusti libri IIII,* ed. G. H. Pertz, *MGH. SS* 2 (Hanover, 1829), pp. 466–516.

Eugippius, *Vita S. Severini,* ed. T. Mommsen, *MGH. SSRG* 26 (Berlin, 1898).

Eunapius, ed. and trans. R. C. Blockley, *The Fragmentary Classicising Historians of the Later Roman Empire,* vol. 2, ARCA Classical and Medieval Texts, Papers and Monographs 10 (Liverpool, 1983), pp. 2–127.

Eutropius, *Breviarium ab urbe condita,* ed. F. Ruehl (Stuttgart, 1975).

Finnsburg, ed. A. J. Wyatt and R. W. Chambers, *Beowulf and the Finnsburg Fragment* (Cambridge, 1925), pp. 158–62.

Fragmentum Annalium Chesnii, ed. G. H. Pertz, *MGH. SS* 1 (Hanover, 1826), pp. 33–4.

Genesius, *Regum Libri Quattuor,* ed. A. Lesmueller-Werner and I. Thurn, *Corpus Fontium Historiae Byzantinae* XIV (Berlin-New York, 1978).

Gesta Abbatum Fontanellensium, ed. S. Loewenfeld, *MGH. SSRG* 28, (Hanover, 1886).

Gildas, *De excidio et conquestu Britanniae,* ed. M. Winterbottom (London, 1978).

Gregory of Tours, *Historiarum Libri X,* ed. W. Arndt and B. Krusch, *MGH. SSRM* 1 (Hanover, 1885), pp. 31–450.

—*Liber in gloria martyrum,* ed. B. Krusch, *MGH. SSRM* 1 (Hanover, 1885), pp. 484–561.

Hydatius, *Chronicon,* ed. A. Tranoy, *Hydace,* Sources Chrétiennes 218 (2 vols, Paris, 1974).

Incerti panegyricus Constantio Caesari dictus, in *Panégyriques Latins,* ed. and trans. E Galletier (3 vols, Paris, 1949–55) vol. 1, pp. 82–100.

Ionae Vitae Sanctorum Columbani, Vedastis, Iohannis, MGH. SSRG 37, ed. B. Krusch (Hanover-Leipzig, 1905).

Isidore of Seville, *Historia Gothorum,* ed. T. Mommsen, *MGH. AA* 11 = *Chronica Minora* II (Berlin, 1894), pp. 268–95.

Jerome, *Chronicon,* ed. R. Helm (Die Griechischen Christlichen Schriftsteller 47 = Eusebius Werke, 7: *Die Chronik des Hieronymus* (Berlin, 1956)).

John of Biclar, *Chronica,* ed. T. Mommsen, *MGH. AA* 11 = *Chronica Minora* II (Berlin, 1894), pp. 207–23.

John the Deacon, *Chronicon Venetum,* ed. G. H. Pertz, *MGH. SS* 7 (Hanover, 1846), pp. 4–38.

Jordanes, *Getica,* ed. T. Mommsen, *MGH. AA* 5.i (Berlin, 1882), pp. 53–138.

Julian, *Panegyric in Honour of Constantius,* ed. and trans. W. C. Wright, *The Works of the Emperor Julian,* Loeb Classical Library (3 vols, London, 1913), vol. 1, pp. 4–127.

—*Letter to the Athenians*, ed. and trans. J. Bidez, *L'empereur Julien: oeuvres complètes, vol. 1.i = Discours de Julien César* (Paris, 1932), V, pp. 206–35.

Julian of Toledo, *Historia Wamba regis*, ed. B. Krusch and W. Levison, *MGH. SSRM* 5 (Hanover, 1910), pp. 501–26.

Leo III, *Epistolae*, ed. K. Hampe, *MGH. Epp.* 5, pp. 85–104.

Liber Historiae Francorum, ed. B. Krusch, *MGH. SSRM* 2 (Hanover, 1888), pp. 215–328.

Liber monstrorum de diversis generibus: De Hyglaco Getorum rege, in R. W. Chambers, *Beowulf: An Introduction*, 3rd edn (Cambridge, 1959), p. 4.

Mamertinus, *Panegyricus Maximiano Augusto dictus*, in *Panégyriques Latins*, ed. and trans. E. Galletier (3 vols, Paris, 1949–55), vol. 1, pp. 24–37.

—*Panegyricus Genethliacus Maximiano Augusto dictus*, in *Panégyriques Latins*, ed. and trans. E. Galletier (3 vols, Paris, 1949–55), vol. 1, pp. 50–67.

Martial, *Epigrammata*, ed. W. M. Lindsay (Oxford, 1929).

Maurice, *Strategikon*, trans. G. T. Dennis (Philadelphia, 1984).

Nazarius, *Panegyricus Constantino dictus*, in *Panégyriques Latins*, ed. and trans E. Galletier (3 vols, Paris, 1949–55), vol. 2, pp. 166–98.

Nennius, *Historia Brittonum*, ed. J. Morris (London, 1980).

Nithard, *Historiarum libri IIII*, in R. Rau (ed.), *Quellen zur karolingischen Reichsgeschichte*, (Darmstadt, 1974), vol. 1, pp. 383–461.

Notitia Dignitatum, ed. O. Seeck (Berlin, 1876).

Notker the Stammerer, *Gesta Karoli Magni*, in R. Rau (ed.), *Quellen zur karolingischen Reichsgeschichte*, (Darmstadt, 1974), vol 3, pp. 322–427.

Orosius, *Historiarum adversum paganos libri VII*, ed. C. Zangmeister (Leipzig, 1889).

Pacatus, *Panegyricus Theodosio dictus*, in *Panégyriques Latins*, ed. and trans. E Galletier (3 vols, Paris, 1949–55) vol. 3, pp. 68–114.

Pactus Legis Salicae, ed. K. A. Eckhardt, *MGH. LL* 4.1 (Hanover, 1962).

Paul the Deacon, *Historia Langobardorum*, ed. L. Bethmann and G. Waitz, *MGH. SSRL* 3 (Hanover, 1878).

Philippe de Commynes, *Mémoires*, trans. M. Jones (Penguin Classics, Harmondsworth, 1972).

Pliny, *Natural History*, ed. and trans. H. Rackham, Loeb Classical Library, revised edn (London, 1968).

Poeta Saxo, ed. G. H. Pertz, *MGH. SS* 1 (Hanover, 1826), pp. 225–79.

Priscus, ed. and trans. R. C. Blockley, *The Fragmentary Classicising Historians of the Later Roman Empire*, vol. 2, ARCA Classical and Medieval Texts, Papers and Monographs 10 (Liverpool, 1983), pp. 222–400.

Procopius, *History of the Wars*, ed. and trans. H. B. Dewing, Loeb Classical Library (5 vols, London, 1913–28).

Prosper Tironensis, *Epitoma Chronicon*, ed. T. Mommsen, *MGH. AA* 9 = *Chronica Minora* I (Berlin, 1892), pp. 341–485.

Rau, R. (ed.), *Quellen zur karolingischen Reichsgeschichte* (3 vols, Darmstadt, 1974/1972/1969).

Ravennatis Anonymi Cosmographia, ed. J. Schnetz in *Itineraria Romana II* (Leipzig, 1940), pp. 1–110.

Rimbert, *Vita S. Anskarii,* ed. D. C. F. Dahlmann, *MGH. SS* 2, (Hanover, 1829), pp. 683–725.

Saxo Grammaticus, *Gesta Danorum,* ed. J. Olrik and H. Raeder (2 vols, Copenhagen, 1831).

Scriptores Historiae Augustae, ed. E. Hohl (2 vols, Leipzig, 1965).

Senchus Fer n Alban, ed. and trans. J. Bannerman, *Studies in the History of Dalriada* (Edinburgh, 1974), pp. 41–9.

Sidonius Apollinaris, *Carmina et epistolae,* ed. and trans. W. B. Anderson, Loeb Classical Library (2 vols, London, 1936–65).

Strabo, *Geography,* ed. and trans. H. L. Jones, Loeb Classical Library, vol. 3 (London, 1924).

Suetonius, *De Vita Caesarum,* ed. and trans. J. C. Rolfe, Loeb Classical Library (2 vols. London, 1914).

Symmachus, *Epistolae,* ed. O. Seeck, *MGH. AA* 6 (Berlin, 1883).

Tacitus, *Agricola,* ed. R. M. Ogilvie and I. Richmond (Oxford, 1967).

—*Annales,* ed. and trans. C. H. Moore, Loeb Classical Library (4 vols, London, 1963).

—*Germania,* ed. and trans. M. Hutton, Loeb Classical Library, rev. edn (London, 1970).

—*Historiarum libri,* ed. C. D. Fisher (Oxford, 1911).

Thegan, *Vita Hludowici imperatoris,* in R. Rau (ed.), *Quellen zur karolingischen Reichsgeschichte,* (Darmstadt, 1974), vol. 1, pp. 215–53.

Theophanes, *Chronographia,* trans. H. Turtledove, *The Chronicle of Theophanes* (Philadelphia, 1982).

Translatio S. Alexandri auctoribus Ruodolfo et Meginharto, ed. G. H. Pertz, *MGH. SS* 2 (Hanover, 1829), pp. 673–81.

Vegetius, *Epitoma rei militaris,* ed. C. Lang (reprint, Stuttgart, 1967).

Velleius Paterculus, *Res gestae divi Augusti,* ed. and trans. J. Hellegouarc'h, *Histoire Romaine* (2 vols, Paris, 1982).

Venantius Fortunatus, *Carmina,* ed. F. Leo, *MGH. AA* 4 (Berlin, 1881).

Versus de Asia et de Universi Mundi Rota, anonymously edited in *Corpus Christianorum, Series Latina* CLXXV, *Itineraria et alia geographica* (Turnhout, 1965), pp. 435–54.

Vita Bonifatii auctore Willibaldo presbytero, in *Vitae Sancti Bonifatii archiepiscopi Moguntini,* ed. W. Levison, *MGH. SSRG* 57 (Hanover-Leipzig, 1905), pp. 1–58.

Vita Columbani, Liber I, ed. B. Krusch, *MGH. SSRG* 37 (Hanover-Leipzig, 1905), pp. 148–224.

Vita Genovefae, ed. B. Krusch, *MGH. SSRM* 3 (Hanover, 1896), pp. 204–38.

Vita Liudgeri, ed. G. H. Pertz, *MGH. SS* 2 (Hanover, 1829), pp. 403–25.

Vita Richarii, ed. B. Krusch, *MGH. SSRM* 7 (Hanover, 1920), pp. 438–53.

Vita Viviani, ed. B. Krusch, *MGH. SSRM* 3 (Hanover, 1896) pp. 92–100.

Widukind of Corvey, *Res gestae Saxonicae*, ed. G. Waitz and K. A. Kehr, rev. P. Hirsch, *MGH. SSRG* 60 (Hanover, 1935).

Zosimus, *New History*, ed. and trans. F. Paschoud, *Zosime: Histoire Nouvelle*, Collection des universités de France (3 vols, Paris, 1971–79).

Secondary Sources

Abel, S. and Simson, B., *Jahrbücher des fränkisches Reiches unter Karl dem Grossen* (2 vols, Leipzig, 1888, 1883: reprint Berlin-Munich, 1969).

Abels, R. P., *Lordship and Military Obligation in Anglo Saxon England* (Berkeley, 1988).

Ahmad, A., A history of Islamic Sicily (Edinburgh, 1975).

Åkerlund, H., *Nydamskeppen* (Gothenburg, 1963).

- Alcock, L., *Arthur's Britain* (London, 1971).

Alföldi, A., 'The invasions of peoples from the Rhine to the Black Sea', in *The Cambridge Ancient History*, vol. 12 (Cambridge, 1939), pp. 138–64.

Andersen, H., 'Det bjerg der kaldes Gamle Lybæk', *Skalk* II (1979), 9–13.

Bachrach, B. S., *Merovingian Military Organisation, 481–751* (Minneapolis, 1972).

—*Liber Historiae Francorum* (Lawrence, 1973).

Bakka, E., 'Scandinavian-type gold bracteates in Kentish and continental grave finds', in V. I. Evison (ed.), *Angles, Saxons and Jutes*, (Oxford, 1981), pp. 11–38.

Balil, A., 'Las invasiones germánicas en Hispania durante la segunda mitad del siglo III D. D. J. C.' *Cuadernos de Trabajos de la Escuela Española de Historia y Arqueología en Roma* IX (1957), 95–143.

—'Hispania en los años 260 a 300 D. D. J. C.' *Emerita* XXVII (1959), 269–95.

Bang-Andersen, A. (ed.), *The North Sea* (Stavanger-Oslo, 1985).

Bannerman, J., *Studies in the History of Dalriada* (Edinburgh, 1974).

Barnes, T. D., *The Sources of the Historiae Augustae*, Collections Latomus vol. 155 (Brussels, 1978).

Bartholomew, P., 'Fourth-century Saxons', *Britannia* XV (1984), 169–85.

Bass, G. F. (ed.), *A History of Seafaring Based on Underwater Archaeology* (London, 1972).

Bendixen, K., *Denmark's Money* (Copenhagen, 1967).

Bengston, H., (ed.), *Grosser Historischer Weltatlas, 1, Vorgeschichte und Altertum* (Munich, 1972).

Besta, E., *La Sardegna medioevale* (2 vols, Palermo, 1908).

Birley, A. R., 'The third-century crisis in the Roman empire', *Bulletin of the John Rylands University Library of Manchester* LVIII (1975), 253–81.

Bliss, A., 'The Aviones and Widsith 26', in P. Clemoes (ed.), *Anglo-Saxon England* 14 (Cambridge, 1985), pp. 97–106.

Blockley, R. C., 'The date of the "Barbarian Conspiracy"', *Britannia* XI (1980), 223–5.

—*The Fragmentary Classicising Historians of the Later Roman Empire*, vol. 1, ARCA Classical and Medieval Texts, Papers and Monographs 6 (Liverpool, 1981).

Bloemers, J. H. F. *et al.*, *Verleden Land* (Amsterdam, 1981).

Blok, D. P. *et al.* (eds), *Algemene Geschiedenis der Nederlanden 1, Middeleeowen* (Haarlem, 1981).

Böhme, H. W., 'Das Ende der Römerherrschaft in Britannien und die angelsächsische Besiedlung Englands im 5. Jahrhundert', *JRGZM* XXXIII (1986), 469–574.

Braunfels, W. (ed.), *Karl der Grosse: Lebenswerk und Nachleben 1* (ed. H. Beumann): *Persönlichkeit und Geschichte,* 3rd edn, (Düsseldorf, 1967).

Brøgger, A. W. and Shetelig, H., *The Viking Ships*, 2nd edn (Oslo and London, 1971).

Brønsted, J., *Danmarks oldtid III, Jernalderen* (Copenhagen, 1966).

Brooks, N., 'The development of military obligations in eight- and ninth-century England', in P. Clemoes and K. Hughes (eds), *England Before the Conquest* (Cambridge, 1971), pp. 69–84.

Brown, H. F., *Venice; An Historical Sketch* (London, 1893).

Bruce-Mitford, R., *Aspects of Anglo-Saxon Archaeology* (London, 1974).

—*The Sutton Hoo Ship Burial, vol. 1. Excavation, Background, the Ship, Dating and Inventory* (London, 1975).

Buck. P. H., *Vikings of the Pacific* (Chicago, 1959).

Bullough, D., *The Age of Charlemagne* (London, 1965).

Burn, A. R., 'Procopius and the island of ghosts', *English Historical Review*, LXX (1955), 258–61.

Bury, J. B., 'The naval policy of the Roman empire in relation to the western provinces from the 7th to the 9th century', in *Centenario della nascita di Michele Amari II* (Palermo, 1910), pp. 21–34.

Cameron, P. N., 'Saxons, sea and sail', *IJNA* XI (1982), 319–32.

Carver, M. O. H., 'Pre-Viking Traffic in the North Sea', in McGrail (ed.), *Maritime Celts, Frisians and Saxons*, 117–25

— 'Boat burial in Britain: ancient custom or political signal?' in O. Crumlin-Pedersen and B. Munch Thye (eds), *The ship as symbol in prehistoric and medieval Scandinavia*, Publications of the National Museum, Studies in Archaeology and History, vol. 1 (Copenhagen, 1995), pp. 111–24.

Casson, L., *Ships and Seamanship in the Ancient World* (Princeton, 1971).

Chadwick, H. M., *The Origins of the English Nation* (Cambridge, 1907).

—*The Heroic Age* (Cambridge, 1912).

Chadwick, N. K., *The British Heroic Age* (Cardiff, 1976).

Chambers, R. W., *Widsith. A Study in Old English Heroic Legend* (Cambridge, 1912).

—*Beowulf: An Introduction,* 3rd edn (Cambridge, 1959).

Chase, C. (ed.), *The Dating of Beowulf,* Toronto Old English series 6 (Toronto, 1981).

Christensen, A. E., 'Scandinavian Ships from Earliest Times to the Vikings' in G. F. Bass, *A History of Seafaring Based on Underwater Archaeology* (London, 1972), pp. 159–72.

Christensen, A. E., 'Proto-Viking, Viking and Norse craft' in A. E. Christensen (ed.) *The earliest ships* (London, 1996), pp. 72–88

Clarke, J., 'Vegetius, The military institutions of the Romans', in T. R. Phillips (ed.), *Roots of Strategy* (Harrisburg, 1944), pp. 35–94.

Cleere, H., 'The *classis Britannica*', in D. E. Johnston (ed.), *Saxon Shore*, CBA Research Report Research Report 18 (London, 1977), pp. 16–19.

Cotterill, J., 'Saxon Raiding and the Role of the Late Roman Coastal Forts in Britain', *Britannia* XXIV (1993), 227–39

Courtois, C., *Les Vandales et l'Afrique* (Paris, 1955).

Crickmore, J., *Romano-British Urban Defences* BAR BS 126 (Oxford, 1984).

Crumlin-Pedersen, O., *From Viking Ships to Hanseatic Cogs*, The third Paul Johnstone Memorial Lecture (Greenwich, 1983).

—'Boats and ships of the Angles and Jutes', in S. McGrail, *Maritime Celts, Frisian and Saxons*, CBA Research Report 71 (London, 1990), pp. 98–116.

Cunliffe, B., *The Regni* (London, 1973).

—*Excavations at Portchester Castle*, vol. 1, (Roman), Reports of the research committee of the Society of Antiquaries of London 32 (London, 1975).

—'Lympne: a preparatory statement', in D. E. Johnstone (ed.), *Saxon Shore*, CBA Research Report 18 (London, 1977), , pp. 29–30.

—'The Saxon Shore: some problems and misconceptions', in D. E. Johnston (ed.), *Saxon Shore*, CBA Research Report 18 (London, 1977), pp. 1–6.

—'Excavations at the Roman fort at Lympne, Kent 1976–78', *Britannia* XI (1980), 227–88.

Deanesly, M., *A History of Early Medieval Europe from 476 to 911* (London, 1956).

de Laet, S. J., 'Wooden animal heads of Carolingian times found in the river Scheldt (Belgium)', *Acta Archaeologica* XXVII (1956), 127–37.

de la Roncière, C., 'Charlemagne et la civilisation maritime au IXe siècle', *Le Moyen Age* X (1897), 201–23.

Demougeot, E., *La formation de l'Europe et les invasions barbares: Des origines germaniques à l'avènement de Dioclétien* (Paris, 1969).

Derolez, R., 'Cross Channel language ties' in P. Clemoes (ed.), *Anglo-Saxon England* 3 (Cambridge, 1974), pp. 1–14.

de Weerd, M. D., 'Ships of the Roman period at Zwammerdam/*Nigrum Pullum*, Germania Inferior', in J. du Plat Taylor and H. Cleere (eds), *Roman Shipping and Trade: Britain and the Rhine Provinces*, CBA Research Report 24 (London, 1978), pp. 15–21.

Diesner, H. J., *Das Vandalenreich* (Stuttgart, 1966).

Dill, S., *Roman Society in Gaul in the Merovingian Age* (London, 1926).

Domaszewski, A. V., 'Inschrift eines Germanenkrieges', *Mitteilungen des kaiserlich deutschen archäologischen Instituts, Römische Abteilung* XX (1905), 156–63.

Bibliography

Dove, C. E., 'The first British navy', *Antiquity* XLV (1971), 15–20.
Dralle, L., *Slaven an Havel und Spree* (Berlin, 1981).
Drinkwater, J. F., *Roman Gaul: The Three Provinces 58 BC-AD 260* (London, 1983).
—*The Gallic Empire*, Historia Einzelschriften 52 (Stuttgart, 1987).
Drucker, P., *Indians of the Northwest Coast* (New York, 1963).
Drury, P. J., 'Roman Chelmsford: *Caesaromagus*', in W. Rodwell and T. Rowley (eds), *The Small Towns of Roman Britain*, BAR 15 (Oxford, 1975), pp. 159–73.
Duby, G., *The Early Growth of the European Economy* (London, 1974).
Dufraigne, P., edition and translation of Aurelius Victor, *Livre des Césars* (Paris, 1975).
Dumville, D. N., 'The chronology of *De excidio Britanniae*, book 1', in M. Lapidge and D. N. Dumville (eds), *Gildas: New Approaches* (Woodbridge, 1984), pp. 61–84.
du Plat Taylor, J. and Cleere, H. (eds), *Roman Shipping and Trade: Britain and the Rhine provinces*, CBA Research Report 24 (London, 1978).
Edwards, D. A. and Green, C. J. S., 'The Saxon Shore fort and settlement at Brancaster, Norfolk', in D. E. Johnston (ed.), *The Saxon Shore*, CBA Research Report 18 (London, 1977), pp. 21–9.
Eicholz, D. G., 'Constantius Chlorus' invasion of Britain', *Journal of Roman Studies* XLIII (1953), 41–47.
Eickhoff, E., *Seekrieg und Seepolitik zwischen Islam und Abendland. Das Mittelmeer unter byzantinischer und arabischer Hegemonie 650–1040* (Berlin, 1966).
Ekroll, Ø. 'Bât I myr – eit eldre jernalders båtfunn fra Nordhordland' in *Arkaeologiske Skrifter. Historisk Museum, Bergen* 4 (1988), 390–401.
Ellmers, D., 'Keltischer Schiffbau', *JRGZM* XVI (1969), 73–122.
—*Frühmittelalterliche Handelsschiffahrt in Mittel- und Nordeuropa* (Neumünster, 1972).
—'Nautical archaeology in Germany', *IJNA* III (1974), 137–145.
—'Nautical archaeology in Germany II', *IJNA* IV (1975), 335–43.
—'Shipping on the Rhine in the Roman period: the pictorial evidence', in J. du Plat Taylor, *Roman Shipping and Trade: Britain and the Rhine Provinces*, CBA Research Report 24 (London, 1978), pp. 1–14.
—'Frisian and Hanseatic merchants sailed the cog', in A. Bang Andersen (ed.), *The North Sea* (Stavanger-Oslo, 1985), pp. 79–95.
Evison, V. I., *The Fifth-Century Invasions South of the Thames* (London, 1965).
—(ed.), *Angles, Saxons and Jutes* (Oxford, 1981).
Fahmy, A. M., *Muslim Sea Power in the Eastern Mediterranean from the Seventh to the Tenth Century AD* (Cairo, 1966).
Fenwick, V., *The Graveney Boat*, BAR BS 53 (National Maritime Museum, Archaeological Series 3, Greenwich, 1978).
Fiebiger, O., 'Frankeneinfall in Nordafrika', *Germania* XXIV (1940), pp. 145–6.
• Frere, S. S., *Britannia*, 3rd edn (London, 1987).

Fulk, R. D., 'Dating *Beowulf* to the Viking age', *Philological Quarterly* LXI (1982), 341–59.

Gaggero, G., *Le invasioni scito-germaniche nell'Oriente Romano dal 251–282 DC* (Genoa, 1973).

Galliou, P., 'Western Gaul in the third century', in A. King and M. Henig (eds), *The Roman West in the Third Century*, BAR IS 109 (Oxford, 1981), pp. 259–86.

Ganshof, F. L., 'L'historiographie dans la monarchie franque sous les Mérovingiens et les Carolingiens', *Settimane* XVII, *La storiografia altomedievale* (2 vols, Spoleto, 1970), vol. 2, pp. 631–85.

—*Frankish Institutions Under Charlemagne* (New York, 1970).

—*The Carolingians and the Frankish Monarchy* (London 1971).

Gerberding, R. A., *The Rise of the Carolingians and the Liber Historiae Francorum* (Oxford, 1987).

• Gibbon, E., *The History of the Decline and Fall of the Roman Empire*, ed. J. B. Bury (8 vols, London, 1897).

Gifford, E. & J., 'The sailing characteristics of Saxon ships as derived from half-scale working models with special reference to the Sutton Hoo ship', *IJNA* 24 (1995), 121–31.

—'The sailing performance of Anglo-Saxon ships as derived from the building and trials of half-scale models of the Sutton Hoo and Graveney ship finds', *Mariner's Mirror* (1996), 131–53.

Goelzer, H. (ed. and trans.), *Tacite: Histoires* (2 vols, Paris, 1965–8).

Goffart, W., *Barbarians and Romans: The Techniques of Accommodation* (Princeton, 1980).

—'Hetware and Hugas: datable anachronisms in *Beowulf*', in C. Chase (ed.), *The Dating of Beowulf*, Toronto Old English series 6 (Toronto, 1981), pp. 83-101.

—*The Narrators of Barbarian History (AD 550–800): Jordanes, Gregory of Tours, Bede and Paul the Deacon* (Princeton, 1988).

Goodburn, R. and Bartholomew, P. (eds), *Aspects of the Notitia Dignitatum*, BAR Supp. Ser. 15 (Oxford, 1976).

Gosselin, J. Y. and Seillier, C., '*Gesoriacum Bononia*: de la ville du Haut-Empire à la ville du Bas-Empire', *Revue Archéologique de Picardie*, III–IV (1984 = *Les villes de la Gaule Belgique au Haut-Empire*), pp. 259–64.

Göttlicher, A., 'Roman ship on Runic bone', *IJNA* 18 (1989), p. 73.

Green, C., *Sutton Hoo. The Excavation of a Royal Ship Burial*, (London, 1963).

Green, H. J. M., 'Roman Godmanchester', in W. Rodwell and R. Rowley (eds), *The Small Towns of Roman Britain*, BAR 15 (Oxford, 1975), pp. 183–210.

• Greenhill, B., *The Archaeology of the Boat* (London, 1976).

Greenhill, B. with Morrison, J., *The Archaeology of Boats and Ships* (London, 1995),

Grundtvig, N. F. S., 'Om Bjovulfs Drape', *Dannevirke* II (1817), 284–6.

Gysseling, M., *Toponymisch Woordenboek van België, Nederland, Luxemburg, Noord-Frankrijk en West Duitsland 1*, Bouwestoffen en studiën voor de

Geschiedenis en de Lexicografie van het Nederlands VI, 1 (Tongeren, 1960).
—'De oudste Friese toponymie', *Philologica Frisica Anno 1969* (Grins, 1970), pp. 41–51.
—'Germanisering en taalgrens', in Blok, *Algemene Geschiedenis der Nederlanden* 1, pp. 100–15.
Haldon, J. and Byrne, M., 'A possible solution to the problem of Greek fire', *Byzantinische Zeitschrift* LXX (1977), 91–9.
Halphen, L., *Etudes critiques sur l'histoire de Charlemagne* (Paris, 1921).
—*Charlemagne and the Carolingian Empire* (Amsterdam-New York-Oxford, 1977).
Hassal, M., 'Britain and the Rhine provinces: epigraphic evidence for Roman trade', in J. du Plat Taylor and H. Cleere (eds), *Roman Shipping and Trade: Britain and the Rhine Provinces*, CBA Research Report 24 (London, 1978), pp. 41–8.
Hedeager, L., 'A quantitative analysis of Roman imports in Europe north of the *limes* (0–400 AD) and the question of Roman-Germanic exchange', in K. Kristiansen and C. Paludan Müller, *New Directions in Scandinavian Archaeology*, Studies in Scandinavian Prehistory and Early History 1 (Copenhagen, 1979), pp. 191–216.
—'Processes towards state formation in early Iron Age Denmark', in K. Kristiansen and C. Paludan-Müller, *New Directions in Scandinavian Archaeology*, Studies in Scandinavian Prehistory and Early History 1 (Copenhagen, 1979), pp. 217–23.
Heidinga, H. A., *Medieval Settlement and Economy North of the Lower Rhine* (Assen Maastricht, 1987).
Herrmann, J., 'The northern Slavs', in D. M. Wilson (ed.), *The Northern World* (London, 1980), pp. 183–206.
Hill, D., *A History of Engineering in Classical and Medieval Times* (London, 1984).
Hlawitschka, E., *Franken, Alemannen, Bayern und Burgunder in Oberitalien (774–962)*, Forschungen zur oberrheinischen Landesgeschichte 8 (Freiburg, 1960).
Höckmann, O., 'Spätrömische Schiffsfunde in Mainz', *Archaeologisches Korrespondenzblatt* XII (1982), 231–50.
—'Zur Bauweise, Funktion und Typologie der Mainzer Schiffe', in G. Rupprecht (ed.), *Die Mainzer Römerschiffe*, 3rd edn (Mainz, 1984), pp. 44–77.
—*Antike Seefahrt* (Munich, 1985).
—'Römische Schiffsverbände auf dem Ober und Mittelrhein und die Verteidigung der Rheingrenze in der Spätantike', *JRGZM* XXXIII (1986), 369–416.
—'Late Roman Rhine vessels from Mainz, Germany' in *IJNA* XXII (1993) pp. 125–135.
Hodges, R., *Dark Age Economics* (London, 1982).

Hofmann, H. H., 'Fossa Carolina: Versuch einer Zusammenschau', in W. Braunfels (ed.), *Karl der Grosse: Lebenswerk und Nachleben 1* (ed. H. Beumann): *Persönlichkeit und Geschichte*, 3rd edn (Düsseldorf, 1967), pp. 437–53.

• Hollister, C. W., *Anglo-Saxon Military Institutions on the Eve of the Norman Conquest* (Oxford, 1962).

Hornell, J., *Water Transport; Origins and Early Evolution* (Cambridge, 1946).

Hutchinson, J. N. et al., 'Combined archaeological and geotechnical investigation of the Roman fort at Lympne, Kent', *Britannia* XVI (1985), 209–36.

James, E., *The Franks* (Oxford, 1988).

Jankuhn, H., 'Karl der Grosse und der Norden', in W. Braunfels (ed.), *Karl der Grosse: Lebenswerk und Nachleben 1* (ed. H. Beumann): *Persönlichkeit und Geschichte*, 3rd edn (Düsseldorf, 1967), pp. 699–707.

—*Haithabu. Ein Handelsplatz der Wikingerzeit*, 5th edn (Neumünster, 1972).

Jellema, D., 'Frisian trade in the Dark Ages', *Speculum* XXX (1955), 15–36.

Jelski, G., 'Les niveaux antiques et la céramique du chartier du commissariat central d'Arras', *Revue du Nord* LXII (1980), 830–50.

Jensen, J., 'The Hjortspring boat reconstructed', *Antiquity* LXIII (1989), 531–5.

• Johnson, S., *The Roman Forts of the Saxon Shore* (London, 1976).

—'Channel commands in the *Notitia*', in R. Goodburn and P. Bartholomew (eds), *Aspects of Notitia Dignitatum*, BAR Supp. Ser.15 (Oxford, 1976), pp. 81–102.

—'Late Roman defences and the *limes*', in D. E. Johnston (ed.), *The Saxon Shore*, CBA Research Report 18 (London, 1977), pp. 63–9.

Johnston, D. E. (ed.), *The Saxon Shore*, CBA Research Report 18 (London, 1977).

Johnstone, P., *The Seacraft of Prehistory* (London, 1980).

Jones, C. W., 'Bede and Vegetius', *The Classical Review* XLVI (1932), pp. 248–9.

• Jones, G., *A History of the Vikings* (Oxford, 1973).

Jones, M. E., 'The logistics of the Anglo-Saxon invasions', in M. Daniel (ed.), *Papers of the Sixth Naval History Symposium held at the U. S. Naval Academy on 29–30 September 1983* (Wilmington, 1987), pp. 62–9.

Jones, M. E. and Casey, J., 'The Gallic Chronicle restored: A chronology for the Anglo-Saxon invasions and the end of Roman Britain', *Britannia* XIX (1988), 379–97.

Jones, M. U., 'Saxon Mucking: a post-excavation note', in S. C. Hawkes (ed.), *Anglo-Saxon studies*, BAR BS 72 (Oxford, 1979), pp. 21–37.

Jørgensen, E. and Rieck, F., 'Mere fra Mosen' in *Skalk* 6 (1997), 5–9, p. 9.

Kaul, F., *Da våbnene tav* (Copenhagen, 1988).

Keay, S. J., 'The *Conventus Tarraconensis* in the third century', in A. King and M. Henig (eds), *The Roman West in the Third Century*, BAR IS 109 (Oxford, 1981), pp. 451–86.

• Kemp, P. (ed.), *The Oxford Companion to Ships and the Sea* (Oxford, 1976).

Kessler, H. L., *The Illustrated Bibles from Tours*, Studies in Manuscript Illumination 7 (Princeton, 1977).

Bibliography

King, A. and Henig, M. (eds), *The Roman West in the Third Century* BAR IS 109 (Oxford, 1981).

King, P. D., *Law and Society in the Visigothic Kingdom* (Cambridge, 1972).

—*Charlemagne* (London, 1986).

—*Charlemagne: Translated Sources* (Lambrigg, 1987).

König, I., *Die gallischen Usurpatoren von Postumus bis Tetricius* (Munich, 1981).

• Kossack, G., 'The Germans', in F. Millar (ed.), *The Roman Empire and its Neighbours*, 2nd edn (London, 1981), pp. 294–320.

Kristiansen, K. and Paludan-Müller, C. (eds), *New Directions in Scandinavian Archaeology*, Studies in Scandinavian Prehistory and Early History 1 (Copenhagen, 1979).

Laistner, M. L. W., *Thought and Letters in Western Europe. AD 500 900* (London, 1931).

Lambert, A. M., *The Making of the Dutch Landscape*, 2nd edn (London, 1985).

Lammers, W., 'Die Stammesbildung bei den Sachsen', in *idem* (ed.), *Entstehung und Verfassung des Sachsenstammes* (Darmstadt, 1967), pp. 263–332.

Latouche, R., *The Birth of Western Economy* (London, 1961).

Lebecq, S., 'De la protohistoire au haut moyen âge: le paysage des "terpen" le long des côtes de la Mer du Nord', *Revue du Nord* LXII (1980), 125–54.

—*Marchands et navigateurs frisons du haut moyen âge* (2 vols, Lille, 1983).

Leighton, A. C., *Transport and Communication in Early Medieval Europe* (Newton Abbot, 1972).

Levison, W., *England and the continent in the Eighth Century* (Oxford, 1946).

Lewis, A. R., *Naval Power and Trade in the Mediterranean AD 500–1100* (Princeton, 1951).

—*The Northern Seas* (Princeton, 1958).

Lewis, A. R. and Runyan, T. J., *European Naval and Maritime History, 300-1500* (Bloomington, 1985).

Lewis, D., *We, the Navigators* (Canberra, 1973).

Lintzel, M., 'Zur Entstehungsgeschichte des sächsichen Stammes', *Sachsen und Anhalt* III (1927), 1–46.

Logan, F. D., *The Vikings in History* (London, 1983).

Longnon, A., *Géographie de la Gaule au VIe siècle* (Paris, 1878).

Longworth, P., *The Rise and Fall of Venice* (London, 1974).

Lorren, C., 'Des Saxons en Basse-Normandie au VIe siècle', *Studien zur Sachsenforschung* II (1980), 231–60.

Louwe Kooijmans, L. P., 'Archaeology and coastal change in the Netherlands', in F. H. Thompson (ed.), *Archaeology and Coastal Change*, pp. 106–33.

McGrail, S., *Log Boats of England and Wales,* BAR BS 51 (Oxford, 1978).

—(ed.) *The Archaeology of Medieval Ships Hnd harbours in Northern Europe*, BAR IS 66 (Oxford, 1979).

—*Ancient Boats in North West Europe* (London, 1987).

—'Boats and boatmanship in the late prehistoric southern North Sea and Channel', in *idem, Maritime Celts, Frisians and Saxons*, CBA Research Report 71 (London, 1990), pp. 32–48.

—(ed.) *Maritime Celts, Frisians and Saxons* CBA Research Report 71 (London, 1990).

McKitterick, R., *The Frankish Kingdoms Under the Carolingians, 751–987* (London, 1983).

—*The Carolingians and the Written Word* (Cambridge, 1989).

Magoun, F. P., 'The geography of Hygelac's raid on the lands of the West Frisians and the HættWare, *c*. 530 AD', *English Studies* XXXIV (1953), 160–63.

Malone, K., '*Ubbo Fresicus* at Bravellir', *Classica et Mediaevalia*, VIII (1946), 116–120.

Mann, J. C., 'What was the *Notitia Dignitatum* for?' in R. Goodburn and P. Bartholomew (eds), Aspects of the *Notitia Dignitatum*, BAR Supp. Ser. 15 (Oxford, 1976), pp. 1–9.

—'*Duces and comites* in the fourth century', in D. E. Johnston (ed.), *The Saxon Shore*, CBA Research Report 18 (London, 1977), pp. 11–15.

—'The Reculver inscription – a note', in D. E. Johnston (ed.), *The Saxon Shore*, CBA Research Report 18 (London, 1977), p. 15.

Marcus, G. J., *The conquest of the North Atlantic* (Woodbridge, 1980).

Marsden, P., 'Ships of the Roman period and after in Britain', in G. F. Bass, *A History of Seafaring Based on Underwater Archaeology* (London, 1972), pp. 112–32.

—'A re-assessment of Blackfriars ship 1', in S. McGrail (ed.), *Maritime Celts, Frisians and Saxons*, CBA Research Report 71 (London, 1990), pp. 66–74.

—'A hydrostatic study of a reconstruction of Mainz Roman ship 9' in *IJNA* 22 (1993), pp. 137–41.

Martindale, J. F., *The Prosopography of the Later Roman Empire. Volume 2, AD 395–527* (Cambridge, 1980).

Mertens, J., 'Oudenburg and the northern sector of the continental *litus Saxonicum*', in D. E Johnston (ed.), *The Saxon Shore* CBA Research Report 18 (London, 1977), pp. 51–62.

• Millar, F., *The Roman Empire and Its Neighbours*, 2nd edn (London, 1981).

Mollat, M., 'Les marins et la guerre sur mer dans le nord et l'ouest de l'Europe (jusqu'au XIIe siècle)', *Settimane, XV, Ordinamenti militari in occidente nell'alto medioevo* (Spoleto, 1967), vol. 2, pp. 1009–42.

—*La vie quotidienne des gens de mer en Atlantique (Ix^e–XVIe siècle)* (Paris, 1983).

Morcken, R., *Langskip, knarr og kogge* (Bergen, 1983).

• Morris, J., *The Age of Arthur* (London, 1973).

Mott, L. V., *The Development of the Rudder* (London, 1997).

Müllenhoff, K., 'Die austrasische Dietrichssage', *Zeitschrift für deutsches Altertum* VI (1848), 435–59.

• Musset, L., *The Germanic Invasions* (London, 1975).

—'Deux invasions maritimes des Îles Britanniques: des Anglo-Saxon aux Vikings', in *Settimane* XXXII, *Angli e Sassoni al di qua e al di là del mare* (Spoleto, 1986), pp. 29–69.
Myres, J. N. L., *Anglo Saxon Pottery and the Settlement of England* (Oxford, 1969).
—*The English settlements* (Oxford, 1986).
Myhre, B., 'Boathouses and naval organization' in A. Nørgård Jørgensen and B. L. Clausen (eds), *Military aspects of Scandinavian society in a European persepective AD 1–1300*, Publications of the National Museum, Studies in Archaeology and History, vol. 2 (Copenhagen, 1997), pp. 169–83.
Neifeind, H., *Verträge zwischen Normannen und Franken im neunten und zehnten Jahrhundert* (Heidelberg, 1971).
Nelson, J. L., 'The Last Years of Louis the Pious' in P. Godman and R. Collins (eds), *Charlemagne's Heir* (Oxford, 1990), pp. 147–59.
Neumann, H., 'Jutish burials in the Roman Iron Age', in V. I. Evison (ed.), *Angles, Saxons and Jutes* (Oxford, 1981), pp. 1–10.
Norberg, D., *La poésie latine rythmique du haut moyen fge*, Studia Latina Holmiensis 2 (Stockholm, 1954).
Norden, E., *Die germanische Urgeschichte in Tacitus Germania* (Leipzig-Berlin, 1923).
Nylén, E., *Bildstenar*, 2nd edn (Visby, 1987).
Odegaard, C. E., *Vassi and Fideles in the Carolingian Empire* (New York, 1972).
Ormerod, A. H., *Piracy in the Ancient World* (Liverpool, 1969).
Paschoud, F., *Zosime: Histoire nouvelle*: see Primary Sources under 'Zosimus'.
Pauly-Wissowa, *Realenzyklopädie der klassischen Altertumswissenschaft* (reprint, Stuttgart, 1958).
Percival, J., *The Roman Villa* (London, 1976).
Philp, B. J., 'Dover', in D. E Johnston (ed.), *The Saxon Shore* CBA Research Report 18 (London, 1977), pp. 20–1.
—*The Excavation of the Roman Forts of the Classis Britannica at Dover, 1970-1977*, Kent monograph series no 3 (Dover, 1981).
Pirenne, H., *Mohammed and Charlemagne* (London, 1939).
Plechl, H. *et al.* (eds), *Orbis Latinus*, (3 vols, Brunswick, 1972).
Porter, H., 'Environmental change in the third century', in A. King and M. Henig (eds), *The Roman West in the Third Century*, BAR IS 109 (Oxford, 1981), pp. 353–62.
Pritsak, O., 'The Slavs and the Avars', *Settimane* XXX, *Gli Slavi occidentale e meridionale nell'alto medioevo* (Spoleto, 1983), vol. 2, pp. 353–432.
Pryor, J. H., *Geography, Technology and War. Studies in the Maritime History of the Mediterranean, 649–1571* (Cambridge, 1988).
Ramm, H., *The Parisi* (London, 1978).
Reece, R., 'Coinage and currency in the third century' in A. King and M. Henig(eds), *The Roman West in the Third Century*, BAR IS 109 (Oxford, 1981), pp. 79–88.

Reuter, T., 'Plunder and tribute in the Carolingian empire', *TRHS* 5th Series, XXXV (1985), 75–94.

Rieck, F. and Crumlin-Pedersen, O., *Både fra Danmarks Oldtid* (Roskilde, 1988).

Rieck, F., *Jernalderkrigernes Skibe. Nye og gamle udgravninger I Nydam Mose* (Roskilde, 1994).

Rieck, F. and E. Jørgensen, 'Non-military equipment from Nydam', in A. Nørgård Jørgensen and B. L. Clausen (eds), *Military aspects of Scandinavian society in a European persepective AD 1–1300,* Publications of the National Museum, Studies in Archaeology and History, vol. 2 (Copenhagen, 1997), 220–25, p. 222.

Roberts, W. I., *Romano-Saxon Pottery* BAR BS 106 (Oxford, 1982).

Robertson, A. S., 'Romano-British coin hoards; their numismatic, archaeological and historical significance', in J. Casey and R. Reece (eds), *Coins and the Archaeologist* BAR 4 (Oxford, 1974), pp. 12–36.

—'The bridges on the Severan coins of AD 208 and 209', in W. S. Hanson and L. J. F. Keppie (eds), *Roman Frontier Studies 1979*, BAR IS 71 (3 vols, Oxford, 1980), vol. 1, pp. 131–9.

Rodwell, W., 'Trinovantian towns in their setting: a case study', in W. Rodwell and T. Rowley, *The Small Towns of Roman Britain*, BAR 15 (Oxford, 1975), pp. 85–101.

Rodwell, W. and Rowley, T. (eds), *The Small Towns of Roman Britain* BAR 15 (Oxford, 1975).

Roesdahl, E., *Viking Age Denmark* (London, 1982).

Rouche, M., 'Les Saxons et les origines de Quentovic', *Revue du Nord* LIX (1977), 457–78.

Rule, M., 'The Romano-Celtic ship excavated at St Peter Port, Guernsey', in S. McGrail (ed.), *Maritime Celts, Frisians and Saxons*, CBA Research Report 71 (London, 1990), pp. 49–56.

- Runciman, S., *The Fall of Constantinople, 1453* (Cambridge, 1965).

Russchen, A., 'Jutes and Frisians', *It Beaken* XXVI (1964), 26–37.

—'Warns, Heruli, Thuringians', *It Beaken* XXVI (1964), 301–6.

Sabbe, E., 'Les relations économiques entre Angleterre et le Continent au haut moyen âge', *Le Moyen Age* LVI (1950), 169–93.

Salway, P., *Roman Britain* (Oxford, 1981).

Sanquer, R., 'The *castellum* at Brest (Finistère)', in D. E Johnston (ed.), *The Saxon Shore* CBA Research Report 18 (London, 1977), pp. 45–50.

- Sawyer, P. H., *The Age of the Vikings*, 2nd edn (London, 1971).
- —*Kings and Vikings* (London, 1982).

Schmid, P., 'Some bowls from the excavations of the terp at Feddersen Wierde near Bremerhaven', in V. I. Evison, *Angles, Saxons and Jutes,* (Oxford, 1981), pp. 39–58.

Schmidt, L., *Geschichte der deutschen Stämme bis zum Ausgang der Völkerwanderung: Die Westgermanen* (2 vols, Munich, 1938–40).

Scholz, B. W. and Rogers, B., *Carolingian Chronicles* (Ann Arbor, 1972).

Bibliography

Schönberger, H., 'The Roman frontier in Germany: an archaeological survey', *Journal of Roman Studies* LIX (1969), 144–97.

Seillier, C., 'Fouilles de Boulogne-sur-Mer (*Bononia*)', *Revue du Nord* LIII (1971), 669–79.

—'Boulogne and the coastal defences in the fourth and fifth centuries', D. E Johnston (ed.), *The Saxon Shore* CBA Research Report 18 (London, 1977), pp. 35–8.

Shiel, N., *The Episode of Carausius and Allectus: the Literary and Numismatic Evidence*, BAR 40 (Oxford, 1977).

Simmons, B. B., 'Iron Age and Roman coasts around the Wash', in F. H. Thompson (ed.), *Archaeology and Coastal Change* (London, 1980), pp. 56–73.

Singer, C., 'East and west in retrospect' in C. Singer and E. J. Holmroyd (eds), *The Oxford History of Technology, vol 2, The Mediterranean Civilizations and the Middle Ages* (Oxford, 1979), pp. 753–76.

Smyth, A. P., *Warlords and Holy Men* (London, 1984).

Sproemberg, H., 'Die Seepolitik Karls des Grossen' in idem, *Beiträge zur belgisch-niederländischen Geschichte*, Forschungen zur mittelalterlichen Geschichte 3(Berlin, 1959), pp. 1–29.

Starr, C. G., *The Roman Imperial Navy*, 2nd edn (Cambridge, 1960).

—*The Influence of Sea Power on Ancient History* (New York, 1989).

Stenton, F. M., *Anglo-Saxon England*, 3rd edn (Oxford, 1971).

Stevens, W. M., *Bede's Scientific Achievement*, Jarrow Lecture 1985 (Jarrow, 1985).

Storms, G., 'The significance of Hygelac's raid', *Nottingham Medieval Studies* XIV (1970), 3–26.

Stroheker, K. F., 'Die Alamannen und das spätrömische Reich' in W. Müller (ed.), *Zur Geschichte der Alemannen* (Darmstadt, 1975), pp. 20–48.

Tarradell, M., 'Marruecos antiguo: nuevas perspectivas', *Zephyrus* V (1954), 105–39.

Thoen, H., *De Belgische kustvlakte in de Romeinse tijd*, Verhandel ingen van de Koninklijke Academie voor wettenschappen. Letteren en schone kunsten van Belgie. Klasse der Letteren, XL (1978) no. 88.

—'The third-century Roman occupation in Belgium: the evidence of the coastal plain', in A. King and M. Henig (eds), *The Roman West in the Third Century*, BAR IS 109 (Oxford, 1981), pp. 245–57.

Thompson, E. A., *The Early Germans* (Oxford, 1965).

—'Britain, AD 406–10', *Britannia* VIII (1977), 303–18.

—*Romans and Barbarians* (Madison, 1982).

—*Saint Germanus of Auxerre and the End of Roman Britain* (Woodbridge, 1984).

Thompson, F. H. (ed.), *Archaeology and Coastal Change* (London, 1980).

Thorpe, L., *Gregory of Tours, History of the Franks* (Harmondsworth, 1974).

Thorvildsen, K., *The Viking Ship of Ladby* (Copenhagen, 1961).

Thouvenot, R., 'Une inscription latine du Maroc', *Revue des études latines* XVI (1938), 266–8.

Todd, M., *The Coritani* (London, 1973).

—*The Northern Barbarians 100 BC–AD 300*, revised edn (Oxford, 1987).

Unger, R., *The Ship in the Medieval Economy, 600–1600* (London-Montreal, 1980).

van Dam, R., *Leadership and Community in Late Antique Gaul* (Berkeley, 1985).

van Doorninck, F., 'Byzantium, mistress of the sea', in G. F. Bass (ed.), *A History of Seafaring Based on Underwater Archaeology* (London, 1972), pp. 133–53.

van Doorselaer, A., 'De Romeinen in de Nederlanden', in D. P. Blok *et al.* (eds), *Algemene Geschiedenis der Nederlanden 1, Middeleeowen* (Haarlem, 1981), pp. 21–98

van Es, W. A., *De Romeinen in Nederland* (Bussum, 1972).

van Es, W. A. and Verwers, W. J. H., *Excavations at Dorestad 1. The Harbour: Hoogstraat 1* (Amersfoort, 1980).

van Werveke, H., 'De oudste Burchten aan de Vlaamse en de Zeeuwse Kust', *Mededelingen van de Koninklijke Vlaamse Academie voor Wetenschappen, Letteren en Schone Kunsten van Belgie, Klasse der Letteren*, XXVII.1 (1965) pp. 3–22.

Verbruggen, J. F., 'L'armée et la stratégie de Charlemagne' in Braunfels (ed.), *Karl der Grosse: Lebenswerk und Nachleben 1* (ed. H. Beumann): *Persönlichkeit und Geschichte*, 3rd edn (Düsseldorf, 1967), pp. 420–36.

Vercauteren, F., 'Comment s'est-on défendu, au IXe siècle dans l'empire franc contre les invasions normandes?', *Annales du XXXe Congrès de la Fédération Archéologique de Belgique* (1936), pp. 117–36.

Vernadsky, G., *Ancient Russia* (New Haven, 1943).

Vierck, H. E. F., 'The origin and date of the ship's figurehead from Moerzeke-Mariekerke, Antwerp, *Helinium* X (1970), 139–49.

Vogel, W., *Geschichte der deutschen Seeschiffsfahrt 1,* (Berlin, 1915).

von Uslar, R., *Westgermanische Bodenfunde* (Berlin, 1938).

Wacher, J. S., *Roman Britain* (London, 1978).

— *The Towns of Roman Britain* (2nd revised edn, London, 1995).

Wallace-Hadrill, J. M., *The Fourth Book of the Chronicle of Fredegar* (London, 1960).

—*The Long-Haired Kings* (London, 1962).

—*The Barbarian West, 400–1000*, 3rd edn (London, 1967).

Webster, G., 'Small towns without defences', in W. Rodwell and T. Rowley (eds), *The Small Towns of Roman Britain*, BAR 15 (Oxford, 1975), pp. 53-66.

Weidmann, K., 'Zur Interpretation einiger kaiserzeitlicher Urnenfriedhöfe in Nordwestdeutschland', *JRGZM* XII (1965), 84–92.

Wenskus, R., *Stammesbildung und Verfassung* (Cologne-Graz, 1961).

Bibliography

—*Sächsicher Stammesadel und fränkischer Reichsadel,* Abhandlungen der Akademie der Wissenschaften in Göttingen, Philologisch-Historische Klasse: Folge 3: 93 (Göttingen, 1976).

White, D. A., *Litus Saxonicum* (Madison, 1961).

Whitelock, D., *The Audience of Beowulf* (Oxford, 1951).

Wightman, E., 'The fate of Gallo-Roman villages in the third century', in A. King and M. Henig (eds), *The Roman West in the Third Century*, BAR IS 109 (Oxford, 1981), pp. 235–43.

—*Gallia Belgica* (London, 1985).

Williams, S., *Diocletian and the Roman Recovery* (London, 1985).

Wilson, D. M., 'England and the Continent in the eighth century; an archaeological viewpoint', *Settimane* XXXII, *Angli e Sassoni al di qua e al di là del mer* (Spoleto 1986), pp. 219–44.

Wolfram, H., *History of the Goths* (Berkeley Los-Angeles, 1988).

Wood, I. N., *The Merovingian North Sea,* Occasional Papers on Medieval Topics 1 (Alingsås, 1983).

—'The fall of the western empire and the end of Roman Britain', *Britannia* XVIII (1987), 251–62.

—'The Channel from the 3rd to the 7th centuries AD', in S. McGrail (ed.), *Maritime Celts, Frisians and Saxons*, CBA Research Report 71 (London, 1990), pp. 93–7.

Yorke, B., 'The Jutes of Hampshire and Wight and the origins of Wessex', in S. Basset (ed.), *The Origins of Anglo-Saxon Kingdoms* (London, 1989), pp. 84-96.

Zöllner, E., *Geschichte der Franken bis zur Mitte des sechsten Jahrhunderts* (Munich, 1970).

Index

A

Aachen, 157, 163, 174
Aardenburg, 27, 48
Abodrites, 136, 173, 175–77
Adriatic, 156, 161
Adriatic Sea, 74, 152–56
Aegean Sea, 51, 52
Aelle, 85
Aelmere, 119, 127, 129
Aetius, 82, 83, 86
Agricola, 18, 19
Alamanni, 42, 66, 78, 139; boats, 42, 75
Alfred the Great, 89, 111, 112
Alicante, 54
Alisni, 143
Allectus, 61–65, 73
Alleluia battle, 82
Als boat. *See* Hjortspring boat
Altmühl, R., 141, 147–52
Amalfi, 159, 161
Amiens, 26
Ammianus Marcellinus, 67, 73, 145
Ampurias, 158
Amsivari, 43
Andalusia, 89
Angers, 86, 87
Angiloi. See Angles
Angles, 13, 16, 78, 88, 92, 105, 124; ships of, 93–103
Anglesey, 90
Anglo-Saxons, 15, 105, 134; migration and settlement, 82–85, 98, 107–9, 185, 186; piracy and raiding, 77, 88, 90, 91, 111, 124; royal navy, 110–12; ships, 93–98, 100–110, 112, 185
Annaba, 160
'Antonine fires', 26, 27
Antwerp, 132, 170

Arabs: piracy, 156–63; ships, 92
Årby boat, 75
Arras, 27
Asclepiodotus, 63
Ashby Dell boat, 104
Asia Minor, 41, 51, 52
Athelstan, king of England, 112
Athelstan, king of Kent, 111
Athens, 51
Attacotti, 68
Attoari. *See* Chattuari
Avars, 135, 136, 139, 142, 150, 175; naval activity, 140
Aviones, 44, 60, 67

B

bagaudae, 26, 55, 169
Baghdad, 153, 154
Balearic Islands, 126, 152, 153, 157, 161
ballista, 57
Baltic Sea, 103
barbarian conspiracy, the, 68–70, 77–80, 113
Barcelona, 146, 152
Bardowick, 175
barges, 34–36, 180
Bari, 161
barrels, 144
bastion towers, 29, 57, 58, 69
Batavi, 17, 24
Batavia, 25, 119
Bavai, 27, 48
Bavarians, 126, 131, 136, 141, 142, 163
Bayeux Tapestry, 100, 101
beacons, 121, 165, 182
Beatus, 153, 154
Beauvais, 27, 87
Bede, 78, 83, 90, 110, 111, 145

Belgica, 23, 26, 27, 35, 46, 49, 53–55, 57, 59, 114
Benevento, 152, 161
Beorht, ealdorman, 90
Beowulf, 43, 110, 116–22
Berhard, 160, 163
Bessin, 86–88, 123
Betuwe. *See* Batavia
Bibles: *San Paolo*, 180, 181; *Vivian*, 181
Billericay, 26
bireme, 19, 25
Biscay, Bay of, 26
Björke boat, 33
Black Sea, 14, 41, 51, 64
Blackfriars boat, 36, 72
Bohemians, 136, 138
Boniface, count, 129, 160, 163
Boorne, river, 121, 129
Bosphorus, 52
Bouin, 168
Boulogne, 29, 56, 61–63, 163, 164, 166
Boulonnais, 86, 88, 123
bow-sweep, 181
Bradwell, 56
Braintree, 26
Brancaster, 28, 29, 56, 57
Brandenburg, 138
Brest, 57
Bretons, 87, 88, 125
bridges, 136, 143, 169; defended, 111. *See also* pontoon bridges
Britain *passim*
Britons, 82–85, 92
Brittany, 26, 30, 53, 54, 57, 88, 125, 131, 182
Brittenburg, 28, 29
Brough-on-Humber, 27, 56
Bructeri, 15, 17, 19, 24, 43
Bruges: boat, 35, 36, 39, 72; Roman fort, 28
Bulgar fleet, 140
Burchard, 158, 163
Burgh, 56, 58
Burgundians, 78, 126, 144
burial customs, 31, 42, 45. *See also* ship burial
Byzantine: bridge building, 144; empire, 152–56; navy, 140, 152–56, 159, 161, 162; warships, 161, 162

C

Cadwallon, 90
Caesar, 35
Caister by Yarmouth, 29
Caistor by Norwich, 27
Caithness, 166
Calabria, 159
canal, Regnitz-Altmühl, 141, 147–52
capitularies, 147, 161, 164, 167, 175
Carausius, 58–65, 73
Carolingian, 15
Carthage, 52, 90, 126, 160
carvel-building, 34, 35, 70, 71, 75, 189
Catalaunian plains, 86
caulking, 35, 71, 72, 146, 189
Celtic shipbuilding, 34, 35, 71, 72, 75, 134, 186
Cephalonia, 155
Cerdic, 85
Chaibones. *See* Aviones
Chamavi, 43, 66
chamber lock, 149
Channel, the *passim*
Charlemagne *passim*
Charles Martel, 114, 128, 129, 131, 138
Charles the Bald, 143, 145, 165, 180, 182, 183
Chattuari, 43, 116, 117, 118, 120
Chauci, 16, 17, 19–25, 27, 30, 32, 37, 39, 41, 43–45, 66, 67, 186; piracy, 14, 22–26, 29–31, 34, 39, 45, 186; ships, 31
Chelmsford, 26, 27
Childeric the Saxon, 88
Childeric, king of the Franks, 87
Chilperic, 125
Chlochilaic. *See* Hygelac
Chramn, 125
Cilician pirates, 52
Civilis, 24–26, 38, 39
Civitavecchia, 158
classis Anderetianorum, 59, 80

Index

classis Britannica, 29, 56, 60
classis Germanica, 24, 25, 28, 29, 60
classis Pannonica, 60
classis Sambrica, 80, 123
Claudius, 23
clench nails, 33, 36, 72, 95, 96, 98, 104
clinker-building, 32–34, 38, 71, 93–104, 186, 189
Clovis, 88, 114, 118, 120, 124, 130
Cnut, 91
coastguards, 107, 160, 165, 167, 169, 171, 176, 181, 183
cogs, 36, 72, 74, 75, 103, 139, 180, 181, 186
coin hoards, 15, 26, 52–54, 61
coins, 22, 53, 54, 56, 58, 64, 73, 81, 110, 125, 134, 144, 173, 178–80
Cokingi, 165, 181
Cologne, 18, 24, 48, 60, 120, 128
Columbanus, St, 130
Comacchio, 154
Comes Litoris Saxonici. See Saxon Shore; count of the
Comes Maritimi Tractus, 68
Constans, 65
Constantinople, 105, 124, 140, 154
Constantius, 62–64
Corsica, 126, 152, 157–60
Croats fleets, 156
customs posts, 175

D

Dacia, 41
Dæghrefn, 118
Dagobert, 88
Dalmatia, 74, 152–55
Dalriada, 91
Danes, 13, 84, 112, 116, 121, 122, 125, 127, 134, 151, 163, 168, 171–78; fleets, 115, 120–24, 167
Danevirke, 172, 174
Danube, river, 41, 51, 60, 66, 75, 81, 131, 139–42, 144, 147
de Oude Werelde, 28, 29
Denmark, 18, 19, 22, 23, 32–34, 37, 60, 89, 98, 116, 165, 172, 176–78, 180

depopulation, 46, 48, 52, 108
Didius Julianus, 26
Diocletian, 46, 61
diplomacy, 153, 172–78
Dorestad, 119, 126–28, 166, 170, 182; coinage of, 134, 178; mint at, 126, 171
Dover: *classis Britannica* fort, 29, 56; Saxon Shore fort, 56; Straits of, 58, 63, 65, 107, 166
Dragowit, 136
dromons, 161, 162
Drusus, 17
dug-out boats. *See* logboats
Dunkirk II, 22, 28, 42, 46, 48, 49, 55

E

Ealdwulf, papal legate, 168
Ealhhere, ealdorman, 111
East Anglia, 27, 56, 69, 82, 98, 104, 108, 111, 116
Ebro, river, 146
Ecgfrith, king of Northumbria, 90, 91, 111
Eddius Stephanus, 109
Edgar, king of England, 112
Edward the Confessor, 112
Edwin, king of Northumbria, 90
Egyptian shipbuilding, 95
Einhard, 139, 165
Elbe, river *passim*
elephant, 153, 158
Ems, river, 15, 17, 21, 44, 121
Enns, river, 131
epidemic, livestock, 140
Ercanbald, 163
Essex, 26, 27, 84
Euric, 88, 90
Everard of Friuli, 145

F

famine, 147, 150, 151
Farne Islands, 110
Feddersen Wierde, 22, 31

federates: Anglo-Saxon, 83–86; Frankish, 113
Fens, the, 49
ferry-boats, 142
figureheads, 34, 110, 121, 132, 133, 179
Finn, 122
fire, destruction by, 24, 26, 27, 51, 64, 129
Fishbourne palace, 55
fishing, 134, 164
Flanders, 165, 168, 169
food prices, 151
fortifications: Carolingian, 15, 121, 130, 131, 168; Danish, 165; Roman, 27–30, 55–59, 65, 69, 77, 86, 107, 166
Franks, 15, 105, 111; campaigns: Adriatic, 152–56; Arabs, 156–63; Danes, 172–78; Frisians, 126–30; Vikings, 163–71; coastal defences, 121, 122, 135–83; navy, 118–21, 123–26, 130, 131, 134–46; origin myths, 52, 114; origins, 16, 17–19, 24, 42, 43; piracy and raiding, 13, 26, 30, 41, 44, 45, 48–55, 57, 59–61, 63–70, 73, 87, 113; settlement, 51, 113, 114, 116, 118, 119; ships, 70, 73–76, 106, 107, 131–34, 146, 161–63, 178–81, 186
Fraxinetum, 161
Freculph of Lisieux, 145
Fredegund, 88
Frisia, 48, 110, 116, 118, 119, 121, 122, 126, 127, 129, 138, 164, 168, 170, 174, 177, 183; geography of, 128
Frisian islands, 45, 121, 142, 166, 167, 175
Frisians, 14, 16, 18, 21, 23, 43, 44, 48, 60, 62, 118, 120–23, 126–31, 134, 139, 141, 151, 167, 171, 174, 186; naval activity, 17, 24, 122, 123, 128–30, 136, 138, 141, 142; piracy, 13, 48, 60, 82, 127; settlement, 126; ships, 36
Fyn, 175

G

Gabinius (governor of Belgica), 23
galleys, 18, 19, 24, 25, 58, 71, 73, 74, 95, 101, 156, 161, 180
'Gallic' empire, 49–53, 58
Gallienus, 46
Gannascus, 23, 31, 39
Garonne, 87, 106, 125, 164, 166, 182
Gascony, 88, 89, 152
Gaul passim
Geats. See Jutes
Genoa, 158
Germanus, St, 82
Germany passim
Gestingthorpe, 26
Ghent, 164
Gildas, 69, 83–85
Godfred, 172–77
Godmanchester, 64
Gokstad ship, 100, 101, 103, 169
Goldsborough, 81
Goths, 14, 41, 52, 86, 88, 114, 116, 125; boats, 41
Gotland picture stones, 95, 98, 110
Grado, 153
Grannona, 28, 56, 59, 80
Graveney boat, 101
Great Chesterford, 26
Gredstedbro ship, 104
Greece, 41, 51, 52
Greek fire, 162
Gregory of Tours, 115, 116, 121–23, 131
Gregory, governor of Sicily, 159
Groningen, 48, 118
Guadalquivir, river, 125
Guernsey, 36, 87

H

Hadeln, 22, 138, 143
Hadrian's Wall, 69
Hadumar, count of Genoa, 158, 163
Halsnøy boat, 33
Hamburg, 182
Harlow, 26

Harun al Raschid, 153
Havel, river, 136
Hedeby, 173–75; coinage, 110, 180
Helier, St, 87
Hemming, 174, 176
Hengist, 83, 85
herikochun, 74, 181
Heriold, 176, 177
Heruls, 14, 43, 60, 90; pirate raids, 13, 14, 89, 124; ships, 92, 97
Hetware. *See* Chattuari
hide, waterproof, 86, 146
Hjortspring boat, 32, 33, 34
hogging truss, 95, 96, 189
Horic, 177, 178, 182
Hugas, 118, 119
Hugmerki, 118
hulks, 179, 180
Humber, 27, 49, 77, 82, 109
Huns, 86, 144
Huntcliff, 81
Hygelac, 115, 114–24

I

Ijssel, river, 42, 43, 119, 120
inscription: funerary, 29
inscriptions, 29, 37, 50, 51, 77, 98
Ireland, 67, 68, 90, 111, 130, 145, 166
Irish Sea, 90, 91
Irmingar, 158
Ischia, 159
Isidore of Seville, 125
Isle of Man, 90
Istria, 152, 155
Itzehoe, 174

J

Jerome, St, 79, 181
Julian, emperor, 66, 67, 113
Justinian, 124, 125
Jutes, 78, 83, 116, 125
Jutland, 14, 16, 34, 43, 72, 89, 96, 104, 107, 108, 116, 127, 172, 173, 175

K

Kapel Avazath barges, 34
Karlby ship carving, 96
keels, 38, 39, 71, 75, 95–97, 100, 101, 103–5, 185, 189
Kelvedon, 26
Kollerup cog, 72
Kongsgårde ship, 96
Kouadoi, 66, 67

L

Ladby ship, 100, 103
laeti, 77
Lahn, river, 42, 122
Lampedusa, 159
Leck boat, 31
Leo III, pope, 157
Liber Historiae Francorum, 115, 116, 118
Liber monstrorum, 116, 118
Liburnian (galley), 18, 19, 73, 74, 161
lighthouse, 164
Liguria, 153
limes, 22, 59, 65
Lindisfarne, 13, 110, 163, 172
Linones, 143
lintres, 31
Lippe, river, 18, 25, 42
Litus Saxonicum. See Saxon Shore
Locus Quartensis sive Hornensis, 56, 80
logboats, 31, 34, 35, 39, 74, 142
Loire, river, 86–89, 130, 131, 164, 166, 169, 182
Lolland, 175
Lombards, 44, 135, 136, 140
London, 36, 63, 68, 84
Lothar, emperor, 165, 182
Lothar, king of the Franks, 125, 159, 161
Louis II, king of Italy, 161, 182
Louis the Pious, 111, 121, 141, 157, 160, 165, 168–72, 175–78, 182
Lugo, 89, 97
Lupus, duke, 122
Lusitania, 54

lusoria, 72
Lympne, 29, 56, 65

M

Magdeburg, 136, 138
Magister Peditum per Gallias, 80
Magnentius, 65
Main, river, 16, 141, 147
Mainz, 42; bridge, 143; Roman ships, 70–75, 101, 133, 181, 186
Majorca, 158
Malamocco, 154
Marcian, 83
Marcis, 28, 56, 80
Marcomanni, 78
marine transgression. *See* Dunkirk II
Marsas, 87
Marseilles, 159, 160
mast step, 35, 36, 72, 75, 100, 103
Maximian, 60–63
Mediterranean Sea, 13, 41, 50, 52, 90, 126, 146, 152, 153, 156–63
Mediterranean shipbuilding, 34, 71, 73, 74
Meginfred the Chamberlain, 139, 141
Middelzee, 129
mint, 81, 125, 126
mobilisation of troops, 25, 29, 81, 136, 139, 141, 142, 145, 147, 152, 167, 169
Moerzeke, 132, 133
Moors, 50, 135, 146; pirate raids, 156–63
Morocco, 50
Mount Badon, 89
Mucking, 84

N

Nantes, 57, 87, 130, 182
Naples, 159, 161
Narbonne, 131, 157
Nechtansmere, 111
Nennius, 80, 86

Nicaea, 51
Nice, 158
Nicephorus I, 153
Nicetas, Byzantine naval commander, 153
Nicomedia, 51
Nijmegen, 48, 116, 119, 170, 171
Nîmes, 125
Noirmoutier, 169, 170, 182
Nordic shipbuilding, 32, 34, 71, 100
Noricum, 81
Normans, 85
North Africa, 50, 152, 156, 159
North American Indians, use of sail by, 38
North Sea *passim*
Northumbria, 13, 90, 109, 168
Northumbrian fleet, 90, 91
Norwegians, 163, 166
Notitia Dignitatum, 56, 79, 80, 123
Nydam Moss, 93
Nydam ships, 14, 73, 74, 96, 100, 104, 107, 133; oak ship, 33, 95, 96, 98, 100, 104; pine ship, 97

O

oars, 19, 25, 33, 34, 38, 70, 72, 74, 76, 95, 97, 98, 100, 101, 104, 105, 107, 110, 125, 133, 156, 161, 179–81, 189
Obelerius, 153, 154
Octha, 86
Odovacer, 86, 87
Oldeboorn, 129
Omayyads, 157, 161
Oostergo, 129
Oost-Souburg, 165
Orkney Islands, 79, 80, 91, 166
Orleans, 87, 88
Orosius, 50, 51, 79
Oseberg ship, 100, 110
Oswiu, 109
Otlingua Saxonica, 86
Otto I, 161
Oudenburg, 28, 56

Index

P

Pactus Legis Salicae, 124
paddles, 38, 75, 76
paddling, advantages and disadvantages of, 75
Pannonia, 139, 140
Paul, *dux*, 154
paved boats, 142
Pentapolis, 153, 161
Pentland Firth, 19
Pevensey, 59, 65, 80, 81
Phoenicia, 78, 79
Picts, 67–69, 79, 80, 83–85, 91, 111
Pippin II, 114, 127, 128
Pippin III, 114, 129, 131
Pippin, king of Italy, 154, 155
Pisans, 160
Pliny the Elder, 31, 32, 35
plunder, importance of, 156–63
Po, river, 154
Polynesian boats, 38, 76
pontoon bridges, 131, 142–45
Pontus, 51, 60, 63
Ponza, 159
Populonia, 154
Port, Saxon leader, 85
Portchester, 56, 58, 59, 65
Postumus, 49, 50, 58
pottery, 22, 28, 76; Elbe-Weser, 31; Romano-Saxon, 77, 78; Samian, 75
prisoners of war: Avars, 150; Saxon, 79
Probus, 51, 53, 58, 60
Procopius, 88, 105, 106
Provence, 127, 157, 161
Ptolemy's *Geography*, 43

Q

Quadi, 66
Quentovic, 134, 166, 178, 180, 182
Quintianus, 115

R

Rába, river, 140
Radbod, *dux* of Frisia, 127, 128
Rædwald, king of East Anglia, 98
ram, 72–75, 162, 181
ransom, 168
Ravenna, 126, 129, 153
Reculver, 28, 29, 57
Regensburg, 139–42, 149
Regnitz, river, 141, 147, 149, 152
Reric, 173–75
Reudingi, 44
Rezat, river, 147, 149, 150
Rhé, 170
Rheims, 179, 180
Rhine, river *passim*:
    changing course of, 119
Rhône, river, 157, 161
Richborough, 56, 58, 81
Ripuarii, 43
Riquier, St, 88
Roman: ships, 25, 28, 51, 66, 71, 73, 95, 133, 181
Roman Empire, third century crisis in, 45
Roman fleets, 15, 17–19, 25, 60, 63, 123, 126
Rome, 29, 46, 83, 126, 152, 157, 160, 171
Rouen, 181
rowing, 19, 31–33, 74–76, 93–95, 98–109; energy efficiency of, 75
rowlocks, 33
rudders, 93, 97, 100, 101, 133, 178, 181
Rüstringen, 177

S

Sæ Wylfing, 101, 185
sails, 25, 35–39, 70, 95–98, 100–110, 178–81, 185, 186; lateen, 72, 162; square, 96, 102, 162, 180
Salians, 43, 67, 113, 120, 121
Sandwich, 111
Saracens, 131
Sardinia, 126, 158, 157–59, 160
Saxon Shore, 27, 28, 55–60, 63–65, 67–69, 77–81; count of the, 68, 80
Saxons, 138, 139, 172; origins, 16, 19, 30, 42–45; piracy and raiding, 13,

41–45, 48, 49, 52, 57, 59–62, 65–70, 77–82, 86, 91, 92, 123, 124, 186; settlement, 78, 82–86, 88, 89, 109, 123; ships, 73, 74, 93, 97, 106, 107, 186
Saxony, 86, 88, 89, 142, 153, 174, 176
scafa exploratoria, 72
Scandinavia, 14, 22, 33, 37, 60, 101, 127, 185
scara, 139
Scheesel, 175
Scheldt, river, 26, 28, 48, 57, 114, 120, 121, 132, 166
Schlei, river, 172, 173
Schleswig, 31, 173
Scotland, 18, 19, 67, 166
Scots, 67, 68, 79, 83–85, 91
Seine, river, 54, 63, 143, 144, 165, 166, 168, 169, 181, 183
Senchus Fer n Alban, 91
Severus, 46, 144
Seville, 125
Shetland Islands, 166
ship burial, 105
shroud rings, 100
Sicily, 52, 126, 153, 159, 160
Sidonius Apollinaris, 106
Sieg, river, 42
Sigfred, 172
signal stations, 69, 81
Sisebut, 125
Sjælland, 175
Skegness, 56
slaves, 18, 88, 124, 158, 172
Slavs, 135, 136, 140, 143, 175; naval activity, 138, 155
Smeldingi, 143, 174
Snape boat, 104
Sorbs, 136, 138
Sousse, 160
Spain, 50–52, 54, 63, 64, 89–91, 125, 127, 146, 152, 156–59, 172
St Peter Port, ship, 36
Stilicho, 80, 81
Stockholm tar, 72
Stör, river, 174
Stour, river, 111

Strathclyde, 91
Suiones, 38
Sunderland, 69
Sutton Hoo ship, 97–105, 109, 185
Svein, 91
Swabians, 150
Swedes. See *Suiones*
Syagrius, 130
Symmachus, 79
Syracuse, 51, 52

T

Tacitus, 14, 18, 19, 21, 24–26, 31, 38, 43, 145, 186
Tarragona, 50
Tencteri, 24
terpen, 21
Tetuán, 50
Texel, 117, 165
Thames, river, 27, 28, 49, 56, 69, 77, 82, 84, 85, 109
Theodoric, Count, 139, 141
Theodoric, king of the Franks, 89, 115
Theodoric, king of the Visigoths, 87
Theodosius, Count, 68, 69
Thérouanne, 26
Theudebert, 115, 130
Theuderic, king of the Franks, 130
Thrasco, 175
Thuringians, 139
tile stamps, 60, 73
tolls, 147, 165
Tortosa, 146
Tournai, 27
Toxandria, 67, 113
trade, 21; Danish, 22, 175; Frankish, 114, 125, 127, 134; Frisian, 19; Roman, 22, 23; Venetian, 154
trading: Frankish, 126
Treene, river, 172, 174
Trelleborg, 165
trenails, 31, 104
Treviso, 154
tribute, 90, 134, 151, 155, 167, 174
Trier, 62, 68, 75, 76
triremes, 24, 73

Index

Trojans, 52
Tubantes, 43
Turks, 144
Twihantes, 43

U

Ubbo, the Frisian, 127
Ubii, 35
urban fortifications, 26, 27, 57
Usipi, 14, 17–19, 24, 43
Utica, 160
Utrecht, 48, 74, 128, 170; boat, 178–80; charters, 181; Psalter, 179

V

Vaaler Moor boat, 31, 32
Valence, 161
Valentinian I, 67, 68
Valentinian III, 83
Valerian, 45, 49, 52
Valkenburg, 24, 48
Vandals, 14, 50, 51, 78, 90, 114
Vecht, river, 119, 128, 129
Vegetius, 72, 145
Venantius Fortunatus, 125
Vendeuil-Caply, 27
Vendsyssel bowl, 34
Venice, 152–56, 161, 174
Verden, 167
Verdun, Treaty of, 170, 182
vici, destruction of, 55
Vikings, 13–15, 39, 52, 66, 77, 84–87, 89, 91, 92, 111, 112, 121, 130, 142, 143, 163–72, 181–87
villas, abandonment and destruction of, 26, 54, 55
Visigoths, 87, 125; fleet, 86

Voorburg, 27, 46
Vortigern, 83

W

Waal, river, 25, 119–21, 183
Waddensee, 127
Wala, 163
Walcheren, 28, 29, 165, 171, 177
Wales, 79, 166
Walton, 56
Wamba, 125
Warni, 88
Wash, the, 28, 49, 56, 65
water transport, 142, 147
Werinofeld, 138
Weser, river *passim*: bone carving, 37
Wessex, 85, 112
Westergo, 129
Wickford, 26, 27
Widukind, 89, 172
Wihmodia, 143
Wilfred, St, 109
Wiltzites, 136, 138, 143, 173, 177
Witla, 170
Würzburg, 149

Y

York, 49, 69

Z

Zara, 153
Zele, 132, 133
Zosimus, 23, 51, 66, 67
Zuyder Zee, 16, 19, 42, 119
Zwammerdam boats, 34, 35, 38, 39

First Steps in Old English: An easy to follow language course for the beginner
Stephen Pollington

A complete, well presented and easy to use Old English language course that contains all the exercises and texts needed to learn Old English. This course has been designed to be of help to a wide range of students, from those who are teaching themselves at home, to undergraduates who are learning Old English as part of their English degree course. The author is aware that some individuals have little aptitude for learning languages and that many have difficulty with grammar. To help overcome these problems he has adopted a step by step approach that enables students of differing abilities to advance at their own pace. The course includes exercises to test the students progress. A correspondence course is also available.

£19   ISBN 1–898281–19–X   250mm x 175mm/10" x 7"   224 pages

Ærgeweorc: Old English Verse and Prose
read by Stephen Pollington

This audiotape cassette can be used with *First Steps in Old English* or just listened to for the sheer pleasure of hearing Old English spoken well.
Tracks: 1. Deor. 2. Beowulf – The Funeral of Scyld Scefing. 3. Engla Tocyme (The Arrival of the English). 4. Ines Domas. Two Extracts from the Laws of King Ine. 5. Deniga Hergung (The Danes' Harrying) Anglo-Saxon Chronicle Entry AD997. 6. Durham 7. The Ordeal (Be ðon ðe ordales weddigaþ) 8. Wið Dweorh (Against a Dwarf) 9. Wið Wennum (Against Wens) 10. Wið Wæterælfadle (Against Waterelf Sickness) 11. The Nine Herbs Charm 12. Læcedomas (Leechdoms) 13. Beowulf's Greeting 14. The Battle of Brunanburh 15. Blacmon – by Adrian Pilgrim.

£6·90   ISBN 1–898281–20–3   C40 audiotape

Wordcraft: Concise English/Old English Dictionary and Thesaurus
Stephen Pollington

This book provides Old English equivalents to the commoner modern words in both dictionary and thesaurus formats. The Thesaurus presents vocabulary relevant to a wide range of individual topics in alphabetical lists, thus making it easily accessible to those with specific areas of interest. Each thematic listing is encoded for cross-reference from the Dictionary. The two sections will be of invaluable assistance to students of the language, as well as to those with either a general or a specific interest in the Anglo-Saxon period.

£9·95   A5   ISBN 1–898281–02–5   256pp

An Introduction to the Old English Language and its Literature
Stephen Pollington

The purpose of this general introduction to Old English is not to deal with the teaching of Old English but to dispel some misconceptions about the language and to give an outline of its structure and its literature. Some basic knowledge of these is essential to an understanding of the early period of English history and the present form of the language.

£3·95   A5   ISBN 1–898281–06–8   48pp

An Introduction to Early English Law
Bill Griffiths

Much of Anglo-Saxon life followed a traditional pattern, of custom, and of dependence on kin-groups for land, support and security. The Viking incursions of the ninth century and the reconquest of the north that followed both disturbed this pattern and led to a new emphasis on centralized power and law, with royal and ecclesiastical officials prominent as arbitrators and settlers of disputes. The diversity and development of early English law is sampled here by selecting several law-codes to be read in translation - that of Æthelbert of Kent, being the first to be issued in England, Alfred the Great's, the most clearly thought-out of all, and short codes from the reigns of Edmund and Æthelred the Unready.

£6·95   A5   ISBN 1–898281–14–9   96pp

The Battle of Maldon: Text and Translation
Translated and edited by Bill Griffiths

The Battle of Maldon was fought between the men of Essex and the Vikings in AD 991. The action was captured in an Anglo-Saxon poem whose vividness and heroic spirit has fascinated readers and scholars for generations. *The Battle of Maldon* includes the source text; edited text; parallel literal translation; verse translation; a review of 103 books and articles. This new edition has a helpful guide to Old English verse.

£5·95   A5   ISBN 0–9516209–0–8   96pp

Beowulf: Text and Translation
Translated by John Porter

The verse in which the story unfolds is, by common consent, the finest writing surviving in Old English, a text that all students of the language and many general readers will want to tackle in the original form. To aid understanding of the Old English, a literal word-by-word translation is printed opposite the edited text and provides a practical key to this Anglo-Saxon masterpiece.

£7·95   A5   ISBN 0–9516209–2–4   192pp

The English Warrior from earliest times to 1066
Stephen Pollington

This important new work is not intended to be a bald listing of the battles and campaigns from the Anglo-Saxon Chronicle and other sources, but rather it is an attempt to get below the surface of Anglo-Saxon warriorhood and to investigate the rites, social attitudes, mentality and mythology of the warfare of those times.

The book is divided into three main sections which deal with warriorhood, weaponry and warfare respectively. The first covers the warrior's role in early English society, his rights and duties, the important rituals of feasting, gift-giving and duelling, and the local and national military organizations. The second part discusses the various weapons and items of military equipment which are known to have been in use during the period, often with a concise summary of the generally accepted typology for the many kinds of military hardware. In the third part, the social and legal nature of warfare is presented, as well as details of strategy and tactics, military buildings and earthworks, and the use of supply trains. Valuable appendices offer original translations of the three principal Old English military poems, the battles of *Maldon*, *Finnsburh* and *Brunanburh*.

The latest thinking from many disciplines is brought together in a unique and fascinating survey of the role of the military in Anglo-Saxon England. The author combines original translations from the Old English and Old Norse source documents with archaeological and linguistic evidence to present a comprehensive and wide-ranging treatment of the subject. Students of military history will find here a wealth of new insights into a neglected period of English history.

£14·95   ISBN 1–898281–10–6   272pp   10" x 7" (250 x 175mm) with over 50 illustrations

A Handbook of Anglo-Saxon Food: Processing and Consumption
Ann Hagen

For the first time information from various sources has been brought together in order to build up a picture of how food was grown, conserved, prepared and eaten during the period from the beginning of the 5th century to the 11th century. Many people will find it fascinating for the views it gives of an important aspect of Anglo-Saxon life and culture. In addition to Anglo-Saxon England the Celtic west of Britain is also covered. Now with an extensive index.

£8·95   A5   ISBN 0–9516209–8–3   192pp

A Second Handbook of Anglo-Saxon Food & Drink: Production and Distribution
Ann Hagen

Food production for home consumption was the basis of economic activity throughout the Anglo-Saxon period. This second handbook complements the first and brings together a vast amount of information on livestock, cereal and vegetable crops, fish, honey and fermented drinks. Related subjects such as hospitality, charity and drunkenness are also dealt with. There is an extensive index.

£12·50   A5   ISBN 1–898281–12–2   432pp

Spellcraft: Old English Heroic Legends
Kathleen Herbert

The author has taken the skeletons of ancient Germanic legends about great kings, queens and heroes, and put flesh on them. Kathleen Herbert's extensive knowledge of the period is reflected in the wealth of detail she brings to these tales of adventure, passion, bloodshed and magic.

The book is in two parts. First are the stories that originate deep in the past, yet because they have not been hackneyed, they are still strange and enchanting. After that there is a selection of the source material, with information about where it can be found and some discussion about how it can be used.

£8·95   A5   ISBN 0–9516209–9–1   292pp

Peace-Weavers and Shield-Maidens: Women in Early English Society
Kathleen Herbert

The recorded history of the English people did not start in 1066 as popularly believed but one-thousand years earlier. The Roman historian Cornelius Tacitus noted in *Germania*, published in the year 98, that the English (Latin *Anglii*), who lived in the southern part of the Jutland peninsula, were members of an alliance of Goddess-worshippers. The author has taken that as an appropriate opening to an account of the earliest Englishwomen, the part they played in the making of England, what they did in peace and war, the impressions they left in Britain and on the continent, how they were recorded in the chronicles, how they come alive in heroic verse and jokes.

£4·95   A5   ISBN 1–898281–11–4   64pp

Looking for the Lost Gods of England
Kathleen Herbert

Kathleen Herbert sifts through the royal genealogies, charms, verse and other sources to find clues to the names and attributes of the Gods and Goddesses of the early English. The earliest account of English heathen practices reveals that they worshipped the Earth Mother and called her Nerthus. The tales, beliefs and traditions of that time are still with us and have played a part in giving us *A Midsummer Night's Dream* and *The Lord of the Rings*.

£4·95   A5   ISBN 1–898281–04–1   64pp

Rudiments of Runelore
Stephen Pollington

This book provides both a comprehensive introduction for those coming to the subject for the first time, and a handy and inexpensive reference work for those with some knowledge of the subject. The *Abecedarium Nordmannicum* and the English, Norwegian and Icelandic rune poems are included in their original and translated form. Also included is work on the three Brandon runic inscriptions and the Norfolk 'Tiw' runes.

£5·95   A5   ISBN 1–898281–16–5   Illustrations   88pp

English Martial Arts
Terry Brown

By the sixteenth century English martial artists had a governing body that controlled its members in much the same way as do modern-day martial arts organisations. The *Company of Maisters* taught and practised a fighting system that ranks as high in terms of effectiveness and pedigree as any in the world.

In the first part of the book the author investigates the weapons, history and development of the English fighting system and looks at some of the attitudes, beliefs and social pressures that helped mould it.

Part two deals with English fighting techniques drawn from sources that recorded the system at various stages in its history. In other words, all of the methods and techniques shown in this book are authentic and have not been created by the author. The theories that underlie the system are explained in a chapter on *The Principles of True Fighting*. All of the techniques covered are illustrated with photographs and accompanied by instructions. Techniques included are for bare-fist fighting, broadsword, quarterstaff, bill, sword and buckler, sword and dagger.

£25   ISBN 1–898281–18–1   250mm x 195mm / 10" x 7½"   220 photographs   240 pages

The Hallowing of England
A Guide to the Saints of Old England and their Places of Pilgrimage
Fr. Andrew Philips

In the Old English period we can count over 300 saints, yet today their names and exploits are largely unknown. They are part of a forgotten England which, though it lies deep in the past, is an important part of our national and spiritual history. This guide includes a list of saints, an alphabetical list of places with which they are associated, and a calendar of saint's feast days.

£4·95   A5   ISBN 1-898281-08-4   96pp

The Rebirth of England and English: The Vision of William Barnes
Fr. Andrew Phillips

English history is patterned with spirits so bright that they broke through convention and saw another England. Such was the case of the Dorset poet, William Barnes (1801–86), priest, poet, teacher, self-taught polymath, linguist extraordinary and that rare thing – a man of vision. In this work the author looks at that vision, a vision at once of Religion, Nature, Art, Marriage, Society, Economics, Politics and Language. He writes: 'In search of authentic English roots and values, our post-industrial society may well have much to learn from Barnes'.

£9·95   A5   ISBN 1-898281-17-3   160pp

Anglo-Saxon Books

Frithgarth, Thetford Forest Park, Hockwold-cum-Wilton, Norfolk IP26 4NQ
Tel: 01842 828430   Fax: 01842 828332   email: asbooks@englisc.demon.co.uk
A full list of our titles is available on our web site at www.englisc.demon.co.uk or send us a s.a.e.

We accept payment by cheque, Visa, Eurocard and Mastercard. Please add 10% for UK delivery, up to a maximum charge of £2·50. For delivery charges outside the UK please contact us or see our web site.

Most titles are available in North America from bookstores.
Our North American distributor is: Paul & Company Publishers Consortium Inc.
c/o PCS Data Processing Inc., 360 West 31 St., New York, NY 10001 tel: (212) 564 3730 ext. 295

Angelcynn

The fifth to ninth centuries were some of the most turbulent of British history. This was the time when England was born, the time of Hengest and Horsa, Beowulf, Redwald of Sutton Hoo, St. Augustine, King Offa, King Alfred, the Viking Invasions and the foundation of the English church. Angelcynn is a living history society that aims to recreate all aspects of life in the period; food, crafts, warfare, pastimes, in fact everything that made up the life of these first English people. We are a society that attracts people from all walks of life, young and old, who come together in a spirit of historical re-creation.

Further information from: Ben Levick, 2 Prospect Row, Old Brompton, Gillingham, Kent, ME7 5AL England
e-mail: angelcyn@hrofi.demon.co.uk - web: www.geocities.com/Athens/2471/

Regia Anglorum

Regia Anglorum is a society that was founded to accurately re-create the life of the British people as it was around the time of the Norman Conquest. Our work has a strong educational slant and we consider authenticity to be of prime importance. We prefer, where possible, to work from archaeological materials and are extremely cautious regarding such things as the interpretation of styles depicted in manuscripts. Approximately twenty-five per cent of our membership, of over 500 people, are archaeologists or historians.

The Society has a large working Living History Exhibit, teaching and exhibiting more than twenty crafts in an authentic environment. We own a forty foot wooden ship replica of a type that would have been a common sight in Northern European waters around the turn of the first millennium AD. Battle re-enactment is another aspect of our activities, often involving 200 or more warriors.

For further information see www.regia.org or e-mail kim_siddorn@compuserve.com
or write to K. J. Siddorn, 9 Durleigh Close, Headley Park, Bristol BS13 7NQ, England

Þa Engliscan Gesiðas - *The English Companions*

Þa Engliscan Gesiðas is a historical and cultural society exclusively devoted to Early English (Anglo-Saxon) history. Its aims are to bridge the gap between scholars and non-experts, and to bring together all those with an interest in the Anglo-Saxon period so as to promote a wider interest in, and knowledge of, its language, culture and traditions. The Fellowship publishes a journal, *Wiðowinde,* which helps members to keep in touch with current thinking on all relevent topics. The Fellowship enables like-minded people to keep in contact by publicising conferences, courses and meetings that might be of interest to its members.

For further details see www.kami.demon.co.uk/gesithas/ or write to:
The Membership Secretary, Þa Engliscan Gesiðas, BM Box 4336, London, WC1N 3XX England.

Bede's World at Jarrow

Bede's world tells the remarkable story of the life and times of the Venerable Bede, 673–735 AD. Visitors can explore the origins of early medieval Northumbria and Bede's life and achievements through his own writings and the excavations of the monasteries at Jarrow and other sites. Location – 10 miles from Newcastle upon Tyne, off the A19 near the southern entrance to the River Tyne tunnel. Bus services 526 & 527

Bede's World, Church Bank, Jarrow, Tyne and Wear, NE32 3DY
Tel: 0191 489 2106; Fax: 0191 428 2361; Website: www.bedesworld.co.uk

Sutton Hoo near Woodbridge, Suffolk

Sutton Hoo is a group of low burial mounds overlooking the River Deben in south-east Suffolk. Excavations in 1939 brought to light the richest burial ever discovered in Britain – an Anglo-Saxon ship containing a magnificent treasure which has become one of the principal attractions of the British Museum. The mound from which the treasure was dug is thought to be the grave of Rædwald, the English king who died in 624/5 AD.

The Site is Open to Visitors for Guided Tours Only
Weekend tours – Guided tours start at the site at 2pm and 3pm every Saturday, Sunday and Bank Holiday Monday from Easter Saturday until the end of October. There is no need to book, just turn up for the tour. Access by foot only – one mile walk along a footpath from the B1083. Tours can be booked at other times for organised parties. For details write to:-

The Sutton Hoo Guiding and Visits Secretary, Tailor's House, Bawdsey, Woodbridge, Suffolk IP12 3AJ
e-mail: visits@suttonhoo.org - website: www.suttonhoo.org

The Sutton Hoo Society

Our aims and objectives focus on promoting research and education relating to the Anglo Saxon Royal cemetery at Sutton Hoo, Suffolk in the UK. The Society publishes a newsletter SAXON twice a year, which keeps members up to date with society activities, carries resumes of lectures and visits, and reports progress on research and publication associated with the site. If you would like to join the Society please write to:

Membership Secretary, Sutton Hoo Society, 28 Pembroke Road, Framlingham,
Woodbridge, IP13 9HA, England   website – www.suttonhoo.org

West Stow Anglo-Saxon Village

An early Anglo-Saxon Settlement reconstructed on the site where it was excavated consisting of timber and thatch hall, houses and workshop. Open all year 10a.m.–4.15p.m. (except Yule). Free taped guides. Special provision for school parties. A teachers' resource pack is available. Costumed events are held at weekends, especially Easter Sunday and August Bank Holiday Monday. Craft courses are organised.

For further details tel: 01284 728718 or see www.stedmunds.co.uk/west_stow.html or contact:
The Visitor Centre, West Stow Country Park, Icklingham Road, West Stow Bury St Edmunds, Suffolk IP28 6HG